Understanding Terrorism
Threats in an Uncertain World

❖

Edited by

Akorlie A. Nyatepe-Coo
Dorothy Zeisler-Vralsted

University of Wisconsin-La Crosse

PEARSON

Prentice
Hall

Upper Saddle River, New Jersey 07458

Library of Congress Cataloging-in-Publication Data

Nyatepe-Coo, Akorlie A.

  Understanding terrorism : Treats in an uncertain world / Akorlie A. Nyatepe-Coo and Dorothy Zeisler-Vralsted.

    p. cm.

Includes bibliographical references and index.

  ISBN 0-13-112098-0

  1. Terrorism. 2. Terrorism—History. 3. September 11 Terrorist Attacks, 2001. 4. Islam and terrorism. I. Zeisler-Vralsted, Dorothy. II. Title.

  HV6431 .N93 2004

  303.6'25—dc21

                                  2003010488

Publisher: Stephen Helba
Executive Editor: Frank Mortimer, Jr.
Assistant Editor: Korrine Dorsey
Production Editor: Nicholas Angelides/
  Pine Tree Composition, Inc.
Production Liaison: Barbara Marttine Cappuccio
Director of Manufacturing and Production: Bruce Johnson
Managing Editor: Mary Carnis
Manufacturing Buyer: Cathleen Petersen

Creative Director: Cheryl Asherman
Cover Design Coordinator: Miguel Ortiz
Editorial Assistant: Barbara Rosenberg
Marketing Manager: Tim Peyton
Formatting and Interior Design:
  Pine Tree Composition, Inc.
Printer and Binder:
  R.R. Donnelley & Sons

Pearson Education LTD.
Pearson Education Singapore, Pte. Ltd
Pearson Education, Canada, Ltd
Pearson Education–Japan
Pearson Education Australia PTY, Limited
Pearson Education North Asia Ltd
Pearson Educaçion de Mexico, S.A. de C.V.
Pearson Education Malaysia, Pte. Ltd

10 9 8 7 6 5 4 3 2 1
ISBN 0-13-112098-0

Contents

❖

Foreword

--- ❖ ---

On Tuesday morning, September 11, 2001, our university community was in the first weeks of the fall semester with the usual hum of activities—students preparing for Homecoming and Parents' Weekend and faculty zealously discussing the nuances of their disciplines. The familiarity of these routines gave us all a sense of security about the world we lived in. But all of that changed in the span of a few hours, and professors who planned to discuss topics ranging from the birth of civilization to aquatic biology were now struck by their irrelevance. Students, shaken by the horror and the unexpectedness of the events of September 11, flooded professors and staff with phone calls to ask whether class was dismissed, if it was safe to travel, or for help in finding a friend or family member in New York City.

Later that day, I called a meeting with colleagues from across campus. By this time we had started to learn about the magnitude of these tragedies, and also that several of our faculty and staff were affected personally. One of the first questions that came up was about how we could, as educators, help our community better understand some of the factors that prompted the terrorist attacks. Not only did we realize the need to deepen our own knowledge of the Middle Eastern world, emerging technologies, and the prolonged effects of terrorism, but we also felt compelled to share these insights with the broader community. Thus within one week of 9-11 we began a multidisplinary lecture series that spanned the next seven weeks and formed the basis of this text. The lecture series reached out to the public, inviting community members and friends of the university to join with faculty and students in discussing various fears and concerns about terrorism. As expected, the series met with outstanding success. Many of the lectures were packed with audiences comprised of university faculty, students, and members of the local community. We saw in the interactions a search for answers and a need to engage with others in trying to understand why and how something like 9-11 could happen. Thus, topics that only a few weeks earlier were seldom discussed became subjects of debate.

But the lectures did more than educate people on obscure facts. The weekly presentations also helped to allay the community's fears and place the challenges ahead in broader perspective. For many, the threat of another terrorist attack, whether in the form of biological warfare or the scale of destruction experienced on September 11, appeared all too imminent. Several of the lecturers attempted to address these fears. For example, William Schwan, a microbiologist, did not dismiss the possibility of an attack with biological weapons, but assured the audience that a major anthrax outbreak was not very probable. In simple layman's terms, he articulated what was probable and improbable. Complementing his presentation was the lecture by University of Wisconsin System legal counsel, Patricia Brady, who gently reminded the audience of the importance of civil liberties in a democratic society. In the months following 9-11, the suspension of civil rights for certain groups in the United States had the appeal of a quick fix that would ensure the country's safety. In Brady's talk, however, we were cautioned that this very easy solution might destroy more than it resolved.

Psychologist Carmen Wilson Van Voorhis helped us to understand the natural human responses and reactions to terrorism, the threat of bioterrorism, and a willingness to suspend certain civil rights. Van Voorhis provided a primer on how to cope with stressful situations. She reviewed symptoms of stress that many of us experienced in the aftermath of 9-11 and offered mechanisms to help alleviate the stress.

These examples show how the University of Wisconsin-La Crosse community did what universities do best—using our intellectual capital to explain the world around us. By distilling topics such as cyberterrorism with user-friendly vocabulary, we can make an increasingly complex world a little more comprehensible and maybe a little less frightening. While an improved understanding in no way diminishes the horror or scope of what happened on September 11, 2001, it can further your knowledge and prepare you for a post 9-11 world. Hopefully, the following essays will help.

Douglas Hastad, Chancellor
University of Wisconsin-La Crosse

Acknowledgments

❖

This reader would not be published without the inspiration and prompting of Winston Beauchamp. Thanks to Winston's keen interest in learning more about the events of September 11, the idea for this manuscript was conceived. Several members of the community attended the lectures offered at the University of Wisconsin-La Crosse in the wake of the terrorist attacks. However, Winston was the first person to suggest the possibility of using the presentations as the nucleus of a reader. Thus, we are indebted to Winston for his guidance in getting the project started and for his support throughout the editorial process. The responsibility, however, for any errors in the text lies entirely with us.

Chancellor Hastad provided leadership in organizing the lecture series that would form the basis for the reader. We thank Interim Provost/Vice Chancellor Ronald Rada, and later, Provost/Vice Chancellor Elizabeth Hitch for making institutional resources available for the project. We are grateful to Frank Mortimer, Executive Editor, Prentice Hall, for making our collective vision a reality. Susan Beauchamp provided valuable insights into the business of publishing and worked hard to keep us on track.

On a personal note, Akorlie Nyatepe-Coo would like to thank Stella and Tumanyanelu for enduring through broken dates and absences during the course of this project. In the same spirit, Dorothy Zeisler-Vralsted again thanks family members, Jim, Robert, and Nora, for helping her realize the fruits of a fulfilling and productive career.

We would also like to thank the following reviewers:

James Albrecht, Sam Houston State University, Huntsville, TX; Alex del Carmen, University of Texas, Arlington, TX; Thomas Phelps, California State University, Sacramento, CA; and John Walsh, Vanderbilt University, Nashville, TN.

About the Contributors

---------------------------------- ❖ ----------------------------------

Karin Bast has over thirty-five years of experience in information systems. She has managed a computer company and consulted with industry for twenty years in the areas of technical corporate training and information systems management. She is currently a lecturer of Information Systems at UW-La Crosse, where she also serves as the manager of PC support and networking for the College of Business Administration.

Patricia A. Brady, J.D., University of Wisconsin-Madison, is the General Counsel, University of Wisconsin System. Before joining the University of Wisconsin System, she served as an Assistant Attorney General in North Carolina. She is a regular speaker on legal issues in higher education and has taught higher education law at the University of Wisconsin-Madison.

Jess Hollenback is currently an associate professor of history at the University of Wisconsin-La Crosse. He received his Ph.D. in history from UCLA in 1988 with a primary field of specialization in the history of religions. He is also the author of a book on comparative mysticism entitled *Mysticism: Experience, Response, and Empowerment,* published by Penn State Press in 1996.

Ronda L. Knox, Ph.D., Kent State University, is an associate professor in Communication Studies at the University of Wisconsin-La Crosse. Her areas of specialization are organizational communication and instructional communication.

Eric Kraemer, Ph.D., Brown University, is professor and chair of the Philosophy Department and Director of the International Studies curriculum at the University of Wisconsin-La Crosse. His areas of expertise include ethics and philosophy of mind.

Tim Kullman is currently a lecturer in the Sociology Department at the University of Wisconsin-La Crosse. Kullman teaches courses in sociology and criminal justice and writes on political extremism and terrorism.

H. Matthew Loayza received his Ph.D. from Purdue University in 1999. He is currently a lecturer in the History Department at the University of Wisconsin-La Crosse. He specializes in U.S. diplomatic history, cold war history, and Inter-American relations.

Akorlie A. Nyatepe-Coo, Ph.D., Northern Illinois University, is professor of Economics and Interim Director of Institutional Research at the University of Wisconsin-La Crosse. His research interests lie in the areas of international development, applied macroeconomics, and financial institutions.

Lalita Pandit, Ph.D., State University of New York, Buffalo, is a professor of English at the University of Wisconsin-La Crosse. Her research and publication areas include Shakespeare, literary theory, Indian literature and culture, and comparative aesthetics. Pandit also writes and publishes poems, short stories, and creative nonfiction.

Jim Rodgers is professor of Political Science at Saint Mary's University of Minnesota. Rodgers teaches courses in political and social thought and public policy and writes in the area of terrorism studies.

William Schwan received his Ph.D. from Northwestern University and is currently an assistant professor in the Department of Microbiology at the University of Wisconsin-La Crosse. Dr. Schwan teaches courses in pathogenic bacteriology and a class on bioterrorism. His research interests are in *Staphylococcus aureus* and type 1 pilus regulation in *Escherichia coli.*

Sheldon Smith received his Ph.D. in Anthropology and Latin American Studies from the University of Oregon. He is currently professor of Sociology at the University of Wisconsin-La Crosse. Dr. Smith is the author of *A World in Disorder,* published by University Press of America, and *Cultural Anthropology: Understanding a World in Transition,* published by Allyn and Bacon in 1998.

Mary M. Step, Ph.D., Kent State University, is an instructor of Communication Studies in the Department of Communication Science at Case Western Reserve University. Dr. Step's research interests reflect the role of emotion and other affective processes in human communication. She is particularly interested in contexts where interpersonal communication and media intersect.

Carmen R. Wilson Van Voorhis, Ph.D., Iowa State University, is an associate professor in the Department of Psychology at the University of Wisconsin-La Crosse. Dr. Wilson Van Voorhis teaches courses in adult and child psychopathology as well as counseling theories and techniques. Her research interests include emotional well-being after exposure to traumatic events.

Kimberly A. Vogt, Ph.D., University of New Hampshire, is a sociologist specializing in the field of criminology. Dr. Vogt teaches courses in criminology, criminal justice, delinquency, deviance, and health care and illness at the University of Wisconsin-La Crosse. Her research interests are in the areas of homicide and nonlethal violence, hate crime, and health risk behaviors among gay, lesbian, bisexual, and transgender youth.

John Weinzierl, Ph.D., Florida State University, is assistant professor of Modern European History at Lyon College, AR. His area of specialization is nineteenth century

Europe, with special emphasis in the French Revolutionary and Napoleonic periods. Dr. Weinzierl also teaches courses on the Middle East and the evolution of war.

Kuang-Wei Wen holds a doctorate in architecture and decision and information systems from Carnegie Mellon University. He is currently chair and associate professor of Information Systems at the University of Wisconsin-La Crosse. Dr. Wen's research interests lie in the area of artificial intelligence, especially in the use of beam search algorithms and neural networks to solve decision problems.

Dorothy Zeisler-Vralsted, Ph.D., Washington State University, is professor and chair of the History Department at the University of Wisconsin-La Crosse. Her research interests include twentieth-century U.S. and environmental history, resource use, and modern Germany.

Introduction

$$\clubsuit$$

Was September 11, 2001 a defining moment in U.S. history? Will the events of that day—the destruction of the World Trade Center, the attack on the Pentagon, and the crash of hijacked United Airlines flight 93 in Pennsylvania—be seen as the beginning of a new era in U.S. history or as three more episodes in a century marked by violence and bloodshed? The events of September 11 will continue to dominate the collective consciousness of Americans for some time to come. However, the tragedies of that day, though not of the same magnitude as the world wars or genocides, reflected an era that extended through most of the twentieth century. Over the last century, the world has witnessed devastation and loss of life at unimaginable levels. Wars and genocides with millions of combatant and civilian mortalities have all been part of this era. These events have been interpreted by political figures and the general public largely in the rhetoric of a world comprised of good and evil, with few nuances. For example, World War I was explained as a conflict prompted by German aggression, while 1930s fascist regimes in Germany and Italy rested on political ideologies with a dualistic worldview. Similarly, the Holocaust was explained in these simplistic terms as the work of a madman. Placed in this broader context, perhaps the tragedies of September 11 are not isolated incidents, and the reactions by Americans and their statesmen reflect continuity with the past.

Yet, in the aftermath of September 11, as initial reactions of shock and horror subsided, scholars all over the world wrestled with the larger meaning of these tragedies. Without diminishing the heinous nature of the attacks, academics of various persuasions sought to move away from simplistic "us versus them" rhetoric toward more comprehensive explanations. In the ensuing discussions, several questions arose. For example, what are the roots of Islamic rage against the West in general, and the United States in particular? What would lead young, well-educated men or women to become suicide bombers? Can we expect more terrorist attacks in the future, and what weapons will be used? Are nuclear, biological, or chemical attacks the next forms of terrorism? Is the use of violence to achieve political goals effective? How can we prevent future terrorist attacks? This reader provides in-depth examinations of these and other questions relating to the current wave of international terrorism.

While artists, writers, and academics worldwide have sought to lend meaning and understanding to the ongoing events, relatively few of these efforts have been consolidated in one text. The multidisciplinary approach of this reader is unique because it offers a broader context for analysis of the events of September 11 and its aftermath. By linking subjects as diverse as film and philosophy and approaches ranging from the literary to scientific, the reader provides a number of disciplinary tools for analysis of various aspects of terrorism. Although viewpoints from several disciplines are presented, the coverage of terrorism is not exhaustive. The approach in the reader is to provide diverse and unique perspectives on the events of September 11, and in the process, broaden the scope of ongoing discussions of international terrorism. This text is the result of a truly remarkable effort to reach out across disciplines, an endeavor that is evident in the diversity of approaches to understanding the significance of that day. For example, the events of September 11 are explained in some chapters by studying similar events from the recent past. In other chapters, the approach is to analyze the motives of terrorists. Other contributors look at the issues by considering the consequences of terrorism, or predicting the future.

Despite the multiplicity of perspectives, however, several important themes emerge. One of the more pervasive themes concerns the threat to the integrity of the democratic process in societies embarking on anti-terrorism campaigns. Several authors acknowledge that without the liberties assured to Americans, terrorists and advocates of right-wing ideologies would have limited opportunities to plan assaults such as the September 11 attacks and the Oklahoma City bombing of 1995. Yet, two of the contributors recognize that if these long-cherished civil liberties were curbed in the fight against terrorism, the losses to Americans would exceed any potential gains. A second recurring theme deals with the role of religion as a motivating factor in the activities of terrorists. Whether by pointing out the long history of the use of violence as a political strategy by people of different faiths, or by providing insights on the diversity of Islam, the authors undermine a popular stereotype linking terrorism to Islam.

Within these discussions, another theme emerges regarding the effectiveness of violence as a political strategy. Without reaching consensus, the authors' opinions range from selective past successes of terrorists to a belief that terrorism is detrimental to the cause of its practitioners. A fourth theme deals with the issue of motive and addresses the question of rationality of terrorist behavior. The contributions in Part II begin with the premise that regardless of the heinousness and apparent futility of the crimes that ensured the deaths of its architects, the perpetrators of the September 11 engaged in carefully selected actions designed to maximize certain objectives. But what is rational about behavior that is inimical to self-interest? These are just some of the more obvious themes; the reader is encouraged to search for others. Some of the tools of analysis discussed in the contributions can be used to explore other issues relating to the threat of international terrorism.

One of the issues discussed in the reader deals with the collective response of the U.S. public and how the media shaped the memories of September 11. Haunting images of the collapsing Twin Towers were played over and over again, perhaps contributing to stress-related disorders in sections of the population. The constancy of the images combined with endless news reporting helped to shape perceptions about potential causes of the attacks, the extent of the devastation, and what actions, if any, should be taken in retaliation. There is concern that some of the coverage in the immediate aftermath of the attacks was deficient in objectivity and diversity of points of view. Throughout the text, the contributors emphasize the need for an informed citizenry in the modern world. In the chapters that follow, special effort is made to bring the reader closer to that goal.

The first part of the reader provides historical context for understanding terrorism. In Chapter 1, titled "Islam and the West," historian Jess Hollenback reviews the core beliefs and practices of Islam and discusses earlier interactions between the Arab world and the West. This is followed by a study of the roots of Muslim anger against the West and Muslim responses to Western culture. Some readers may be surprised to learn that Islam and Christianity share many of the same beliefs. Further, before modernization of the Western world, the Arab Empire preserved much of the Greek and Roman classics during a period when most of Western Europe lived in ignorance. In addition to the historical perspective, Hollenback emphasizes the diversity of Islam. Because Islam is not monolithic and includes moderates as well as fundamentalists, Hollenback is guardedly optimistic about future relations between Islam and the West.

Further historical background is offered in Chapter 2, an essay by historian John Weinzierl entitled "Terrorism: Its Origin and History." Weinzierl introduces the reader to the origins of terrorism, focusing on the activities of earlier terrorist groups, such as the ancient Zealots, as well as more recent activities of certain Israeli groups. Within this broader context, the reader is led to the conclusion that terrorism has a long, and in some instances, effective history not limited to the Arab world. In this respect, the terrorist group al-Qaeda is not unique. The causes of terrorism might also be longstanding—Weinzierl identifies apathy, frustration, and indignation as the seeds of contemporary terrorism. The overriding theme in most of the chapter is whether the use of violence to achieve political and/or religious ends is effective.

As an extension of the inquiry into how events of September 11 occurred, the second part of the reader examines the behavior and motives of terrorists. This section broadens the discussion by considering philosophies, motives, incentive structures, potential triggers, and organizational structures of domestic terrorists as well as international groups. In many cases, the only link among the groups is their approval of violence as a strategy to achieve political ends. Drawing upon their expertise in sociology and criminal justice, Jim Rodgers and Tim Kullman, in Chapter 3, profile domestic terrorists as typically uneducated and lower income individuals who perceive themselves as being disenfranchised. These demographics contrast sharply with those of the terrorists behind September 11. Yet, similarities exist, and the authors are thorough in their review of domestic terrorists' biases such as anti-Semitism—a prejudice shared by many international terrorists. At the end of the chapter, the reader is reminded of the pervasiveness of terrorism and its domestic presence.

In another look at the behavior of terrorists, Chapter 4, written by anthropologist Sheldon Smith, examines the attacks of September 11 within the broader context of *jihads* against globalization and Western influence. In this chapter, titled "Terrorism, True Believers, and the Attack on Globalization," Smith reviews the philosophical justifications for the activities of international terrorist groups such as al-Qaeda, Hamas, and Hezbollah. Returning to the theme of the effectiveness of terrorism, the author contends that the rise

of Islamic fundamentalism in the Middle East and the consequent use of violence for political objectives will not significantly impact U.S. influence or the trend toward globalization. Instead, Smith concludes that in the long run, acts of terrorism are more damaging
to countries in the Middle East. The discussion of the effects of terrorism in the Middle
East complements the discussion of U.S. foreign policy in the concluding Chapter 15.

Under the general heading of motives, Chapter 5, "Economic Implications of
Terrorism," strikes a different tone from the previous ones. Using an economic model of
criminal behavior, economist Akorlie Nyatepe-Coo suggests that the decision to engage in
a terrorist act is based on assessment of costs and benefits. This author identifies two main
factors in the development of terrorist intent: environments that create a predisposition toward criminal acts and organizational structures that recruit, mobilize, and indoctrinate
members. This piece may be challenging for some readers, but the reader is rewarded with
the expanded insight into the factors involved in the transformation of otherwise law-
abiding citizens into the authors of incredible crimes. From studying the actions of terrorists from the perspective of what incentives and the organizational dynamics sustain
terrorist groups, the text shifts next to what goes on in the minds of terrorists and their organizations. By the end of the second section, a conceptualization of modern-day terrorists has evolved drawing upon the work of historians, sociologists, and economists.
Beginning with the often-troubled history between Islam and the West, the long-standing
use of terrorist tactics, the linkage between domestic and international terrorists (demonstrating further terrorism's prevalence) and the external factors that have promoted the
birth and existence of groups such as al-Qaeda, and finally, an examination of internal factors that ensure the preservation of the organization, the reader has a foundation to explore
the more abstract inquiries into the nature of terrorism.

Chapters 6 and 7 expand the boundaries of traditional scholarship on terrorism and
September 11. In Chapter 6, "Inside the Mind of a Suicide Bomber: Santosh Sivan's *The
Terrorist,*" Lalita Pandit, a professor of English, reviews an Indian film based on the 1991
assassination of Rajiv Gandhi by a suicide bomber. Because the film is a fictional account,
filmmaker Sivan is able to speculate on various aspects of the motivation for this form of
terrorism. Using the approach of a literary critic, Pandit sheds light on the private life of a
terrorist: the disconnectedness from secular thought as well as various aspects of the link
with humanity. The main character, Malli, grows up in a society whose sole purpose is the
achievement of a certain political end. Lost in this single-mindedness, Malli is divorced
from the rhythms of everyday life. In the conclusion, Sivan introduces Malli back to a humanity rich in culture and daily rituals. A different view of terrorism is provided as Sivan
explores what might stop a terrorist from committing an act of terrorism. In summarizing
the film, Pandit also draws parallels between terrorist organizations in Sri Lanka and other
emerging nations and considers the legacy of colonialism. Throughout the review, Pandit
provides the tools necessary for sophisticated film analysis, which should serve the reader
in the study of other films.

Although the next chapter is somewhat removed from the immediacy of a terrorist's
life, Eric Kraemer, a professor of philosophy, complements Pandit's essay through his reasoned examination of how to define evil. In Chapter 7, titled, "A Philosopher Looks at
Terrorism: Evil, Religion, and World Ethics," Kraemer offers valuable insights into how to
assess human actions. The difference between intent and result is recognized, but the author argues that evil can still be defined in the actions of the September 11 terrorists.

Further, by accepting the definition of evil suggested in the chapter, the acts of the September 11 terrorists cannot be dismissed as irrational, making the crimes of September 11 even more heinous. In an approach similar to that used in Chapter 6, Kraemer concludes with specific suggestions on what could be done (from a philosophical perspective) to help prevent further attacks from occurring. Although this suggestion—that is, a world ethics perspective—is more academic and abstract than that found in Sivan's film, both authors are unique in looking beyond the traditional economic, political, or military resolutions to prevent future terrorist attacks. Like Pandit, Kraemer provides students with additional tools to assess the world around them. Taken together, the two essays are imaginative inquiries as to how societies can shape collective responses to a changing world.

In Part III, four authors investigate some of the responses in the aftermath of September 11. These chapters deal with some of the immediate reactions to September 11 and include studies of the role of the media, psychological responses, the activities of hate groups, and the efforts by some to curb civil liberties in the United States. In contrast to the contributions in the previous section, which were more hypothetical with respect to the causes of terrorism, the studies in this part deal with the immediate reality of September 11 and challenge the reader to question the legacy of this day for U.S. society. Chapter 8 is a contribution by communications studies professors Mary Step and Ronda Knox titled "Media Portrayals of September 11, 2001 and Beyond." The authors note that events of September 11 provided the media with unprecedented challenges and opportunities. With that underlying emphasis, they review typical media coverage of a disaster, media conventions that resulted, the media responses from disparate groups, and how audiences reacted to the media coverage of the terrorist attacks. In addition to this introduction to the inner workings of the media, the authors explore the consensus reached by the media in its coverage of September 11. Using the response to one political commentator's comments on U.S. actions after September 11, Knox and Step point to some of the weaknesses of the September 11 coverage by commercial U.S. media.

In another examination of the impact of September 11 on the lives of individuals, psychologist Carmen Wilson VanVoorhis in Chapter 9 offers the reader a practical guide to living after experiencing disasters on the scale of September 11. She describes stress-related disorders and symptoms and suggests responses for individuals and communities. VanVoorhis writes in an easily accessible style, giving the reader useful information and insights on behaviors observed in the months following the attacks as well as various aggravating or ameliorating factors. Although written more with the individual in mind, VanVoorhis' article underscores the long-term effects of terrorism. After the destruction to life and property, populations can continue to experience long-lasting psychological damage. Again this raises the question, how effective are acts of terrorism? Another expression of the effects of terrorism was seen in the growth in hate crimes against certain groups in the aftermath of September 11. Drawing on her expertise in criminal justice, Kim Vogt's Chapter 10, "Hate Crime as a Reaction to the Terrorist Attacks of September 11, 2001," discusses the evolution of individuals and groups that commit hate crimes. This study discusses different factors that can cause hate crimes and presents profiles of individuals or groups usually associated with these crimes.

Chapter 10 provides an introduction for Chapter 11 by attorney Patricia Brady, titled "The Impact of the September 11, 2001 Terrorist Attacks on Civil Liberties." Brady's essay reflects contemporary debate regarding U.S. civil liberties and the new restrictions placed on Americans and other groups—for example, international students. The essay provides insightful commentary regarding the nature of a democratic society and is framed around the question "To what degree should Americans be willing to accept limits on civil liberties in order to achieve victory over terrorism?" After reviewing the origins of U.S. civil liberties and discussing current challenges such as the USA Patriot Act, the author concludes with a reminder of the role of universities in the preservation of civil liberties. Brady believes that it is important for universities to encourage the expression of diverse points of view and continue to pursue knowledge regarding the causes of terrorism. Within this framework of the search for truth, she offers hope that civil liberties can be protected even in the midst of the fight against terrorism.

By reviewing emerging trends in contemporary terrorism, the chapters in Part IV approach the discussion of terrorism from yet another perspective. In the wake of September 11 and the subsequent anthrax scare, many Americans became increasingly anxious over forms of terrorism yet to be experienced. The news media heightened awareness of the possibility of biological, chemical, and nuclear warfare and the belief that terrorist groups may possess these types of weapons became an ever-present concern. A text on terrorism without an informed discussion on forms of terrorism would be a serious omission. Chapter 12 provides a general discussion of the potential use of emerging technologies to further the terrorist agenda. This is followed by two chapters examining the crimes of cyberterrorism and bioterrorism. Chapter 12, titled "Technology and the Transformation of Terrorism," by Jess Hollenback cautions the reader about the power of emerging technologies, especially when these technologies get into the possession of individuals with malicious intent. Hollenback reviews a wide range of possible attacks and emphasizes how, for the first time in history, small groups have the means to wage warfare. While some of the scenarios outlined in this chapter are hypothetical, Hollenback poses thoughtful questions regarding the consequences of unrestrained technological development.

Using a more functional approach, experts in information systems, Karin A. Bast and Kuang-Wei Wen examine the threat of cyberterrorism in Chapter 13, titled "Cyberterrorism: A New Reality in the Information Age." In clear, concise language, the authors introduce the frequently discussed but often misunderstood subject of cyberterrorism. They offer suggestions on how to defend against a cyberattack and recommend follow-up actions in the event that a cyberattack is successful. While acknowledging the threat of cyberterrorism and underscoring the inherent dangers to democratic societies dealing with its worst effects, the authors suggest that by taking practical steps, such as more cooperation between law enforcement agencies, the damage from a cyberattack can be minimized. One of the themes in this chapter concerns the potential loss of civil liberties in the fight against cyberterrorism.

Complementing the expertise of Bast and Wen is Chapter 13, "Bioterrorism: Should I Be Worried?" by microbiologist William Schwan. The author, while recognizing the potential damage from a bioterrorist attack, suggests that the probability of a successful attack is diminished due to difficulties with weaponization of various biological agents. Schwan begins with the premise that the more that is known about a subject, the less vulnerable people are to fear. The author discusses concerns and misconceptions regarding biological agents or "germs" and treatments available to either prevent or treat illnesses caused by the agents. Finally, Schwan offers practical advice on what the average person needs to know in the event of a biological attack.

What does the future hold in the arena of international relations? The final chapter, by historian H. Matthew Loayza, titled "Terrorism in the 21st Century," provides an informed foreign policy perspective. In this review of real and potential terrorist threats, the author offers suggestions on how the United States might avert future attacks. Applying a historical perspective to contemporary foreign policy, Loayza reminds the reader of earlier mistakes caused by U.S. misconceptions of Soviet actions and intent—misconceptions that resulted in the Cold War. The author cautions Americans not to oversimplify past events. Looking toward the future, Loayza contends that a world that includes terrorism will be part of contemporary life and that the role of government, in the form of increased spending on the military, technology, and intelligence, will be changed as a result.

In summary, the essays have universal appeal as thought-provoking responses to the events of September 11. The multidisciplinary approach informs the reader of the many facets of terrorism and explores perspectives not usually considered in conventional texts. This reader represents the efforts of a handful of academics to provide some insights on why the attacks of September 11 occurred, the historical significance of the events, and the implications in an increasingly intricate and challenging world.

Dorothy Zeisler-Vralsted

PART I

INTERNATIONAL TERRORISM IN HISTORICAL CONTEXT

1

Islam and the West

Jess Hollenback

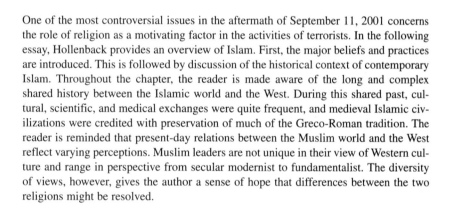

One of the most controversial issues in the aftermath of September 11, 2001 concerns the role of religion as a motivating factor in the activities of terrorists. In the following essay, Hollenback provides an overview of Islam. First, the major beliefs and practices are introduced. This is followed by discussion of the historical context of contemporary Islam. Throughout the chapter, the reader is made aware of the long and complex shared history between the Islamic world and the West. During this shared past, cultural, scientific, and medical exchanges were quite frequent, and medieval Islamic civilizations were credited with preservation of much of the Greco-Roman tradition. The reader is reminded that present-day relations between the Muslim world and the West reflect varying perceptions. Muslim leaders are not unique in their view of Western culture and range in perspective from secular modernist to fundamentalist. The diversity of views, however, gives the author a sense of hope that differences between the two religions might be resolved.

It must have been a deep and passionate fury that drove nineteen Muslim hijackers in the prime of their lives to seize the controls of four airliners on September 11 and fulfill their grim suicidal missions that destroyed not only their own lives but also the lives of thousands of innocent people. Before we can ever begin to comprehend what happened on September 11, 2001, we must understand the historical roots of this pervasive and deep-seated anger against the West that looms so prominently and menacingly in the cultural landscape of the contemporary Islamic world. But, we must also realize that this stereotyped image of an enraged Islam is only part of the story. While it is true that conflict has been a prominent theme in relations between the two civilizations for many centuries, both ancient and modern history show that some degree of cultural symbiosis between the two great civilizations has also been a part of that relationship. It is especially true that modern Muslim responses to the West have actually been more complex and nuanced than the media stereotypes of an enraged Islam would suggest.

OBJECTIVES OF THIS STUDY

This study has four principal objectives: First, it will give the reader a brief overview of the cardinal assumptions, practices, and beliefs of Islam, that religion whose adherents are known as Muslims. Second, it will discuss both the early policies of Muslim rulers toward their Christian subjects as well as some of the early intellectual encounters between Islam and neighboring civilizations with special attention to the ways that Islam and Western Europe exchanged scientific and philosophical ideas, medical knowledge, and technologies. The third objective of this study is to trace the roots of Muslim anger against the West, beginning with the Crusades and Spanish Reconquista and continuing through the period of modern Western European colonialism and imperialism. What sorts of actions and stereotypes of Islam and Muslims emerged in the West during these long centuries of civilizational conflict and how have they contributed to the present-day climate of conflict and misunderstanding? Fourth, this chapter concludes with an analysis of some of the principal ways that Muslim leaders and intellectuals have responded both to Western cultural influences and to the forces of modernization since the nineteenth century. These responses—while almost always rejecting Western political and military domination of Muslim lands—display a broad spectrum of attitudes to Western culture and Western cultural institutions. Some, like the secular modernists and Islamic modernists, find much to admire in Western culture, whereas other groups—who are commonly labeled as Islamic "fundamentalists"—stress Islamic self-sufficiency and find almost nothing in Western culture that is worthy of emulation. In short, this study concludes that Islam is not monolithic in its response to the West and that there are genuine reasons to hope for an eventual amelioration of conflict between the Islamic world and the West.

ISLAM: CORE PRACTICES, BELIEFS, AND ASSUMPTIONS

Islam is an Arabic word that means "submission," more specifically, submission to the will of God. It is also the name of that religion that originated from the seventh century Arabian prophet Muhammad (570–632) and that is now the second largest religion in the world today in terms of the numbers of its followers, who call themselves "Muslims." Although, historically, Islam appeared in the seventh century, Muslims claim that Islam is not a new religion at all but rather a very old religion that God has repeatedly revealed to prophets like Noah, Abraham, Isaac, Moses, David, John the Baptist, and Jesus. Muslims therefore believe that there were Muslims before Muhammad and that "any human being who . . . submits and obeys [God's will] is, therefore, a Muslim in a moral state of Islam" (Abdalati, n.d., p. 10).

Islam, like Judaism and Christianity, is an exclusivist form of monotheism. The sole object of worship in Islam is Allah, an Arabic word that simply means "God." Muslims therefore claim that they worship the same God as the Jews and Christians and that this same God gave the same revelation that He communicated to Muhammad through the angel Gabriel to the other Old and New Testament figures whom Muslims regard as prophets.

Islam also has other close religious connection to Judaism and Christianity. For instance, all three religions worship the same God and regard Him as the exclusive object of their worship. Many of the figures honored as prophets in Islam are also honored in Judaism and/or Christianity. Further, they share the common premise that obedience to God's will is supremely important and that those things are good that conform to God's will, and those things are evil or impure that fail to conform to His will. Finally, all three assume that God created the universe out of nothing by an act of His sovereign will and that, for that reason, all of creation is utterly dependent upon Him.

Further connections exist between Christianity and Islam. Both believe in the existence of an eternal afterlife in either Paradise (Heaven) or Hell and they maintain that one's post-mortem destiny is determined by whether one obeyed God's will. They also believe in the bodily resurrection of the dead and in the existence of a Last Judgment where those who acted in conformity to God's will be rewarded by a blessed eternity in Heaven or Paradise and where the wicked who disobeyed His will will be punished by an eternity of torments in Hell.

The religion of Islam has as its holy scripture the Qur'an (Koran). Muslims maintain that *Muhammad did NOT create the Qur'an; instead the Qur'an is a divine creation.* God created the Qur'an and the prophet Muhammad simply served as the passive mouthpiece through whom God's angel, the Holy Spirit Gabriel, spoke His word to humankind (Abdalati, p. 193). It is God who is talking to us in the Qur'an, not Muhammad. Furthermore, God brought His word to humankind in Arabic. For this reason, Muslims have an intense reverence for Arabic and until recently, the translation of the Qur'an from Arabic was discouraged. Those who know the Qur'an in the original Arabic emphasize its incredibly beautiful sound and rhythm, which cannot be communicated in any translation. This extraordinary beauty of the sound of the Qur'an is believed by devout Muslims to be proof of its divine rather than human origin. The Qur'an is the single most important foundation for Muslim behavior and belief.

How do Muslims regard the scriptures of the Jews and the Christians? Muslims contend that God gave the earlier prophets—and this includes Jesus—basically the same message that He gave to Muhammad. Thus the Qur'an tells us:

> Say [to them]: "We believe in God, and in what has been revealed to us and what was revealed to Abraham, Isma'il [Ishmael], Isaac, Jacob, and the Tribes, and in (Books) given to Moses, Jesus, and the Prophets, from their Lord; we make no distinction between one and another among them . . ." (Qur'an 3:84).

In other words, the message that God gave to the earlier prophets before Muhammad was an authentic message that showed those peoples the true path of obedience to God's will. Unfortunately, Muslims contend, the people who received these earlier revelations of God from their prophets corrupted the scriptures that they had received from Him by losing or concealing the books, omitting portions of God's original revelation, or by adding human inventions of their own to the revealed word. Because they have been tampered with in this fashion, Muslims maintain that the Torah of the Jews and the Bible of the Christians are not authentic records of God's word. The only message from God that has been preserved without adding or deleting anything is the Qur'an. From the Muslim perspective, if one wants to know what Moses or Jesus really said or did, one must consult the stories about those figures that appear in the Qur'an rather than relying upon the Bible.

Muslims have a tremendous reverence for the prophet Muhammad. When devout Muslims mention Muhammad's name, they often follow it with the expression "upon whom be peace" as a sign of reverent respect for him. It is a very serious cause of offense to Muslims for anyone to defame or vilify Muhammad or the members of his family. Although Muslims deeply revere Muhammad, they do not worship him. He is only a human being like the rest of us. Muhammad is called the "seal of the prophets," that is to say, he is the last in a long line of prophets who have received God's revelation. There will be no other revelations of God's will since the Qur'an as revealed through Muhammad is complete.

Muslims deeply revere Muhammad because they regard him as the perfect and sinless model of what human life in obedience to God's will should be like. He is the perfect exemplar of Islam, submission to the will of God. Indeed, the Qur'an tells us this when God asserts "Ye have indeed in the Apostle of God [Muhammad] a beautiful pattern of conduct for anyone whose hope is in God and the Final Day . . ." (Qur'an 33:21). Devout Muslims try to model every facet of their public and private behavior in accordance with God's will. Seyyed Hossein Nasr has described this phenomenon in the following words:

> For nearly 1400 years Muslims have tried to awaken in the morning as the Prophet awakened, to eat as he ate, to wash as he washed himself, and even to cut their nails as he did. There has been no greater force for the unification of the Muslim peoples than the presence of this common model for the minutest acts of daily life (Nasr, 1975, pp. 82–83).

This is an extremely important statement about Islam because it points to its comprehensive character as a religion. Islam is submission to God's will not just when it comes to such "important" matters of life as the proper way to treat other people, but also in even the minutest and most seemingly insignificant details of private life, such as how one eats, cuts one's nails, and washes oneself. The example of the prophet Muhammad (also known as the Sunnah of the Prophet) provides Muslims with that model for performing even the minutest details of private life in a way that is pleasing to God and in conformity to His will.

Central to Islamic practice are the *five pillars of Islam,* consisting of the following: The first pillar is the *shahada* or declaration of faith, "There is no God but God and Muhammad is His messenger." This is a statement of Islam's uncompromising monotheism and an acknowledgment that Muhammad is God's faithful transmitter of God's message to humankind.

The second pillar of Islam is *salat* or prayer five times a day around dawn, noon, midafternoon, sunset, and nightfall. Prayers are said in Arabic and contain verses from the Qur'an. These prayers must be performed in the prescribed manner with the head facing the sacred city of Mecca, with the prescribed words in Arabic, at the prescribed times, and in a state of ritual purity. These prayers, by interrupting one's routine five times a day, are a powerful means of eliciting remembrance of God and a sense of thankfulness towards Him.

The third pillar of Islam is *zakat* or almsgiving. Islam is deeply concerned with social justice and with the plight of the unfortunate. *Zakat* is an obligatory payment that amounts to about 2.5 percent of one's capital. By paying *zakat,* one is not only helping the needy but also purifying one's wealth and possessions.

The fourth pillar is fasting during the daylight hours of the holy month of Ramadan, a month made sacred because of the fact that it was the month the first Qur'anic verse came to Muhammad. One abstains from all food, drink, and sexual activity during the period from first light until last light after sundown. This, too, is a powerful means of calling one to remembrance of God, and it is a ritual that powerfully bonds the members of the Islamic community in a common struggle to realize God's will when one's bodily instincts are tempting one to break the fast.

The fifth pillar of Islam is the *hajj* or greater pilgrimage to the sacred city of Mecca that ought to be performed once in one's lifetime. This obligation is only binding upon those who have the financial means and health to do so. It must be performed during a several-day period in the twelfth month of the Islamic lunar year. It is a powerful means of enhancing Islamic solidarity since millions of Muslims from all parts of the world converge on Mecca to perform the series of rituals that fulfill this obligation to God.

Some words must be said about *jihad,* an exercise or struggle that some people regard as a kind of "sixth pillar" of Islam. First, the Arabic word *jihad* has a variety of meanings besides the usual one of "holy war" on behalf of Islam. It is an Arabic word that means "struggle" or "exertion" to realize God's will. This struggle can be of different kinds. There is the "*jihad* of the heart," which is the constant struggle of humans against their base instincts that hinder them from realizing God's will. There is a tradition where Muhammad is alleged to have said that this form of *jihad* was the "greater *jihad*" and that, compared to this struggle, engaging in holy war was the "lesser *jihad.*" There is the "*jihad* of the tongue and hand," which is the struggle of Muslims to persuade people to do what is good in God's eyes and to avoid evil. There is the "*jihad* of the pen," which is the peaceful struggle to convert non-Muslims to Islam. And finally, there is the "*jihad* of the sword," which is holy war in defense of Islam.

Islam is not a pacifist religion. It recognizes that there are times when warfare is necessary, such as when someone attacks the Islamic community. Indeed, the Qur'an makes it clear that warfare is obligatory for Muslim males if the Islamic community is attacked. The vast majority of modern Muslims, however, maintain that the Qur'an does not justify aggressive warfare against non-Muslims but only defensive warfare. They can cite such passages in the Qur'an as 2:256, which declares that "there shall be no compulsion in religion," as well as other passages such as Qur'an 2:190, which proclaims that "God has no love for those who embark upon aggression." In a Saudi Arabian book put out by the Islamic Teaching Center to acquaint non-Muslims with Islam, the author has this to say about *jihad:*

> Islam never tolerates aggression from its own side or from any other side, nor does it entertain aggressive wars or the initiation of aggressive wars. Muslims are commanded by God not to begin hostilities, or embark on any act of aggression, or violate the rights of others (Abdalati, n.d., p. 142).

Nevertheless, certain extremist elements in Islam such as al-Qaeda and the Islamic Jihad organization interpret certain sayings attributed to the prophet Muhammad and certain Qur'an verses as a justification for their belief that Muslims must wage war on both those Muslims who refuse to live in strict accord with the Qur'an and the example of the prophet Muhammad and on non-Muslims. For example, Muhammad al-Salam Faraj, the author of an extremist tract entitled *Neglected Duty* and a member of the Islamic Jihad organization that assassinated Egyptian president Anwar Sadat in 1981, denies that *jihad* is defensive only. In support of his position he cites Qur'an 9:5, the so-called "sword verse," which reads: "Fight and slay the pagans wherever ye find them and seize them, beleaguer them and lie in wait for them in every stratagem in war." He also cited Qur'an 47:4, which reads: "So when you meet those who have disbelieved, (let there be) slaughter until ye have made havoc of them, bind them fast, then (liberate them) either freely or by ransom." He contends that since Qur'an 9:5 and Qur'an 47:4 came from God to Muhammad later in the prophet's career than the earlier verses like Qur'an 2:256 and 2:190, which emphasize the defensive character of *jihad,* the milder verses have therefore been abrogated by the "sword verses" (Jansen, 1986, pp. 193–198). Faraj also justifies his view that *jihad* can be aggressive by citing certain actions of Muhammad such as his letter to the Christians of Najran inviting them to accept Islam or risk war. The relevant text of this letter reads: ". . . From Muhammad . . . to the Bishop and people of Najran . . . I call upon you to let yourselves be ruled by God, and not by men. When you refuse, then a head tax. When you refuse (this, too), be apprised of war" (Jansen, 1986, p. 194). Both the militant extremists and the advocates of purely defensive *jihad* are being selective in their usage of texts from the Qur'an in support of their viewpoint.

This selective use of scripture, however, is not unique to Islam. Every religious tradition pivots around the central question of how its scriptures and sacred traditions are interpreted and reinterpreted in light of changing historical circumstances. Further, every religious tradition consists of various different groups who selectively interpret the scriptures and sacred traditions to suit their particular agendas. Thus, there are Muslims who interpret the Qur'an to advance their view that Islam is against offensive warfare; others interpret the Qur'an to argue that it is in favor of offensive warfare; and finally, Islamic pacifists like the Sri Lankan sufi Muhammad R. W. Muhaiyadeen interpret the Qur'an in such a way as to make it serve their pacifist agenda (Muhaiyadeen, 1987). Christians have done the same thing with the Bible. Some have cited and interpreted the Bible to support pacifism and others have cited and interpreted that same Bible to support imperialism or the enslavement of non-European peoples.

One of the most important contrasts between Islam and Christianity concerns their respective beliefs about Jesus. Islam has a deep reverence for Jesus as a prophet, messiah, and as a miracle worker. In addition, the Qur'an teaches that Jesus was born of a virgin. The Qur'an, however, denies that Jesus was divine or that He was the Son of God. Muslims also regard the Christian doctrine of the Holy Trinity as a kind of covert polytheism. Furthermore, the Qur'an denies that Jesus was crucified. The Qur'an also teaches that Jesus "received" the Gospels in much the same way that Muhammad received the Qur'an from the angel Gabriel. This contradicts the Christian belief that the Gospels were not given to Jesus but rather were written about Him after He had been crucified. There is also a story about the Last Supper in the Qur'an where God lowers a table full of food to Jesus and His disciples after they ask Jesus to have God do this as a proof of His miraculous powers. There are also stories about Jesus animating clay birds and speaking in the cradle (Qur'an 5:112–115; 5:110; 19:29–33). These last two stories are not found in the Bible, but they are found in the noncanonical *First Gospel of the Infancy of Jesus Christ,* 15:1–6 and 1:2–3, respectively.

Another very profound difference between Islam and Christianity is the legalistic character of Islam. Like Orthodox Judaism today and the Judaism of the Pharisees in Jesus's day, Islam is a religion that places tremendous emphasis on following a God-given code of law called the *shari'a* that ideally should govern the minutest details of how one lives one's public and private life. In contrast, Jesus ridiculed the Pharisees for what He thought was their obsessive concern with the minute details of Mosaic Law, such as whether one should wash one's hands before eating. To Jesus, the details of the letter of the Law were not really all that important compared to its spirit. Furthermore, Paul taught that Christians no longer had to worry about following the minute details of Mosaic Law, such as avoiding pork, because Jesus's redemptive death on the Cross redeemed Christians from bondage to the Law so that they are saved by faith alone and not by works. In Islam, however, you are NOT saved by your faith alone but also by your works, by what you do, and by whether what you do is in accordance with God's will as revealed in the Qur'an and the Sunnah of the Prophet (the example of the prophet Muhammad). Devout Muslims do concern themselves with what to Christians seem nitpicking details like washing themselves the same way Muhammad washed himself and cutting their nails they way he cut his. This stems from the comprehensive character of Islam and the *shari'a.*

The *shari'a* is a divinely ordained code of behavior based upon two primary foundations: the Qur'an and the Sunnah of the Prophet. It is the principal objective of all present day Islamic revivalists (or fundamentalists) to implement this *shari'a* and make it the law of the land. It is important to emphasize that this second major foundation of Muslim behavior and the *shari'a,* the Sunnah of the Prophet, is based on collections of thousands of individual anecdotes called *hadith* that were collected by devout Muslims in the first two centuries after the Prophet's death. Those *hadith* are individual anecdotes about what Muhammad is supposed to have said or done on particular occasions. For instance, there are anecdotes about how Muhammad prayed and there are even anecdotes about Muhammad telling his followers how to wash a bowl that a dog has contaminated by licking it (*Sahih Muslim,* vol. 1, ch. 111). The sum total of all of these thousands of *hadith* that the Islamic community has deemed to be authentic constitutes what is called the example of the Prophet or the Sunnah of the Prophet.

As mentioned earlier, Islam is a comprehensive way of life that, ideally, ought to shape *every* facet of one's public and private behavior as well as the forms that political and social life ought to take. In other words, it is important to realize Islam is not just a matter of private belief. Instead, as the Universal Islamic Declaration of 1976 states [my emphasis], "Islam is a complete code of life suitable for all people and all times, and Allah's mandate is eternal and universal and applies to *every sphere of human conduct and life, without any distinction between the temporal and the spiritual*" (quoted in Hunt & Crotty, 1991, p. 107). Consequently, the separation of "church" and state is alien to Islam because Islam ought to dictate not just what a Muslim believes about God and the afterlife, but also the forms of social and political organization he or she lives under.

Islamic law, the *shari'a,* is not just a comprehensive code of behavior and regulations modeled upon the Qur'an and the Sunnah of the Prophet. It is also a code of law where God is the sole legislator. The laws and regulations that constitute the *shari'a* do not derive their legitimacy from the fact that they reflect the will of the people or the will of any king but instead, from the fact that they have been ordained by God. Under the *shari'a* humans simply execute the laws that God has ordained in the Qur'an and the example of the prophet Muhammad.

EARLY ENCOUNTERS BETWEEN ISLAMIC CIVILIZATION AND NEIGHBORING CIVILIZATIONS

A stunning feature of Islam was the incredible speed with which it spread out of Arabia to incorporate vast areas of the Middle East, north Africa, central Asia, and even Spain into its empire within the first century that followed the death of the Prophet Muhammad in 632 C.E. During the first thirty years after the Prophet's death, the Christian Byzantine empire, though it managed to keep control of its vital agricultural heartland in Anatolia (present-day Turkey) for several more centuries, permanently lost its former territories in Egypt, Syria, and Palestine to the Arabs. The great empire of the Sassanids fared even worse succumbing completely to the victorious armies of Islam.

Fortunately, the Arab Muslim conquerors were generous in victory. They did not attempt to wipe out the Middle Eastern civilizations whom they had just conquered nor did they attempt to forcibly convert the non-Muslim religious communities to Islam. Instead, the Arabs followed a pattern of cultural assimilation that generously amalgamated various elements derived from the cultures of their diverse subject peoples with elements from their own Arab culture. Moreover, they also pursued a policy of religious toleration towards conquered Christians, Jews, and Zoroastrians provided that these groups paid the *jizyah* or poll tax assessed on all non-Muslim "People of the Book." This policy of toleration and cultural exchange played an important role in creating a rich and vibrant Islamic civilization that reached its peak of intellectual vitality during the first three centuries of the Abbasid caliphate (750–1258 C.E.).

When one talks about Islam's relationship to the West, it is first of all essential to understand how the prophet Muhammad and early Muslim rulers regarded Christianity and the Christian communities whom they had just incorporated into their vast empire. Broadly speaking, Islamic rulers have usually accorded religious toleration toward Christians and Jews, subject to significant, and sometimes humiliating, restrictions. On the one hand, Christians and Jews have generally been given a special covenant of protection (*dhimmah*), and as such protected "People of the Book" (*ahl al-kitab*) they have also been known as *dhimmis. Dhimmis* have usually been permitted to practice their religion, govern themselves, and resolve disputes among themselves in accordance with their own religious law. They have also been guaranteed protection of their persons and property by the Islamic state provided that they pay the *jizya,* a special tax on non-Muslims, remain loyal to the Islamic state, and refrain from proselytizing. It is also worth noting that instances of forcible conversion and persecution of *dhimmis* have been rare. Despite this toleration and protection that the Muslim state accorded to Christians and Jews, however, it is also clear that when one compares the way that the Muslim state treated its Muslim subjects with the way that it typically treated its Christian and Jewish subjects, the latter were treated as though they were second-class citizens in terms of both prestige and social position.

The Qur'an passage that has been most important in defining traditional Muslim rulers' behavior towards Christians and Jews is Qur'an 9:29, which reads as follows:

> Fight those who believe not in God nor in the Last Day, nor hold that forbidden which
> hath been forbidden by God and His Apostle, nor acknowledge the religion of truth, (even
> if they are) of the *People of the Book,* until they pay the Jizya with willing submission,
> and feel themselves subdued.

Here it is clear that Christians and Jews, the People of the Book, are to be fought until they acknowledge Muslim political supremacy and display this submission to Muslim authority by paying the *jizya.* This divine commandment was carried out by the Prophet Muhammad when he conquered the Byzantine frontier town of Tabuk as well as on other occasions. After Tabuk surrendered to his armies, he imposed this *jizya* on the Christians of that town (Vaziri, 1992, p. 44), and this precedent was followed by later caliphs (heads of the Islamic state after the death of Muhammad). With the payment of this tax, they were allowed to practice their religion and given protection of their lives and property by the Muslim state.

It is important to emphasize that the religious toleration that Christians and Jews were accorded under Muslim rule was not the same thing as religious freedom as we envision it in the United States today. Yet the traditional Muslim treatment of religious minorities was indeed a model of toleration compared to the extreme forms of bigotry toward religious minorities that occurred in the Christian world, such as the decision by Ferdinand and Isabella of Spain to expel all Jews and Muslims in Spain who refused to convert to Christianity and the vicious pogroms against the Jews that have periodically been carried out in Czarist Russia and medieval Germany. Nevertheless, Muslim toleration of Christians and Jews was often contingent upon the *dhimmis* abiding by other conditions besides payment of the *jizya.* For example, when Muhammad imposed the *jizya* upon the Christians of Tabuk, he also required, among other things, that they abstain from slanderous or malicious talk about Islam, himself, or the Qur'an; that they avoid Muslim women; that they avoid behavior offensive to Muslims such as drinking wine in public or bringing pigs into the marketplace; that they abstain from carrying weapons and riding horses; that they abstain from drawing attention to their places of worship by ringing church bells or reading the Bible loudly in front of Muslims; and that they wear special clothing to distinguish themselves from Muslims (Vaziri, 1992, p. 44.). Under some later caliphs, these extra conditions for toleration and protection were deliberately intended to humiliate. For example, the medieval Muslim historian al-Tabari records that in 850 C.E. caliph al-Mutawakkil issued an edict ordering that Christians and Jews wear honey-colored hoods and turbans to distinguish themselves from Muslims, that any new churches that they had built were to be destroyed, and that wooden images of devils should be nailed to the doors of their houses to distinguish their houses from the houses of Muslims. He also forbade them from working for the government in situations where they might have power over Muslims (Goddard, 2000, pp. 66–67). There were also times when the *jizya* was collected in a manner that was clearly intended to humiliate the *dhimmi.* Thus, both the twelfth-century Muslim writer al-Zamakhshari and the very influential twentieth-century militant Islamic fundamentalist Sayyid Qutb assume that the purpose of the *jizya* referred to in Qur'an 9:29 is a kind of punishment designed to emphasize their inferiority to Muslims. Indeed, al-Zamakhshari states that to humiliate the *dhimmis,* they should be required to come to pay the tax on foot rather than riding on a mount and that they should not be allowed to sit while paying the tax but should stand while the tax collector sits. Then the tax collector "should seize him by the scruff of the neck, shake him, and say, 'Pay the jizyah!' cuffing him on the back of the head once the tax has been paid" (Cornell, 1995, p. 377).

Thus religious toleration in the Muslim world was not the same as equality before the law in the United States today. Furthermore, religious toleration in premodern Islam did not extend to proselytization. As a result, Christians in a Muslim state were not allowed to proselytize Muslims, and any Muslim who converted from Islam to Christianity would lay himself or herself open to the capital offense of apostasy from Islam.

One of the most important ways that early Islamic civilization interacted with both its Western and Asian neighbors was by voraciously assimilating much of their scientific, philosophical, mathematical, and medical knowledge. This process of assimilation required, first of all, that the Muslims undertake a massive effort to translate the texts containing this scientific and philosophical knowledge from the Greek, Syriac, Persian, and Sanskrit languages into Arabic, the language of the Islamic state. During the eighth and ninth centuries of the Common Era, Muslim rulers subsidized massive translation projects, the most famous being the *Bait al-Hikmah* (House of Wisdom) sponsored by caliph al-Mamun (813–833). The number of ancient Greek philosophical, medical, scientific, and mathematical works translated from Greek and Syriac into Arabic by these translators was simply enormous. As a result, almost all of surviving mathematical and scientific learning of ancient Greece became part of the intellectual legacy of Islamic civilization. As one scholar of Islamic civilization, Philip Hitti, put it:

> All this took place while [Western] Europe was almost totally ignorant of Greek thought and science. For while al-Rashid and al-Mamun were delving into Greek and Persian philosophy, their contemporaries in the West, Charlemagne and his lords, were reportedly dabbling in the art of writing their names (quoted in Stanton, 1990, p. 67).

Not only were the Arabs busy translating Greek works into Arabic, they were also doing the same thing with the voluminous literatures of the Persians and the Indians. For example, in the 760s a group of learned men from India came to Baghdad to teach the Arabs about Indian science, philosophy, and mathematics and to translate texts in astronomy and mathematics from Sanskrit into Arabic (McClellan & Dorn, 1999, p. 106). Exchanges of this kind were the most likely route by which the superior Indian system of numerical notation—which includes a number for zero—came into the Islamic world and later was transmitted to Europe as the so-called "Arabic" system of numbering.

The Arabs did much more than just preserve—and later on, serve as conduits for transmitting—this enormous corpus of mathematical and scientific literature from the Greeks, Persians, and Indians to the Latin-speaking western Europeans in the twelfth and thirteenth centuries of the Common Era. They also considerably enhanced and refined that knowledge with mathematical and scientific discoveries of their own. The most important one occurred when Islamic mathematicians introduced the so-called Arabic system of numbers that we use today. Because it contains the number zero, this system of numeration could generate decimal fractions and was therefore far superior to other systems of numbers like Roman numerals. Just compare dividing 298 by 17 both in Arabic numerals and in Roman (CCXCVIII by XVII) numerals! When one does this, the extraordinary superiority of the Arabic system of numbers and its placeholder for zero immediately becomes self-evident. In physics, the optical investigations of Abu ibn al-Haitham (965–1039) were truly remarkable advances over anything that the Greeks had done. He noted that the eye was a lens, that vision was a result of this lens focusing light rays. He also realized that the speed of light depends upon the medium through which it is transmitted (McClellan & Dorn, 1999, p. 106). Al-Haitham, al-Biruni (973–1051), and the alchemist Jabir ibn Hayyam (721–815) also share the noble distinction of being early advocates of experimentation in the investigation of nature.

A significant portion of this enormous body of Greek, Indian, and Muslim scientific, philosophical, medical, and mathematical knowledge that was preserved in Arabic made its way into western Europe through Latin translations in the twelfth and thirteenth centuries. These translations took place in Spain, Sicily, and southern Italy where Christian armies had just conquered areas that had been under Muslim rule for several centuries (McClellan & Dorn, 1999, p. 184). As a result, European science, philosophy, and technology owe an enormous debt to the world of classical Islam. Prior to the influx of Arabic materials on science, mathematics, and medicine in the twelfth and thirteenth centuries, the state of scientific and mathematical knowledge in early medieval western Europe was simply abysmal. One of the most prominent sources of information about nature in the early medieval West, Isidore of Seville, labored under the delusion that the sun illuminated stars. Even as late as the eleventh century, two European scholars, "Regimbold of Cologne and Radolf of Liege, could not fathom the sense of the elementary proposition from geometry that 'the interior angles of a triangle equal two right angles.' The terms 'feet,' 'square feet,' and 'cubic feet' had no meaning for them" (McClellan & Dorn, 1999, p. 95). Medical practice was very primitive—based on herbal concoctions and incantations. Astronomy was based on folklore rather than on the discoveries of the ancient Greek, Indian, and Muslim astronomers, and early medieval western European chemistry was restricted to the smelting of metals and dying of cloth (McClellan & Dorn, 1999, pp. 146–147).

The translation from Arabic into Latin of the scientific, medical, and mathematical learning of the Islamic world and its intellectual forebears would radically transform the medieval western Europeans' understanding of mathematics, medicine, and nature. For example, now through the Arabs the medieval Europeans would be introduced to the zero and the Arabic system of numbers, to algebra, and to trigonometry. Medieval western European chemical knowledge would be powerfully enhanced by incorporating the Muslim alchemists' knowledge of chemical processes. The enormous dependence of later medieval western European science and medicine upon their Muslim predecessors is immediately evident when one realizes that al-Khwarazmi's books on algebra were the principal texts for teaching algebra in western Europe up until the seventeenth and eighteenth centuries (McClellan & Dorn, 1999, p. 158) and that the great Muslim physician Ibn Sina's [also known as Avicenna (980–1037)] *Canon* on medicine "became the most widely accepted text in medicine during the medieval period, with editions continuing in use until the seventeenth century" (McClellan & Dorn, 1999, p. 160).

It is also important to stress that many important technological innovations came to western Europe through the Muslims. For example, the ability to make paper came from the Chinese into the Islamic world around 750, and then gradually spread throughout the Islamic world, reaching Spain in 1150 (McClellan & Dorn, 1999, p. 109). Shortly afterwards, paper manufacture made its way into Western Europe either from Spain or the Byzantine Empire (Shaffer, 1997, p. 842), both of which had depended upon diffusion of that technology from the Muslim Middle East. By about 1250, the Muslims had also introduced Europeans to the use of the compass as a navigational tool, an instrument that they had, in turn, borrowed from Chinese civilization as early as the ninth century (Shaffer, 1997, p. 844). Several other extremely useful navigational aids came to the medieval western Europeans from their Islamic neighbors: the astrolabe and the lateen or triangular sail. By combining the traditional European square sails with the Arab lateen sail, later medieval Europeans' ships could now head into the wind rather than simply sail with the wind. Without this new combination sails, Columbus's ships would never have been able to cross the Atlantic, and the fifteenth- and sixteenth-century Spanish and Portuguese voyages of discovery that so radically transformed our world would not have been possible (Watt, 1972, p. 20). Europeans were also introduced to a wide variety of new agricultural products through their cultural contacts with the Muslims, specifically, rice, sugar cane, melons, cotton, and citrus fruits (McClellan & Dorn, 1999, p. 103).

Medieval European philosophy and theology was also profoundly transformed by the translation of Arabic materials into Latin. The western Europeans recovered most of the Greek philosopher Aristotle's works from the Arabs; they also translated into Latin many of the writings of prominent classical Muslim rationalist philosophers. The fuller corpus of the works of Aristotle made available to the Europeans through the Muslims and the writings of both ibn-Sina and ibn-Rushd powerfully shaped St. Thomas Aquinas's epochal attempts to harmonize faith and reason in his great *Summas,* the most important philosophical works to come out of medieval Europe. More specifically, ibn Rushd, ibn-Sina, and Aquinas, despite their confessional and intellectual differences, are engaged in a common quest to employ the philosophy of Aristotle in an attempt to harmonize faith and reason (Stanton, 1990, pp. 157–158).

Two things stand out about these early scientific and mathematical exchanges between the classical Islamic world (ca. 750–1258 C.E.) and western Europe: First, they show that antagonism has not always been the norm between Islam and the West. The relationship between Europe and Islam in these two domains of inquiry was symbiotic rather than antagonistic insofar as both civilizations enjoyed mutual benefits from their contacts with one another. Muslim science, philosophy, medicine, and mathematics were all stimulated by translating and assimilating what the ancient and Hellenistic Greeks had discovered in those branches of knowledge. On the other hand, medieval Europeans benefitted immensely by being reintroduced through the Muslims to much of the Greek intellectual heritage that they had lost after the collapse of the Western Roman Empire and by being exposed to the new scientific, medical, and mathematical discoveries of Muslim thinkers and scientists that went beyond anything that the Greeks had known. Second, this "Golden Age" of Muslim science and intellectual vitality was a product not of cultural isolation from the non-Muslim world but was, instead, a result of Islamic civilization's willingness to open itself to non-Muslim cultural influences. This simple but important fact needs to be mentioned, since much of present-day Islamic fundamentalist discourse stresses the contrary view that Islam is or ought to become culturally self-sufficient and that it ought to isolate and emancipate itself from Western cultural influences in order to realize its full potential.

WESTERN EUROPEAN ENCOUNTERS WITH ISLAM DURING THE CRUSADES AND SPANISH RECONQUISTA (*CA.* 1050–1492)

When one reads Usama bin Laden's "Declaration of War against the Americans . . ." of August 23, 1996 (Alexander & Swetnam, 2001, Appendix 1A) and a related proclamation of *jihad* issued in the name of the World Islamic Front dated February 23, 1998 (Alexander & Swetnam, 2001, Appendix 1B), the phrase "Zionist–Crusaders alliance" occurs repeatedly as an inflammatory synonym for the Israelis and the United States and its allies. In a different context, when President Bush, in a public statement about Operation Enduring Freedom, described this operation against terrorism as a "crusade," his use of this emotionally loaded term elicited an immediate outcry from his Muslim allies. These two different examples indicate that the images of the medieval European crusader and the Crusades themselves remain an extraordinarily potent memory for the Arabs in the Middle East despite the passage of many centuries. Indeed, one scholar who has studied Muslim perspectives on the Crusades confirms this impression of their lasting impact on shaping Muslim–Christian relations. After citing how numerous influential twentieth-century Muslim leaders, thinkers, and groups such as Sayyid Qutb, Moammar Qaddafi, Saddam Hussein, Khomeini, and Hamas have drawn parallels between the Crusades and the situation of Muslims in the present day, Hillenbrand concludes her book with the observation that:

> It is an unpalatable fact that, just as many deep-seated Western prejudices can be traced back to attitudes molded in the period of the Crusades, so too Muslim opinion about the West has been profoundly influenced by Islam's encounter with western Europe in the twelfth and thirteenth centuries (Hillenbrand, 2000, p. 612).

The historical associations that the Crusades and the crusaders bring to the Arab Muslim's mind still have a great deal of power to enkindle passions of humiliation, anger, and revenge. Arab Muslims today draw many parallels between their situation under the European imperialism of the medieval crusaders and the still raw and humiliating memories that they have from the age of western European imperialism during the nineteenth and twentieth centuries. In both cases non-Muslims contemptuous of Islam invaded the Middle East and occupied the holy city of Jerusalem; in both cases the non-Muslim conquerors from the West divided the occupied portion of the Middle East among themselves without consulting the wishes of the Arabs; in both cases the non-Muslim invaders employed dehumanizing or degrading stereotypes of the Muslims and their beloved Prophet Muhammad to justify their acts of aggression against them; and finally, in both cases—with the exception of the Israelis—the non-Muslims occupying the Middle East ended up retreating. To label a supposed enemy of Islam as a "crusader" continues to have such powerful emotional resonance among Arab Muslims because it simultaneously calls forth old memories of humiliation, profanation, and anger while at the same time conveying the idea that the invaders' successes will only be temporary and that the Muslims will eventually bring them to defeat.

The medieval Crusades were a series of eight armed pilgrimages initially sponsored by the Papacy and conducted by western European kings and knights to liberate the Christian people and holy places in Palestine from atrocities and acts of profanation. These alleged crimes were supposedly committed by the Seljuk Turks upon the Christians and their places of worship after they had inflicted a disastrous defeat upon the Byzantine Empire's armies at the Battle of Manzikert in 1071. From the fall of Jerusalem to the crusaders in 1099 until the last crusader stronghold at Acre fell in 1291, the western Europeans precariously controlled a series of small kingdoms in what is now Palestine, Syria, and Lebanon.

The Crusades were part of a much broader western European military expansionism that began in the eleventh century. A victim of aggression during the early Middle Ages, western Europe began to reverse roles and become the aggressor starting in the eleventh century and continuing up through the heyday of Western imperialism in the nineteenth and twentieth centuries. From the eleventh century through the end of the fifteenth century, western European military aggression became manifest through the numerous crusades that were launched to the Holy Land in the eleventh through thirteenth centuries, by the eleventh-century reconquest of Sicily and Sardinia from the Muslims, and through the Spanish Reconquista, a centuries-long effort by the Christians of northern Spain to wrest control of the rest of Spain and Portugal from the Muslim powers that had controlled it since 711. This Spanish Reconquista began in the middle of the eleventh century and culminated in 1492 when Ferdinand and Isabella defeated the last Muslim stronghold in Spain and shortly afterwards expelled the Jews and Muslims from Spain. Unlike the Crusades, which ultimately ended in defeat for invading Europeans, the Spanish Reconquista ended up being a lasting defeat for the Muslims and Jews of Spain, since they were both expelled unless they chose to convert to Christianity.

Both the Crusades and, to a lesser extent, the Spanish Reconquista left legacies that have embittered Muslim–Christian relations ever since. Imperialism, whether it be Christian or Muslim, will always leave some legacy of bitterness in its wake among the defeated peoples. Still, the Crusades were conducted in a way that guaranteed that they would leave a lasting legacy of anger and serious cultural misunderstanding.

First of all, Pope Urban II mobilized the knights and the populace of medieval Europe for the First Crusade (1095–1099) by spreading highly inflammatory and probably exaggerated stories of Muslim atrocities against the Christian peoples who lived in the Holy Land and against the Christian holy places. In one example, he described details of various tortures that the Muslim invaders had allegedly inflicted upon the hapless Christians of the Holy Land:

> When they wish to torture people by a base death, they perforate their navels, and dragging forth the extremity of the intestines, bind it to a stake; then with flogging, they lead the victim around until the viscera having gushed forth, the victim falls prostrate upon the ground (quoted in Weber. p. 216).

Furthermore, he appealed to the Frankish knights by promising them if they went on the Crusade they could redeem the Holy Land from desecration by the heathen, acquire fertile land for themselves at the Muslims' expense, and assure themselves of salvation by taking up the Cross and going on this armed pilgrimage (Weber, 1959, pp. 216–218).

Second, the Crusaders' extreme brutality when they successfully conquered Jerusalem in 1099 was never forgotten. Although the defending troops were given a safe conduct out of the city, the entire Muslim and Jewish population of the city was slaughtered. One Christian eyewitness stated that when he went to the site of the Temple, he had to slog through knee-deep piles of blood and dead bodies (Goddard, 2000, p. 85). Muslims do not fail to point out the contrast between the revolting fanaticism of the Christians in victory and the chivalrous behavior of the Muslim leader Saladin when he retook the city from the Crusaders in 1187 after the battle of Hattin. Saladin spared the noncombatants and made a successful effort to prevent looting and harassment of the Christian populace of the city (Goddard, 2000, p. 88).

Finally, the Crusades and Spanish Reconquista played a major role in spreading throughout western Europe distorted and dehumanizing images of Muslims and Islam that have persisted for centuries and poisoned relations between the two civilizations. Literary works and travelogues that were composed during the time of the Crusades and shortly thereafter continued to depict Islam in a completely distorted way. The people are described as savage and not a civilization with a venerable and splendid past.

One other problematic legacy of the Crusades and the caricatures of Islam and Muslims that they spawned was a tendency for western European writers to vilify and demonize the Prophet Muhammad. This has been especially offensive to Muslims because, although they do not regard Muhammad as divine, they do accord him the greatest respect and veneration and consider any defamation of his character to be a terrible act of blasphemy deserving the severest punishment. Yet the tendency to vilify Muhammad persisted as later medieval western European writers carried scurrilous fantasies about Muhammad to grotesque extremes.

ISLAM AND ITS ENCOUNTER WITH MODERN WESTERN EUROPEAN IMPERIALISM

While it is true that the Crusades and the Spanish Reconquista left a very persistent legacy of misunderstanding and hostility between western European Christians and the Islamic world, these events and their literary residues did not pose a serious military, economic, or cultural threat to Islam.

For several centuries, until the middle of the nineteenth century, Islamic civilization was untouched. Thanks to the Scientific Revolution of the seventeenth century and the Industrial Revolution that began in England around 1750 and rapidly spread thereafter to the rest of western Europe and the United States, the Europeans now possessed a deep understanding of nature and its laws as well as a superior technology of rapid-fire weapons, railroads, steamships, telegraphs, and telephones that enabled them to dominate cultures that did not possess this scientific and technical knowledge. Between 1830 and 1962, many parts of the Islamic world such as Algeria, India, Malaya, and Indonesia would become colonies under the direct military and administrative control of one of the European powers, while others such as Iran and Ottoman Empire, though avoiding direct military and administrative control, would nonetheless find themselves economically dependent on the European powers and subject to various forms of economic exploitation by them. A once proud and vibrant civilization that had always Islamicized previous invading groups like the Turks and the Mongols suddenly found itself subjugated to and humiliated by an infidel culture that held them in contempt. This was a shattering blow from which the present-day Islamic world is still trying to recover. Indeed, one cannot understand the current wave of Muslim anger against the West unless one realizes that much of that anger stems from specific events that took place when Europeans militarily and economically dominated the Muslim world.

It is an appalling experience to be conquered by another nation. It is even more appalling and unbearable when that conquering power is blinded by an overweening sense of its own racial and cultural superiority so that it utterly despises you and openly proclaims that it regards both you and your culture as intellectually, spiritually, and morally inferior to their own. This was exactly what the western European powers did to Islam—just as they had done to the Native Americans, the Australian Aborigines, Africans, and other indigenous peoples. The Europeans used this assumption that "Oriental" peoples were culturally, spiritually, and morally inferior to whites in order to justify their domination and economic exploitation.

Some remarks of Lord Cromer, the top British colonial administrator in Egypt from 1882 to 1907, serve as a perfect illustration of these racist assumptions that were so typical of European colonial officials. Speaking of Oriental peoples in general, he told his audience that "Accuracy is abhorrent to the Oriental mind. . . . Want of accuracy, which easily degenerates into untruthfulness, is in fact the main characteristic of the Oriental mind." He went on to draw an unfavorable contrast between the superior European who "is a close reasoner" and who makes statements "devoid of any ambiguity" and the present-day Arabs who "are singularly deficient in the logical faculty." Elsewhere he describes his Egyptian subjects as "devoid of energy and initiative," as well as "lethargic and suspicious" (quoted in Said, 1978, pp. 38–39).

Since European colonial administrators were usually racists who assumed that they were vastly superior morally, culturally, and intellectually to their Muslim and Oriental subjects, their policies were often shockingly indifferent to the welfare and cultural sensitivities of their subject peoples. The disdainful treatment of Muslim religious charities and educational institutions in Algeria and the dispossession of many Muslim Algerians from much of their land by the French and the successful but flagrantly self-serving efforts of the British in extracting oil from Iran for many years at very low prices and paying the Iranian government very low royalties for this non-renewable resource from their country are two classic illustrations of this indifference.

While it is certainly true that the disdainful racism that animated the administrative policies of the European colonialists was a constant irritant to the subject peoples, the most disturbing thing about modern Western European imperialism for Muslims was its inevitable association with the twin processes known as modernization and Westernization. The modernization wrought by European occupation brought the indigenous peoples exposure to modern secular-scientific education and its worldview. This differing worldview was a powerful challenge to tradition. Moreover, colonization brought the Industrial Revolution with its railroads, factories, rapid and massive urbanization, modern hygiene, and the rapid population increases resulting from that as well as powerful economic disruptions caused by the massive influx of machine-made goods competing at much cheaper prices with traditional handmade manufactures. Along with modernization came an equally disruptive and revolution force, Westernization. European notions and political ideologies such as a

separation of church and state, democratic liberalism, nationalism, and socialism conflicted with traditional Islamic conceptions of the proper relationship between religion and
politics. Postwar European notions of women's equality with men, the free mixing of the
sexes in public, and Western dress codes conflicted with traditional Islamic gender expectations. And finally, western European conceptions of private property when introduced as
the law of the land by European powers upset traditional forms of communal or tribal land
tenure. These transformations of worldview and these powerful social, economic, and
technological forces unleashed by either contact with or domination by Western Europeans
were, for good or ill, transformative agents of extraordinary power that would, in time,
elicit deep and powerful responses from Islam.

Of all the troublesome legacies of the age of Western European imperialism, the one
that continues to generate the most persistent and visceral Muslim anger and bitterness directed toward the West was the decision to create the state of Israel out of Arab Palestinian territory. This single event, coupled with the consequences of the 1967 Arab–Israeli Six
Day War—the Israeli occupation of the Arab-dominated West Bank and Gaza Strip, the
Israeli occupation of east Jerusalem, Israeli control of the land on which the al-Aqsa
mosque is located, and the construction of Jewish settlements in the occupied West Bank—
has provided much of the emotional fuel that energizes present-day Islamic terrorism. As
these details are reviewed by Dr. Weinzierl in Chapter 2, there is no need to go into more
specifics here.

FOUR FORMS OF MUSLIM RESPONSE TO MODERNIZATION AND WESTERNIZATION

Loosely following Esposito (Esposito, 1988, pp. 196–199), one can classify the responses of nineteenth- and twentieth-century Muslims to the twin processes of
Westernization and modernization triggered by their encounters with Western imperialism
into four main categories: (1) conservatives, (2) secular modernists, (3) Islamic modernists, and (4) Islamic revivalists (also commonly referred to by the terms Islamic fundamentalists or Islamists). One should realize that sometimes it is difficult to know exactly
which of these four categories is the most appropriate one for a particular Islamic group,
since there is often considerable overlap between them, especially between some groups
of Islamic revivalists and conservatives.

The Islamic conservative response to Westernization and modernization was especially strong among the *ulama,* those learned men of the Islamic religious schools who
were experts in Islamic law, the Qur'an, and the Sunnah of the Prophet. The conservatives
are predominately rejectionist in their response to modernity, Western cultural influences,
and modern science and technology. They are very suspicious of innovation (*bida*), and
they are adherents to *taqlid,* the practice of following the legal precedents of medieval
Muslim jurists on matters of Islamic law. In short, they do not believe that the Islamic
world needs to adapt itself to the modern world, since they believe that the cumulative
body of rulings and interpretations of the Qur'an and the Sunnah of the Prophet developed
by the medieval jurists during the early centuries of Islamic civilization provides the
Islamic community of today with all it really needs in order to realize God's will.

At the opposite end of the spectrum from the conservative response to
Westernization and modernization one encounters the orientation of the secular mod-

ernists. Best exemplified by Mustafa Kemal Ataturk, the man who created the modern nation–state of Turkey and modernized it in the 1920s and 1930s, the secular modernists were the most accommodating of all Muslims to Western cultural influences. They believed that religion and its influence should be restricted solely to the private sphere and family law (e.g., issues of divorce, inheritance) and play little or no role at all in public life. Consequently, they felt completely free to accept any Western cultural influences such as secular education; Western political ideologies like liberalism, socialism, and nationalism; Western styles of dress for men and women; and the free mixing of men and women in public, without worrying about finding an Islamic—that is, a Qur'anic or Prophetic—rationale for them.

Most of the leaders who created the new nation–states in the Islamic world after they had gained their independence from European rule after World War II were Western-educated and sympathetic to the cultural values of the West even as they fought against Western imperialistic domination. Gamal Abdul Nasser in Egypt, Muhammad Ali Jinnah in Pakistan, Ataturk in Turkey, Achmed Sukarno in Indonesia, and Ahmed ben Bella in Algeria were all leaders of this type who were largely secularist in their religious orientation. While many of these leaders would not go as far as Ataturk in proclaiming a complete separation of religion from politics and the public sphere, most of them only paid lip service to the idea that Islam was the official religion of the newly independent state. Most of these newly independent nation–states created criminal and civil law codes modeled upon the West rather than upon the traditional Islamic law codes. The only main exception to this Westernization of the law codes was in family law (i.e., related to matters of divorce, marriage, and inheritance), which, in many cases, still remained in the hands of the *qadis*.

The Western political ideology of nationalism affected most of the secular modernist leaders of the Islamic world. One of the core ideas of European nationalism as it emerged out of the experience of the French Revolution was the notion of citizenship—the idea that all citizens in the nation are equal before the law. This meant that the law was blind to religious affiliation. This was very different from the way that the law had worked in traditional Islamic societies and in the old Ottoman Empire where each religious community was governed by its own court systems that adjudicated conflicts between co-religionists. Many of the more traditionally minded Muslims were unhappy with this secular modernist notion of citizenship with its assumption that non-Muslims in a nation should be treated equally before the law with Muslims. This is one reason why many Islamic revivalists have been so hostile to nationalism.

Islamic modernism constitutes the third principal Muslim orientation to Westernization and modernization. Both the secular modernists and the Islamic modernists find much to admire not only in modern science and technology but also in Western European social, educational, and political institutions and the openness to innovation. In this way, they both differ markedly from the reactionary orientation of the conservatives who reject innovation and reject modernization and Western cultural institutions. What principally differentiates the Islamic modernists from the secular modernists is that the Islamic modernists want to be more selective in integrating elements of Western thought, culture, and technology into Islam. Whereas secular modernists like Ataturk separated religion from politics and government and introduced major changes without worrying about whether those innovations could be given an Islamic rationale, the Islamic modernists insist that innovations be compatible in some way with a creatively reinterpreted Islam.

Furthermore, Islamic modernists tended to celebrate both reason and science as noble pursuits and they saw no intrinsic incompatibility between Islam, reason, and science.

As already indicated above, the Islamic modernists were extremely critical of the conservative *ulama,* whom they blamed for much of the backwardness of Islam vis-à-vis Europe. The modernists also repudiated one of the cornerstones of the conservative *ulama*'s conception of Islam when they rejected the latter's reliance on *taqlid,* the practice of adhering to medieval precedent when it came to interpreting the Qur'an and prophetic Sunnah and/or applying those texts to particular issues like how women should dress or how one should treat someone guilty of apostasy. When it came to interpreting the Qur'an and Sunnah of the Prophet and applying them to modern situations and circumstances, Islamic modernists rejected *taqlid* in favor of *ijtihad. Ijtihad* was the intellectual struggle involved in exercising one's own *independent* judgment in either interpreting what a particular passage of the Qur'an or prophetic Sunnah really meant or how it was to be applied to the particular situation or issue that one was facing. Muslims exercising *ijtihad* are not worried about following what their medieval predecessors might have done because they have faith that as sincere Muslims knowledgeable about their own scriptures and traditions, they are just as capable of knowing how to understand what God wants them to do in a particular situation as any legal scholar.

Furthermore, Islamic modernists stress the importance of being creative in their reinterpretation of sacred texts and their application to modern circumstances. Most Islamic modernists would contend that there is no reason that the most "progressive" Western institutions and practices like democracy, women's rights, and free speech are incompatible with Islam, the Qur'an, or the Sunnah of the Prophet. The types of "creative" textual interpretation that characterized Islamic modernist thought emphasized that proper interpretation of a text involved not only understanding the letter of the text but also its spirit, something that modernists criticized the *ulama* for failing to do. Islamic modernist exegesis of the Qur'an and prophetic Sunnah was also very sensitive to the particular historical contexts that generated an individual scriptural passage, prophetic precedent, or medieval jurist's legal judgment. For example, when the Islamic modernist Asghar Ali Engineer wanted to argue in favor of women having the right to take positions of leadership in government, he had to contend with a prophetic *hadith* in which Muhammad supposedly said that "a nation can never prosper which has assigned its rule to a woman." This *hadith* was often cited by religious conservatives as evidence that Islam was incompatible with women as heads of state. How could Engineer claim to be a good Muslim and ignore such a statement from Muhammad? He stressed, among other things, that "one does not know in what context this was said (as context makes all the difference, ignoring which wrong inferences could be drawn) and how it was understood by the narrator from the Prophet" and that it also contradicted a passage in the Qur'an (27:32–44) "which speaks highly of a woman ruler, the Queen of Sheba" (Engineer, 1992, p. 17).

Most Islamic modernists, though they favor harmonizing modern cultural institutions with Islam, would reject the idea so dear to the Islamic revivalists that the *shari'a* should become the law of the land. The Malaysian politician Anwar Ibrahim contends that

> [Southeast Asian Muslims] would rather strive to improve the welfare of the women and children in their midst than spend their days elaborately defining the nature and institutions of the ideal Islamic state. They do not believe that it makes one less a Muslim to promote

economic growth, to master the information revolution, and to demand justice for women (quoted in Esposito, 2002, p. 135).

It is also worth noting that, in contrast to the often-intolerant hostility to the West that characterizes much of the rhetoric of contemporary Islamic revivalism (or fundamentalism), Ibrahim favors an inclusive and pluralistic Islam that is tolerant of all faiths and civilizations and is engaged in serious and respectful dialogue with them (Esposito, 2002, pp. 135–136).

With the more militant forms of Islamic fundamentalism hogging the headlines, it is important to remember that a liberal strain of Islamic modernism is an important, pervasive, and vigorous element of contemporary Islam. As one contemporary scholar of Islam put it, "'Liberal Islam' may sound like a contradiction in terms" (Kurzman, 1998, p. 3) but it is out there, though its presence is quiet. The tendency of both the press and even scholars of Islam to overlook this important group of Muslims is regrettable because they share with most educated Americans an "opposition to theocracy, support for democracy, guarantees of the rights of women and non-Muslims in Islamic countries, freedom of thought, and belief in the potential for human progress" (Kurzman, 1998, p. 4).

The fourth form of Muslim response to Westernization and modernization is that of the Islamic revivalists, who are also frequently called Islamic fundamentalists or Islamists. This particular Islamic response to modernization and Western culture has become especially prominent since the 1970s and is the one that gets the greatest degree of media coverage. What most sharply differentiates the Islamic revivalists from both the secular modernists and the Islamic modernists is their ultimate goal of making the *shari'a* the law of the land—that is to say, they want to replace man-made law codes, especially those of Western origin, with the divinely mandated law code embodied in the Qur'an and the Sunnah of the Prophet. To put it another way, they want what they call "Islamic government," a truly Islamic state ruled by the Qur'an and the Sunnah of the Prophet. Making the implementation of the *shari'a* the central item in their reformist platform guarantees that the Islamic community will modernize in its own authentically *Islamic* way rather than doing so in a manner that merely apes the West and undermines Islam.

Islamic revivalists believe that the economic and social problems of the present-day Islamic world are rooted in the legacies left by Western imperialism and Westernized Islamic rulers and elites who have replaced Islamic law codes and institutions with Westernized ones. They also maintain that the problems the Islamic world faces today are a result of their own failure to follow the true Islam of the Qur'an and the Sunnah of the Prophet and the earliest Muslim community of the Prophet and his companions. Given these assumptions, the Islamic revivalists stridently insist upon the need to purge Islamic culture of all those alien Westernized accretions incompatible with Islam that have crept into it since the encounter with Western imperialism. As Sayyid Qutb contended in his influential work *Milestones,* the Islamic community of today "is crushed under the weight of . . . false laws and customs which are not even remotely related to the Islamic teachings" (quoted in Esposito, 2002, p. 58). In another one of his works, *Social Justice in Islam,* Qutb elaborates further by telling his readers that "We should not go to French legislation to derive our laws, or to communist ideals to derive our social order, without first examining what can be supplied from our Islamic legislation which was the foundation of our first form of society" (Donohue & Esposito, 1982, p. 125). As this quote indicates, Islamic revivalists are not against modernizing Islam. They just want to be sure that any changes to Muslim society that are necessary to adapt it to modern technologies and economic forces are consistent with the Qur'an and Sunnah of the Prophet and that those two sources are consulted first before any changes are implemented.

In addition to their primary goal of implementing the *shari'a,* Islamic revivalists utterly repudiate Western secularism with its separation of religion and government. Islamic revivalists never tire of insisting that Islam is a comprehensive system governing *every* facet of life, both public and private, so that all public and private institutions and actions are in accordance with God's will as manifest in the Qur'an and prophetic Sunnah. Moreover, Muslim revivalists also differ from most modern European social reformers by regarding any system of social institutions and laws that are man-made as being intrinsically inferior to that which is divinely created or divinely ordained. Unlike Western-style democracies, which assume that the laws derive their legitimacy from the will of the people, Islamic revivalists operate from the traditional Islamic assumption that God is the sole legislator and that laws and moral codes ultimately derive their legitimacy and obligatory character from the fact that they originated from God. In drawing a contrast between "Islamic government" and Western-style democracies and republics, Ayatollah Khomeini stated that whereas in a republic "the representatives of the people . . . engage in legislation, in Islam the legislative power and competence to establish laws belongs exclusively to God almighty" (Khomeini, 1981, p. 55). Human beings simply execute the laws that God laid down in the Qur'an or made manifest in the behavior of the Prophet Muhammad.

Islamic revivalists like Ayatollah Khomeini, Mawlana Mawdudi, Sayyid Qutb, and Hasan al-Banna contend that Islam is self-sufficient and has no need of the West in order to modernize nor does it need to adapt its institutions to conform to Western cultural expectations. However, this emphasis on Islamic self-sufficiency does not mean that Islam has to wall itself from the rest of the world. Indeed, Islamic revivalists are perfectly willing to use modern science and technology to better their society and spread their religious message. Thus Zaynab al-Ghazzali asserts that a good Muslim woman must "raise her son in the conviction that he must possess the scientific tools of the age, and at the same time must understand Islam, politics, geography, and current events" (Comstock, 1995, p. 363). Nevertheless, though Islamic revivalists embrace modern technologies, they often display an ambivalence about science. For example, during the early 1990s, a committee of Pakistani Islamic revivalists managed to develop what they regarded as a completely Islamicized science curriculum for the country. It is worth quoting one of their recommendations:

> There is latent poison present in the subheading Energy Causes Changes because it gives
> the impression that energy is the true cause rather than Allah. Similarly it is unIslamic to
> teach that mixing hydrogen automatically produces water. The Islamic way is this: When
> atoms of hydrogen approach atoms of oxygen, then by the will of God water is produced
> (quoted in Comstock, 1995, p. 54).

The parallels between their ambivalence about science and trying to harmonize it with scripture and the similar efforts of the creationists in the United States are striking. Needless to say, some Islamic revivalist regimes have passed laws prohibiting the teaching of evolution.

It is very important to stress the social activism of the Islamic revivalists; it is also very important to emphasize that most Islamic revivalist groups such as the Jamaat-i-Islami in Pakistan and the majority wing of the Egyptian Muslim Brotherhood are willing to work within the established system to transform society from below into their ideal Islamic state. Most modernized and Westernized states in the Middle East have simply been unable to cope with the massive social and economic problems—such as widespread unemployment, widespread poverty, illiteracy, poor health care, and the lack of other vital social services—that modernization has triggered in the Islamic world. Consequently, Islamic revivalist groups have created their own "educational facilities, psychiatric, dental, and drug rehabilitation clinics, nurseries, legal aid societies, subsidized housing, food distribution, banking and investment houses" (Esposito, 1984, pp. 227–228) alongside those of the state. Furthermore, as one Egyptian sociologist has noted, these Islamic revivalist social welfare institutions "are better run than their state/public counterparts, less bureaucratic and impersonal . . . more grass-roots oriented, far less expensive . . ." (quoted in Esposito, 1984, p. 228). These Islamic revivalist organizations are like a state within a state, much like Christianity was a state within a state during the declining centuries of the Roman Empire. Through these social welfare institutions, the Islamic revivalists are sincerely struggling to bring about a truly just and humane social order founded upon the ideals of social justice present in the Qur'an and the example of the Prophet Muhammad. What is true of Egypt is true elsewhere in the Islamic world of today.

One can divide the Islamic revivalists into two major groups: the moderates described above who attempt to Islamicize society through peaceful means by working within the established system and the extremist fringe of militants who stress that the ideal Islamic order cannot be established without the use of violence.

The terrorists that one reads about in the headlines today come from this militant extremist wing of the Islamic wing of the Islamic revivalists. They are represented by such thinkers as Sayyid Qutb and such organizations as Osama bin Laden's al-Qaeda network and Egypt's Islamic Jihad group responsible for the assassination of President Sadat in 1981. These militant extremist groups within the Islamic revivalist camp have been inspired by ideas of the medieval jurist Ibn Taymiyya (1268–1328) and by the premodern eighteenth-century Sunni Muslim revivalist movements that swept through the entire Islamic world from Senegal to India at that time. With respect to the latter, it was especially the teachings of the eighteenth century Arabian reformer Muhammad ibn Abd al-Wahhab (1703–1792) that have been most influential in shaping the actions of modern-day Islamic terrorists like Osama bin Laden. Ibn Taymiyya insisted on a very strict literalist interpretation of the Qur'an and the Sunnah of the Prophet and wanted to purify Islam from the many popular practices and folkways that were inconsistent with or absent from the Qur'an and the Sunnah. One of the things that infuriated Ibn Taymiyya was the Mongols' practice of converting to Islam and yet continuing to follow their *yasa* codes of laws that they had received from Genghis Khan. It was inconceivable to Ibn Taymiyya that a true Muslim would refuse to live by the *shari'a* founded upon the Qur'an and prophet Sunnah and instead follow a pre-Islamic law code from the times of their polytheistic ancestors. As a result, he issued a *fatwa* (an Islamic legal judgment) against the Mongols proclaiming them to be apostates from Islam and therefore proper objects for *jihad*. It was the duty of every good Muslim to wage war on such apostate Muslims who refused to live by the *shari'a.* Later generations of Islamic militants, including Osama bin Laden (see Alexander & Swetnam, 2001, Appendix 1A, p. 6), have found inspiration in Ibn Taymiyya's teachings that (1) any Muslim who fails to implement the *shari'a* is an apostate from Islam and no longer to be regarded as a Muslim and (2) that it is the duty of all other Muslims to make war or put to death for apostasy such renegade Muslims (Esposito, 2002, pp. 44–46). It is for this reason that today's Islamic terrorists believe that they are being true Muslims when they assassinate secular modernist or Islamic modernist Muslim rulers who fail to implement the *shari'a* or mix Western cultural institutions with Islamic ones. Ibn Taymiyya's ideas are actually quite revolutionary, because most Muslims in history have been willing to accept a person as a Muslim provided that person acknowledges the prophethood of Muhammad, believes that Allah is the only God, and makes at least a perfunctory effort to abide by the five pillars of Islam. In such cases it is for God to decide who was the true Muslim on the Day of Judgment. The militant Islamic revivalists of today do not agree with this long-established majority viewpoint and join the seventh-century Kharijite schismatics and such eighteenth-century Islamic revivalists as the Nigerian reformer Uthman dan Fodio and the Arabian reformer Muhammad ibn Abd al-Wahhab in calling for warfare against Muslims who deviate from their strict, literalist interpretations of the Qur'an and Sunnah of the Prophet. The result is an intolerant and violent fanaticism exemplified by a statement of Osama bin Laden's mentor Dr. Abdullah Azzam: "'*Jihad* and the rifle alone: no negotiations, no conferences, no dialogues'" (quoted in Esposito, 2002, p. 7). It is important to note, once again, that these militant revivalist views are not mainstream Islamic views.

CONCLUDING REMARKS

This chapter shows that the relationship between Islam and the West is a very complex and nuanced one. Islam, like Christianity and Judaism, is one of the Abrahamic religions and, like both of them, is committed to the creation of a humane and just social order. Like their Christian and Jewish counterparts, Muslims are not agreed on how to create this humane and just social order. Secular modernists, Islamic modernists, Islamic revivalists of both the moderate and militant type, and conservative Muslims have different visions of how this great goal can and ought to be achieved. In short, this study shows that Islam today is not monolithic. Most importantly, the extremist wing of the Islamic revivalists is just that—extremist and out of the mainstream of Islamic tradition and practice. However, that does not mean that the West can afford to ignore the grievances of the militants, because many of them are legitimate and shared by many of the other groups in the Islamic world, even if these groups repudiate the tactics of the terrorists.

The common image of the Islamic world as retrograde and intolerant also stands in need of correction. There are many liberal and modernist voices in the Islamic world that are committed to many of the same things we regard as precious: human rights, better treatment of women, freedom of speech, social justice, a sustainable relationship with our environment, and a commitment to the advancement of scientific knowledge and technological and social progress. These voices do not receive much press but they are there. We in the West must also remind ourselves that the scientific and technological progress that we are so proud of owes a great deal to those Muslims in the medieval world who transmitted their scientific knowledge and that of the Greeks to western Europe.

This study also shows that Islamic revivalism/fundamentalism is not monolithic any more than Islam is. Many Islamic revivalists are peaceful law-abiding citizens willing to transform society from within the established political system just like their devout Christian counterparts. They are motivated by a sincere conviction that a just and humane social order can and must be achieved and they are willing to create at the grassroots level social institutions to actualize their vision of social justice. Given our own common concerns with social justice, certainly some kind of dialogue between the West and those moderate revivalist groups is possible and ought to be initiated. Moreover, the West also needs to realize that even if the Islamic revivalists and their Western counterparts strongly disagree about a great many important things, this right to disagree is an essential part of our democracy. Islamic revivalism has challenged the smug assumption of many Western intellectuals that modernization and secularization necessarily go hand in hand. If Islam forces us to challenge some of our deepest cultural assumptions, that is hardly a crime but rather a prod for us to be more self-critical, the sign of any culture that has true intellectual vitality.

This chapter has also shown that much of contemporary Muslim anger against the West is indeed justified. Muslims are not angry at the West and the United States just because they are an irritable and fanatical people. As this study shows, western European imperialists did terrible and humiliating things to Muslim peoples. Justice and common decency demand that the United States and Europe acknowledge these wrongs and do something to rectify them. This is especially important in the case of the Palestinians and the great wrongs that they have suffered. This does not mean that Israel's security should be compromised or that its quest for recognition of its right to exist from its Arab neighbors should be abandoned. However, at the very least it seems that the United States and Europe should insist upon the right of the Palestinians to a *viable* state on the West Bank. On the other hand, as much as the West needs to acknowledge the unjust and defamatory things it has done to Muslims, it is also incumbent upon Muslims to be more critical of their own shortcomings and take responsibility for them.

A wider perspective about the diversity of voices in the contemporary world together with a deeper appreciation for the common concern that Muslims and Americans share for creating a just and humane society can serve as a powerful antidote to terrorism and inter-religious hostility. This study shows that terrorists' religious ideology based upon the teachings of Ibn Taymiyya threaten not just the United States but also fellow modernist Muslims whom the extremists regard as insufficiently Islamic. Our ability to reach out to these Muslims, to give them greater prominence in our press, and to co-operate with them in fighting this common enemy is essential if we are to win the war on terrorism. Muslim terrorists armed with weapons of mass destruction will not just be a threat to the United States and Europe. Sooner or later, they will also be a threat to those in the Muslim world who disagree with them. In other words, moderate Muslims and Americans have a common enemy. For this reason, it is urgent that we get to know each other better, that we understand their grievances against us and sincerely try to rectify whatever wrongs we may have done to them, and that those who formulate U.S. foreign policy make the establishment of mutually respectful relations with moderate Muslims, both modernists and revivalists, one of their highest and most urgent priorities.

DISCUSSION QUESTIONS

1. Discuss three similarities between Islam and Christianity.
2. Why is the author of this chapter optimistic regarding future relations between the Islamic world and the West? Do you share this optimism? Why or why not?
3. Which elements of the Islamic faith have been used to justify the actions of the September 11 terrorists? What do these elements have in common with Judeo-Christian beliefs?

REFERENCES

ABDALATI, H. (n.d.). *Islam in focus.* Riyadh, Saudi Arabia: Islamic Teaching Center.

ALEXANDER, Y., & SWETNAM, M. (2001). *Usama bin Laden's al-Qaida: Profile of a Terrorist Network.* Ardsley, NY: Transnational Publications.

COMSTOCK, G. (1995). *Religious autobiographies.* Belmont, CA: Wadsworth Publishing Company.

CORNELL, V. (1995). Jizyah. In *The Oxford encyclopedia of the modern Islamic world* (Vol.2, pp. 377–378). New York: Oxford University Press.

DONOHUE, J., & ESPOSITO, J. (1982). *Islam in transition: Muslim perspectives.* New York; Oxford: Oxford University Press.

ENGINEER, A. (1992). *The rights of women in Islam.* New York: St. Martin's Press.

ESPOSITO, J. (1984). *Islam and politics* (3rd. ed.). Syracuse, New York: Syracuse University Press.

———. (1988). *Islam: The straight path* (expanded ed.). New York: Oxford University Press.

———. (2002). *Unholy war: Terror in the name of Islam.* New York: Oxford University Press.

The First Gospel of the Infancy of Jesus Christ. (1974). In *The lost books of the Bible and the forgotten books of Eden.* [s.l.]: William Collins & World Publishing Co.

GODDARD, H. (2000). *A history of Christian-Muslim relations.* Chicago: New Amsterdam Books.

HILLENBRAND, C. (2000). *The Crusades: Islamic perspectives.* New York: Routledge.

HUNT, A., & CROTTY, M. (1991). *Ethics of world religions* (Rev. ed.). San Diego: Greenhaven Press.

JANSEN, J. (1986). *Neglected duty: The creed of Sadat's assassins and Islamic resurgence in the Middle East.* New York: Macmillan; London: Collier Macmillan.

KHOMEINI, A. (1981). *Islam and revolution: writings and declarations of Imam Khomeini.* Berkeley: Mizan Press.

KURZMAN, C. (ed.). (1998). *Liberal Islam: A sourcebook.* New York: Oxford University Press.

MCCLELLAN, J., & DORN, H. (1999). *Science and technology in world history: An introduction.* Baltimore & London: The Johns Hopkins University Press.

MUHAIYADEEN, M. (1987). *Islam and world peace: Explanations of a sufi.* Philadelphia: The Fellowship Press.

NASR, S. (1975). *Ideals and realities of Islam* (2nd ed.). London: George Allen & Unwin.

Qur'an. (1992). *The Holy Qur'an: English translation of the meanings of the Qur'an with notes.* Trans. by Abdullah Yusuf Ali. Indianapolis: H & C International.

Sahih Muslim. (199?). Riyadh, Saudi Arabia: International Islamic Publishing House.

SAID, E. (1978). *Orientalism.* New York: Vintage Books.

SHAFFER, L. (1997). A concrete panoply of intercultural exchange: Asia in world history. In A. Embree & C. Gluck (Eds.), *Asia in western and world history: A guide for teaching* (pp. 810–866). Armonk, NY & London: M.E. Sharpe.

STANTON, C. (1990). *Higher learning in Islam: The classical period, 700–1300.* Savage, MD: Rowman & Littlefield Publishers.

VAZIRI, M. (1992). *The emergence of Islam: Prophecy, imamate, and messianism in perspective.* New York: Paragon House.

WATT, W. (1972). *The influence of Islam on medieval Europe.* Edinburgh: Edinburgh University Press.

WEBER, E., ed. (1959). *The Western Tradition.* Boston: D.C. Heath.

2

Terrorism: Its Origin and History

John Weinzierl

❖

The second chapter outlines the history of terrorism. Although living with the threat of terrorist attacks is a recent development in U.S. society, many parts of the world regard terrorism as part of the political landscape. Further, the use of violence to achieve political and/or religious goals dates back to the first century of the common era. In this chapter, Weinzierl provides historical context for understanding contemporary terrorism. One of the most compelling questions posed to the reader asks whether terrorism is effective. This essay reveals not only the longstanding use of violence as a political strategy, but the inadequacy of conventional means to stop terrorism. In this examination of the usefulness of violence as a political tool, the author provides an accessible and informative survey of the modern history of the Middle East.

On September 11, 2001, the United States experienced the brutal reality of terrorism. In the aftermath, many asked how could this happen. Is this a new kind of war and, if so, can we win? However, what many Americans do not realize is that these same questions have been asked for generations because terrorism is not new. It has a history that has been all too often ignored. Perhaps this is because terrorism has resurfaced in the late twentieth century after a period of relative calm. Before the challenges of terrorism can be understood, it is important to establish a historical context.

In addition to providing a historical perspective, the second objective of this chapter is to investigate the effectiveness of terrorism. History teaches us that terrorism is more effective today than ever before. As a result, an explanation of the methods, motivations, and objectives of contemporary terrorist groups—in particular, Hezbollah, Hamas, and al-Qaeda—is necessary. The future implications of terrorism are horrifying when one considers the ever-expanding availability of chemical, biological, and nuclear weapons. Can this new trend be stopped? The vast military and economic resources of the United States are intimidating and effective if brought to bear against a conventional military foe, however, international terrorist groups and networks do not fit this model.

DEFINITIONS

Arriving at a generally accepted definition of terrorism is not easy. Is it a term used by Western nations to condemn and define enemies of the state? Is terrorism just something you recognize and label when you see it, like bombings, assassinations, kidnappings, and skyjackings? Or, to quote the now common phrase, "Is one person's terrorist another person's freedom fighter?" Despite the difficulty in arriving at a precise definition, there are threads of commonality. Acts of terrorism are intended to evoke a response and generate fear from an audience much wider than the immediate victim. The psychological component of seeking to create fear as a primary goal, whether in an individual, a community, or a state, is essential to the concept of terrorism. It is difficult to measure this sense of terror, but what is clear is that there are advantages to be gained from it. Terrorism is also a potent way not only to communicate, but to send a message in an age dominated by the mass media (Weinberg & Davis, 1989, pp. 1–6).

Another important characteristic of terrorism is that it usually involves a well-planned, organized action, not a random, impulsive act of violence. Al-Qaeda has demonstrated this fact and set a new standard for terrorist effectiveness. Another element that needs to be understood is that terrorism is a feasible method of combat for groups and states that would not stand a chance in a conventional war against a particular opponent. In this respect terrorism provides a low-cost, low-risk, and potentially high-yield alternative. Lastly, a disturbing characteristic of terrorism, especially contemporary terrorism, is that it goes beyond the accepted rules in regard to humanitarian constraints. In other words, terrorist attacks cause the death of innocent people. This is above all true when considering the attacks of suicide bombers. Of course, this disregard of human life gives terrorism its shock power (Hoffman, 1998, p. 40).

Below are two definitions of terrorism. The first is official, while the second definition is scholarly. The second definition in particular tightly defines terrorism's major characteristics.

> Terrorism is the threat of violence and the use of fear to coerce, persuade, and gain public attention (National Advisory Committee, 1976, p. 3).

> Political terrorism is the use, or threat of use, of violence by an individual or a group, whether acting for or in opposition to established authority, when such action is designed to create extreme anxiety and/or fear-inducing effects in a target group larger than the immediate victims with the purpose of coercing that group into acceding to the political demands of the perpetrators (Wardlaw, 1982, p. 16).

Terrorism is not an ideology but a strategy that may be used by individuals, groups, or states for different purposes. It is a strategy that is often confused with guerrilla warfare. Although both rely upon unconventional military means with which to attack their opponents, there are differences between the two. Guerrilla war is rural in character, with guerrilla fighters establishing bases far from the reach of state power. Guerrilla war is typically a conflict between the insurgent guerrillas and the government. In the early phases of hostilities, guerrillas may turn to the strategy of terrorism to bring attention to their cause and show government vulnerability; however, as the chances for success improve, terrorism is likely to be used less. Ultimately, with popular support mounting, a "people's army" will rise up and defeat the government's regular forces and seize control of the state (Crozier, 1960, pp. 159–191).

The strategy of terrorism, on the other hand, avoids attacking government forces directly, preferring instead to commit acts of violence against unarmed civilians in hopes of achieving political change indirectly through fear and coercion. Terrorism, unlike guerrilla warfare, is typically an urban phenomenon, simply because cities offer targets that are more dramatic: public buildings, government apparatus, vulnerable populations, and full media coverage, all of which serve to generate publicity and magnify the crucial element of fear.

ORIGIN AND HISTORY

The earliest forms of terrorism, drawn from Jewish and Muslim histories, are religiously motivated and seek to influence not only the masses, but also God. Specifically, early terrorism focuses on the roles of the Sicarii, an extreme Jewish Zealot sect, in provoking a revolt against Rome (66–70 A.D.), and the Assassins, a radical Shiite Ismaili sect, which waged a campaign aimed at the purification of Islam for almost two centuries (1090–1275 A.D.) (Weinberg & Davis, 1989, p. 19).

Roman-Jewish historian Josephus Flavius tells of the Sicarii's unorthodox tactics, such as attacking enemies in broad daylight, preferably when crowds gathered on holidays in Jerusalem. Their weapon of choice was the dagger (*Sicarii* means dagger-wielders), which was hidden under the coat. It was thought that the crowd provided a sort of cover or anonymity for the assassin, who would simply blend in after the murder was committed (Laqueur, 2001, p. 7). Their actions created an environment of fear where no one was to be trusted and everyone was feared. The message of the Zealots–Sicarii was that all fellow Jews who accommodated with the Romans would be killed. Zealots mainly assassinated other Jewish moderates, but Greeks living in Judea and Roman rulers were targets as well. Their immediate goal was to eliminate Roman influence, but their ultimate goal was to initiate the coming of the Messiah by forcing an apocalyptic confrontation between Rome and the Jewish nation. The Zealots believed that by provoking such a crisis they could force God's direct intervention to save the people of Israel. Their God was a crucial part of the wider audience they were trying to influence.

The desired revolt began in 66: however, by 70 A.D. it was a catastrophe with thousands of Jews dead, the second Temple in ruins, and the Jewish state destroyed. The last of the Zealots fled and took refuge on top of Masada near the Dead Sea, where they committed mass suicide in 73 A.D. rather than surrender to the Romans besieging them. Like many religious extremists today, the Sicarii embraced their martyrdom as something joyful. Although the Zealots never witnessed the coming of the Messiah, the memory of their struggle and deep commitment persisted.

The medieval Assassins represent another religious sect that used terrorism in the eleventh and twelfth centuries. Some of the features of this movement remind one of contemporary terrorist movements. Their origins are found in the division among the followers of the Shiite tradition and in particular with the formation of a sect known as the Ismalis (centered in modern day Israel, Syria, and Iran). Followers of this group believed in the need for a purification of the Muslim community in order to hasten the arrival of the

Imam "the heir of the Prophet, the Chosen of God, and the sole rightful leader of mankind," who would establish a new and just society (Lewis, 1967, p. 27).

Outnumbered by the orthodox Sunni Muslim rulers, the Assassins sought to achieve their ends by unconventional means. Their leader, Hassan I Sabah, developed a strategy of using isolated mountain strongholds as bases to stage protracted campaigns of terror against Sunni religious and political leaders. According to the Assassins, these Sunni leaders had usurped leadership of Islam and corrupted its meaning (Weinberg & Davis, 1989, p. 21).

Acting as instruments of God, the Assassins would seek out and kill "enemy" leaders, despite the certainty of their own death. Using a short dagger, they would kill the enemy and, rather than flee, the Assassin would calmly await capture and execution. Most of the victims were Sunnis, but some Christians were taken as well, the most celebrated being Marquis Conrad of Montferrat, ruler of the kingdom of Jerusalem, who was killed by a group of Assassins disguised as monks. To counter the awe and respect these bold attacks generated among the common people, the Abbasids Arab dynasty spread rumors that the Assassins were not acting of their own accord but were really acting under the influence of hashish.

Overall, the impact of the Assassins was insignificant. They made few converts and never succeeded in reforming the Islamic faith. One of the greatest legacies of terror left behind by the Assassins was the origin of the suicide mission and the strategy of disguise or deception. For his martyrdom, the devout Assassin was promised admission to paradise—the same reward that motivates members of al-Qaeda, Hamas, Hezbollah, and other Islamic extremists today. The legends of the Assassins deeply impressed contemporaries and subsequent generations.

Throughout the Middle Ages and the subsequent religious wars of the fifteenth and sixteenth centuries in Europe, there was tremendous violence in which religious and political leaders were killed: however, there are no examples of terrorism equaling the sustained campaign of the Zealots or the Assassins. Perhaps one exception was the fanatical Anabaptist groups who represented the left wing of the sixteenth-century Reformation. Besides challenging infant baptism, they emphasized adherence to scripture and strict church discipline as ranking higher than the law of the state. The most spectacular example of Anabaptist success was the seizing of Münster (1533–1535) and the establishment of the "Kingdom of Saints." After gaining control of the city, the Anabaptists waged a campaign of terror against its "heretical" inhabitants in order to establish God's kingdom. "Christ will give the sword and revenge to them, the Anabaptists, to punish all sins, stamp out all governments, communize all property and slay those who do not permit themselves to be rebaptized" (Cohn, 1970, p. 255). This violence did much to discredit the movement and only redoubled the efforts of both Roman Catholics and Protestants to crush the movement.

So far, we have considered the earliest manifestations of terrorism associated with extreme religious beliefs. These terrorist activities, directed at both divine and human audiences, were intended to improve human existence both politically and religiously. But the purposes of these groups, though religiously inspired, were not exclusively religious in objective. Whether it was to seize political control or maintain it, overthrow the dominant wealthy class, or rid an area of Roman influence, secular objectives were inevitably part of the religious agenda. Much like the Islamic extremist groups today (Hezbollah, Hamas, al-Qaeda, and others), the religious terrorists of the ancient and medieval period attempted to modify the political order in the name of an ultimately religious purpose. There can be no doubt, however, that the members of these sects believed and saw their activities as serving God's will (Weinberg & Davis, 1989, p. 23).

MODERN TERRORISM

The late eighteenth century saw the nature of terrorism change with the coming of the French Revolution. The "Reign of Terror" did not initiate the Revolution but maintained and protected it from counterrevolution by spreading fear through violence. "The Terror" was a policy carried out by the French state and is an example of terrorism from above, or state terrorism. The state terrorism of the French Revolution pales in comparison to that practiced by Nazi Germany and Stalinist Russia, but nonetheless it established a precedent in the history of terrorism.

The French Revolution and the Terror were not legitimized in the name of God, but in the name of the *people*. With this concept, the motivational foundations for terrorism changed dramatically. In the century following the events in France, revolution against the established order was often justified by its proponents in the name of the people, the masses, or the proletariat. Like God for the religious fanatic terrorists, the people's will came to be viewed as transcendent—a substitute for God, in whose name everything was justifiable. With these developments came new definitions of citizen and state, and concepts such as nationalism and self-determination. All of this helped establish an intellectual climate that would give rise to the more radical political ideologies of Marx and Bakunin. In short, the French Revolution sparked an intellectual revolution that transformed terrorism from a religious to a predominantly secular phenomenon (Weinberg & Davis, 1989, pp. 24–25).

Modern non–state-sponsored terrorism, or terrorism from below, emerged during the last third of the nineteenth century because liberal, revolutionary changes failed to materialize. Frustration mounted as the revolutions of 1830 and 1848 failed to bring sweeping changes—Russia remained an autocracy controlled by the Czar, the French Republic was perverted into empire, and Germany remained unchanged. In addition, the masses seemed apathetic and the proletariat never rose up as Marx said they would. Some felt that terrorism could reignite the flame to unleash social or national revolution (Weinberg & Davis, 1989, p. 26).

Czarist Russia offers the first manifestations, both in theory and practice. The Russians Michael Bakunin and Sergey Nechayev published *Revolutionary Catechism* (1869), which provided an idealized guide that would be used by later generations as a model of a terrorist dedicated to his or her cause. According to Bakunin and Nechayev, the terrorist was a lost soul without an identity or ties to family and friends. The terrorist had broken with society and its laws and conventions and was consumed with only one passion: the revolution. All had to be sacrificed for the revolutionary cause. Reminiscent of Assassin tactics, the *Catechism* advised infiltration by way of disguise and dissimulation. The army, the bureaucracy, capitalists, and especially the church and royal palace were all targets. It was recommended to kill the most capable and intelligent enemies first, for such assassinations would inspire fear among society and government. The *Catechism* also defined anarchism by stressing the need for the total destruction of institutions, social structures, and civilization (Westwood, 1993, pp. 109–119).

Modern terrorism was first practiced by the Russian terrorist group Narodnaya Volya, or the People's Will. Its members were basically middle-class student–revolutionaries who had become disenchanted with the indifferent peasants, police repression, czarist tyranny, and absence of constitutional freedoms. In this light, terrorism in Russia was merely a manifestation of a general crisis in Russian society. The People's Will launched a terror campaign in 1878 against the Russian czarist regime culminating in the assassination of the Czar Alexander II in 1881. Instead of reviving the revolution, the only result of these efforts was a new more repressive czar. One can conclude that the terrorism of the People's Will, although a powerful statement of dissatisfaction, was ineffectual and indeed counterproductive. The assassination only shut the door to a political solution of the Russian crisis. The unrest did not spread and most of the members of the People's Will were quickly apprehended and executed. The demise of the People's Will effectively ended terrorism in Russia for two decades (Borcke, 1982, pp. 48–62).

The period between 1878 and 1914 saw a wave of terrorist activities carried out by anarchists (including the activities of the People's Will). They practiced the concept of "propaganda by deed," which believed that the most effective means of propaganda to draw people into the struggle was a violent deed. They felt that workers did not need to read—in other words, the propaganda of the idea had little effect—and violence is what awoke the consciousness, drew attention to, and generated publicity for a cause. Didactic violence would ultimately rally the masses behind the revolution. The deeds of the anarchists preoccupied public opinion, police chiefs, psychologists, and writers all over Europe for many years. Not only were bombs thrown into cafes, theaters, and parades, but there were many attempts on the lives of leading statesmen. U.S. presidents Garfield and McKinley were killed. There were attempts to assassinate Bismarck and Emperor William I of Germany. French President Carnot was killed in 1894; Antonio Canovas, the Spanish prime minister, in 1897; Elizabeth, Empress of Austria in 1898; and King Umberto of Italy in 1900 (Laqueur, 1999, p. 20). These examples, however, were isolated acts of violence and not part of a coordinated campaign of terror. Despite the deeds of violence, the social revolution never came, and in this respect the anarchists failed. Instead of mobilizing the masses, the violent deeds increased passivity, leaving people with the impression that these violent acts were the revolution, not a spark to ignite it (Joll, 1980, pp. 99–129).

Nationalism also became a powerful motive for terrorism in late nineteenth and early twentieth century. Nationalists who practiced terrorism targeted the multinational empires of Britain, Austria–Hungary, and Ottoman Turkey. The objective was statehood for the respective nationalities under imperial control. Perhaps the most notorious example was the assassination of the Archduke Ferdinand in 1914. Young Gavrilo Princip, part of the Pan-Serbian secret society known as the Black Hand, hoped to further the cause of the southern Slavs by killing the Austrian heir. This act of terrorism precipitated a world war that directly led to the downfall of the Austrian Empire. Viewed in this light, the assassination of the archduke was extremely effective; however, it can be argued that war was inevitable because of the international rivalries (specifically Anglo-German antagonisms) of the time.

Between the world wars a new motive emerged as a major cause of terrorism in Europe. Until World War I, terrorism was mainly a left wing strategy, however, now groups seeking to preserve the status quo or prevent change turned to right wing or reactionary terrorism. The Ku Klux Klan provides an example of such terrorism; founded in 1865, it is still operational today. In Europe many people reacted to the Bolshevik Revolution in Russia (1917) with the fear that communism would take over the world. The objective became the repression of anyone who threatened the status quo: socialists, communists, liberals, and so on. The fascist movement, with its nationalistic, violent, and anticommunist ideology, arose and flourished in this climate. Eventually, the fascist and nazi movements established totalitarian regimes in Italy and Germany respectively. Along with Stalinist Russia, these totalitarian states used terrorism to repress and control the masses. Persecution of Jews, communists, and other "enemies of the state" was typical and ensured submissive compliance among the people (Hoffman, 1998, p. 24). During this period anarchists did not disappear entirely; however, many national terrorist groups derived ideological as well as material support from the fascists.

After World War II, the feared neo-Nazi or neo-Fascist specter never rose from the ashes, and terrorist activities shifted from Europe to North Africa, Middle East, and Asia where anticolonialism and nationalistic sentiments were gathering strength. Violent campaigns were launched by nationalist groups striving for independence. Terrorism had occurred in the Middle East before, but now with the weakening of colonial powers, terrorism only gained momentum. Successes, like the fall of Singapore, demonstrated that the once mighty empires of the West were vulnerable (Laqueur, 1999, p. 23).

In the British mandate of Palestine, Irgun and the Stern Gang (both of which were Zionist paramilitary organizations dedicated to the expulsion of the British forces and the Arab population from Palestine in efforts to establish a Jewish state) escalated their use of terrorism after the British White Paper of 1939, which severely restricted Jewish immigration to the Palestine region. The White Paper effectively closed one of the few remaining avenues of escape for European Jews fleeing the Holocaust (Ovendale, 1999, pp. 77–79).

The leader of Irgun, Menachem Begin, realized that a handful of men and few weapons could never hope to challenge the British Army on the battlefield. Instead, Irgun would launch a terrorist campaign and utilize the urban landscape of Palestine to blend in until the time was right to strike. Begin's objective was not to defeat Britain militarily, but to use terrorism to undermine Britain's prestige and confidence. If it cost the British too much prestige and too many young soldiers to control the mandate of Palestine, Begin was confident that the British public would insist upon withdrawal. Irgun bombed various British offices in Jerusalem, Tel Aviv, and Haifa frequently. The 1946 bombing of Jerusalem's King David Hotel, the site of the British Army headquarters, was the most spectacular operation of Irgun. Ninety-one people were killed in this tragedy that still holds the distinction of one of the world's single most deadly terrorist attacks (Hoffman, 1998, p. 51). Unwilling to enforce military rule, Britain turned Palestine over to the United Nations in 1947. Success vindicated Begin's strategy; the exclusive use of terrorism forced the British from Palestine. Interestingly, Menachem Begin later became prime minister of Israel, thus providing an excellent example of a terrorist leader achieving legitimate political success.

The Israelis were not alone in experiencing success. Mao Tse-tung in China, Ho Chi Minh in Vietnam, and Fidel Castro in Cuba had also emerged victorious in their struggle for national liberation or social revolution. Their strategy for success, unlike Irgun's terrorist campaign, was a rural-based guerrilla war. Terrorism was used in these struggles, but it played a decidedly secondary role and was not a major factor in determining the outcome.

CONTEMPORARY TERRORISM

Terrorism is one of the greatest threats facing the world today, particularly when one considers the catastrophic potential of coupling a suicide bomber with a weapon of mass destruction (nuclear, biological, or chemical). Unlike war, terrorism is not a relatively constant factor in human history. Its violent outbreaks are unpredictable, sometimes with years, decades, or even centuries elapsing without much activity. It is evident that from the late 1960s to the present we have lived in an active period or a so-called "age of terrorism" (Weinberg & Davis, 1989, pp. 38–47). Many factors have contributed to this reality.

Technological innovation, in a sense, freed terrorism from any geographic or regional constraints. The 1960s saw the introduction of international commercial jet travel and the incredible proliferation of television. Terrorists could now strike at international targets of their choice and in a matter of hours have their message received by a mass audience—a situation undreamed of by the most dedicated Zealot, Assassin, or anarchist. Selecting the 1972 Munich Olympic Games and the 1978 World Cup Soccer tournament in Argentina as terrorist targets was no accident. In both cases, television audiences were estimated to number almost 800 million people (Weinberg & Davis, 1989). News coverage of these terrorist acts, especially when innocent victims were involved, created a major media event.

The ever-increasing use of jet aircraft to carry large numbers of people at great speeds and according to predetermined schedules created a situation vulnerable to skyjackings. Terrorists now had the opportunity to purchase their tickets and travel rapidly to other locations where new unsuspecting target populations could be exploited. Modern advances in communication (satellite/television) and transportation (commercial jet travel) effectively internationalized terrorism. These developments, particularly the emergence of modern communications (and its future development), go along way in explaining why we live in an "age of terrorism" (Weinberg & Davis, 1989).

Another dynamic force changing terrorism was the technological development in weaponry. Cold war competition created ballistic missiles and nuclear powered submarines, but it also yielded a completely new class of small weapons such as plastic explosives, armor-piercing bullets, hand-held rocket launchers, and the miniaturization of other existing weapons (Weinberg & Davis, 1989). Such improvements not only made daggers obsolete but made it easier for terrorists to conceal these weapons until they were ready for use or to detonate explosives from a safe distance. Among other things, the modern commercial jetliner has proven vulnerable to these new developments in explosives. It does not take an accomplished physicist to realize that only a small amount of explosives is needed to bring down an aircraft, while substantial quantities are required for a target on land (an estimated six tons for the 1983 attack on the U.S. Marine headquarters in Beirut). In short, these technological advances in weaponry increased the power of the terrorist to kill and become more difficult to detect.

International cold war competition between the Soviet Union and the United States was an important mechanism in the development of contemporary terrorism. In the 1980s, some regarded terrorism as a calculated means of the communist world to destabilize the West (Sterling, 1983). At the time this seemed plausible and the U.S. government was receptive to this conspiracy theory. By the middle of the decade, however, with a series of suicide bombings directed against many U.S. diplomatic and military targets in the Middle East, it became obvious that more than the Kremlin was funding terrorism. Attention began to shift to Iran, Iraq, Libya, and Syria as states sponsoring terrorism. With this development, one can see weaker states using terrorism as an alternate or "surrogate" form of warfare to inflict significant damage on the great power of the world without the risk of retribution (Hoffman, 1998, p. 27).

Another factor contributing to terrorism today is hostility toward the United States. During and after the cold war many peoples of the world began to perceive the United States as the imperialist power of the modern era. The growth of multinational corporations, the stationing of U.S. troops, and the coercive use of economic sanctions all strengthened this perception. In addition, tremendous differences between the levels of wealth and consumer consumption further accentuated the growing disparity between the developed world and the underdeveloped, or "third-world." Feeling economically exploited by U.S. capitalism, underdeveloped countries increasingly detested the intrusive foreign policy exercised by the United States (Hoffman, 1998, p. 80). Such impressions were destined to spawn feelings of intense antipathy, frustration, and indignation; these are the seeds of terrorism.

Today many frustrated people in third-world countries feel that the United States has so thoroughly monopolized and so formidably consolidated its global standing that there is no means of turning the tables besides terrorism. Terrorism is a ferocious strategy indeed, but many terrorists feel the situation is so irretrievable that any chance of change demands such tactics. No terrorist group—or country, for that matter—can hope to fight and win a conventional war against the United States; terrorism represents a feasible alternative (Baudrillard, 2001).

One of the most distinct features of contemporary terrorism is the resurgence of radical religious movements and terrorism of the extreme right. This should not come as a surprise, because religion was the original motivation for terrorism, as demonstrated by the examples of the Zealots and Assassins. Unfortunately, terrorism generated by religious motivation typically leads to greater bloodshed and destruction. This is especially true where violence is seen as a divine duty. In this situation, the religious terrorist is given unlimited means to legitimize and justify his or her actions. The terrorist feels no longer constrained by temporal morality and respect for fellow humans. The taking of innocent lives or his or her own life is not something to avoid; it is simply a means to a divinely directed end (Hoffman, 1998, p. 88).

TERRORISM IN THE MIDDLE EAST

Throughout history, religious fanaticism and terror are not exclusive to any one religion. Christian cults exist in the United States that spew hate propaganda of white supremacy and anti-Semitism and armed opposition to the federal government. It was precisely this type of attitude that was responsible for the bombing of the federal building in Oklahoma. Judaism also has its extremists. In 1984 Jewish extremists attempted to bomb the Dome on the Rock, one of the holiest sites in Islam; the plot was thwarted by Israeli security. In 1994, a Jewish fundamentalist massacred twenty-nine Muslims in a crowded mosque at Hebron. In 1995, a Jewish extremist assassinated Prime Minister Yitzhak Rabin two years after he signed the Oslo Peace Accords (Wilkinson, 2001, p. 59).

Although the current resurgence of religious terrorism is largely identified with the Muslim and Arab world, it would be ridiculous to associate mainstream Islamic religion with the terrorism of its most extreme elements. It is interesting to point out that, even though the anti-Western attitude of Islamic extremists is important, most violence practiced by extreme Muslims is directed against other Arabs or Muslims. Iraq, Afghanistan, and Algeria are examples of the *jihad* turning inward to destroy domestic evil before turning against the infidel abroad. Having stated this, one cannot overlook the fact that Muslim countries lead the world in terrorist activities. The frequency of Islamic/Arab-inspired terrorism is striking. In the last year alone the activities of Hezbollah, Hamas, and al-Qaeda have shaken Israel and the West to its core. It is interesting to note that of all armed conflict on the globe in 1999, Islam was involved in 80 percent. Of thirteen United Nations peace missions, nine concerned Muslim countries or interests (Laqueur, 1999, p. 129). It is for these reasons that discussion will now focus upon Islamic terrorism.

In the Middle East, discontent revolves around the survival of the Israeli state that was created by a U.N. resolution in 1948. Islamic and specifically Palestinian terrorism grew out of the resistance movement against Israel. There had been attacks against Israeli settlements since the state was created, mainly small raids across the border, but it was only after the Six Days' War of 1967 and the Israeli occupation of the West Bank, Gaza, and the Golan Heights that a major terrorist campaign began. It was after 1967, when a substantial number of Arabs came under Israeli rule, that well-organized terrorist groups with substantial budgets, sophisticated weapons, and their own intelligence services came into being. It can be concluded that the inability of the Arab states to effectively coordinate their military efforts and defeat Israel was a potent catalyst for terrorism in the Middle East (Laqueur, 1999, p. 134).

The Palestinian Liberation Organization (PLO) is an umbrella organization comprising Palestinian political and guerrilla groups. It remains the recognized governing institution of the Palestinian people. Yasser Arafat is not only Chairman of the PLO (since 1969), but founder of Fatah, the military branch and current dominant member of the PLO. The current goals of the PLO are to establish an independent, *secular* Palestinian state on part of historic Palestine liberated from Zionist occupation. The PLO accepts the existence of Israel.

The PLO has engaged in many notorious operations: Munich Olympics of 1972, blowing up jets at Dawson field in Jordan 1970, and other miscellaneous bombings and ambushes. These major operations brought reprisals from both Jordan and Israel; however, the PLO gained a considerable amount of international recognition. After Munich, because of international television broadcasting, the whole world was aware of the Palestinians and their cause. They could no longer be dismissed as insignificant. The PLO brought terrorism to the world and was an example to all future terrorist groups.

With this in mind, the 1980s witnessed the emergence of two of the more well-known extremist groups: Hezbollah in Lebanon and Hamas in Gaza and the occupied territories. Both of these groups are Muslim fundamentalist in origin and have caused far greater problems for Israel than Fatah or any other group. Their emergence was part of the wave of fundamentalism sweeping through the Muslim world, because of the recent success of the revolution in Iran. The Iranian revolution is held up as an example to Muslims worldwide that the West's intrusion into the Middle East can be resisted. The success of this revolution also gave strength to the reassertion of the fundamentalist teachings of the Qur'an (Laqueur, 1999).

Hezbollah, which means "party of God," was directly connected with the victory of Ayatollah Khomeini and his Shiite followers in Iran. The Iranian state helped to found and fund Hezbollah, hoping that this group would export the goals of Iran's successful Islamic revolution to Lebanon and create an exclusively Islamic state there. Another objective of Hezbollah is to drive Israel from the occupied territories. Hezbollah believes it is fighting a defensive struggle sanctioned by God and struggles against what it considers the arrogance and depravity of the West. The United States is perceived as the "great nemesis behind all problems of the region, due to its support for Israel and because it distances itself from all causes of liberty and freedom in the area" (Fadlallah, 1986, pp. 4–13).

Hezbollah was established by a contingent of 2,000 troops (Islamic Revolutionary Guards) sent to Lebanon in the summer of 1982 to expel an international force (Israeli, French, and United States) engaged in the war there. Eventually, Hezbollah gained substantial popular support and established a real political presence in Lebanon. This popular support was achieved by providing social services to its followers, such as schools and medical services. Providing such services has bolstered Hezbollah's image as the champion of the poor and oppressed; however, its sectarian, religious character has prevented it from becoming too powerful in Lebanon, although it has held tremendous sway over the Shiite minority there. It has engaged in a variety of business ventures, including supermarkets, bakeries, drugs, and farming to help finance its terrorist activities. While some of its income comes from wealthy Shiites in Lebanon, most comes from Iran (Laqueur, 1999, p. 137).

In 1983, Hezbollah conducted a lethal terrorist campaign against the Israeli, French, and U.S. military contingents in Lebanon. Its suicide bombings, which used vehicles packed with explosives, included attacks on the U.S. embassy in West Beirut (killing 61 persons), the U.S. Marine camp at Beirut Airport (killing 241), the French contingent's headquarters (killing 74), and the Israelis forces headquarters in Tyre (killing 30). Hezbollah was also responsible for numerous other activities such as hijackings and the keeping of hostages. The effectiveness of Hezbollah, especially during its early days, is impressive. The suicide bombings induced the United States and France to withdraw their forces from Lebanon. However, the ultimate objective of establishing an exclusive Islamic state remains elusive. Hezbollah has remained active during the 1990s, most prominently engaging in border warfare against Israel in south Lebanon. Using rockets and roadside bombs, Hezbollah has made life difficult for Israelis in the north and has continued fighting against Israeli forces in southern Lebanon. In May 2000, Israeli forces withdrew from Lebanon, vindicating the efforts of the Hezbollah guerrilla fighters.

The rise of Hamas was tied to the *intifada* that erupted in 1987. The *intifada* refers to the popular uprising of the Palestinians in the Gaza Strip and the West Bank against the Israeli occupation. This uprising broke out against the backdrop of twenty years of Israeli military occupation, during which the Palestinian population had met with frustrating political, economic, and social deprivation. While the early stages of the uprising involved youngsters throwing stones and taunting Israeli soldiers, it eventually spread and involved organized demonstrations, civil disobedience, and boycotting of Israeli goods and services. The magnitude and resilience of the *intifada* surprised Israel. Daily clashes attracted world media attention, which further fueled the fire of the grassroots movement. The international community began to sympathize with the Palestinian cause and voice concerns about alleged Israeli state terror perpetrated against Palestinians.

Hamas was the driving force behind the *intifada,* and in 1987, it formally declared its existence. Hamas is actually an acronym for the Arabic phrase "Islamic Resistance Movement." From the outset, the Sunni fundamentalist Hamas set a moral and political challenge to the national secular PLO. It insisted in remaining out of the PLO and soon became its primary opposition in the Palestinian political arena. One of the keys to Hamas's popularity is its large-scale welfare arm. Like Hezbollah, Hamas provides educational, medical, and other desperately needed welfare services in impoverished West Bank and Gaza towns, creating a marked contrast with the corrupt and ineffectual image of Arafat's administration (Sela, 1999, pp. 276–280).

Since the conclusion of the Israel–PLO Oslo Agreement in 1993, Hamas, through its armed struggle against Israel, has constituted a serious challenge to the peace process. The PLO's desire to establish a secular Palestinian state and its willingness to compromise and co-exist with Israel was unacceptable to Hamas, which called for nothing less than the complete destruction of the Jewish state. The ultimate goal is to create an Islamic state in all of pre-1948 Palestine (which includes all of Israel). The short-term objective is to drive the Israelis out of all the occupied territories. Hamas believes that the Palestinian struggle is part of the religious duty of *jihad* incumbent on all Muslims (Sela, 1999).

In the mid-1990s in response to the Oslo Agreement, Qassam units (Hamas military/terrorist units) carried out a number of suicide attacks against Israeli targets. Qassam operates entirely on a clandestine basis, and it is believed to have up to 500 young volunteers for suicide missions. Lack of resources, Israeli counterterrorism, and PLO authority, however, hampered their efforts. Not ready to fight the PLO as well as Israel, in the summer of 1997, Hamas made it known it would cooperate with Arafat. Although it will not abandon suicide attacks against Israel, it has agreed to refrain for defined periods. While it refuses the authority of the PLO domestically, it does accept Arafat's leadership in representing the Palestinians internationally. Both the PLO and Hamas want to avoid a Palestinian civil war, in which both sides feel Israel would be the winner (Laqueur, 1999, pp. 138–140).

While Hamas may be a lukewarm ally of the PLO in the day-to-day battle against Israel, it is resolutely opposed to restoring the peace process. Their latest *wave* of suicide attacks (2000–2002) is designed to sabotage the peace process and force Israel from the occupied territories. From October 2000 to June 2002, Hamas is thought to be responsible for no less then twenty-two suicide bombings in Israel targeting restaurants, malls, buses, and bus stations. Casualties from these bombings total over 1,000 people (175 dead and over 900 wounded). The Israeli military response has brought charges of state terrorism, particularly in the case of the Jenin refugee camp. The international pressure on Arafat to answer for and halt this latest round of suicide attacks has sent him on a collision course with Hamas. Arafat has little chance of controlling or eliminating Hamas. Opinion polls find 70 percent of Palestinians in support of the suicide bombings and opposed to a ceasefire. Many Palestinians feel that the suicide bombings are a means to an end and their only means of resistance. In fact, Arafat's own Fatah regards Hamas as comrades-in-arms against the Israelis, and there is little enthusiasm for the task of arresting Hamas leadership.

Another terrorist group involved in Middle Eastern politics is the organization or network known as al-Qaeda (Arabic for "the base"). This organization was created in 1990 by the Saudi multimillionaire Osama bin Laden to recruit Arab Muslims to fight against the Soviets in Afghanistan. In fact, the United States actually engaged in state sponsorship and helped train and fund al-Qaeda during the last phase of the cold war, hoping to defeat the Soviets indirectly. Al-Qaeda is a revolutionary group with the stated objective to unite all Muslims and establish a government under Sunni Muslim precepts. To achieve this goal it is thought that all Muslim governments, "corrupted by Western influence" (i.e., the Saudi government) must be overthrown by force. Eventually, Muslim state boundaries will be erased and replaced with a unified pan-Islamic state under the rule of the caliphs (Alexander & Swetnam, 2001, p. 2).

Al-Qaeda's activities are largely supported by the personal fortune of Osama bin Laden, (rumored to be worth upwards of $300 million), which he received from the bin Laden Group, his father's construction company. Bin Laden has augmented his fortune with various successful companies (construction, agriculture, investment, transportation) that he has established. Al-Qaeda also receives donations from all over the world to continue its *jihad*. Bin Laden, for all practical purposes, acts as the chief executive and chief financial officer of a loosely affiliated group of terrorist extremists who share resources and expertise and come together for an operation and then disperse. Al-Qaeda is just the most visible head of this international terrorist network (Cilluffo & Rankin, 2002, p.13).

In 1996, bin Laden issued a Declaration of Jihad against the United States and the Saudi government. He has endorsed a *fatwah* (religious ruling) stating that Muslims should kill Americans and their allies, military and civilian, anywhere in the world where they can be found. Al-Qaeda, and more generally all Islamic fundamentalist groups, detests U.S. global hegemony, the continued U.S. presence on the Arabian Peninsula following the Gulf War, and its seemingly unreserved support of Israel (Alexander & Swetnam, 2001, Appendices, pp.1–22).

In its efforts to spread *jihad* to all corners of the globe, al-Qaeda has been linked to many terrorist operations, such as the 1993 World Trade Center bombing in New York; the 1993 attack on U.S. troops in Somalia; the 1996 bombing of the Khobar Towers in Saudi Arabia; the 1998 U.S. embassy bombings in East Africa; the 2000 attack on the *USS Cole* in Aden, Yemen; and the 2001 assassination of Ahmad Shah Massoud, leader of the Northern Alliance in Afghanistan. In addition, al-Qaeda masterminded the September 11, 2001 attacks on the World Trade Center and the Pentagon, where nineteen suicide bombers hijacked four U.S. domestic flights and crashed three of them into their targets. The fourth flight crashed following an apparent struggle between hijackers and passengers. Almost 3,000 people perished in this most deadly terrorist attack in history.

How effective is al-Qaeda? It has not yet won its *jihad,* but it has won some skirmishes toward that ultimate objective. Al-Qaeda has done what no terrorist group has: It has successfully attacked and hurt the United States on American soil and demonstrated U.S. vulnerability. The propaganda from this deed automatically gives al-Qaeda a respect and visibility afforded to no other contemporary terrorist group. The United States, for all practical purposes, has won the war in Afghanistan and has crushed the Taliban, but although al-Qaeda has been wounded and forced from Afghanistan, it is impossible to ascertain its strike capabilities. Even if Osama bin Laden is captured or killed, al-Qaeda will survive and continue its activities. Al-Qaeda is an international terrorist network; it will take more than apprehending one of its chief lieutenants to stop it. It is important to understand that the United States has a difficult task because it must completely exterminate al-Qaeda to "win," while al-Qaeda merely has to survive to "win."

The al-Qaeda network has effectively exploited advances in technology unlike any other terrorist group. The ability to use the internet and satellite communications to recruit, propagandize, and coordinate strikes is impressive, but when you add to this the exceptional ability to organize globally, build clerical support, and attract recruits willing to martyr themselves, al-Qaeda becomes the most daunting terrorist organization to date. No single event better illustrates this fusion than the attacks of September 11.

Bin Laden is increasingly deified by many in the Islamic community. The headmaster of one the largest religious schools in Pakistan stated that Osama bin Laden is a "hero because he raises his voice against the outside powers that are trying to crush Muslims" (quoted in Bergen, 2001, p. 31). The young students at this school, needless to say, share this same view. In an interview before September 11, General Pervez Musharaf, the ruler of Pakistan, summarized bin Laden's appeal:

> The Western demonization of Osama bin Laden . . . made him a cult figure among Muslims who resent everything from the decline in moral values as conveyed by Hollywood movies and TV serials to America's lack of support for Palestinians being killed by Israeli occupation forces. . . . It is a very long list of complaints that has generated a strong persecution complex that the Osama bin Laden cult figure has come to embody. He is a hero figure on the pedestal of Muslim extremism (quoted in Bergen, 2001, p. 34).

What has caused U.S. officials great concern recently are the reports stating that al-Qaeda, Hezbollah, and Hamas are cooperating and may be in the process of establishing an alliance (Nasser, 2002). Such an alliance would be unprecedented and allow the organizations to collaborate on explosive and tactics training, money laundering, weapons smuggling, and sharing intelligence. If these organizations stood together, they could be more resilient in the "War on Terrorism" just begun by the United States. As an example, if al-Qaeda has been hobbled because its bases in Afghanistan are destroyed, members could assimilate into Hamas or Hezbollah and not only survive and continue to train and plan, but strengthen the global terrorist network. Hezbollah leadership categorically denies any link with al-Qaeda. Such a link would have to overcome different interpretations of Islam (al-Qaeda is Sunni, Hezbollah is Shiite)—not an easy task. However, Hamas has developed a working relationship with the PLO in order to focus better upon its enemy; perhaps Hezbollah and al-Qaeda will do the same (Nasser, 2002).

All of these organizations display a remarkable religious or ideological enthusiasm, resulting in fanatical acts such as suicide bombing. To Hezbollah, Hamas, and al-Qaeda, the suicide bomber is a martyr who believes his or her cause is both worthy and invincible. Because the secular cultures of the West place so much emphasis upon individual worth and freedom, it is perhaps more difficult to understand such a seemingly desperate strategy. In the United States in particular, where the media and, in some cases, government officials have given the impression that a clean, high-tech war can now be fought with almost no casualties, empathy is impossible.

Yet suicide missions have existed for as long as wars have been fought. The Assassins, discussed above, were a much-dreaded group that specialized in suicide missions. Most of the nineteenth-century anarchists were on suicide missions as well. Their bombs had to be thrown from short distances to be accurate, thus, the explosion would kill them, too. In fact, all attacks against public officials in countries that have capital punishment are suicide missions. The attacks have to be carried out at close range and the chances for the assassin to escape are poor (Laqueur, 1999, p. 140). Considering the above examples, it should not be a surprise that contemporary terrorist organizations use suicide missions, even though the media treated it as a new phenomenon in the early 1980s.

Islamic theological conflict surrounds the use of suicide bombers. The Qur'an does not permit suicide in principle; however, it can be interpreted as a religious duty to fight and die for Allah and Islam. In theory, the martyr is to submit to the will of Allah by his or her own free will and die an unavoidable and unsought death. In practice the candidates for martyrdom are heavily indoctrinated, selected by group leadership, and given a target. The typical suicide bomber is a male between the ages of 16 and 28. Most bombers come from poor families or refugee camps where living conditions are miserable. In most cases the main motivation is religious with patriotism and nationalism only secondary considerations. A very disturbing aspect of the September 11 attacks was that the suicide bombers involved did not follow the typical pattern. They all were generally middle-class, well educated, technically savvy young men who assimilated all too well into the communities in California and Florida. In fact, some of these men had been living unnoticed in the United States for several years and even learned how to fly passenger jets in the United States (Bergen, 2001, pp. 27–28). Suicide bombers in general present a difficult problem for authorities to defend against, because ordinarily authorities depend on the natural human fear of death as a deterrent, but the suicide bomber has already embraced death (Anderson & Sloan, 2002, p. 470).

It is important to understand that terrorists willing to martyr themselves, coupled with the development of weapons of mass destruction (WMD; biological, chemical, and nuclear), constitute one of the greatest threats to national security and humanity. The use of WMD has the potential to give terrorism unprecedented publicity, coercive power, and effectiveness. Incidences like the 1995 nerve gas attack on the Tokyo subway system, the 1995 bombing in Oklahoma City, and the devastating 2001 attack on the Pentagon and World Trade Center betray this reality and indicate the more lethal direction that terrorism is unfortunately headed. Such destructive power only a decade ago was monopolized by the nation–state; we are now on the brink of a new era where this type of destructive capability is increasingly in the hands of a few.

Another disturbing factor is the availability of material needed to make WMD. There is a great amount of fissionable material unaccounted for, mainly from the former Soviet Union, which has now entered the black market. Although much of this material is not suitable for constructing a nuclear weapon, it could be used to build a "dirty bomb"—in other words, coupling radioactive agents with conventional explosives. Although the device would fail to reach nuclear yield, it would nonetheless spread radioactive contamination with devastating economic and psychological consequences. The fallout would cause panic and people would have to stay inside to avoid it. Authorities would have to clean a tremendous amount of square miles. Buildings would have to be scrubbed, topsoil removed, and so on. The cost of such a cleanup would be unfathomable (Stern, 1999, p. 3).

Biological or chemical attack has the potential to be as devastating as a nuclear bomb. This type of attack is much more likely because the methods for making such weapons are simple and accessible. The formula for Sarin (nerve gas) is on the internet, and the materials and education needed to create other crude biological and chemical weapons are cheap and basic. At a different level, weaponized anthrax (which is difficult to create), if disbursed under optimal conditions in an urban setting, could kill several million people. Unlike a nuclear attack, however, some biological and chemical agents can be reversed if the population is aware of the attack and well-prepared medical personnel and vaccines or antidotes are on hand. The real danger of the biological threat lies in the highly infectious nature of its agents. If undetected, diseases such as smallpox or the plague can multiply exponentially and spread through a population. By the time the symptoms are recognized, it could be too late to contain an epidemic (Cilluffo & Rankin, 2002, p. 13).

Every modern society is vulnerable to terrorist attack. The United States is especially vulnerable because of its free and open nature. First Amendment protections allow the dissemination of printed materials that can help terrorists. The Bill of Rights that makes Americans free also makes terrorism more difficult to combat (Stern, 1999, p. 5). The above two statements are a reality. The question is, what is the balance between civil liberties and public safety? In June 2002, an ABC news poll reported that 79 percent of Americans feel it is more important to investigate terrorism, even if it means intruding on personal privacy. Just 18 percent said it was more important not to intrude on privacy, even if it limits counterterrorism efforts. The frequency of terrorist success in the United States will directly alter that cherished balance between civil liberties and public safety. If there are more attacks like September 11 and other landmark bridges or buildings crumble, or if there is a successful terrorist deployment of a weapon of mass destruction, measures will be called for that may well violate civil rights. These measures could include a more active FBI and CIA, curtailing the right of free speech, expanding the role of the military, and increasing surveillance and phone tapping.

In combating terrorism in the future, it is necessary to recognize that the terrorist threat is a permanent condition. The United States will always be vulnerable because of its openness, its huge urban centers, and its transportation systems. In this respect, complacency must be avoided and vigilance maintained. One of the most pressing needs of the United States is to improve intelligence capabilities. Accurate and timely information, coupled with proper analysis, is crucial in defending against terrorism and infiltrating terrorist groups. Terrorism is a dynamic and evolving force; so too must a nation's capabilities and responses improve and adapt. The area of human intelligence is critical. Technological gadgets are helpful to be sure, but to effectively combat terrorism the intelligence community needs up-to-date, accurate information from human agents and informants. There is also a wealth of information to be tapped in open literature and from the private sector. Journalists and entrepreneurs who work in "problem" areas of the world have a wealth of information to contribute (Hall & Fox, 2001/2002, p. 10).

Strengthened international cooperation is crucial as well. The coalition established to fight terrorism after September 11 still exists, but it has wavered at times. In this era of globalization and increasing interdependence, almost every terrorist campaign has an international dimension. It will take a long-term international commitment to effectively combat the terrorist threat that exists today. The United Nations' measures on human rights could be used to combat terrorism. The *Universal Declaration of Human Rights* (1948) specifically guarantees the right to life, liberty, and the security of the person. Several other U.N. covenants stress the right to enjoy "freedom from fear" (Wilkinson, 2001, p. 189). These provisions could be more rigorously enforced to help blunt terrorist success and establish a united international front (Hoffman, 1998, p. 211).

States that sponsor terrorism must be held accountable. If nations such as Iraq, Iran, Libya, Syria, and North Korea refuse to be brought into the international community and insist on funding terrorism, they are a large part of the problem and they must be stopped. How to do this is another matter; economic sanctions, diplomacy, and military action have been used in the past with varying results.

Shortly after September 11, the United States created the Office of Homeland Security to deal with the vulnerability of U.S. society. This unprecedented national response to the modern terrorist threat represents a new course for U.S. security. Congress appropriated a $40 billion Emergency Response Fund to wage war against al-Qaeda, help efforts to rebuild New York and Virginia, compensate victims, and strengthen home defenses. A total of $10 billion was dedicated to homeland security for such things as increased security for airports, nuclear facilities, dams, and bridges; employment of sky marshals on airlines; production of vaccines; installation of detection equipment in major mail sorting facilities; and many other measures. Another important objective for the Office of Homeland Security is to improve the use and coordination of intelligence across all levels of government (Bush, 2002, pp. 2–20). Only the future will demonstrate how effective these security efforts will be.

CONCLUDING REMARKS

As we have seen, terrorism can be defined in many ways because there are many types of terrorism. Terrorism has appeared in conjunction with a civil war or guerrilla warfare. It has been waged by religious and secular groups, by the left and the right, by nationalists and internationalist movements, and by state governments. Terrorism, unlike guerrilla movements, has rarely ever reached its final objective or changed the course of nations. Overall, the impact of terrorism on history has been minor. Then why use terrorism? Maybe some terrorists are poor students of history and continue to hope for an exceptional Irgun-like success. The likely answer is that the strategic limitations of terrorism are understood, but the tactical, short-term rewards (publicity, expression of belief, exhilaration, and revenge) make it worthwhile, at least to the terrorist (Laqueuer, 1999, pp. 46–48).

What the future holds for terrorism is unknown. Will the abysmal record of accomplishment continue? The answer is probably not. Over the last twenty-five years, terrorist attacks have become much more lethal. What began with hijackings soon escalated to sabotage bombing of jumbo jets, then to car and truck bombs capable of killing hundreds of people, and finally to commercial jet aircraft being used as weapons and flown into skyscrapers. What could be next? Everyone's fear, of course, is the use of WMD. If and when they are used, the potential for terrorism to reach its long-term, final objectives will increase dramatically.

To counteract this "age of terrorism," the international coalition must effectively mobilize its resources and ingenuity. The task is enormous and requires efforts on many fronts: law enforcement, military, intelligence, homeland security, health care. The international community can and must triumph over terrorism.

DISCUSSION QUESTIONS

1. What role has religion played in terrorist attacks over the last twenty years? Why is religion a key ingredient in the current wave of international terrorism?
2. What would you consider as an effective terrorist action? Why is terrorism more effective today than in the past?
3. What are the seeds of contemporary terrorism? The author recommends certain policies for governments trying to combat terrorism. Outline three of these policies. What are the potential problems with implementing these policies?

REFERENCES

ALEXANDER, Y, & SWETNAM, M. (2001). *Usama Bin Laden's al-Qaida: Profile of a terrorist network.* Ardsley, NY: Transnational Publishers.

ANDERSON, S., & SLOGAN, S. (2002). *Historical dictionary of terrorism* (2nd ed.). Lanham: The Scarecrow Press.

BAUDRILLARD, J. (2001, November 2). "L'esprit du terrorisme." *Le Monde* (Paris).

BERGEN, P. (2001). *Holy war, inc.* New York: The Free Press.

BORCKE, A. (1982). Violence and terror in Russian revolutionary terrorism: The Narodnaya Volya, 1879–83. In W. Mommsen & G. Hirschfeld (Eds.), *Social protest, violence and terror in nineteenth and twentieth century Europe* (pp. 48–62). New York: St. Martin's Press.

BUSH, G. (2002). Securing the homeland, strengthening the nation. *www.whitehouse. gov/homeland/homeland_security_book.html,* retrieved 7/1/2002

CILLUFFO, F., & RANKIN, D. (Winter 2001/2002). Fighting terrorism. *NATO Review,* 12–15.

COHN, N. (1970). *The pursuit of the millennium.* New York: Oxford.

CROZIER, B. (1960). *The rebels.* Boston: Beacon Press.

ESPOSITO, JOHN. (1998). *Islam: The straight path.* Oxford: Oxford University Press.

FADLALLAH, M. H. (1986). Islam and violence in political reality. *Middle East Insight, 4,* 4–5.

HALL, R., & FOX, C. (Winter 2001/2002). Fighting terrorism. *NATO Review,* 8–11.

HOFFMAN, B. (1998). *Inside terrorism.* New York: Columbia University Press.

JOLL, J. (1980). *The anarchists.* Cambridge, MA: Harvard University Press.

LAQUEUR, W. (2001). *A history of terrorism.* New Brunswick: Transaction Publishers.

_____. (1999). *The new terrorism.* Oxford: Oxford University Press.

LEWIS, B. (1967). *The Assassins: A radical sect in Islam.* New York: Oxford University Press.

_____. (1997). *The Middle East.* New York: Simon and Schuster.

NASSER, C. (2002, July 1). Hizbullah denies Al-Qaeda link again; *Washington Post* claims groups 'coordinating.' *The Daily Star. www.hizbollah.org/english/press/p2002/p20020701.htm,* retrieved 7/4/2002.

National Advisory Committee on Criminal Justice Standards and Goals. (1976). *Report of the Task Force on Disorders and Terrorism.* Washington, DC: U.S. Government Printing Office.

OVENDALE, R. (1999). *The Arab-Israeli wars* (3rd ed). London: Longman.

PETERS, R. (1996). Jihad *in classic and modern times.* Princeton: Markus Wiener Publishers.

SELA, AVRAHAM. *Political Encyclopedia of the Middle East.* Continum: NY, 1999.

STERLING, C. (1983). *The terror network: The secret war of international terrorism.* New York: Holt, Rinehart & Winston.

STERN, J. (1999). *The ultimate terrorists.* Cambridge, MA: Harvard University Press.

WARDLAW, G. (1982). *Political terrorism: Theory, tactics, and counter-measures.* Cambridge, UK: Cambridge University Press.

WEINBERG, L., & DAVIS, P. (1989). *Introduction to political terrorism.* New York: McGraw Hill.

WESTWOOD, J. (1993). *Endurance and endeavor: Russian history 1812 to 1992* (4th ed.). Oxford: Oxford University Press.

WILKINSON, P. (2001). *Terrorism versus democracy.* London: Frank Cass.

PART II

UNDERSTANDING
THE MOTIVES AND BEHAVIOR
OF TERRORISTS

3

Networks of Hate

Tim Kullman and Jim Rodgers

❖

This chapter provides an overview of current issues surrounding political extremism and international terrorism. The authors suggest that political extremists and terrorists tend to target the same groups, usually ethnic minorities and susceptible noncombatants. But in comparing the demographics between domestic terrorists and those responsible for September 11, the authors note a striking difference—while the former are often uneducated with moderate means, many of the latter represent a well-educated middle class. Still, the rhetoric of the two has similarities with both espousing many of the same prejudices, such as anti-Semitism. The authors explore the historical development of these right-wing extremists and their increasingly global reach.

Terrorism has a long history as a tool of political strategy. For many Americans, however, it took the events of September 11, 2001 to bring this threat to public view. While many Americans were unclear as to why the United States had become a target for terrorist groups, what is unmistakable is that the United States has been catapulted into the sad reality of terrorism as a global fact. Historically, the United States has known the boundaries and borders of its enemies, but this enemy has become invisible and ubiquitous. The purpose of this chapter is to discuss the activities and expanding fluidity of domestic and international extremist and terrorist networks.

In recent years, increased communication and coalition building among groups that previously operated independently have occurred. Technological development in communication capabilities and weapons production allow terrorist organizations to greatly expand their reach and influence. Terrorism and extremist political activity has become global and borderless. In addition to the similarity of techniques in communication and weapons use among divergent groups, another factor that these groups all possess is their bias and targeting of specific groups. Special attention will be given to explaining anti-Semitism as a continuing theme in both international and domestic terrorist motivation.

The next section will provide an overview of current issues surrounding political extremism and terrorism. In the "Historical Figures" section, we will review some of the U.S. historical figures that first began to communicate with Neo-Nazi and Fascist groups in Europe. The "International Activities of Domestic Extremists" section will analyze some of the major right-wing domestic extremist individuals and organizations that are regularly meeting with European right-wing groups to develop a global strategy for a white supremacist ideology. "Right-Wing Politics in Europe" will look at the impact of right-wing thought on current European politics, and the section titled "Global Expansion of Terrorism" will review the global expansion of international terrorist organizations.

CURRENT ISSUES

The nature and dynamics of global geopolitical systems have been radically altered in the 1990s by developments in information technologies, immigration rates, and rapidly fluctuating political structures. Globalization can be defined as growing interconnectedness and linkages across national borders (Passas, 2000). These transnational linkages allow for a significant increase in all types of economic and political activities, both legitimate and illegitimate. Cross-border flows of information and goods, cultural and political forces, people, and ideas can increase power inequalities and weaken governmental effectiveness in combating international criminal activities.

Terrorism and political extremism have become high tech, where all one needs is a computer and cell phone to begin global operations. With the constant flow of people and economic goods across national borders, the opportunity to move individuals and materials illegally has increased the potential for future terrorist strikes.

The *American Political Dictionary* defines terrorism as "actions undertaken by governments, individuals, or groups using violence or threats of violence for political purposes" (1993, p. 561). Political extremism can be broadly defined as beliefs in the political process that occur at either end of the political spectrum. It is important to clarify that all terrorist activities are rooted in extremist beliefs, but very few individuals who have extremist beliefs become terrorists. Even though a very small portion of the extremist population carries out terrorist activity, it is vital to realize that extremist beliefs can contribute to terrorist activities.

Complicating the problem in the United States are the political freedoms the Constitution allows. As a result, any individual or group can align with any political or religious organization, and, provided that violent action is not undertaken or the overthrow of the government is not proposed, their beliefs are legal. Terrorism, however, is a violent behavior against society, not simply a belief.

Political extremism in the United States has a long history that can be found in virtually every era of U.S. history. The majority of U.S. political extremist activity is right-wing in nature and calls for a return to some previous time in the past that was perceived as better than current conditions. U.S. political extremism, or *Nativism,* originates when groups of individuals feel threatened by changing social, political, or cultural conditions. Oftentimes, people feel a profound anxiety over some massive change in their lives that they did not control. This anxiety may be caused by a loss of privilege or status, either real or imagined, or rapid social change provided by industrialization, modernization, or migration patterns. When individuals feel threatened by changing social and political conditions, they search for scapegoats to blame. All Nativist activity attempts to reduce complex social conditions to simple problems.

In the United States, Nativist scorn has been anti-immigrant, anti-foreigner, and racist in nature. Anyone perceived by Nativist groups as being nonwhite is viewed as a potential threat to the White/Anglo-Saxon/Protestant (WASP) lifestyle. Some examples of early Nativist groups include the Know-Nothings established in the 1830s, the first Ku Klux Klan movement established in 1866, and the American Protective Association organized in 1887. These groups were also anti-Catholic because of practitioner allegiance to the Vatican, which was seen as a foreign power and not to be trusted (Lipset & Raab, 1970).

Today in the United States, the central issues that connect many right-wing extremist groups include distrust of U.S. government policies concerning immigration, actions toward globalization, multiculturalism and diversity, and policies supporting Israel. There has been a long history of anti-Semitism in the United States, and this belief is coupled with a U.S. foreign policy that is seen as favoring Israel. One interpretation of the origins of anti-Semitism contends that anti-Semitism was a result of the competition for converts between Judaism and Christianity beginning in the second century A.D. As the struggle unfolded for adherents, Jews were portrayed as a people possessing evil, which evolved to Jews being defined as the children of Satan. Many early leaders of the Christian church taught that a Jew would be the Antichrist. As the Christian church expanded in following centuries, the myth of the Jews as sons of Satan continued to gain popularity. By the Middle Ages, the belief in the existence of a secret Jewish government surfaced. This secret Jewish government was believed to be a hidden network of organizations and agencies that allegedly had the ability to control political and economic activities (Cohn, 1966).

As Europe's social and political landscape experienced massive change with the rise of industrialization and urbanization in the eighteenth and nineteenth centuries, traditional land-based ways of life were forever altered. Consequently, the struggle between traditional rural lifestyles clashed with the new mobile society. Because Jews had primarily been urban dwellers, they were once again blamed for much of the social and cultural upheavals. After World War I, Europe suffered devastating setbacks, such as rising inflation, a breakdown of infrastructures, and food shortages, to name a few. All of these blows contributed to the rise of Hitler in Germany, and his Nazi propaganda machine revived the belief in the Jewish world conspiracy. Using this propaganda, the Third Reich developed policies of genocide against the Jewish people.

Another area where anti-Semitism can be found is in the modern Arab world, where scholars link the growth of anti-Semitism to the establishment of the Jewish State of Israel by the United Nations in 1948 and the first Arab–Israeli War in 1949. The crushing defeat of the Arab states by the Israeli army triggered a mass exile of Palestinian refugees from the newly created Jewish state. Estimates of Palestinian refugees entering Jordan, Syria, Lebanon, and Egypt range from 700,000 to 950,000 (Hoffman, 1998). The Arabs and Israelis have fought two additional wars and have been in perpetual conflict for the last fifty years with hundreds of acts of violence on both sides that indicate no sign of ending. The United States has been a longtime supporter of Israel, which has made the United States a target of terrorism. In addition to support for Israel, the United States is perceived as a symbol of global economic and military hegemony that uses it power to achieve its own political and economic goals, with little concern for Arab or Palestinian interests.

Both anti-Semitism and anti-American sentiments are not limited to an international audience—these prejudices are also found within the doctrines of domestic extremist groups. For example, many domestic groups are hostile toward any form of government above the county level; believe that Jews and non-whites are the children of Satan; advocate (to the point of obsession) religious and racial purification in the United States; believe in a conspiracy theory of powerful Jewish interests controlling the government, banks, and the media; and support the overthrow of the U.S. government or the ZOG (Zionist Occupation Government). This last point reiterates the extremist belief that Jews have significant influence in the policies and activities of the U.S. government (Hoffman, 1998).

The most horrific example of right-wing anti-government extremism can be seen in the bombing of the Alfred P. Murrah Federal Building in Oklahoma City, Oklahoma, on April 19, 1995. Convicted for the attack were Timothy McVeigh and Terry Nichols—both espousing sympathies for right-wing extremist paramilitary groups in the U.S. One of the primary inspirations of McVeigh and Nichols was the fictional work *The Turner Diaries,* which described a civil war in the United States. The book detailed bands of U.S. patriots in their battle against all non-whites and Jews and a corrupt federal government that was a mere pawn for ZOG (Zionist Occupation Government). At the time of McVeigh's arrest, a short time after the bombing of the Alfred P. Murrah Federal Building, a copy of *The Turner Diaries* was found in his possession. William Pierce, the author of *The Turner Diaries,* is a prominent figure in the development of race hate domestic extremism and will be discussed further in Part III.

Since September 11, U.S. attitudes toward many groups of foreigners have turned to hatred and distrust, which has resulted in numerous incidents of violence toward innocent individuals simply because of the color of their skin. When individuals feel threatened, they will look to simplified causes for the perceived threat. When a violent reaction toward individuals because of their racial or ethnic origin can be legitimized, a serious threat occurs to the American way of life. Prior to World War II, all U.S. right-wing extremist groups espoused a profound distrust toward any foreign individual or group. But the post–World War II political landscape was so radically altered that for the first time, right-wing extremist groups began reaching out to European right-wing neo-Nazi and fascist organizations that also espoused a race-based nationalist theory. The strategy was to create race-pure national states called pan-Aryan states in an attempt to keep the bloodlines clean of foreign influence. Despite the defeat of Hitler's Nazi Germany in 1945, plans were immediately developed to carry on Hitler's idea of race-based nationalism.

HISTORICAL FIGURES

The first attempt to internationalize the Nazi viewpoint occurred in 1949 by U.S.-born Francis Parker Yockey. Yockey's life is one of mystery and intrigue as he moved around the world as a promoter of Nazi and fascist propaganda, avoiding many U.S. government agencies, including the Federal Bureau of Investigation (F.B.I.) and U.S. Army counterintelligence. His influence can be found within Nazi and fascist circles in Europe and the United States from the end of World War II to the present. Born in Chicago in 1917, Yockey first surfaced in 1939 when F.B.I. reports have him meeting with several right-wing Nazi organizations such as William Dudley Pelley's Silver Shirts, the German-American Bund and the America First movement (Lee, 2000). The F.B.I. would track Yockey for his Nazi sympathies for over twenty years before he was finally captured in 1960. Despite his opposition to the U.S. involvement in World War II, Yockey enlisted in the U.S. Army. His time in the military reflected his shadowy and covert life when he disappeared for several months in 1942 and the F.B.I. suspected him of being on a spy mission for the Nazis in Mexico City. Regardless of his dubious actions, he received an honorable discharge in 1943 due to a nervous breakdown (Lee, 2000).

Yockey's political belief is reflected in his massive treatise *Imperium,* which was published in 1949. *Imperium* is a 600-page attempt to legitimate anti-Semitic attitudes and the creation of a Third Force to counterbalance the development of Western capitalism and Eastern European communism. Yockey proposed the end of nationalism because nationalist boundaries weakened countries against superpowers. He is also opposed to democracy because it dilutes political power by giving a voice to the lower classes that, in his opinion, have no right or intelligence in governance. Yockey proposed the creation of a Third Force or empire that will extend from Ireland to Eastern Russia and be able to challenge the two superpowers for global domination. Yockey saw the United States as a dupe for the Jewish financial power that controlled most of the Western world and polluted the Aryan culture. He called for a "world-historical struggle," of which the primary goal is the removal of all Jews from Europe (Lee, 2000, p. 98).

With *Imperium* being praised as the best work on race nationalism since Adolf Hitler's *Mein Kampf,* Yockey moved throughout Europe and the United States to gather support for his new movement by creating the European Liberation Front (E.L.F.). He received support from neo-Nazi and fascist groups in and out of Europe, but fell short of his goal for unification. On June 6, 1960, Yockey was captured in Oakland, California with numerous phony passports and birth certificates. Eleven days later, Yockey was found dead in his cell from a cyanide overdose. The mystery that surrounded his life followed him after his death. Despite his early demise, his legend and ideology are currently being promoted long after his death.

Willis Carto, the founder of the anti-Semitic organization the Liberty Lobby, met Yockey days before his death. Carto was so impressed with him that he decided to reprint *Imperium* and continue the message of anti-Semitism and race nationalism. Carto's racism differed from Yockey's in that for Carto, racism was based on genetics, whereas Yockey based racism on the soul of the culture. Yockey believed some cultures were superior due to an inherent spiritual sense at the core of the culture (Lee, 2000). Carto has been involved with right-wing movements for nearly fifty years and continues to be active in 2002. Carto has established a number of right-wing publications and organizations that always espouse an anti-Semitic and racist position. Carto suffered a substantial setback in July 2001, when he was forced to close Liberty Lobby and his newspaper *The Spotlight* due to eight years of court battles ending in bankruptcy (SPLC, 2001). Regardless of his financial and legal difficulties, Carto remains an active force in anti-Semitic circles.

One of the primary goals of anti-Semitic hate groups is to promote the idea that the Holocaust was a hoax fabricated by Jewish power holders to gain world sympathy. To advance this goal, Carto established the Institute for Historical Review in 1978. Carto claims IHR is a value-free legitimate center for historical research, but a review of the literature produced by their *Journal of Historical Review* revealed a rabid anti-Semitic sentiment.

Even though he has recently severed his relationship with IHR, Willis Carto remains one of the primary organizers in the right-wing anti-Semitic movement in the last half-century. Carto has successfully utilized technological developments such as short-wave radio and the Internet to spread his message of hate and racial purity. Carto and Francis Parker Yockey represent an important ideological bridge in understanding the dynamics and interrelationships of neo-Nazi and fascist hate groups in the twenty-first century.

INTERNATIONAL ACTIVITIES OF DOMESTIC EXTREMISTS

The Southern Poverty Law Center, a major watchdog organization that monitors hate groups and racism, has reported on the continuing expansion of U.S. and European extremist groups aligning themselves with each other to develop a global strategy of creating a race nationalist agenda (SPLC, 2001). They believe that a global race war is inevitable and that the Caucasian race is at risk of eventual extinction. Only with pan-Aryanism—the development of Caucasian nation-states—can racial purity and superiority be preserved. Despite the patterns of continued global multicultural diversity, this race separatist belief exists in more than the extreme right-wing.

The 1990s saw a substantial increase in domestic extremist leaders traveling abroad to spread their message. The following overviews represent a small sample of current extremist global activities that includes a mixture of neo-Nazis, Skinheads, white supremacists and Klansmen, beginning with William Pierce, the founder of the neo-Nazi National Alliance and author of *The Turner Diaries,* who has traveled to Europe to meet with neo-fascists in Greece, the neo-fascist N.P.D. Youth Congress in Germany, and the neo-fascist British National Party. In 1997, Pierce was banned from the United Kingdom. He has been successfully utilizing the latest in technology to spread his message of race hate. In addition to his information website, *The Turner Diaries* is now online. *The Turner Diaries* is a fictional account of the coming war against minorities and government conspirators. This was the book that allegedly inspired Timothy McVeigh. In 1999, Pierce acquired control over the Swedish white power music label Nordland (SPLC, 2001), and in 2002 he began distributing a hate-based video game called Ethnic Cleansing (Godinez, 2002).

Another domestic extremist leader with international interests is Lincoln, Nebraska-based neo-Nazi Gary Lauck, who spent two decades traveling to Europe to distribute Nazi propaganda. He was banned from several European countries and in 1995 was arrested in Denmark and extradited to Germany to stand trial for inciting hatred. In 1996, Lauck was sentenced to four years for inciting race hatred; he returned home in 1999 (SPLC, 2001). Still another figure is former Ku Klux Klan leader David Duke, who traveled to Russia to promote his latest book on race supremacy called *The Ultimate Supremacism: My Awakening on the Jewish Question.* Duke feels that Russia is the key to advance his "world-wide revolution of White awareness." Duke allied himself with the anti-Semitic organization Russian Action and other ultra-nationalist groups. Because of legal problems in Louisiana, for the present it appears that he has made Russia his home.

The neo-Nazi British National Party also developed a strategy for U.S. support by creating an alliance with the American Friends of the British National Party (BNP). Their intention was to fund-raise in the United States so that BNP candidates can pay the necessary fees to be eligible for local and national elections. The primary organizer, Mark Cotterill, demonstrated considerable organizational skills by bringing together a wide array of race supremacists including former Klansmen David Duke and Don Black, members from the National Alliance, Richard Kelly Hoskins from the anti-Semitic Christian Identity organization, and Jared Taylor from the race-based American Renaissance (SPLC, 2001).

RIGHT-WING POLITICS IN EUROPE

One of the primary motivations that contributed to the growth of right-wing ideologies in European politics has been immigration (legal and illegal) into much of Europe. Individuals fleeing a variety of inhumane conditions and political conflict have sought refuge in the European community. Often, the immigrants are young with limited technical or language skills, making their assimilation difficult. The increased burden on social welfare programs and a rising crime rate have made immigrants unwelcome in much of Europe, resulting in an increasing legitimacy of right-wing groups in mainstream European politics.

While racial prejudice and hatred can be found in both the right-wing European political parties and the domestic extremist groups outlined in Part III, what distinguished them was their attitude towards parliamentary democracy. Very few of these groups espoused an anti-democratic platform (*Economist,* April 27, 2002).

While mainstream European politics is experiencing an increasing presence of right-wing ideologies, the trend fluctuates country by country. Perhaps the most startling showing, however, was in France, when in April, 2002, far right Jean-Marie Le Pen placed second with 17 percent of the vote in a field of sixteen and sent shock waves throughout Europe (Daley, 2002). His surprising success can be attributed as much to the French voters' disgust with the mainstream political parties as to Le Pen's virulent anti-immigrant law-and-order approach.

Other European countries are also witnessing a growth in right-wing parties, as illustrated by Austria's far-right Freedom Party, led by Jorg Haider. The party posted significant gains in recent years by winning between 22 to 27 percent in general elections and placing second overall in 1999 (*Economist,* April 27, 2002). In Switzerland, the far-right Swiss Peoples Party led by Christoph Blocher came in first during parliamentary elections in 1999 (SPLC, 2001).

But the gains achieved in recent years were offset by losses as well. The Italian far-right party the National Alliance (not to be confused with U. S.-based National Alliance of William Pierce), led by Gianfranco Fini, has slipped in the polls in recent years after receiving 12 percent of the vote in parliamentary elections in 2001 (SPLC, 2001). Regardless of their current losses and gains, the right-wing presence in European politics, fueled by economic instability and a massive immigrant influx, remains a central concern for the hope of a unified Europe. The message of racial and ethnic hatred portrayed in the right-wing movements in Europe and the United States may lead to terrorist attacks on individuals and organizations. The majority of attacks, however, are often spontaneous actions by individuals acting on their own and generally not part of an overall global network of terror. These groups are potentially capable of widespread terror, however, but have not taken widespread terrorist actions. Part V will review the global terrorist threats that al-Qaeda represents.

GLOBAL EXPANSION OF INTERNATIONAL TERRORISM

Despite the American–British alliance's success in routing Taliban forces and various terrorist operatives in Afghanistan, evidence points to the continued viability of the terrorist network in general and al-Qaeda and its links in particular. On Tuesday, March 19, 2002, the media reported that CIA Director George Tenet told the U.S. Senate Armed Services Committee that despite worldwide efforts to arrest people with ties to al-Qaeda, the core leadership of the terrorist organization remained at large and was actively trying to reconstitute itself as a threatening and menacing group vis-à-vis the United States.

But activities of al-Qaeda–linked groups have caused concern in many places far from the conflict in Afghanistan. One news story reported that Singapore responded to an apparent terrorist conspiracy in January 2002 by detaining fifteen suspects (including one Malaysian) who had bomb-making information and photographs and video clips of U.S. businesses and the U.S. embassy in their possession. Papers linking the suspects to bin Laden's al-Qaeda network were also present. Furthermore, since September 2001, the U.S. military has undertaken a major effort to assist the Philippine military's Southern Command to root out Abu Sayyaf guerillas in the jungles of the country, due to the suspected ties of the Filipino rebels to al-Qaeda. Philippine President Arroyo is very supportive of the U.S. effort in part because U.S. economic aid and private investments were pledged to follow the $100 million in U.S. military aid already committed to that country (Bello, 2002) .

On Saturday, January 26, 2002 the Fox News Channel reported that Singapore's efforts in foiling alleged terrorist plots had, among other things, prevented U.S. military personnel from being killed and naval vessels of the United States, as well as other facilities, from being destroyed. In early February the Associated Press translated an eleven-volume manual titled *Manual of Afghan Jihad,* which provided instructions to potential terrorists on the kinds of places to target in the U.S. for maximum value—industry, skyscrapers, and sports stadiums.

The abovementioned events and circumstances, together with the continued uncertainty as to the whereabouts or condition of Osama bin Laden, support the idea that the terror network stemming outward from al-Qaeda in tentaclelike fashion is vast and remains a serious danger to the security of the Western powers. Most especially, Tom Ridge, as Director of Homeland Security, and the FBI and CIA directors, Mueller and Tenet, respectively, face continuing pressure to develop more effective and up-to-date intelligence-gathering operations and to begin steps that strengthen U.S. security of vital sites around the country. For example, one of bin Laden's suspected top lieutenants, Abu Zabaydah, was wounded and apprehended in Pakistan.

Compounding the West's search for and elimination of al-Qaeda links around the globe is the recent resurrection of widespread violence—and, indeed, terrorism—in the Middle East. The organization Hezbollah, which receives financial, material (arms shipments), and moral support for its efforts from Iran, continues its campaign of sporadic violence against Israeli civilian buses and Israeli political and military targets in northern Israel and the West Bank area. Hezbollah's political goal of instability in Palestine is shared by other groups, such as Hamas and other elements sometimes associated with Yasir Arafat's own Palestinian authority. Israel's hard-line government, led by Prime Minister Sharon, has seen fit to respond to the outbreaks of violence through the most substantial, sweeping military actions in Gaza, Jerusalem, along the West Bank, and in northern Israel. Limited deployments and cautious diplomacy by either side have given way to action and reaction with heavy violence from all sides on the Palestinian issue, as President George W. Bush tries to reestablish the dialogue of peace in the region through the efforts of Vice President Cheney, Ambassador Anthony Zinni, Secretary of State Powell, and others.

Hezbollah, for its part—though primarily a conservative Shia group within Islam—has made a strange fellowship with drug smugglers in the tri-border area of South America where Argentina, Brazil, and Paraguay are joined. Hezbollah has used this rugged frontier as a place to hide suspected terrorists; a place to plot new violent adventures; and a source of drug-running and fund-raising from which to continue its terror campaign in Palestine (Miller & File, 2001, p. 44). Like al-Qaeda has proven to be, Hezbollah is extremely resourceful in keeping its strategies of chaos and disorder alive and well supported. The U.S. State Department believes that Iran and Syria each lend financial, material, and/or moral support to Hezbollah.

To be sure, the terrorism the world has been made so painfully aware of since September 11, 2001 is in part the work of a significant network of terrorist operatives, many of whom have their roots in the Afghanistan of 1979–1989 and the Afghan war against the Soviet Union. In his book *Taliban: Militant Islam, Oil and Fundamentalism in Central Asia* (2000), Ahmed Rashid ably reports how Algerian Afghans who fought the Soviets and were assisted by bin Laden returned to Algeria to orchestrate the Armed Islamic Group (GIA) wreaking havoc throughout Algeria and destabilizing North Africa and France with their brand of radical Islam (Rashid, 2000, pp. 135–136). Funded in part through bin Laden and his friends, the GIA has become notorious for its ruthless brutality and has been tied to the killing of 75,000 Algerian citizens and the disappearance of 20,000 more since 1993 (Miller & File, 2001, p. 26). Bin Laden, alone, as Rashid recounts, has had significant connections not only to the latter-day Algerian extremists but also to radical groups in Egypt, Sudan, Gaza and the West Bank, Bangladesh, Chechnya, Kenya, Hezbollah in Lebanon, Pakistan, and the Philippines, and to the sons of blind cleric Omar Abdel Rachman. Bin Laden's efforts seem to have involved coordination, financing, organization, and moral support for the operations, planning, and critical training of the many and varied terrorist factions working in and out of Afghanistan prior to the U.S.-led war on terrorism.

Because the various ways in which the terrorist network is connected to Afghanistan are so complex and extensive, the subsequent demands on U.S. policy in terms of effective response are very great. Traditional policies of no-compromise, go-it-alone Yankee resolve and seek-and-destroy will unlikely be sufficient to root out the vestiges of al-Qaeda and its terrorist comrades. Flexibility of response in diplomatic and military terms is called for in the effort to combat terrorism. Containment of the terrorist activities and establishment of key alliances with developing and developed nations will be needed to succeed in this new war. There is a need to recognize that the terrorists have a long-term plan to rid the developing world of the major, corrupting influences of the United States and other infidel powers. This commitment to the goal of purging much of the world of Western economic, political, and social influences will remain, regardless of whether Osama bin Laden is personally found and dealt with or not. The goals of the current terrorist network are not dependent on the leadership of any one person or one group of elites. Further, strict Islamic beliefs are sometimes relegated to secondary importance by the actions of terror groups (e.g., Hezbollah) in the planning and operations in places such as the Middle East. As CIA Director Tenet has pointed out to Congress, alliances are very likely to be formed between Sunni and Shiite groups in the future, due to their common interest in going after the United States and its allies. Indeed, as staff writers Dana Priest and Douglas Farah have pointed out on a *Washingtonpost.com* news story on June 29, 2002, the actions of Hezbollah and al-Qaeda now involve such things as coordination of training, smuggling of weapons, money laundering, ad hoc tactical support, and information sharing. Intense opposition to the United States and the West creates an ever-expanding network of terror, with former rivals cooperating in an opportunistic manner to secure greater surprise and surer tactical advantage over the democratic-capitalist countries. As Russian imperialism persisted during the cold war, so terrorist commitment to the destabilization of Western interests will likely continue into the foreseeable future.

As Robert Schulzinger (1994) has pointed out, the cold war containment policies advocated by foreign service officer George Kennan in his celebrated, anonymous X article in *Foreign Affairs* in July 1947 and followed by virtually every presidential administration through a variety of tactics from Truman to Reagan were based on the notion of an enduring Russian imperialism (Schulzinger, 1994, p. 208). Such imperialism, U.S. policymakers came to believe, would be a more significant obstacle to peace and U.S. interests than either the Marxist–Leninist ideology or the paranoia and hatred of specific leaders, such as Stalin (Schulzinger, 1994). Thus, the United States, in order to stymie Russian expansionism, developed sets of trip-wires, obstacles, and pressures, with diplomatic and military alliances and outright military efforts as necessary to frustrate, constrain, and eventually wear down the Soviet aggressor.

Similarly, one could argue that tackling the enduring menace of the terrorist aggressors is the future of the new war on terrorism. Long-term strategies and tactics designed to frustrate, constrain, and wear down the aggressor seem to be called for. Eliminating the terror threat altogether is unrealistic. Containing the efforts and effects of terrorism by reshaping the developing world with effective economic, diplomatic, and military alliances that address specific, mutual needs and that present potential terrorists with sets of trip-wires, obstacles, and pressures would seem to be an improvement over the more common action–reaction, we do not compromise, search-and-destroy policies of the 1980s and 1990s in Lebanon and Libya, for example. Short-term approaches seem not to offer effectiveness on the order realized by Kennan, Truman, and Marshall in those fateful days of 1947 when the Soviets were on the rise and long-range U.S. plans were implemented with the creation of the Truman Doctrine and the European Recovery (Marshall) Plan. Certain long-term strategies of the West inevitably involve bureaucratic responses to terrorism. The Bush administration recognized this reality in the development of the proposal to create a new, massive Department of Homeland Security made public on June 6, 2002. The new mega-agency is supposed to be in place by January 1, 2003. The agency would incorporate such existing bureaus as the Coast Guard, the Federal Emergency Management Agency (FEMA), and the Secret Service, as well as immigration and customs functions of the federal government. As widely reported, some $37 billion and more of budget allocations would be involved in the new department.

Importantly, however, the critical intelligence and response arms of the federal government changed with combating terrorism on domestic soil, the CIA and FBI, are omitted from the new security agency structure. Numerous news and political commentators have questioned the wisdom of leaving out the intelligence and law enforcement operations from homeland security apparatus, especially since President Bush intends to have the new agency receive information from the CIA and FBI on an ongoing basis so as to conduct analysis and assessment of the likelihood of a terrorist threat to any significant site or event in the United States. It is reasonable to question whether such a system of information sharing and analysis response will be any better than that in place prior to September 11, when several pieces of information pointed to the possibility of terrorist efforts directed at U.S. soil (e.g., the arrest in August in Minneapolis, Minnesota of Zacarias Moussoui later charged by the feds with being a part of the September conspiracy). Minneapolis Special Agent Coleen Rowley, it may be remembered, was unable to successfully use the normal channels of bureaucratic communication in the FBI to gain federal attention and effort to the Moussoui case *before* September 11.

Since the history and practice of large public bureaucracies in the United States and elsewhere teach the student of policy that adherence to precedents, formal rules, standard operating procedures, and the turf protection of subunits within the agency and between agencies are common practices over time, is it realistic to assume that a homeland security agency will somehow be immunized against these efforts? Crisis response and management efforts of the past in the United States do not offer terribly reassuring examples of bureaucratic success. Efforts to create an energy czar in the 1970s under Nixon and Ford proved so ineffective that President Carter proposed and ultimately secured Congressional creation of the Department of Energy in 1977. (Note the similar pattern in homeland security as President G. W. Bush tried a czar-like approach under former governor Ridge of Pennsylvania and then proposed a new Cabinet-level agency.) Hardly anyone, aside perhaps from the already powerful and entrenched interest groups involved in energy production, has found the Department of Energy a beacon of bureaucratic success, and President Reagan attempted unsuccessfully to abolish the agency in the 1980s. More recently, President Clinton's Secretary of Energy, Bill Richardson of New Mexico, came under great fire from Republicans and Democrats alike (especially from the senior Senate Democrat, Robert Byrd of West Virginia) for the sloppy departmental management of secrets regarding the U.S. nuclear research and development programs at the Los Alamos National Laboratory.

Perhaps the Bush administration and students and observers of public policy issues hope that the Department of Homeland Security will resemble more the can-do, task orientation of the National Aeronautics and Space Administration (NASA) created in the Eisenhower years, empowered by President Kennedy with a clear vision, and sustained over time (even through disasters such as the explosion of the space shuttles Challenger and Columbia) through dynamic and creative applications of research and technology to space exploration more and more broadly defined by effective leadership. Citizens and students will no doubt judge the new Department of Homeland Security as they have judged NASA, the Energy Department, and other bureaus, on the results of its functions and operations. In the final analysis, the new agency will rise or fall based upon its accumulated track record in securing domestic tranquility in the face of continuing terrorist threats.

CONCLUDING REMARKS

The complexity in understanding political extremism and terrorism is represented in the wide variety of topics, organizations, and ideas reviewed in this chapter. Our attempt has been to show how terrorism and political extremism, despite their different forms and roots, have been able to utilize developments in communication technologies, global financial systems, and access to new weaponry to expand their operations. A second goal has been to show the similarities in the targets of terrorism and political extremism. Anti-Semitism and anti-American government sentiments are prime motivators for both international and domestic groups. Terrorism and political extremism can take a multiplicity of forms and structures. The nature of terrorism is fluid, dynamic, and adaptable. Combating these new forms of terrorism will take a complete reassessment of our strengths and vulnerabilities. Our open and democratic lifestyle will always leave us somewhat vulnerable. Whatever the source of extremist or terrorist action, we need to be more aware of the potential threats these sources pose to our way of life and to the future of the world and all its citizens.

DISCUSSION QUESTIONS

1. Are there any similarities between domestic and international terrorist groups?
2. What factors motivate the activities of right-wing extremist groups in Europe? How important are these factors in the activities of U.S. extremist groups?
3. Discuss the prevalence of anti-Semitism in the propaganda of U.S. right-wing extremist groups and international terrorists.

REFERENCES

BELLO, W. (2002, March, 18). A second front in the Philippines. *The Nation.* Vol. 274 No. 10 pp. 18–22.

COHN, N. (1966). *Warrant for genocide: The myth of the Jewish world-conspiracy and the protocols of the elders of Zion.* New York: Harper & Row.

DALEY, SUZANNE. (2002, April 22). "Protests over La Pen's Success Growing across a shocked France." *New York Times.*

Fox Report (2002, January 26). *Fox News Channel.*

GODINEZ, V. (2002, March 17). Racist groups pitching high-tech hate to teens. *Wisconsin State Journal,* p. A-7.

HOFFMAN, B. (1998). *Inside terrorism.* New York: Columbia University Press.

LEE, M. (2000). *The beast reawakens.* New York: Routledge.

LIPSET, M., & RAAB, E. (1970). *The politics of unreason: Right-wing extremism in America, 1790–1970.* New York: Harper & Row.

MILLER, M., & FILE, J. F. (2001). *Terrorism factbook: Our nation at war.* Peoria, IL: Bollix Books.

PASSAS, N. (2000, Summer). Global anomie, dysnomie, and economic crime: Hidden consequences of neoliberalism. *Social Justice,* 1–5.

PLANO, JACK C. and MILTON GREENBERG (eds.). (1993). *American Political Dictionary*. New York: Brace.

PRIEST, DANA and DOUGLASH FARAH. (2002, June 29). Terror alliance has U.S. worried. *The Washington Post*. Retrieved from www.washingtonpost.com/A23–24.

RASHID, A. (2000). The *Taliban, militant Islam, oil and fundamentalism in Central Asia*. New Haven: Yale University Press.

SCHULZINGER, R.D. (1994). *American diplomacy in the twentieth century*. (3rd ed.). New York: Oxford University Press.

Southern Poverty Law Center. (2001, Fall). Intelligence report. Retrieved from www.spicenter.org/intelligenceproject/ip-index.html.

"Toxic but containable." (2002, April 27). *The Economist*.

4

Terrorism, "True Believers," and the Attack on Globalization

Sheldon Smith

The previous chapter compared the motivations of terrorists with political extremists. In the following chapter, Smith explains the attacks of September 11, 2001 as reactions to the spread of globalization and Western influence in the Islamic world. This chapter explores the role of radical Islam in the current wave of international terrorism and suggests that the growth of groups such as al-Qaeda is as much a backlash against the spread of Western values as a reaction to autocratic, corrupt, and ineffective regimes supported by the West. Smith argues that in the long run, the real losers from international terrorism are the people of the Middle East because the spread of radical Islam threatens to disrupt the emergence of cultures supporting peace, democracy, and open markets in the region.

THE "TRUE BELIEVERS" AND GLOBALIZATION

The September 11, 2001 attacks are explained as *jihads* against U.S. materialism by terrorists and their supporters. Terrorist leaders such as Osama bin Laden encourage Muslims all over the world to carry out attacks against globalization and the spread of Western influence. In this respect, bin Laden and his followers may be regarded as "true believers" in a radicalized Islam that is unacceptable to most Moslems. There are actually two types of *jihad,* a "greater *jihad*" and a "lesser *jihad.*" The first is one's search for salvation through faith in Allah. The second sanctions rebellion against an unjust ruler. Ahmed Rashid argues that bin Laden, the Taliban, and al-Qaeda and its supporters have ignored the greater *jihad* and debased the lesser *jihad.* Rashid writes:

. . . nowhere does *jihad* sanction the killings of innocent non-Muslim men, women and children, or even fellow Muslims, on the basis of ethnicity, sect or belief. It is this perversion of *jihad*—as a justification to slaughter the innocent—which in part defines the radical new fundamentalism of today's most extreme Islamic movements (Rashid, 2000).

In the war against terrorism, the U.S. public has been given an opportunity to view what societies controlled by true believers look like. For the sake of an extremist form of Islam, supporters of terrorism in the Middle East are creating exactly the forms of political and economic organization that have spelled poverty and injustice for Muslims throughout the twentieth century and the early part of the twenty-first century. The extreme poverty created by state-controlled economies ruled by ruthless and corrupt leaders is blamed on the United States and on globalization. It is important to find ways to reduce poverty in these regions as part of the overall strategy to combat terrorism.

Despite the scale of the 9-11 attacks, it is unlikely that terrorists will have any long-term impact on the United States, its allies, or the processes of globalization. This chapter explores the nature of international terrorism and radical Islam. Its main argument is that the real threat of radical Islam and terrorism is to the well-being of the people of the Middle East. Why? Because radical Islam is a threat to newly emerging political cultures supporting peace, democracy, and open markets in the Middle East. *Jihads* on globalization do more damage to the countries of the Middle East than they do to the United States and other economically successful countries.

POLITICAL CULTURES OF POWER AND THE CIVIL SOCIETY

A decade ago, anthropologist Joan Vincent took anthropology to task for ignoring the study of power and politics (Vincent, 1990). That critique of anthropology can be extended to other social sciences. While Vincent's critique still applies, a new and younger generation of European anthropologists, such as Wil G. Pansters of the Netherlands, has pursued the cultural study of politics and power; his discussion is appropriate here. Pansters has turned to political scientists Gabriel Almond and Sidney Verba's concept of political culture (1963). Following Almond and Verba's work, Pansters defines political culture as ". . . a people's predominant belief, attitudes, values, ideals, sentiments, and evaluations about the political system of its country, and the role of the self in that system" (Pansters, 1997, p. 5). The same concept has been used in a recent analysis of the democratization of Latin American political cultures (Smith, 2003 Latin America in transition: The influence of culture on ecology, power and diversity). Political culture should not be confused with political institutions or forms of political organization. Political culture is what lies behind specific systems of power and determines their organizational structures.

In his study of Mexican political culture, Pansters demonstrates that the ability to use, manipulate, or acquire power is culturally conditioned. Political culture limits the range of political systems that can be brought into existence in a given society. This is another way of saying that there are cultural limits on certain political activities. He argues that Mexico has been dominated by the "political culture of the pyramid." Latin American political culture was center oriented and vertically structured. The cement that held it together is called *personalismo* (or *caudillismo* or *caciquismo*). That is, it is the personality of the "strongman," "man of power," or "boss" that holds the pyramid together. He argues that Mexican political culture was based on *the use of power,* not the rule of law (Pansters, 1997).

Recently, Mexico has experienced the initial stages in the development of a second competing set of values. Out of an authoritarian culture, one can see the slow evolution of liberal–democratic "political culture of citizenship" (or civil society). Much of what is written about the cultures of the pyramid in Mexico applies to the countries in the Middle East, with the possible exception of Israel and Turkey. Civil society, according to Pansters, ". . . is oriented towards multiple power centers and is horizontally structured by institutions" (Pansters, 1997, p. 9). Among the most important characteristics of this newly emerging form of political culture is *the rule of law,* a feature that has been missing during most of Latin America's history. The history of the development of civil societies in the Middle East is much more discouraging than in much of Latin America and Asia.

The countries of the Middle East appear based on political cultures that favor strongman rule and rule by force, not law. The only country with a civil society is Israel, and while politicians in Turkey appear to want the same political system, the use of state terror against the Kurds prevents the appearance of the rule of law. Israel's recent return to the use of violence against Palestinians, as well as the reverse, has pushed back the further development of civil society into the future. Compliance with the Oslo Accords will be the first step in both societies to adapt the rule of law.

THE ISRAELI–PALESTINIAN CONFLICT AND SECULAR INTERNATIONAL TERRORISM

Force, not law, rules most of the countries of the Middle East. In 1948, Israel came into being during a spasm of violence that continues to plague the region today. Israel survived its own birth pangs, but the war was a loss to all who participated. Israel, as well as its neighbors, stooped to the use of terrorism. The failure of Middle Eastern states to win the war was blamed on corrupt monarchies, which brought about a change in the political culture of the Middle East directly after World War II. In 1954, young military officers in Egypt overthrew King Farouk and made Gamel Abdel Nasser prime minister. Between 1954 and today, the political cultures of the Middle East shifted from supporting totalitarian monarchies to supporting secular, authoritarian, and socialist one-party states. Only a handful of royal kingdoms managed to keep their traditional political systems, but these share many of the features of the radical states in that force is chosen over law.

The model for Middle Eastern political systems was developed for Turkey by its post–World War I president, Mustafa Kemal Ataturk. Directly after World War I, Ataturk blamed Islam for the fall of the Ottoman Empire, of which Turkey was the dominant core. He outlawed religious political parties and established an authoritarian secular and socialist government. Most of the countries in the Middle East followed his model directly after World War II.

With the exceptions of Israel and Turkey, the political cultures of the Middle East chose the rule of force over the rule of law and thus condemned themselves to political corruption and economic underdevelopment. The vast wealth of the oil fields was used to maintain the elites in power, much as had been done during the Ottoman Empire and the colonial period. Wealth was not used to develop democratic and prosperous societies; instead, it was used to purchase weapons. For the following four decades, most of these states received support from the Soviet Union, and a few were responsible for terrorist activities in the 1960s, 1970s, and 1980s. Most of these actions were related to the conflict between Palestine and Israel and are examined below.

Roots of the Conflict between Israelis and Palestinians

The origins of conflict between Palestinians and Israelis began with the British Balfour Declaration of November 2, 1917. This document stated that the British government, which after World War I controlled the lands called Palestine, "view with favor the establishment in Palestine of a national home for the Jewish people," thus giving support to the Zionist movement (Zionism is a socialist political movement to make the region of Israel a Jewish homeland). Ideally, Zionism was socialist and secular. But most Muslims consider Zionism as nothing more or less than the extension of U.S. capitalist control through the Jews of present day Israel.

In the mid-1930s, the scale of Jewish immigration into Palestine increased (as a consequence of the rise of Hitler, fascism, and anti-Semitism in Europe). Civil war between Jews and Palestinians occurred in 1937, and then again after World War II in 1947. International conflict followed between the new state of Israel and the surrounding Arab states. Although small in number, the *Yishuvs* (Jewish communities) were far stronger than Palestinian communities. The announcement of partition in November 1947 had helped restore a measure of unity to the Arabs of Palestine, but that unity was the consequence of opposition to Israel rather than true political unity. Arab communities throughout the Middle East were left in confusion, and cooperation was generally lacking.

Civil conflicts led to the Palestinian/Israeli war of 1947–1948. No longer a battle between Jews and Palestinians, Egypt, Syria, Iraq, and Jordan joined with Palestinians in a war against Israelis and were defeated. Rumors of Israeli atrocities spread, and by 1948 more than three-quarters of the Arabs who had lived in the region had become refugees in the surrounding Arab countries or in the Jordanian controlled West Bank (Peretz, 1977, p. 22).

Over the next twenty years, from 1949 to 1969, exiled Palestinians went through considerable social and economic change. United Nations' representatives in the refugee camps offered young refugees educational and technical opportunities. They broke out of the framework of traditional Arab peasant society. Most Palestinians made the move from illiterate *fellahin* to literate urban dwellers overnight. Generally, more Palestinian Arabs were enrolled in higher education than any other Arab groups (between 80 and 90% compared to 53% in the Arab world as a whole). Palestinians became a quasi-elite in many Arab countries, providing professionals for rapidly developing countries such as Kuwait and Libya (Peretz, 1977, p. 32).

Socialist and secular Egypt, Jordan, Syria, and Iraq competed in their use of the Palestinians for their own purposes (the creation of a Pan-Arab state). Each country had its own Palestinian "leaders," which it backed. The Syrian army assisted in organizing and training commando groups and adopted al-Asifa, the military arm of al-Fatah (the Palestinian terrorist network developed by the present-day president of the Palestinian authority, Yasser Arafat, in attempts to embroil Jordan with Israel [Peretz, 1977, p.38]). However, while the leaders of Arab states embraced the Palestinian cause, many

Palestinians felt they were being cynically used because the same countries that supported their demands for a homeland would not allow them to become citizens. It was not until May 1967 that some unity was restored, when the crisis leading to the June war built to fever pitch. The Arabs, imagining a smashing success against Israel, were willing to co-operate with each other. In addition, many countries that had little interest in the Palestinian problem, such as Morocco, Tunisia, Algeria, Sudan, and the Persian Gulf states, became involved in the conflict against Israel (Peretz, 1977, pp. 42–43).

Israel's defeat of Egypt, Syria, and other Middle Eastern states in what is now referred to as the Six-Day War had a traumatic impact on the Arabs of Palestine. Four hundred thousand Palestinians were displaced from their homes, many for the second time. Most of the refugees fled from the West Bank (which is what was left of Palestine) to Jordan. The West Bank was conquered by Israel, and Israelis began settling the region in 1968. Tens of thousands of Palestinian Arab refugees began life over again in tents. The situation resembled that of the war of 1947–1948. There were urgent appeals for help.

In many respects, the situation was not the same as 1948. Whereas after the first "disaster" only a tiny remnant of Palestinian Arabs remained under Israeli control, now there were about a million and a half. The largest concentrations were on the West Bank and in Gaza; these comprised over half of the two and a half million Palestinian Arabs living in the Middle East. The situation was also radically altered because Israel now held all of Palestine, the West Bank, the Gaza strip, the Egyptian Sinai, and the Syrian Golan Heights. Israel's security was vastly improved with its population far from Arab armies (Peretz, 1977, p. 44).

TRANSNATIONAL TERRORISM

Terrorism is the illegal use of force against civilians who are randomly targeted to create fear. While terrorism has been common in Europe and the Middle East for decades, if not centuries, after the 1967 conflict, terrorist activities took a quantum leap from loose nationalistic operations to those that spanned many countries. The new type of terrorism is called *transnational terrorism* (Wilkinsen, 1979). Terrorist organizations or networks are made up of cells of highly trained professional and disciplined warriors whose goal was the destruction of Israel. The cells capitalized quickly on the mobility afforded them by expanding international transportation and communication systems during the decades following the development of the state of Israel. Thus, the terrorists used the technologies of globalization against their enemies.

In the Middle East, in the period between 1968 and 1990, terrorism was used by secular transnational organizations from various regions such as the Palestinian Liberation Front, Black June of Palestine, the Red Brigades in Italy, the Basque Fatherland in Spain, First of October Anti-Fascist Resistance Group in Spain, Peoples Struggles and People's Resistance Groups in Iran, the Irish Revolutionary Army in Belfast, the Tupamaros of Paraguay and Argentina, and the Shining Path movement in Peru. These secular and socialist movements, with a few exceptions, almost disappeared in the 1990s. However, in the Middle East violence has expanded as Islamic militants, whose agendas are the direct opposites of their secular rulers, have adopted transnational terrorism for their own use.

Most of the terrorists of the period before 1990 can be considered transnational and secular. Their goals, unlike bin Laden and al-Qaeda, were to punish the West for its support of Israel. The terrorists were not Islamic fundamentalists, but secular and often socialist Palestinians with like networks throughout the Middle East. The failure of radical states to defeat Israel led to the organization of Palestinian elements to adopt terrorism in attacks on Israel. The new terrorists joined with other terrorist groups around the world to create truly transnational terrorism.

The July 1968 hijacking of an El Al flight from Rome to Tel Aviv by the Popular Front for the Liberation of Palestine (PFLP) was the first application of the transnational concept of terrorism that became common over the next twenty years. The Black September Organization of Palestine, the Japanese Red Army (JRA), and the Baader-Meinhof group in Germany followed the actions of the PFLP. These helped Palestine Arabs to carry out terrorist attacks around the world. It has been estimated that in the 1980s there were about fifty such groups operating with membership as high as 3,000.

There was no hard evidence of formalized coordination of international terrorists groups, but they did share support apparatus, certain specialists, and expertise in common. Many believed that the Soviet Union backed the radical states, but the kidnapping and killing of Russians in Lebanon and the growing awareness of the importance of Libya, Syria, and Iran in contemporary international terrorism in the Near East made it doubtful that the Soviets were directly responsible for transnational terrorism (Adams, 1986). However, those countries supporting terrorism held down their operatives from escalating violence above a certain acceptable level in fear of retaliation from either the Soviet Union or the United States.

Transnational terrorists share certain characteristics in common. One of these characteristics is training. There is evidence that in the late 1970s and during the 1980s, there were terrorist training camps established in Libya and financed by radical Iran after 1979. The PFLP and al-Fatah shared instruction. According to several analysts of transnational terrorism, Palestinian training was and is the glue that held transnational terrorists together in the 1970s and 1980s. Also, there is a sociological profile that characterizes secular terrorists: They are usually 22 to 25, single, male, university trained, and urban. The vast majority studied humanities and nontechnical fields at European and Near Eastern universities. Islam, for them, was a religion that should not be involved in politics.

Transnational secular terrorists tend to be highly ideological. They tend to be either Marxist or anarchist and share a hatred of Israel and the United States. Many European and Japanese terrorists followed a trend towards nihilism (violence and destruction become ends in themselves). Transnational terrorists cooperated on common causes despite ideological differences. As an example, Iranian terrorists tend to be conservative, anti-Marxist Shiite Muslims, while their allies in Syria tend to be Marxists, and both groups have carried out terrorist attacks.

There is evidence for *quid pro quo* activities—that is, one terrorist group helps another terrorist group in exchange for help. Palestinian and Turkish hit squads assaulted the Lod Airport in Israel, and in exchange, German terrorists attacked Israeli facilities in Frankfurt. Or different terrorist groups performed distinct phases of an operation. For example, the Baader-Meinhof gang/Carlos/JRA cooperated in an assault on a French Embassy.

Another characteristic of transnational terrorism is that it is carefully staged to affect a mass audience. Terrorist acts, such as the "shipnapping" of the Achille Lauro cruise ship, were staged for public consumption. Often this is part of the arbitrary characteristic of terrorist acts. A random act of violence against innocent people is much harder to deal with emotionally than an act of calculated violence against a military installation or a politician. It is the arbitrary quality of terrorist violence that frightens people into not flying to Europe or elsewhere because of the fear that they may "accidentally" be on board a plane targeted for destruction by some "looney" group. It is this arbitrary quality of violence that attracts the attention of the mass media. The actual chance of being killed while traveling abroad by such a terrorist attack is probably much lower than being run over by a taxi cab while walking across a street in lower Manhattan. However, it is irrational fear upon which terrorism feeds for its success.

Paul Wilkinson (1979), a student of terrorism, distinguishes terrorism from guerrilla war (such as occurred in Central America from 1967–1985) and violence in general. Terrorism, for him, is a special mode of violence. It involves the threat of murder, injury, or destruction to terrorize a given target into conceding to the terrorists' will and consists of three basic elements: the decision by perpetrators of violence to use terrorism as a systematic weapon, the threats or acts of extranormal violence themselves, and the effects of this violence on the immediate victims and international opinion.

Terrorism should not be equated with criminal or psychopathological actions. Most terrorists are extremely shrewd and rational. It is also a mistake to think of terrorism as only the activities of fringe movements or individuals. Terror has been used by states; Wilkinson cites France in 1792 and the Bolsheviks in Russia after 1917. States can also plan and use "proxy" terrorism in which a state, such as Libya, pays a terrorist to commit a terrorist act, such as the bombing of the Boeing 747 over Lockerbie, Scotland in 1989, while disclaiming any such activity (Wilkinson, 1979, p. 99).

Terrorism is inherently indiscriminate both in its physical and psychological effects partly because of the destructive nature of modern weapons and partly because of the attempt to deliberately kill randomly (Wilkinson, 1979, p. 100). Another important distinction is that terrorists do not recognize ethical or human limits; all is justified by "the revolution." It is something extranormal (Jenkens, 1985). However, terror, when used by nationalist groups against liberal democracies or indigenous autocracies, has proved almost a total failure in terms of achieving political ends. Only in armed colonial independence struggles against British and French colonials was there success. Britain's relinquishing of Palestine in 1948 and Cyprus in 1960 were the results of terrorism. Terrorism also played a role in British withdrawal from the Suez Canal Zone in 1954, from Aden in 1964, and the French from Algeria in 1962. Part of the reason the English and French gave up was expense; it was not worth the effort to continue to fight against nationalistic terrorism.

Most specialists on terrorism and counterterrorism agree that the hostage taking of the 1980s by Iranian proxy terrorists was largely unprofitable. Iran did not gain very much in return for giving up hostages in 1991. According to Wilkinson, the most dangerous of terrorist strategies is the one designed to provoke and exploit a vicious spiral of violence and counter-violence (such as we see today between Palestinians and Israelis). Terrorism can be used to polarize and to destroy the moderates and compromisers of the political center. This technique was used by the FLN terror squads in Algeria to destroy those groups in the Muslim population in favor of peaceful evolution and cooperation with the French authorities; the same can be said about Hamas in the conflict between Israelis and Palestinians.

Terrorism may also be deployed, as Carlos Marighella [the terrorist "Carlos"] proposed, in an effort to "militarize" a political situation. Here the terrorists' aim is to provoke the authorities into a panic and overreaction. If the government can be trapped into ordering its security forces into general repression and harassment of the civilian population and the suspension of civil rights, the terrorists will seek to exploit the position. They will try to get civilians to blame the violence and disruption on their own government and security forces and proffer themselves as the party of social justice and the defenders of civil rights (Wilkinson, 1979, p. 111). Wilkinson points out, however, that terrorist groups are rarely politically successful and then asks the question, why do they continue? His answers are: Terrorism is remarkably cheap and easy to mount, the risks are surprisingly low, and terrorists gain worldwide publicity. In the 1980s, terrorists succeeded in obtaining blackmail money on massive scales through kidnappings (Wilkinson, 1979, p. 112).

The collapse of the Soviet Union in the late 1980s led to a reduction in the strength of secular terrorists and set loose new Islamic movements in Afghanistan, Turkmenistan, Kazakhstan, and Uzbekistan. With the exception of Afghanistan, these countries had been under the control of the Soviet Union until the late 1980s, and it had made the practice of Islam against the law. Islam, long despised by the Soviets, became a force, sometimes for good and sometimes for bad. Here it is important to note that the new Islamic movements should not be confused with the secular socialist movements of previous decades whose political culture supported a secular form of terrorism, nor is it generally true that they support terrorism today. Most support the development of a Muslim way of life, but not through the use of force (Rashid, 2002). The new parochial movements have as their aim nothing less than the creation of a new Islamic empire controlling lands that were once occupied by the Ottoman Empire. Most of these "fundamentalist" movements are nonviolent, and their leaders practice forms of Islam that disdain violence. Others, such as al-Qaeda, Hamas, and Hezbollah, use terrorism as a major strategy to attack those who appear to be against them.

THE BLOCKING OF DEMOCRATIC REFORM

Political elites and expanding middle classes grasped the need to change their societies as the Soviet Union collapsed. No longer was there a powerful force behind the elites of the Middle East. Ethnic groupings began to run into conflict with one another, sometimes over religion, sometimes over resources. Fearful of ethnic conflicts, elite and middle class movements favored democracy and the rule of law. But there has been little actual movement due to the fear that democratic elections will lead to rule by radical Islamic groups. With exceptions in Israel and Turkey, the countries of the Middle East have failed to merge into the culture of globalization through democratic reform and open markets.

In the Middle East, the new movements to develop democracy and the rule of law are primarily the political cultures of educated political elites and middle classes, not the poverty-stricken lower classes. These want to go in a quite different direction, which we will examine. The elites understand the need to integrate the Middle Eastern economies into the global capitalist system, but the poverty-stricken poor believe globalization will worsen their lives, not improve them. Their *mullahs,* or religious leaders, tell them it is possible to recreate the Ottoman Empire and stand up against materialistic Western civilization. They view the elites and middle classes as corrupt in support of globalization. They fail to recognize the fact that the Ottoman Empire's greatest contribution to the region was peace between ethnic groups that stimulated trade and prosperity.

Terrorism at the end of the twentieth century and the beginning of the twenty-first century is distinct from that of the period before the collapse of the Soviet Union. The new movements are religious, and their worldview is cataclysmic. They do not have any sense of proportion in their acts of terror, and in this they differ profoundly from the secular movements tied to Palestine and Israel.

As social movements among the elites and middle classes appeared, secular terrorism disappeared, only to be replaced by a new form of parochial terrorism, which we will examine. Many of the members of transnational terrorist cells, such as those that formed al-Fatah, abandoned terrorism and were recruited by Yasser Arafat to form his police force in Gaza and parts of the West Bank. Arafat's supporters tend not to be radical Muslims, but are themselves threatened by such organizations as Hamas and Hezbollah. These and other radical movements in Palestine receive support from bin Laden and his terrorist network, but their political acts of violence today are meant to target Israel and destabilize the budding democratic reforms in the Palestinian territories.

THE ROOTS OF RADICAL ISLAM

Paul Magnarella, an anthropologist who worked with the Kurds of eastern Afghanistan, has documented the connection between poverty and Islamic fundamentalist movements. He shows that poverty supplies anti-Western terrorist groups with supporters and operatives. Magnarella looks at what he calls "humankind's susceptibility to indoctrination by ideologies that present faith worlds and faith acts that cannot be empirically validated" (Magnarella, 1993, p. 5). He adopts the psychological theory of political scientist Ted Robert Gurr, who argues that interpretive and informational conditions lead to human discontent, and that a society's inability to correct deficiencies such as rapid population growth, marked differences in the distribution of wealth, an insecure economic situation, demand for improved educational opportunities, and an inefficient and corrupt government will lead to support for those ideologies that condemn their conditions. In short, conditions of poverty lead to ideologies of terrorism (Magnarella, 1993, p. 119).

The real threat is the way that radical Islam blocks political reform in the Middle East. As leaders attempt to confront totalitarian political cultures and create democratic ones, they face a dilemma. The dilemma is found throughout the Middle East, from Algeria and Morocco to Iraq, Egypt, and Syria. It is also found in Jordan, in the newly emerging state of Palestine, and in the kingdoms of Saudi Arabia and Kuwait. If the political leaders of one-party states in the Middle East open the door to democracy, free markets, and trade, this may bring radical Islamic parties into power, against the interests of the political elites. Instead of expanding democracy, the winners in this process may create anti-democratic and Islamic states. The case of the Taliban in Afghanistan is an example.

Another manifestation of the dilemma can be found in Algeria. In the 1950s and 1960s, Algerians fought a war against colonial France. The National Liberation Front (NLF), a Marxist revolutionary party, successfully led them. After the war, the NLF organized Algeria as a secular socialist country and for the most part closed it off from the rest of the world. After the collapse of the Soviet Union, political leaders realized that socialism and one-party political control of the country were not the way to go. In 1989, the Algerian government legalized the Islamic Salvation Front (ISF), an Islamic political party, and offered free elections, which took place in December 1991. The ISF won the first round of the general election. The government, headed by the NLF, canceled the second round, outlawed the ISF, and jailed many of its leaders. The government and its NLF leaders fear an Islamic-dominated government, and many ISF leaders in fact call for a totalitarian Iran or Taliban-style state. Officials realize that they cannot continue opposition to democracy, yet leaders of the ISF deny democracy. Should the government allow the ISF to win elections with the hope that the new government will face the same pressures for democracy, or should it oppose the ISF, thus opposing democracy? Should leader help open their countries to globalization, or should they keep them closed? Similar problems exits in Egypt and Iraq, and in Libya, where Qaddafi, a supporter of secular terrorists a decade ago, tries to open that country to foreign investment.

CONCLUDING REMARKS

This chapter has distinguished between two distinct types of terrorism, one secular and socialist and the other parochial and organized by religious leaders in the Middle East. While these two systems have acted together at times, they view each other with disdain and cooperate only because of their common enemies, the United States as it represents globalization, and Israel in its harsh rule of Palestinians. However, a study of contemporary history shows that whatever the terrorists wish to achieve, they will basically reproduce the same violent and anti-Western values that keep the peoples of the region poor. Until democratic reforms begin to occur and the rule of law replaces rule by force, terrorism will continue to operate, and the countries of the Middle East will continue with corrupt governments and angry lower classes supporting the activities of terrorists.

As pointed out earlier, terrorism, even at the international level, is rarely successful. In Latin America, left-wing terrorists such as the Tupamaros caused considerable hysteria in the 1960s but had virtually no impact on the organization of these societies. Instead, the attacks from the radical left led to military states that were only abandoned in the mid-1980s, once left-wing movements had been destroyed. Instead of achieving a better world, terrorists in Latin America did significant damage to the development of the various economies. Africa is in shambles due to warfare between ethnic groups, but there is little international terrorism. The same is true for Asia, with the exceptions of Pakistan, India, and Sri Lanka. In the continuous conflict over the status of Kashmir, Pakistan and India have used terrorism against each other with the result that their economies continue to produce more poverty than prosperity. Even in small Sri Lanka, a war between the Tamil Tigers and the government led to greater poverty. It is heartening to learn that the two conflict groups have come to realize that terrorism has brought nothing but misery and are in the act of resolving their conflicts without violence.

Finally, while it appears that the United States is doing everything possible to fight terrorism, the long-term solution should include efforts to improve the welfare of poor people in the less-developed nations. In countries where people at the lowest end of the economic scale earn less than $200 a year, what would the injection of several million dollars do? It would not take a great deal to improve the lot of the most seriously impoverished people. This would be an act of generosity, and in the past Americans have been generous once they knew what the problem was.

DISCUSSION QUESTIONS

1. The author regards the September 11 attacks as *jihads* against globalization and Western influence. Do you agree with this assessment? Why or why not?
2. What are some of the features of radical Islam, and what role has this form of Islam played in providing justifications for the latest wave of international terrorism?
3. Do you agree with the author's assessment that in the long run, the real losers from radical Islam and terrorism are the people of the Middle East? Why or why not?

REFERENCES

ADAMS, J. (1986). *The financing of terror.* New York: Simon and Schuster.

ALMOND G. and S. VERBA. (1963). *The civil culture: Political attitudes in five nations.* Princeton: Princeton University Press.

FARR, G. M., & MERRIAN, J. G. (Eds.). (1987). *Afghan resistance: The politics of survival.* Boulder, CO: Westview Press.

HAMMOND, T. T. (1984). *Red flag over Afghanistan.* Boulder, CO: Westview Press.

HYMAN, A. (1984). *Afghanistan under Soviet domination.* New York: St. Martin's Press.

JENKINS, B. (1985). *International terrorism.* Santa Monica, CA: Rand Corp.

LACY, R. (. . .) *The kingdom.* New York: Avon Books.

MAGNARELLA, P. (1993). *Human materialism: A model of sociocultural systems and a strategy for analysis.* 1993 University Press of Florida Gainesville.???

PANSTERS, W. (ed). (1997). "Theorizing political culture in modern Mexico." *Citizens of the Pyramid.* Amsterdam: Thela Publishers.

PERETZ, D. (1977). *The Palestine state.* Port Washington, NY: Kinniket Press.

RASHID, A. (2000). *The Taliban: Militant Islam, oil and fundamentalism in Central Asia.* New Haven, CT: Yale University Press.

RASHID, A. (2002). *Jihad: The rise of militant Islam in Central Asia.* New Haven, CT: Yale University Press.

SMITH, S. (2003). "Latin America in transition: The influence of culture on ecology, power and diversity." Lanham: University Press of America.

SMITH, S. (1995). *World in disorder.* University Press of America.

VINCENT, J. (1990). *Anthropology and politics: Visions, traditions, and trends.* Tucson: University of Arizona Press.

WILKINSON, P. (1979). *Terrorism: Theory and practice.* Boulder, CO: Westview Press.

5

Economic Implications of Terrorism

Akorlie A. Nyatepe-Coo

What motivates terrorists to engage in spectacular acts of violence, such as those witnessed on September 11? What organizational structures exist to support and promote the terrorist agenda? In the following chapter, Nyatepe-Coo suggests that the attacks of September 11 were not random acts by emotionally disturbed individuals, but rather the work of rational beings motivated by the promise of immeasurable rewards. From this premise, the author applies an economic model of criminal activity to explain the effects of various deterrents on criminal behavior. In the second part of the chapter, Nyatepe-Coo examines the organizational structures that support contemporary terrorist groups. With this focus on economic aspects of terrorism, the reader is exposed to another facet of modern terrorism—revealing its complexity and subsequent pervasiveness.

Beginning in the late 1960s, the international community has been rocked by random and yet fairly continuous episodes of violence against civilians and noncombatants. The attacks of September 11, 2001, together with other recent episodes of terrorist activity, reveal certain common trends. The bombing of the U.S. embassy in Beirut in 1983, the downing of the Pam Am flight 103 over Lockerbie, Scotland in 1988, the first World Trade Center bombing of 1993, the gas attack in Tokyo by the Aum Shinrikyo cult and the Oklahoma City bombing of 1995, the bombing of the U.S. embassies in Kenya and Tanzania in 1998, and the attacks of September 11 demonstrate that: (1) Violence was used not as an end in itself, but as means to influence the balance of political power; (2) violence was used not for military advantage, but to create panic and anxiety, and (3) violence was directed not just at immediate victims, but at larger and increasingly diverse international political groups.

   While the use of violence to achieve political objectives is not a recent phenomenon, the current wave of terrorism is unique in terms of the intensity of conflict and global reach. In the recent past, terrorist groups were often limited by fears that excessive violence would alienate some of the audiences they were trying to appeal to. Too much violence, it was felt, would dilute the message. There was also the consideration that excessive violence could provoke retaliatory military responses. With the chemical attacks by the group Aum Shinrikyo in 1995 and the recent attacks, the scale of conflict has been elevated to levels not even contemplated by earlier nationalist terrorist groups. Another aspect of this intensity is expressed in the tendency among more militant groups such as al-Qaeda, Hezbollah, and Aum Shirinkyo to regard mass killings of civilians as not only acceptable but "holy." This trend poses significant long-term risks for the security and stability of the international community.

Two approaches have been used to set standards for the definition of terrorism (Levitt, 1988). The deductive approach establishes a common analytical definition to cover all the acts deemed to contravene codes of international relations. One example describes terrorism as ". . . the deliberate and systematic murder, maiming and menacing of the innocent to inspire fear for political ends" (Netanyahu, 1986 p. 9). The U.S. State Department defines terrorism as ". . . premeditated, politically motivated violence perpetrated against noncombatant targets by subnational groups or clandestine agents, usually intended to influence an audience (U.S. Department of State, 1999)." These and other general definitions of this type may be useful as political rhetoric, but they tend to be too vague and broad to provide the basis for international responses to the crimes committed by terrorists. The inductive approach outlines categories of criminal acts that fall under the umbrella of terrorism. The earliest definitions dealt with acts normally associated with domestic terrorism—assassinations, murder, kidnapping, and so on. This approach has been expanded in recent years to cover some of the prevalent forms of international terrorism—aircraft hijacking and sabotage, attacks on diplomats, and the use of weapons of mass destruction. Paul Pillar, a former deputy chief of the CIA's Counterterrorist Center, suggests that there are four key elements of terrorism: (1) It is premeditated, rather than an impulsive act of rage; (2) it is political, not criminal; (3) it is directed at civilians; and (4) it is carried out by subnational groups, not by the army of a country (Pillar, 2001).

Given the heinous nature of the crimes perpetrated by terrorists, and the fact that most acts are committed against civilians, noncombatants, or people who otherwise have no direct influence on the policies decried by the perpetrators, the common tendency is to describe such acts as works of psychopaths. The prevailing view in modern criminology is that criminal behavior can be ascribed in many instances to "deviant" or "aberrant" motives. According to this approach, the solution to crime may be found in programs designed to reduce or eliminate such psychological imbalances. Improvements in mental health, substance abuse awareness and prevention programs, and various kinds of role modeling for at-risk individuals are all viewed as necessary interventions in crime prevention. Trends in international terrorism over the last decade, however, suggest that while it is difficult to generalize about terrorist personalities, most of the perpetrators of terrorist acts can be regarded as being quite normal. As suggested by Hudson, ". . . [c]ontrary to the stereotype that the terrorist is a psychopath or otherwise mentally disturbed, the terrorist is actually quite sane, although deluded by an ideological or religious way of viewing the world" (Hudson, 1999, p. 91).

The careful planning and execution of the attacks in each of the cases mentioned above would suggest that the terrorists made deliberate choices designed to maximize quite specific objectives. Moreover, as pointed out by Hudson and others, the highly selective recruitment processes of terrorist organizations would tend to identify and remove applicants with signs of mental illness in the early stages of conscription, in the interests of group survival. The results of various investigations into terrorist activities across the globe suggest that in most cases the perpetrators are backed by highly motivated, goal-oriented, well-organized, and globally connected criminal enterprises. It is important for the international community to develop a greater awareness of the motivations and organizational structures of these groups. Economic analysis, without denying that criminal behavior is psychologically deviant, would suggest that the criminal might still respond to incentives in ways that could be regarded as rational. Perhaps, by applying some tools of economic analysis, valuable insights can be gained about the motivations and incentive structures governing the behavior of terrorists, thus resulting in more effective efforts at deterrence. In the aftermath of the turbulence of 2001, it is necessary to take a more objective look at the factors behind the latest conflicts. This chapter will attempt to answer three basic questions.

First, *what motivates an individual to become a terrorist, and what would provoke an individual to engage in suicide attacks?* Documents left by some of the men who flew the planes into the World Trade Center point to "endless happiness" and "infinite prosperity" as rewards for those participating in attacks against the United States. But these documents tell only part of the story. To what extent are ideology and the quest for vengeance against perceived adversaries adequate in explaining the motives of terrorists willing to take part in suicide missions? In this respect, some scholars suggest that the incentives of terrorists pursuing martyrdom may not be very different from the incentives that cause soldiers to participate in risky missions. This implies that the difference between the individual who commits a crime and one who elects to engage in legitimate activity may lie less in motivation or attitudes toward risk and more in terms of some subjective assessment of expected rewards. The first section of the chapter will outline some of the main tenets of the economic theory of criminal behavior. This section will reexamine the qualitative predictions of existing models in light of recent evidence suggesting that the costs and benefits of terrorism may be expressed in nonmonetary terms.

How were the terrorists organized and financed? Preliminary evidence from the media suggests that the perpetrators of the September 11 attacks were backed by intricate networks of business and financial interests. Not much attention has been paid to the role of organizational structure in facilitating the planning and coordination of the attack. In general, suicide missions are not undertaken by isolated individuals but depend on formal or informal organizations to recruit and mobilize individuals, channel their anger and frustrations toward specific causes, and ensure that members follow through with their missions. The second section will examine the organizational and financial infrastructure behind the terrorist networks, the increasing ability of members to tap into emerging technologies to advance their objectives, and the use of enforcement mechanisms to keep members on task.

Why should we be concerned about terrorism? One of the least understood aspects of the terrorist threat concerns the effect on the economy. According to the National Bureau of Economic Research, the attacks of September 11 occurred during a period of recession that began in March 2001. This assessment was borne out in subsequent months by massive job losses and apparent declines in consumer confidence. Economists of various persuasions agree that government budget deficits should be large during temporary economic difficulties such as recessions or wars. Administration officials have already suggested that the federal government can expect to run budget deficits for at least the next three years, and several states, including Wisconsin, are dealing with budget shortfalls. This section will assess the state of the U.S. economy in light of the terrorist attacks and the implications of changing economic priorities for the global economy.

TERRORISM AND ECONOMIC MODELS OF CRIMINAL PARTICIPATION

The crime of terrorism has much in common with other kinds of crime, yet not much effort has been made to apply some of the tools of economic analysis to this kind of behavior. Since the early 1990s, empirical models have been used to study various aspects of terrorist behavior, as in, for example, the effects of metal detector technology on the number of skyjackings (Enders, Sandler, & Cauley, 1990) or the effects of high-profile terrorist events—such as the 1985 hijackings of TWA flight 847 and the Achille Lauro cruise ship—on tourism (Enders, Sandler, & Parise, 1992). However, these studies provide little insight into what motivates the potential terrorist to select this type of criminal endeavor. The basic premise of economic models of criminal behavior is that potential criminals behave "rationally," in the sense of acting in ways designed to maximize their objectives. As discussed above, goal setting and rational behavior are essential to the activities of terrorists. As shown in the attacks of September 11 and in previous terrorist acts, the meticulous preparation and use of sophisticated techniques to conceal plans and divert attention from their activities show that the perpetrators were driven to accomplish their goals at any cost.

One important difference between the current wave of international terrorism and other kinds of crime lies in the predominantly nonmonetary assessment of costs and benefits of terrorist activity. While some evidence exists of the use of property crimes in intermediate stages—for example, robbing banks, gun shops, hospitals, etc.—to stockpile resources for major acts of domestic terrorism, the overwhelming evidence suggests that terrorists are driven primarily by political and religious considerations. Several of the groups have well-defined nationalistic or sectarian goals. The Basque Fatherland and Liberty group (ETA), for example, seeks an independent Basque state in northern Spain and southern France. The Kurdistan Workers' Party (PKK) seeks to establish an independent Kurdish state in southeastern Turkey. The Liberation Tigers of Tamil Ealam (LTTE) seek to establish an independent Tamil state in Sri Lanka. Other groups are motivated by ideology and seek to replace Western-oriented governments with peasant revolutionary regimes. These groups also seek to remove the influences of the United States, European Union, or NATO from the respective countries. Examples of this latter group include the Revolutionary Armed forces of Colombia (FARC), Revolutionary Organization 17 November (Greece), Revolutionary People's Liberation Party/Front (DHKP/C, Turkey), and Shining Path (Peru) (F.B.I., 2002). A third set of terrorist groups uses violence and the threats of violence to pursue religious goals. The latest terrorist attacks against the United States, for example are considered as part of a larger *jihad*, or holy war against Westernization and modernity. In this larger scheme, the United States is viewed as the source of all the crisis and trouble afflicting the Muslim world. By using violence, the terrorists aim to drive the United States from various countries in the Middle East and facilitate the creation of Islamic states. The absence of clear monetary or other economic signals raises difficulties with assessment of costs and benefits of terrorist acts and with efficacy of deterrence.

Another distinguishing characteristic of terrorist activity lies in the passion, the ideological commitment, theological zeal, or religious fervor that drives the terrorist agenda. The essence of this passion is quite evident in the latest terrorist acts. In referring to the new breed of religious terrorists, Bodansky opines that . . . "[t]hey risk life and limb, they risk capture and most likely execution, and in the case of suicidal operations, they face death without flinching. The individual perpetrator-terrorist can overcome these challenges only though psychological tempering and immense conviction in the righteousness of the act to be performed" (Bodansky, 2001, p. 152). Such passions may create a predisposition toward illegitimate and other nonsanctioned activities in ways that may defy conventional analysis.

Economic models of criminal behavior assume that people balance the benefits of any action against costs to determine which action produces the highest welfare or utility. Utility is a measure of the satisfaction received from possessing or consuming goods and services. The benefits and costs of crime are usually defined in monetary terms, but they may also include psychic or nonmonetary equivalents. The risk of punishment, for example, is defined as a psychic cost in addition to other costs and benefits of illegal activity. Thus, the models of criminal behavior are generally presented within the broader context of the theory of rational behavior under uncertainty. The models fall into two main categories. The earliest models were concerned with the allocation of time between legal and illegal activities. These models fall within the general realm of time allocation models, and they analyze crime in terms of the relative costs and benefits to be gained (Pyle, 1983).

The second class of models views the decision to offend as a portfolio selection problem in which the individual chooses what portion of his or her wealth to put at risk by engaging in criminal activity (Allingham & Sandmo, 1972). The portfolio selection models have been used mainly to analyze the crime of income tax evasion. They are especially suited for situations where costs and benefits of crime can be expressed in monetary terms and where the amount of time allocated to the criminal enterprise is fairly small. While some speculation exists about potential monetary gains for the al-Qaeda network from the decline in stock prices after September 11, most of the evidence on expected payoffs refers to nonmonetary rewards such as such as ". . . a happy life in the heavens full of virgins for those who complete a job which is loved by God," or other allusions to spiritual rewards. This implies that the portfolio selection models may not be appropriate for analyzing the crime of terrorism. In what follows, we concentrate on time allocation models, and especially on situations where the costs and benefits of criminal activity are expressed almost exclusively in nonpecuniary terms.

In the time allocation framework, an individual decides to engage in crime not because his or her motivation differs from that of other individuals, but because the conception of the costs and benefits associated with criminal activity, the evaluation of the probability of being caught, or the attitude toward risk is different (Becker, 1968). Criminal activity is risky: The potential criminal does not know in advance if he or she will be caught and punished. This uncertainty is dealt with by assuming that the individual maximizes *expected utility*. A crime will be committed if, in the evaluation of the individual, the expected utility to be gained from the crime is greater than the expected utility from engaging in an alternative legitimate economic activity. If expected utility from committing crime is expressed in terms of net changes to wealth—potential monetary gain plus expected loss to wealth as a consequence of being caught and/or punished—then an increase in the severity of punishment or the probability of being caught will reduce the expected utility from committing offenses and thus reduce the number of offenses committed. This theory supports the notion of deterrence: By increasing severity and certainty of punishment, the cost of committing a crime increases, and thus the time devoted to criminal activities and the number of offenses can be reduced.

The main difficulty with the approach outlined above is the failure to consider psychic or nonmonetary costs of crime. The nonmonetary costs range from the unpleasant nature or disagreeability of criminal activity to such negative consequences as loss of life, freedom, and reputation. As discussed below, it is the minimization of such costs through psychological tempering and conviction that may tip the scale from more conventional forms of crime toward terrorism. In the extension to the time allocation models discussed here, the psychic costs are recognized by including time spent on legal and illegal activities directly in the utility function (Block & Heineke, 1975). Each individual is faced with the problem of allocating time between crime and a legitimate activity. The amount of leisure time is assumed to be fixed, so crime and legitimate employment are competing activities. In this case, the individual's allocation of time between the two activities will depend on the attitude toward risk as well as a certain preference for honest living. The preference for honesty implies that an individual is predisposed to engage in legitimate activity because the utility from legitimate activity exceeds utility from crime. Individuals with an aversion to risk and a preference for honesty are shown to reduce their offending as a result of either an increase in the probability of conviction, increased fines, or improved returns to legitimate activities. However, even with risk aversion, an individual may not be deterred by an increase in the probability of conviction or fines if he or she exhibits a preference for illegal activity.

One of the issues addressed in this version of the time allocation models is the relationship between increases in penalties meted out to convicted offenders and participation in criminal activity. An increase in penalties will reduce the real returns from crime and reduce criminal activity. This is called a *wealth effect*. On the other hand, an increase in penalties may cause the criminal to increase time spent on criminal activity as a way to boost reputation. In this case, crime is regarded as a prestige activity, and the individual substitutes criminal activity for legal occupation in response to an increase in penalties. This is an example of a positive wealth effect. Another effect is indicated if the individual reduces the time spent on criminal activity because the real cost of crime has risen relative to the cost of legal employment. This is the *substitution effect*. Thus, an increase in penalties meted out to convicted offenders may generate wealth and substitution effects in such a way that the net effect on criminal activity cannot be determined. In general, by accounting for psychic costs of crime, the unambiguous results discussed earlier with respect to the effects of deterrence become less definite. What insights can be obtained from extensions of these models to the crime of terrorism?

As discussed above, most acts of terrorism are designed to produce a change in a government's political position or influence political power. Terrorism is regarded as a special case of criminal activity and is treated as such in national laws and international treaties. The terrorist is motivated to act for several reasons: The current political situation is regarded as unbearable, the goal being sought is important enough to dominate all other considerations, or in certain cases, the costs of trying are quite low. Violence is used in lieu of military might as a means to political power. The individual terrorist considers which actions, legal or illegal, will produce the highest expected utility. Maximization of expected utility in this context implies balancing the potential benefits from involvement in a terrorist act against costs. Participation in terrorist activity can be thought of as yielding an increase in the offender's monetary wealth or psychic well-being, or both. Some of the psychic benefits may be defined to include a variety of individual needs: spiritual fulfillment, belonging to a group, enhancement of reputation, and admiration from peers and family. On the other hand, by violating existing national or international laws, the terrorist risks a reduction in wealth or psychic well-being. Monetary penalties for conviction include fines and reductions in earning opportunities from acquiring a criminal record. Psychic costs range from time in prison, with associated losses in freedom, to the ultimate penalty of loss of life.

The individual allocates time between participation in terrorist activity and legitimate employment. Utility is obtained from time spent on legal activities, time spent on terrorist activity, some measure of monetary wealth, and a collection of psychic attributes to terrorist activity. The returns from legal activity would be expected to include a monetary component. However, these returns are subject to risk. Based on conditions in several of the host nations for potential terrorists, periods of unemployment, high inflation, and economic insecurity tend to undermine the value and certainty of rewards from legitimate activity. This explanation of terrorist activity as an alternative to legal occupation is not very different from the commonly held view in the United States that unemployment and lack of opportunities contribute to higher drug offenses among urban youth. Terrorist organizations are typically founded on the premise that existing government institutions and/or market systems are flawed. The members of these organizations do not regard existing arrangements as permanent. Under such circumstances, crime and legitimate activities are not necessarily regarded as competing activities. It is more likely that those drawn to terrorist groups will be individuals with strong feelings about particular issues who are willing to resort to illegal activity to attain their goals. The dispositions toward violence and other types of illegal activity are facilitated in situations where the terrorist can count on the support of the immediate community, or in the case of international terrorism, where crimes against foreigners may be viewed with apathy. Individuals planning terrorist acts often seek out communities where people are sympathetic to the goals of the organization or otherwise indifferent or ignorant. To the extent that membership in a terrorist group may confer on the individual an elevation of social status in some circles, it is possible for the militant to contemplate terrorist acts in relative tranquility, without the stigma associated with illegal activity. As has been the aftermath of September 11, the widespread rhetoric in many parts of the Muslim world about Islamic revivalism and Western decadence can be used as lightning rods for group action.

One psychic cost of terrorism, for example, might be severity of sentence if convicted. Psychic costs in turn are expressed as functions of the probability of failure (i.e., being apprehended before the commission of the terrorist act). In this interpretation, the higher the probability of being caught, the higher the disagreeability of the terrorist acts. On the other hand, the psychic costs are lower with a lower probability of being caught. To the potential terrorist, the end justifies the means. The terrorist, either through a preference for illegal activity or indoctrination within the group, is willing to endure any level of punishment *as long as* the terrorist act is successfully completed. This is consistent with a conditional attitude toward risk: The potential terrorist is risk-averse to the reality of being caught but is willing to take on increasing levels of risk as the magnitude of the terrorist act increases. The psychic benefits include nonmonetary additions to well-being in the form of infinite happiness, enhanced reputation, etc.

The problem is to maximize expected utility subject to a time constraint: The sum of the time allocated to legal activity, terrorism, and leisure should equal 24 hours. As discussed above, the individual's allocation of time between terrorism and legitimate occupation will depend on the attitude toward risk as well as a predisposition toward criminal activity. The preference for criminal activity means that the utility from crime exceeds utility from legitimate activity. In the framework developed above, this predisposition toward terrorism can be explained in several ways. First, the returns of legitimate activity are subject to risk. This may compel individuals to look beyond monetary considerations to sectarian, psychic, or spiritual rewards. Second, the level of indoctrination and socialization is pervasive to the point where terrorist activity is effectively decriminalized in the mind of the militant, and membership in the group is regarded as a higher calling, an elevated state of being. Third, surveillance and law enforcement capabilities may not be adequate in the host countries to detect terrorist crimes, especially where such crimes are committed against outsiders.

Given these factors, the following results can be derived. Individuals with a preference for legal occupation and an aversion for risk will respond to deterrence by reducing the time spent on terrorist activity. On the other hand, even where individuals exhibit an aversion to risk, if they have a preference for illegal activity, they may not be deterred by increases in the probability of conviction, increased fines, or improvements in opportunities for legitimate employment. This result is similar to the ambiguous results discussed above for the case with recognition of psychic costs of crime. The unique finding in this study is that an increase in the probability of failure will result in an unequivocal decline in time spent in terrorist activity because an increase in the probability of arrest before commission of a crime raises the psychic costs of terrorist activity. Furthermore, to the extent that participation in terrorist activity is largely independent of monetary wealth, an increase in the probability of arrest prior to the act will result in a negative effect on the supply of terrorist activity because the criminal will try to substitute away from the higher-cost activity.

The preceding analysis supports the notion of early detection and arrest prior to commission of terrorist acts as the primary deterrent against terrorism. The analysis also explains why other forms of deterrence—for example, increases in the conviction rate, given arrest; increases in restrictions in freedom post-conviction; or more severe penalties after the fact—will not be effective in reducing terrorist activity. The results of this study can be used to provide some justification for the empirical finding that the U.S. bombing of Libya in April 1986 did not have the desired effect of reducing terrorist attacks against the United States and the United Kingdom (Enders, Sandler, & Cauley, 1990). The assumption of decreasing absolute risk aversion with respect to terrorist activity implies an increasing willingness to take on risk as the magnitude and ramifications of the activity increase. This means that terrorists under attack for previous acts are more likely to expand the scope of their activities as the scale of conflict intensifies. The perpetrators of terrorist activities, given their predispositions and indoctrination within the group, are not likely to be intimidated by higher penalties imposed after the fact. What is more likely is that potential terrorists may be deterred from participation if the probability of apprehension *before* commission of the terrorist act is high. The analysis above explains what factors are important in an individual's decision to commit a terrorist act. But is this sufficient to explain why some terrorists are willing to give up their lives or why some terrorists choose to engage in crimes so heinous as to defy imagination, all in pursuit of their goals? The next section reviews organizational theories of terrorism and looks at the role of terrorist organizations in facilitating the commission of incredible crimes.

ORGANIZATIONAL THEORIES AND TERRORIST ACTIVITY

Terrorist acts are seldom random. Individuals who develop a predisposition toward terrorist activity usually do not act in isolation. They seek out groups of like-minded individuals and look to these groups to channel their anger and frustrations toward specific causes and provide the support needed to carry out their objectives. One of the central tenets of organizational process theory is that the fundamental purpose of a political organization is to maintain itself (Crenshaw, 1988). In this interpretation, terrorist organizations exist to ensure that members follow through with fairly specific objectives. While several terrorist organizations have evolved from traditional compartmentalized organizational structures toward decentralized cell-based units, the basic goal-oriented tendencies are still very much in evidence.

The motivation for joining a terrorist group includes a variety of common psychological needs: to belong to a group, to acquire social status and reputation, to make friends and have fun, or to gain material benefits. Under certain conditions, membership in underground organizations may provide social connections that confer respect and admiration from peers and family members. The idea of participating in an organization in order to elevate one's profile relative to others is common in nationalist and sectarian groups, where some degree of empathy exists from those who may deplore the method but applaud the goals of the organization. Since most terrorists are adolescents, joining a terrorist group may start out as a sign of rebellion rather than a political statement. Over time, this rebellion against parental authority may be molded into distrust for political authority. Other incentives for joining a terrorist organization are those intangible benefits of association in a group: a feeling of belonging, acceptance, and solidarity. As discussed above, in situations where the returns to legitimate occupation may be subject to risk, such intangible benefits may take on increasing significance. In the West Bank and other countries of the Middle East, the feeling of empathy has been expressed in more tangible forms—through financial and logistical support for terrorist organizations. It is common for radicals to see their actions as the continuation of a historic struggle of the oppressed, winning respect of other revolutionaries across the globe.

Most terrorist organizations offer a collection of incentives to keep members engaged in the enterprise. The issues or causes may change with the organization's need to offer different incentives to members. The French group Action Directe is a case in point. Since 1979, the group has opposed nuclear energy, imperialism, Israel, the Catholic

Church, and French intervention in Chad (Cordes et al., 1984). In the same vein, some experts expressed surprise at the seeming shift in focus from Western decadence and the presence of U.S. troops in the Arabian Peninsula to the plight of the Palestinians in pronouncements by the leadership of al-Qaeda following the attacks of September 11. Organizational goals are not necessarily consistent. In general, the need for action, no matter what the outcome is, may be the dominant incentive. If an organization is forced into inactivity, substitute incentives must be found. This explains why some groups may be found dealing drugs or running guns, for example.

In the economic theory of organizational imperatives proposed by Hirschman (1970), organizations are fragile; they are engaged in a constant struggle to prevent decline. Hirschman suggests that dissatisfied members of an organization have two options: "exit" or "voice." Exit, as it applies to terrorist groups, refers to the possibilities of joining another organization or splintering off and creating a new group. Members often exit after attempts to persuade the group to follow another direction have failed. Although extremist groups consistently attempt to define exit as betrayal, it is common to find factions of the parent group. The possibility of switching allegiances to a rival group depends on the existence of an attractive alternative. Where there are no competitors, the dissatisfied must create a new group. The exercise of this option apparently occurs when more extremist members feel inhibited by restrictions imposed by the relatively moderate leadership and demand an escalation of violence. The example is given of the Provisional IRA, for example, which developed from the refusal of the parent or "official" IRA to adopt a strategy of terrorism against Protestants and the British.

Most terrorist organizations strongly discourage the expression of discontent. Cohesion and solidarity are important values, both to the organization (for which security is a prime concern) and to the psychological well-being of members for whom belonging is a dominant incentive. Exit results in organizational decline, and procedures are put in place early in the life of the group to ensure complete loyalty. The exercise of voice can also be destructive. Some organizations may therefore be more sensitive to internal disagreement than to defection. The most centralized and secretive organizations are likely to be the least tolerant of dissent. Recent media reports have played on the issue of "blind loyalty" among adherents of a particular cause. In many of the ideological or redemptive organizations, such loyalty is essential because dissent may equal heresy.

Another method by which organizations inhibit defection is to establish what Hirschman calls "severe initiation costs." For members with a lot invested in the organization, the option of exit is costly. Terrorist groups and organized crime syndicates routinely require the commission of an illegal act for precisely this purpose, to eliminate the individual's option of abandoning the group. Psychologists refer to the concept of *deindividuation,* the process of losing one's sense of individuality by becoming submerged in a group (Forsyth, 1983). Some of the earliest studies of the phenomenon pointed to the link between reduction in inhibitions and the subsequent aberrant behaviors by group members (Festinger, Pepitone, & Newcomb, 1952). The combination of incentives, binding oaths of allegiance and high initiation costs, and submergence in the group contribute to suppress individual thinking and expression and, in the process, may instigate otherwise law-abiding individuals to commit incredible acts of violence, such as those seen in the United States on September 11, 2001.

ECONOMICS OF CATASTROPHE: THE ECONOMIC IMPLICATIONS OF THE SEPTEMBER 11 ATTACKS

What impact did the September 11 terrorist attacks have on the U.S. economy? According to the National Bureau of Economic Research, the U.S. economy was already in the throes of a recession dating back to March 2001. The terrorist attacks caused a temporary disruption in the nation's economic activity. Air traffic was halted, consumer spending fell, businesses reduced investment, and companies announced thousands of layoffs. The travel and leisure sector suffered the worst job losses, mainly in the airline, hotel, car rental, and restaurant industries. In the last five months of 2001, for example, the travel industry lost 237,000 jobs (Council on Foreign Relations, 2002). The IMF estimates that the attacks could cost the United States $21 billion in property losses and insurance costs. This estimate does not account for income losses from the massive layoffs, for example. A study by the Milken Institute estimates that the attacks will cost the United States more than 1.8 million jobs by the end on 2002 (Avery, 2002). Months after the attacks, the economy appeared to be recovering. However, the New York metropolitan area continues to suffer from the attacks on the World Trade Center, and the financial markets have been set back in recent months by allegations of corporate misconduct.

Administration officials have suggested that the federal government can be expected to run budget deficits for at least the next three years because of the recession and the high cost of combating terrorism. The large surpluses previously projected will be consumed by tax cuts and other economic stimulus measures, as well as substantial expenditures to increase national security and finance the war on terrorism. The administration's proposed budget for 2003 would increase defense spending by $45 billion, or 13 percent, and would double funding for homeland defense to $36 billion—including $11 billion for border security and $5.9 billion for combating bioterrorism (Council on Foreign Relations, 2002).

One of the key economic issues raised in the aftermath of September 11 concerns the effects of terrorist acts on globalization. Some scholars have tried to attribute the recent attacks to Muslim resentment of the forces of globalization. By targeting the World Trade Center, a symbol of U.S. leadership in the world economy, it would appear that the terrorists were trying to strike a blow against increasing economic integration among countries. Globalization brings with it closer economic ties through trade, travel, immigration, shared information, foreign direct investment and mobility of capital, and accelerated transmission of technology. This hypothesis is not completely valid for several reasons. First, the Arab and Islamic countries are relatively closed to trade and foreign capital, so that adverse economic conditions in these countries can be blamed on too little, rather than too much globalization. Second, many of the participants in the attacks, together with their backers, are quite vested in the global economy. Osama bin Laden, leader of al-Qaeda, is heir to one of Saudi Arabia's largest international conglomerates. What is clear is that the influx of foreign, and especially U.S., companies in some Middle East countries could have produced anger, resentment, and envy.

Historically, major international events such as World War I or the Great Depression have had the effect of stalling trends toward globalization. The attacks of September 11 would probably slow down the pace of globalization. Already countries are taking enhanced security measures with respect to air travel, imported goods, immigration, and information flows. However, as is becoming clear in global responses to the terrorist threat, the future will require greater collaboration in the collection and transmission of information and in policies to deal with issues such as global poverty. The events of September 11 may have stalled the movement toward globalization, but future trends suggest that closer economic integration is inevitable.

CONCLUDING REMARKS

This study identifies two important factors in the transformation of otherwise law-abiding citizens into terrorists: (1) environment, which creates a predisposition toward terrorist activity, and (2) organization, which recruits, mobilizes, and indoctrinates members and ensures that members follow through with their missions. The analysis in this chapter supports the notion of early detection and arrest prior to commission of terrorist acts as the primary deterrent against terrorism. This study also explains why other forms of deterrence will not be effective in reducing terrorist activity. In particular, retaliatory strikes will tend to harden the terrorist position, and may increase expected psychic rewards from terrorist activity.

DISCUSSION QUESTIONS

1. What arguments are used in the chapter to support the idea that contemporary terrorists can be thought of as rational, goal-oriented individuals? With reference to the September 11 attacks, do you agree with this assessment?
2. What are the main differences between property crimes and the crime of terrorism? What are some of the difficulties with applying economic analysis to the study of terrorism?
3. Discuss three environmental factors that could create a predisposition toward terrorist activity. Are such factors present in the United States and other industrialized countries? Why or why not?

REFERENCES

ALLINGHAM, M., & SANDMO, A. (1972). Income tax evasion: a theoretical analysis. *Journal of Public Economics, 1*(1), 323–338.

AVERY, S. (2002). Fallout from attacks expected to cost country 1.8 million jobs by end of 2002. *Associated Press*, January 10.

BECKER, G. (1968). Crime and punishment: An economic approach. *Journal of Political Economy, 76*(2), 169–217.

BLOCK, M., & HEINEKE, J. (1975). A labor theoretic analysis of criminal choice. *American Economic Review, 65*(3), 314–325.

BODANSKY, Y. (2001). *Bin Laden: The man who declared war on America*. Roseville, CA: Prima.

CORDES, B. et al. (1984). *Trends in international terrorism, 1982 and 1983.* Santa Monica, CA: Rand.

Council on Foreign Relations. (2002). *Terrorism: Q & A. http://www.terrorismanswers. com/policy/.*

CRENSHAW, M. (1988). Theories of terrorism: Instrumental and organizational approaches. In D. Rapoport (Ed.), *Inside terrorist organizations* (pp. 13–31). New York: Columbia University.

ENDERS, W., SANDLER, T., & CAULEY, J. (1990). Assessing the impact of terrorist-thwarting policies: An intervention time series approach. *Defense Economics, 2,* 1–8.

ENDERS, W., SANDLER, T., & PARISE, G. (1992). An econometric analysis of the impact of terrorism on tourism. *Kyklos, 45,* 531–554.

Federal Bureau of Investigation (F.B.I.). (2002). The 28 groups on the U.S. State Department's designated foreign terrorist organization list. *http://www.fbi.gov/terrorinfo/ftolist.htm.*

FESTINGER, L., PEPITONE, A., & NEWCOMB, T. (1952). Some consequences of deindividuation in a group. *Journal of Abnormal and Social Psychology, 47,* 382–389.

FORSYTH, D. (1983). *An introduction to group dynamics.* Monterey, CA: Brooks/Cole.

HIRSCHMAN, A. (1970). *Exit, voice, and loyalty: Responses to decline in firms, organizations, and states.* Cambridge, MA: Harvard University.

HUDSON, R. (1999). *Who becomes a terrorist and why: The 1999 government report profiling terrorists.* Guilford, CT: Lyons.

LEVITT, G. (1988). *Democracies against terror: The western response to state supported terrorism.* New York: Praeger.

NETANYAHU, B. (1986). Defining Terrorism. B. Netanyahu, (Ed.), *Terrorism: How the west can win.* New York: Farar, Strauss & Giroux.

PILLAR, P. (2001). *Terrorism and U.S. foreign policy.* Washington, D.C.: Brookings Institution.

PYLE, D. (1983). *The economics of crime and law enforcement* (pp. 8–28). New York: St. Martin's.

United States Department of State. (1999) *Patterns of Global Terrorism,* 1998. Washington, D.C.

6

Inside the Mind of a Suicide Bomber: Santosh Sivan's *The Terrorist*

Lalita Pandit

Another dimension of the issue of motivation is given in the chapter titled "Inside the Mind of a Suicide Bomber: Santosh Sivan's *The Terrorist*," by Pandit. The author examines the recent film, *The Terrorist,* produced by Indian filmmaker, Santosh Sivan, and uses the method of literary criticism to look at both sides of the question, what would make someone do this? The method of literary criticism is used to powerful effect in this chapter because polarizing explanations are rejected in favor of multi-dimensional portraits of the terrorist. *The Terrorist* is based on the assassination of Indian Prime Minister Rajiv Gandhi in 1991. The world was shocked at the news of Gandhi's death at the hands of a suicide bomber, especially upon learning that the assassin was a young woman. In reviewing Sivan's re-creation of this tragedy, the author offers a glimpse into the private, personal world of the terrorist. Sivan's film uncovers the stark existence of many terrorist organizations and their isolation from the normal, reassuring rhythms of daily life. Pandit brings the film alive and makes the terrorist acts comprehensible, if not understandable. Further, the author reveals that certain aspects of contemporary terrorism possess a universality that cuts across regions and nation-states.

Since September 11, 2001, media focus on suicide bombers has been consistent and terrorism as a global phenomenon has become not only an issue of concern, but a source of fear. In parts of South Asia and the Middle East, suicide bombings and terrorist attacks, associated with separatist and insurgent movements, have occurred over the years with some frequency. For this reason, the phenomenon of suicide bombings has been a subject of analysis and discussion in some of these regions. Long before the recent events, an insightful and powerful film focused on a suicide bomber was made in India. Its treatment of the subject, though grounded in local events and history, has consequences for a broader understanding of the global phenomenon of terrorism and suicide bombings. In addition, the historical context of ethnic violence that inspired this film mirrors situations in a broad

91

range of multiethnic societies in other areas of the world. In general, insurgent movements are different from globally spread out mercenary institutions that sponsor terror, though human problems resulting from either kind require humane solutions brought about by an active engagement of a world community. The film that I shall focus on provides many avenues for thought and, as a film, it is also a form of action.

Santosh Sivan, an award-winning cinematographer from India, made his debut film *The Terrorist* in 1998. The film is based on the assassination of Rajiv Gandhi, Prime Minister of India, at Sripurambudur, a town not far from Chennai (Madras) in South India. On May 21, 1991, this assassination, carried out by a female suicide bomber of the Sri Lankan Liberation Tigers of Tamil Elam (LTTE), shocked the country and the world. The word *Elam* in the original language means "a homeland." The movement's initial goal was to form a separate, fully autonomous homeland within the territories of Sri Lanka. Since 1991, the Tamil Elam insurgency has passed through many phases, and its leader, Vellupillai Prabhakaran, is currently working towards a peace process. At a press conference recently, when journalists asked him if the recent "war on terrorism" had any impact on his changed attitude, he said that his group began their work on the peace initiatives long before September 11, 2001 (Iype, 2002, p. 22). It is not unreasonable to assume that Sivan's film contributed to raising an awareness.

According to statements made by him, Santosh Sivan was there when the assassination of Rajiv Gandhi took place in 1991, and it challenged the artist and the humanist in him. To one interviewer, he says: "I used to wonder, how would someone do something like this. What *possibly could make her not do it?*" (Walsh, 1998). In *The Terrorist,* he sets out to explore what might make a suicide bomber, who is all set to kill and to die, desist from her aim. The film focuses on a fictional suicide bomber, named Malli, whose prehistory intersects with the history of the insurgency; the title of the film in Tamil is *Malli,* in English *The Terrorist*. The film narrative takes the viewer through her physical journey and preparation for the assassination, as well as her mental journey to the final point of danger and death. Other characters are Malli's lover, whose name we are not given. For the four days prior to the assassination, she stays with an old farmer, Vasudev, and his farmhand, Gopal. Another key character is Surya/Lotus, who escorts Malli through the jungles to be ferried across; Thyagu and Perumal are fellow insurgents who oversee her rehearsals for the assassination. *The Terrorist* was secured for U.S. release by John Malkovich after he saw it while serving on the jury at the 1998 Cairo Film Festival (Johnson, 2000). The role of Malli is played by Ayesha Dharkar; Vasu by Parmeshwaran; Gopal by Gopal; Thyagu by Vishnu Vardhan; Perumal by Bhanu Prakash; Surya by Vishwas; and the Lover by K Krishna. There is no MPAA rating for the film, and it contains nonexploitative violence. It is in Tamil with English subtitles (Ebert, 2000).

THE LANGUAGE OF FILM FORM

In an age of photojournalism, when majority of what is "news" is brought to us through the visual media, where film art is used manipulatively to slant, foreground, diminish, and enhance factors of whatever situation is being reported or commented on, the viability of film as a discursive text can hardly be doubted. Quite often, aesthetically sophisticated cinema aims to correct the exploitative effect of visual media on spectators. A leading film theorist, David Bordwell, observes: "As an active perceiver, the spectator is constantly testing the work for larger significance, for what it says or suggests." Starting with this assumption about "an active perceiver" inside every passive "spectator," Bordwell identifies various types of film meaning. Out of these, two are particularly relevant for the following analysis of *The Terrorist*. One of these is what Bordwell calls "the referential meaning," which is constituted by the film's overall form. Items of concrete detail, names of characters, language and speech, setting, costumes, and other details clue the viewer to a specific social, cultural context. While referential meaning is often concrete, "symptomatic meaning" is abstract and symbolic. "It situates the film within a trend of thought, a value system," or even a social ideology (Bordwell, 2001, pp. 46–48). Judging from the reviews, it is clear that with regard to *The Terrorist* many "active perceivers" have touched on some of the referential and symptomatic meanings, but the film's larger sociocultural and global significance has not been explored. The purpose of the following analysis is to look at Santosh Sivan's *The Terrorist* as a counternarrative, that is, a narrative that questions, displaces, and shifts habitual patterns of thought generated by historical and media narratives. The insights that this filmmaker provides can be useful for understanding the causes and the human cost of violent struggles. Moreover, the historical context in which this particular insurgency developed reads like a story of any postcolonial nation in crisis, caught between growing ethnonationalism, subnationalism, in the backdrop of identity-negating, assimilative neocolonial forces of globalization.

Unlike History, and more in the manner of Poetry, Film uses a language of indirection. One advantage of this symbolic language is that it frees the creator of this language from confining dichotomies that define the terms in which an issue can be discussed. Often, these terms are narrow and end results are predictable. For instance, leftist and rightist discourses frame issues in terms that are predictable and narrowly defined. It is often difficult for people to think outside of the box, so to say. For this reason many current discussions on terrorism, counterterrorism, and war as a response to terrorism are, to a large extent, locked up in terms dictated by polarized ideological positions. Forms of social communication that use creativity, to some extent—in so far as they do not repeat fossilized conventions—circumvent these limitations and reinvent the terms in which an understanding of an issue can be formulated. Film language works by creating cinematic silence that communicates ideas and articulates issues in terms that go beyond the stated terms of an argument. Film techniques used to create cinematic silence, as well as tools of analysis that help to decode the codes of aesthetic silence, are, no doubt, too numerous. Some of these are familiar and need no explanation, though a few technical terms that are used here merit a preliminary introduction.

The two interrelated terms relevant for the following analysis of *The Terrorist* are **cinematic identification** and **alienation effect.** Cinematic identification refers to various aspects of visual and aural representation that are aimed at making the viewer form an ego-identification with the characters, most often with the hero or the heroine. Through ego-identification, a viewer becomes personally invested in the protagonists' aims and goals. Even with regard to news media, spectator psychology is shaped through a cinematic identification with the anchor person. That is why costume, physical appearance, tone of voice, and connectedness to the target listener/consumer of news broadcasts are all considered important. When news comes to us packaged in visual effects, no matter how minimal, cinematic identification and its relation to spectator psychology play a significant role in shaping our perceptions of reality. In the world of theater, and by extension in filmmaking, the opposite of cinematic identification is a phenomenon that Bertolt Brecht defined as the "alienation effect." The word *alienation,* in this context, does not have a negative connotation. It simply suggests ways, in theatrical practice, to move away from mechanisms of ego-identification with the hero/heroine, and his or her projected aims and goals. While mainstream cinema works mostly through cinematic identification, films that strive towards critical thinking and questioning of habitual modes of thought may use varieties of alienation effect to shift and re-engage viewer attention.

As the following discussion will show, in *the Terrorist,* Sivan moves away from cinematic identification, toward a sort of Brechtian alienation effect. Particular handling of **mise-en-scene,** that is, elements placed in front of the camera to be photographed, such as setting, props, lighting, figure behavior, and costume, can achieve certain attention shifting and distancing effects. A related term, **montage,** emphasizes the dynamic, often discontinuous relationship between shots and the juxtaposition of images to create ideas that are not present in either shot. According to this theory, shots are not only related by succession, but by juxtaposition. Some of the juxtaposition effect can be achieved through **discontinuity editing,** a practice that allows mismatching of temporal and spatial relations, and/or **intellectual montage,** which is a juxtaposition of a series of images that leads to the formation and communication of an abstract idea. It is in these ways that film language can break free from the limitations of discursive language that is often limited by either/or terms of an argument. Music and other sounds in a film frame can either emerge from the story world itself, **diegetically,** or these can be introduced **nondiegetically,** not emerging from the story world, but introduced as external compositional elements. In *The Terrorist,* Sivan uses many of the techniques described above to project a dialectic between an actual incident and its hypothetical simulation, reality and imagination, film and history. A brief overview of the historical context—Sri Lankan history and the shared history of Sri Lanka and India—will help to situate the film in relation to its localized referents. Sri Lankan history, in many ways, mirrors histories of a broad range of postcolonial nation-states in other areas of the world.

HISTORICAL BACKGROUND: SRI LANKA

Sri Lanka has roughly a population of 18 million. Seventy-four percent are Sinhala Buddhists, 18 percent Hindu Tamils, including 6 percent upcountry Tamils who immigrated to Sri Lanka to work at the tea estates owned by the British. Before the British, the Portugese (1505) and the Dutch (1602) came to Sri Lanka. In 1802, Ceylon became a British Crown Colony. A year after India's independence, in 1948, Ceylon became a self-governing Dominion. In the absence of constitutional guarantees, the minorities in Sri Lanka had no protections. Tensions between ethnic groups that were simmering during colonial rule came to play a significant part in policy making. As a result, the Citizenship Act was passed almost immediately. Within a year, the upcountry Tamils were marginalized as a group, ripped of citizenship and the right to vote. Half were forcibly repatriated to the Southern State of India, Tamil Nadu, right across the Palk Strait.

In political terms, the marginalization of the upcountry Tamils can be seen in relation to a mounting concern for making electoral victories of the Sinhala candidates easier
in the tea-estate provinces (Rotberg, 1999, p. 5). With the growth of a majoritarian Sinhala
ethnonationalism and Buddhist revivalism, the Official Language Act that made Sinhalese
the official language was passed in 1956. While this law replaced English, the language of
colonial rule, with Sinhalese, it also disenfranchised Tamil speakers who had proficiency
in Tamil and English, not in Sinhalese. It is easy to see that this sort of false anticolonialism made access to higher education difficult for ethnic Tamils of Sri Lanka. In a different
context, Tariq Ali, a novelist and social historian, identifies hypocritical policy changes
that do not serve a people but vested interests, as "an anti-imperialism of fools" (Ali, 2002,
pp. 126–140). The growing ethnonationalism in Sri Lanka, mixed up with or masked as
anticolonialist reform, led to other policy changes. It was around this time that the
Teachers Training College in Colombo was closed to Tamils. Consequently, the Tamil
Freedom Party was formed in 1949 to oppose these policies, as well as the settlement of
Sinhalese in Tamil-speaking areas, "alleging that this was a deliberate government colonization scheme" (O'Ballance, 1989, p. 4). Mistrust between the ethnic communities aided
the growth of Tamil subnationalism to combat Sinhalese ethnonationalism. The graded na-
ture of these conflicts led to further deterioration of relations between communities
(Wilson, 2000, pp. 6–7).

In response to a demand made by the Tamil minority, through peaceful demonstrations followed by riots, Solomon West Ridgeway D Bandarnaike in 1958 agreed to grant
"home rule prerogatives to Tamils in the northern and eastern provinces." The home rule
provisions included "recognition of Tamil as administrative language in both provinces,"
transfer of "taxing and other important fiscal powers, and search for further ways to assuage Tamil anxieties." However, it is believed that the Buddhist clergy protested furiously
and saw this as appeasement of the minority (Hindu) Tamils. At this time, there "were
widespread racial riots," in which "10,000 Tamils lost their homes and were evacuated to
Jaffna" (Rotberg, 1999, pp. 6–7). Solomon Bandarnaike was assassinated in 1959, and his
wife, Sirimavo Bandarnaike, became the prime minister. In the meantime, the 1961 dead-
line for the implementation of the Sinhala Language Act gave rise to civil disobedience by
Tamils throughout the country. In the Jaffna Peninsula (the Northern Provinces), Tamils
began "organizing their own postal service, selling their own stamps, and forming their
own vigilante groups, while Tamil passengers on the nationalized bus services refused to
pay their fares and Tamil picketing of government offices spread to Trincomalee"
(O'Ballance, 1989, p. 5). Perhaps the transition from peaceful civil disobedience to a violent insurgency was helped by the implementation of emergency regulations.

On May 22, 1972, Ceylon became a fully autonomous republic and reclaimed its old
name, Sri Lanka (the island of resplendent light). In the subsequent decades, due to competing nationalisms, divisive electoral politics, and outside forces playing a part, the country's population became polarized. This polarization fed the flames of a rebellion that had
begun as a legitimate resistance to discriminatory laws. In the meantime, India, with a
large, upwardly mobile, politically aware population of the Tamil Nadu state, just across
the Palk strait, so close to Jaffna, began paying attention. Some historians believe that
Indira Gandhi, the prime minister of India, gave support to Tamil insurgents, as did the suc-
cessive regional governments of Tamil Nadu. Also, in 1982, when Israelis captured documents from the Palestinians in Lebanon, it became known that "300 Tamils had been

trained in the terrorist camps" there (O'Ballance, 1989, p. 15). However, because of closer ties with India, historians of Tamil Elam movement consider Indian involvement as having been more important.

Things reversed in 1987, when Indian Peace Keeping Forces, 52,000 soldiers, were invited to help the Sinhalese government crush the insurgency. Indira Gandhi's son, Rajiv Gandhi, as the prime minister of India, became implicated in this invasive move. While the work of Indian Peacekeeping Forces in Sri Lanka is seen to have been disastrous and intrusive, it is important to keep in mind that India had helped Sri Lanka put down another insurgent movement in the seventies, the JVP (Janata Vimukht Peramuna, or People's Liberation Front). This movement was supported by Maoist China. In some sense, the Tamil Elam insurgent ethos became later superimposed on the former JVP ethos of class struggle. Chinese support of this movement cannot be ruled out, though most historians focus only on India because of the proximity factor. Diplomatically, India's mission was to talk Tamil rebels out of a demand for a fully autonomous Elam, ruled by them, and settle for greater federalist autonomy within the Sri Lankan polity. Militarily, the army was a reinforcement to Sri Lankan troops.

In the late 1980s, India's Peace Keeping Forces made some difference in controlling the rebels, but their presence raised anxieties in the minds of the Sinhalese majority population. They began to see Indian presence as a potential threat to the sovereignty of Sri Lanka. Ironically, the Sinhalese government gave covert support to the rebels to weaken the IPKF. It was in the aftermath of the IPKF intervention that Rajiv Gandhi was assassinated during a campaign rally in Sriperumbudur in Tamil Nadu. There was fear among the LTTE ranks that Rajiv would win the election. They saw him as their prime enemy. A young girl named Dhanu, a member the LTTE "shadow" squad, rehearsed twice before the final event. In April, at a campaign rally on Marina Beach in Chennai, standing along with others on the welcome line, she came close to the target but not close enough. During the second rehearsal, with V.P. Singh, another candidate for the national elections, she got close, placed the garland on the politician's neck, touched his feet, as she would on May 21. Both rehearsals were videotaped and sent to the leader in Sri Lanka for permission to proceed. On May 21, 1991, at the Sriperumbudur rally, everything went as it was planned and a horrific death, in which many others died, was staged for local, national, and international broadcasts. The Tamil Elam insurgency provides a backdrop for Sivan's film, the assassination plot—each and every detail of which was unearthed by the media in the subsequent months and years—is its immediate source.

In the following discussion, various dimensions of this film will be examined in relation to the "referential meaning," which is, no doubt, contextual and evokes a sense of the development of ethnonationalism and subnationalism in Sri Lanka. The film's "symptomatic meaning" is of greater importance in view of the current engagement with suicide bombings, especially the threat associated with them. This meaning, as suggested by Bordwell, places a given film in relation to a value system or an ideology. Since the filmmaker rejects ideological polemics, the symptomatic meaning of *The Terrorist* is suggested by locations of culture, in this case indigenous Tamil culture. It seems that the suicide bomber Malli's moral and emotional awakening takes place when she is aligned with a viable, fully functional lived culture. The neocolonial history, in which she and her contemporaries are trapped, is disconnected from progressive modernity as much as it is disconnected from tradition. The same is true of generations of young people in Algeria,

Egypt, Kashmir, Malaysia, and many other regions and nation-states. For the Tamil minority in Sri Lanka, the Sihalese government's false anti-imperialism, as exemplified by the Language Act, would have made them lose out on both worlds. Their insurgent ethos is inspired as much by the demand for a physical homeland as by their need for a cultural anchor. In the course of the film, Malli is realigned with agencies of indigenous (Tamil) culture. The film's progressive ethos is not informed by a bourgeois global modernity, or postmodernity, but by a revisionist relocation of tradition. It is, as we will see, not so much a return as an arrival.

DETAILED PLOT SUMMARY OF *THE TERRORIST*

At the very outset, the incongruity between the suicide bomber's name, Malli, which means "jasmine," and her career becomes obvious. Malli is 19 years old, her father, we are told, was a famous revolutionary poet, and her brother, Ramu, the first martyr for the cause. During an ambush an entire guerilla camp (Liberation Tigers of the Tamil Elam) is wiped out by Sri Lankan or Indian army, most likely the latter. Toward nightfall, Malli rescues a young man, pulling him out of a puddle. He is wounded, though not fatally. The proximity brings them closer emotionally and sexually. They spend the night together on the forest floor, sort of a hovel that provides a leafy, shadowy shelter. In the morning, when Malli leaves him for a moment to make sure the coast is clear, he is captured. Standing behind a tree, she watches soldiers beating and bloodying him, as he takes his cyanide pill.

When the group's leader decides it is necessary to assassinate a certain VIP, Malli wins the coveted job of the suicide bomber. Once the selection is made from among inmates of Camp Fourteen, Malli departs to meet the leader, whose face is never shown, at Camp One. From there, she is assigned an escort. He is a young man of 13 or 14. His code name is Lotus, and his real name is Surya. With him Malli completes a two-day journey through lush jungles, rivers, and waterfalls. In fictional terms, the locale is the Jaffna peninsula in Sri Lanka. Surya teaches Malli to watch out for landmines and helps her get through dangerous checkpoints. On the way, at one point she kills a soldier rather brutally, and perhaps unnecessarily, shocking Surya and making him afraid that *she too is like the others and won't come back*. Eventually, they reach the shore from where she is to take a ferry to get across. Though the film was shot entirely in rural Kerala and some areas near Chennai, the idea of Malli's passage to India from some other place is suggested. In literal terms she just crosses over to a nearby fishing hamlet. Before Malli's vessel has set sail, when she is still getting adjusted for the ride, she sees soldiers march towards Surya and kill him.

After she reaches a safe house, it is four days to the hour of the assassination: She reaches there on the 16th and the assassination is scheduled for the 20th. Two men, Perumal and Thyagu, meet her and take her to stay with an unsuspecting farmer, Vasudev, who lives with his farmhand, Gopal, and his comatose wife, Padmavathy. A great deal of Malli's time is spent with the co-conspirators, rehearsing in her room. However, much happens in these four days in terms of communication with others, some of which is foreshadowed by Malli's journey with Surya, and her encounter with the wounded insurgent. In Vasu's house, its corridors, rooms within rooms, and courtyard, she becomes aware of a world outside of her metaphorical blindfold in the jungle camps. She realizes what life has to offer outside of the sacrificial, austere, disciplined routines, the shootings, and the sound and fury of war in the midst of a sublime beauty of nature. In Vasu's home she has her first experience of a normal life, appropriate food, sleep, showers, soulful music suited to the time of the day, a neighborhood temple compound and its serene beauty, and a neighbor's children walking to and returning from school.

Vasu is told that Malli is Perumal's cousin, a student of agriculture who is doing research. She stays in his son's room, who, she is told, is a photojournalist. He covers news about riots and demonstrations and is, supposedly, away from home. The relation between Vasu and Malli is at first tentative. Through calming and enriching influences of Karnatak music, small mealtime rituals, domestic order of the house and the backyard, and verbal exchanges with communicative intent, the relation between the two moves toward care and commitment. In this house, which is nothing like a complicit, conspiratorial "safe house" for "a terrorist," Malli's sense of reality changes.

DIALETICAL INTERPLAY OF IMAGES

As the film begins, diegetic sound (that which emanates from the story world) precedes image. We hear a vehicle drive up and unload its cargo, followed by someone yelling out in anguish and anger: "Traitor!" Someone else suggests they should not remove the mask because it would be a bad omen for them "to look at the face of the defector" (Sivan, 1998). When the picture comes on, a man in a white mask removes a black mask from the condemned man's face; he restrains another who is crying out: *Traitor, you killed my brother.* The person in the white mask reads out names of those whose deaths were caused by this act of betrayal. The real-life equivalents of these characters were, no doubt, adversely affected by the Language Act, the Citizenship Act, and other discriminatory laws in Sri Lanka. In addition, many lost families and homes in forced exiles and massacres. Yet, from the start Sivan distances us from that history. The film does not elicit an easy identification-based sympathy for the rebels; it draws attention to a larger, global issue.

Commenting on this aspect of *The Terrorist,* Roger Ebert explains how it is different from other movies based on revolutionaries, criminals, or anyone whom we perceive as hero and heroine and this person is engaged in violence. He says that in most such movies the viewer is made to root for the hero/heroine, and want him or her to succeed in his or her mission. "Films," he says, "are such a first-person medium—they identify so strongly with their protagonists—that they generate sympathy even for evil . . ." The distinctive quality of *The Terrorist,* according to Ebert, is that we do not want Malli to succeed (in her mission). While at the same time, the film "paints her loyalty to her cause, and the possibility that her cause is right." Ebert finds Malli's involvement and loyalty to her cause as more "moral" than the practice "of killing by remote control at long distance and calling it 'modern warfare.' " Further, the film's suicide bomber makes Ebert think of "a condemned prisoner who knows the exact hour of his death." "How much stranger, it must seem," he says, "to be your own willing executioner: to die because an idea is bigger than yourself" (Ebert, 2000).

It is obvious that in this case what Ebert says is only the starting premise, the first stage of a philosophical–psychological process. As the film progresses, for the viewer as well as for the protagonist, the *idea* becomes smaller than the *self* and, in the end, the self emerges as a lot bigger than the idea. As has been noted before, Sivan made this film three years before September 11, 2001; he did not have the current situation and mental attitudes generated from it in mind. Yet, his vision, wisdom, and insight have implication for us now. His words throw further light on how he deals with the issue of violence in film. He says, "Most of the films that deal with violence end up glorifying violence. . . . I wanted to have the audience go through *a process* so that they might say at the end: *No, I don't want to see this blast,* even though that is what they came for (emphasis added)" (Walsh, 1998). Clearly, the rhetoric and composition of the film is informed by the filmmaker's strive to redirect spectator psychology, his attempt to work against viewer anticipation of and interest in (the success of) the suicide bomber's mission.

In "Colonialism, Racism, and Representation: An Introduction," Robert Stam and Louise Spence discuss aspects of cinematic identification technique as it its used in *Battle of Algiers*. They say that the film presents "anti-colonialist terror as a response to colonialist violence" (Braudy & Cohen, 1999, p. 245). When the film was made, that approach was appropriate and consistent with an anti-colonial ideology. The filmmaker, they maintain, makes "us want" the two Algerian women who are planting bombs to complete their task, "not out of political sympathy but out of the mechanism of cinematic identification" (p. 244). This means that *Battle of Algiers* uses cinematic identification to allow their spectators, those who might not be sympathetic with the Algerian cause, to involuntarily support anti-colonialist activity that is revolutionary in nature. For Sivan's film, the context is different. It deals with violence that is a consequence of internal strife among competing ethnic groups of a postcolonial nation. Aware of the dangers of cinematic identification in this case, Sivan departs from the conventions set up by such classics in this genre as *Battle of Algiers*. In contrast, *The Terrorist* seeks to disinvest the viewer from the suicide bomber's aims and goals, even recoil from them, but remain engaged in her as a human subject and the issue that is articulated there. For example, in the opening scene, the masked Malli is introduced as the one who saw (the informant), and she is asked to shoot him. We do not know the background; we have no idea who this masked person is, though it is clear that she is the protagonist. Still, it is not clear if this person is a man or a woman, young or old. In fact, the removal of the mask from the traitor's face makes him more accessible as a person, while Malli in this scene is no more than a masked killer. Malli's masked appearance and her act of shooting the informant creates a space between her and us, a space in which a different kind of engagement with what she represents can occur. Subsequently, she emerges as an allegorical figure for an internally battling and an embattled postcolonial nation.

The visual composition of this sequence illustrates aspects of what Eisenstein describes as the dialectical interplay of shots. Montage for Eisenstein is a conflict between a cinematic shot and it successor. Each shot, in his view, has an energy that expresses itself visually by way of its conflict with its successor (Braudy & Cohen 1999, pp. 25–27). It makes sense that the cinematic technique perfected by the celebrated maker of the silent film would be suitable for Sivan's project. *The Terrorist,* though not a silent film, uses silence as a form of communication. In the opening sequence of the film, for instance, the first shot in its close up format draws attention to the spray of the traitor's blood that sprinkles on Malli's mask, barely missing her eyeball. In the succeeding shot, she removes her mask with a steady motion of her free hand, and her bare face is caught in a torrent of rain.

Again, there is a juxtaposition between the bucolic grandeur of the scene—rain falling through trees and lush foliage, a river at some distance—and the summary execution of a condemned man whose face showed fear, not shame or regret. The shift from what is said, their desire to "not see the defector's face," to the swift action that removes the mask and exposes the face suggests a dialectic.

While the configuration of characters and actions presents a view of the rebel movement, shifts in montage encode references to political processes that preceded the insurgency. In the context of those processes, one might ask who were the traitors, who the executioners, and what was the cause? Was the Sinhalese establishment that passed the Citizenship Act and the Language Act working for the good of the nation? If not, who were they working for? What decolonizing frenzy went into caricaturing the Tamil minority as beneficiaries of the British rule that justified their extreme repression? Were Sinhalese interest groups being patriotic when they reacted violently to Solomon Bandarnaike's attempts to meet the demands of a constitutionally disenfranchised minority? More importantly, are the Tamil insurgents who have launched an armed rebellion traitors or patriots? The traitor of the opening scene is a mirror for all those who are present in this frame, as well as others who are out there in the cities and towns practicing a divisive politics of ethnonationalism. Though the concrete detail of the film form only refers to Sri Lanka and South India, we can draw inferences about similar geopolitical and socioeconomic processes that are carried on in other towns and cities of other nation-states. The ambiguity about who is the traitor and who the patriot expresses a larger, global anxiety: a sense of threat (and guilt) in an uncertain world.

In terms of technique, the symptomatic meaning emerges from the filmmaker's manipulation of visual images, his consistent use of shallow focus and closeup shots that simulate photojournalistic images, while at the same time they emerge as scenes painted onto the screen. Many reviewers of this film have taken note of its painting-like quality and Sivan's movement away from, for the most part, depth-of-field framing. Choice of technique, with regard to a film like this, cannot be an idle choice. Sivan's shift from "depth to flatness" can be seen in relation to what Brian Henderson describes as a " a non-bourgeois" camera style. Henderson maintains that depth-of-field framing projects the "bourgeois world as infinitely deep, rich, complex, ambiguous." A movement away from this convention, for instance, is Jean-Luc Godard's revisionist shift to flatness that "demystifies" by flattening this world into two-dimensionality (Braudy & Cohen, 1999, p. 66). While Sivan's closeup shots might aim for a two-dimensional effect to show the insurgent movement's inflexibility and its sociomoral isolation, he adds something to the flatness that opens a third dimension of a different kind. At one level, the closeup shots present replicas of media coverage of events related to the insurgency. At another level, the flatness of film frames is highly aesthetic, almost ornamental. This visual feature establishes a parallel between film form and (Indian) painting, sculpture, dance (especially Bharat Natyam), music (Karnatak), ancient Indic art forms that are part of a vibrant, lived culture, though Indic ideas have been long discredited and forgotten. They are no longer a part of the intellectual and discursive practices that shape politics and civil life and provide models for social organization. This particular feature of cinematography in *The Terrorist* makes us conscious of the postcolonial disjunction between lived culture and discourse practices that shape social and political institutions in many postmodern nation states in today's world.

In a more positive way, the repetition and variation of shallow focus, closeup shots of Ayesha Dharkar's face achieve an iconic quality; her film form faces resemble faces in Indian painting and sculpture. The cumulative effect transforms the visual aspect of Malli's character into a cinematic "ideograph," to use Eisenstein's term. It denies and defers a vantage point of a realistic identification based on depth of field framing where Ayesha Dharkar, as Malli, might appear to be like us, where she could be situated in relation to a normal gestalt of events and objects. Instead, the iconic quality of Dharkar's face, articulate in its dance-like expressions, accompanied at times by the sound of her breathing on soundtrack, turns her image into an intellectual montage painted onto the screen. An example of a reflective montage, as distinct from intellectual montage, is the extended sequence of shots that focuses on an object associated with Malli's face. Moments after the execution, she is seen washing her blood-stained mask at the river. Rain has stopped, and the sun has come out. A female friend braids Malli's hair and talks to her sweetly; their togetherness associates with scenes of female bonding depicted in Tamil poems and Sanskrit plays. What passes between them, once again, collides immediately with the sound of machine gun fire. Grabbing their weapons, leaving behind Malli's mask, the two scurry away.

We are left with this piece of cloth that has holes in it to match a face; it relaxes on the smooth current, spreads out, and exposes its loose cotton weave. First, the white color catches the light, then it folds up, highlighting the red. The guilt that the masked killer may not be aware of is played out by the imagery of water and light. The mask becomes a substitute for the disappearing face, the absent self. Various aspects of *mise-en-scene*—setting, staging, lighting, movement—are used to frame this object as a counterpoint to water as well as to the human subject. Reviewers of *The Terrorist* have remarked on the pervasiveness of water imagery in the film, its "dewy pantheism" (Hoberman, 2000). The insistent focus on water imagery can also be seen as a genuine neopantheism, rather than an accidental "dewy pantheism." Through these images, the cinematic discourse is associated with ancient texts, now repressed and disowned, that represent water, earth, and fire as primal and symbolically sacred. Visual images of beautiful landscape in *The Terrorist,* where bodies of water are the focal point, conflict with the "killing fields" aspect of these territories. Through these frames, historical reality is juxtaposed with conceptions of a sacred reality, sacred time; the witness *self* (the *atman*) of everyone is seen in conflict with a fiercely politicized ethnonational and subnational *identity*. While water retains redemptive potential, fire has become wholly incriminated in violence to human life as well as to habitats. The only images of fire are gunfire, landmine blasts, columns of flame rising from burning bunkers, and finally, the explosive covered in plastic, wrapped around the waist of the suicide bomber, awaiting a dreadful detonation. Through the use of intellectual montage, visual sequences like these express a gripping, global fear, guilt, anxiety, and a collective sense of threat in an uncertain world, but without the loss of confidence in an integrated world's ability to save itself.

MEMORY AND FILM FORM

The full import of Malli's role in the opening sequence becomes clear later when she is seen hiding behind a tree, watching the soldiers torture her lover. The executed traitor of the opening frame is with them. The look of contempt she throws at his falling body, in this context, becomes a look of recognition. It establishes her credibility. Her fear, shock, and sorrow enter as emotive elements in another frame, where a number of rebels lay dead, layered in folds of foliage. While Malli's gaze is only fixed on the bodies being pulled out, the bloodied vegetation and the earth, as if they were human actors, are brought into an intensified poetic focus for the viewer. The referential context for this incident calls to mind instances from documented events. In 1987, for example, Indian Peacekeeping Forces ambushed a group of guerrillas, who "were preparing to ambush an IPKF convoy" (O'Ballance, 1989, p. 115). This was the first real armed clash between the IPKF and the Tamil rebels. Prior to this incident, 500 Tamil Tigers had been arrested by the IPKF at Batticaloa and another 150 "in the Mullaitivu-Manikulum-Tulvankulam area" (p. 114). The place names themselves signify a fusion of territory with language and culture.

In these and many other ways, codes of action and representation refer to particular incidents of ambush and counter ambush. In addition, the filmmaker threads together stories of displaced and massacred Tamils. An instance of this is the painful story Surya tells Malli. His father was burned alive, his sister and mother killed, and their home was destroyed. The sequence that dramatizes this story uses many elements of *mise-en-scene,* including staging and acting style. Malli, dressed in white, stands near the front porch of this ruined, meager home. Surya has his back toward her. Bent forward in a stylized manner, he speaks of the horror he witnessed as a child. Nondiegetic strains of a music frame a context for the spectator. Surya's mode of delivery resembles formal mourning. Most likely, there is an allusion to the 1983 communal riots "in which 100,000 Tamils became homeless in Colombo and 175,000 elsewhere in the country" (Rotberg, 1999, p. 7). Surya explains why he cannot leave these woods; it is his home. His father was burned alive at that spot. The compositional style abstracts the story from the particular so that it emerges as a global instance. For the perceiver, Surya becomes an exemplar for all those who are similarly displaced and lost, framed in relation to habitats of geopolitically "disputed territories" in other parts of South Asia, in the Middle East, Bosnia, Yugoslavia, and other places in the world.

Apparently, a story like the one Surya tells is supposed to have made a great impression on the young mind of the Tamil Elam movement's leader, Prabhakaran (O'Ballance, 1989, p. 13). This too is a story of a Brahmin priest who was burned alive. The filmmaker presents to the viewer a universal story of loss. The soft blue color contrasts with white clothes of Malli and Surya. The backdrop is of darkening woods and bird song. We don't see Malli's face; Surya's back is toward her. Her silence and distance, as well as her posture of attentiveness, constitute her as witness, rather than co-participant. The nondiegetic strains of a lullaby that do not emerge from the immediate story world make us aware that the child, Surya, has remained a child. Yet, in many ways, he has become an old man. The night that follows the evening when he told his story to Malli, Surya has a nightmare in which he screams: *Don't burn my father.* If father is also fatherland, then the image of a child seeing his father being burned alive gives rise to a sense of his perpetual exclusion from the cultural-symbolic order of his country of birth.

For a better understanding of Surya's situation, it might help to examine an ethnonationalistic term, such as *Bhumiputra* (son of the soil), a phrase originally used to refer to the ethnic Malay, as opposed to the Chinese. In the context of Buddhist nationalism in Sri Lanka, *Bhumiputra* identifies someone as having been born there, while *Buddhaputra* (son of the Buddha) identifies someone as an inheritor of the cultural legacy that has "higher" na-

tionalistic value. In this light, the ethnonationalists, the Sinhalese Buddhists, would see themselves as both the *Bhumiputras,* sons of the soil, as well as *Bhuddhaputras,* sons of the Buddha. They would see ethnic Tamils as only *Bhumiputras,* not *Buddhaputras* (Wilson, 2000, pp. 7–10). This mindset, conscious or unconscious, would make someone like Surya a person who has a (dubious) right only to the "motherland," not to the "fatherland." Seen in this light, Sivan's cinematic inclusion of Tamil (Hindu) culture aims for a symbolic rehabilitation of the culturally disinherited. However, it is important to keep in mind that the rehabilitating counternarrative of Sivan's film erases explicit references to specific nations, regions, and ethnic identities so as to dissociate from ethnonationalisms and hegemonic claims, past and present, of all kinds. The divisive history that Sivan's film bears witness to is indicative of globally relevant and globally practiced majoritarian politics that privileges one cultural tradition over others and considers it more valid to the nation. As the culturally disinherited swell the ranks, subnationalisms emerge and separatist movements are born. This is a threat, and one of its causes is the growth of majoritarian claims of cultural superiority in postcolonial nations and particular regions within these nations. Often, the claims of superiority mimic colonialist and imperialist notions of superiority.

While Surya's story in *The Terrorist* presents a case of cultural disinheritance, in addition to the trauma and tragedy, Malli's own story unfolds through another interplay of motifs after she is chosen to be the suicide bomber. For a final briefing and to share a meal with the leader, she arrives at Camp One. Waiting in the corridor, she overhears parts of an ongoing conversation on the wireless. The leader concludes with an incantation of his commandments: "Our struggle has purpose/Justice is on our side/Our objectives are unique/Our aim has a goal/We are self-confident/Death will not deter us" (Sivan, 1998). At "Death will not deter us," the frame cuts to a funeral scene. It is a very flowery funeral; the film form uses soft light and warm colors. A little girl is looking uncomprehendingly at a decorated corpse fortified by an armed guard. An inexpressible absurdity and sadness is expressed by the sound of her voice when she speaks her name, "Malli." The leader tells her to be proud of her brother. At this point, the frame cuts back to his: "We will shed our blood, not tears/Ramu was fearless in defeat/He will live in our history/Such bravery strengthens our movement." Ramu is, no doubt, Malli's brother, the dead man of the funeral. Through discontinuity editing, the story of Malli when she was 6 or 7 is aligned with her present. This image-schema memory situates Malli's personal history within the glorified myth of the struggle, while Surya's emotion memory evokes an exemplar of systemic oppression that led to the insurgency.

Memory schemas, which are often visual, emerge from what cognitive psychologists classify as "information memory." Information memory covers a broad range of human experience; memory schemas influence our present actions and responses to events. In this case Malli's image schema memory of her childhood, at one level, provides an internal motivation for sacrifice; it makes the cause seem bigger than her life. That is not all, though. The memory scene make the body and full persona of the child Malli cinematically present; this startling presence gives rise to an implicit expectation that is not consistent with the explicit anticipation of the bomb blast. In contrast to image schema memories, episodic and anecdotal memories are by their very nature fragmentary. People often reconstruct them in relation to present circumstances. Surya constructs his emotion memory in terms of an episodic memory to share his past with Malli. In itself emotion memory is not accessible to conscious recall. What may have happened to someone like

Surya may not be exactly what he tells, but the fact that he tells the story shows that there is an unspeakable trauma. This young boy is only a messenger. Unlike Malli, he recoils from scenes of violence. Taken together, the stories of Surya and Malli constitute a dialectic between the history of displacement and genocide and the grandiose myth of personal sacrifice. As the film progresses, other stories unfold and become part of a collective narrative not only of these characters, but internally displaced people in other nation-states and other regions of the world.

LOVE AND DEATH

An absurd aspect of Malli's preparation for the journey and the high-profile assassination is that for the first time in her young life she will don female garb. On the day of the assassination, she will wear perfume, flowers in her hair, earrings, lipstick, and bindi for the first and the last time. An inverted pattern of cross dressing underscores the incongruities of this life. There is no ellipsis between her visit with the leader and the departure. Trivial details of her measurements being taken become part of the *mise-en-scene*. An emphasis like this deflects viewer attention and adds a new dimension to suspense and anticipation. When Malli arrives at her destination, she is handed the suitcase, informed that the measurements were sent through the wireless. It is interesting to note that it was only after Rajiv Gandhi's assassination that the Indian government found out about the elaborate wireless communication system that made it possible for rebel activities to be carried out from Tamil Nadu, India. In the film, this detail is brought up in connection with preparations for Malli's "disguise." The comic irony distracts us from the seriousness of her mission. It distracts her. The viewer shares in her sensual delight in new clothes.

After being driven through the jungles in a truck, Malli waits for her contact. A series of mutually reinforcing depth-of-field shots and closeup shots suggest a transitional phase in her life. Malli is sitting on a boulder, in the middle of a vast river bed, with white water eddying and swirling all around her, lovely hills in the distance. In this sunny solitude, her mind returns to a recent experience. Unlike the image schema memory of her childhood, this is an episodic memory, divided into segments, narrated through discontinuity editing, marked by sharp, sometimes jolting cuts. As has been explained, image-schema memory influences one's actions and responses in the present. Episodic memory reconstructs fragments of a remembered event in relation to a present circumstance. Malli's episodic memory is reconstructed in relation to the present circumstance: her suicide bombing assignment. In other words, the life-logic of an subjective experience interferes with the death-logic of her assigned task. Each segment of the episodic memory is constructed through interior montage (which, in cinema, functions like interior monologue in fiction) that begins in the scene described above; it ends a day before the assassination. Scenes of this embedded romantic tragedy form a parallel relation to daily events. It is like a seed wrapped in the shell of daily events and activities, always present in her body and mind.

A significant nondiegetic element, music, is introduced as a compositional element to this highly intensified sequence. It is a variation of raga *tilanga,* played on soundtrack. Tilanga raga comes from water-song compositions that village girls sing when they "go to wells to fetch water" (Avtar, n.d., p. 18). Needless to say, Malli's situation presents a contrast to the raga motif. The music, emanating from outside the story reality, alludes to tradition and culture that is absent in the story world. In dark blue light, Malli is no more than a shadow in the backdrop of a lake or a pond; hills and forests are in the distance here too. The *alap,* opening part of the raga, is synchronized with this scene. As opposed to the shallow, closeup shots used throughout this segment, these two depth-of-field shots are similar, though the location is different in each, so is the light. In the memory scene, Malli spots a body, dimly floating, caught in reeds, very close to the bank. An outstretched hand stands out, like a muddied water lily. Soldiers are everywhere, as is incessant machine gun fire. She lifts the body out of muddy water, drags it to the forest floor. He is wounded on the side of his face, near the ear, not dead but in some sort of a delirium. She cradles him and cautions him to be quiet. In an ambush at Camp Seven, he says: "They killed everyone."

Just as Malli's and Surya's prehistory is associated with specific phases of the Tamil struggle in Sri Lanka, this young man's story, whatever little there is of it, also refers to something specific. In a semi-conscious state, he says something about books. Later, Malli asks him what it was about books. He says he had always wanted to read a lot of books; that was his dream. At 13 he put all his books in a box, locked and buried it. He promised his mother when the war is over, he will take them out and complete his education. Contextual reference to various policies and laws that blocked access to higher education for ethnic Tamils is hard to miss. If his books were in Tamil and English, with the implementation of the Language Act that made Sinhala the national language, they would be useless for practical purposes. In psychological terms, it seems natural that at this time in his life he would think of unfinished business: a promise to his mother and a commitment to the idea of a motherland—the Tamil *Elam.* He asks Malli what her dream is. She says, "If we get used to seeing reality as a dream, then our dreams will be real." The dialectic between nondiegetic sound (of music) with the diegetic sound, voices, footsteps of soldiers, intermittent shooting, define the terms and conditions of their dream and their reality. The purpose of this storyline is not so much to show the "human" side of the suicide bomber, but to insert an event that would provide a dialectical opposition to her mission.

For this entire sequence, the filmmaker has used a monochromatic color design and hard light, which makes outlines and objects very sharp. Strands of Malli's hair have been described by one reviewer as "venetian blinds." The shades of color are sometimes purple-blue, sometimes blue-black. The blue color in mythic contexts associates with the goddess Kali's blue-black color, her hair. More importantly, the insistent use of blue reminds one of the *kalkuta* poison that, according to legend, has the potential to destroy the entire world. An ancient story of a deadly poison that grows in time and bursts upon the world as a grave problem to be solved has parallels in the means of self-destruction the modern world possesses. According to ancient myth, Shiva supposedly drank this poison, making the world safe; and, in turn, this drink made his throat blue. Further, the *kalkuta* poison that Shiva swallowed to save the world came out of the worldly strivings of *devas* (gods) and *asuras* (demons). In modern terms, the *devas* in any culture are those who we side with and *asuras* those who we are against. To return to Ebert's insightful comments on *The Terrorist,* he says, "if we disagree with them, they are fanatics. If we agree, they are heroes" (Ebert, 2000). While the terms *devas* and *asuras* are not parallel to "fanatics" and "heroes," they are more like our notion of "good guys" and "bad guys," *us* and *them.* Out of the mythic churning of an ocean, by virtue of the collective labors of these two kinds of people, many good things are supposed to have emerged. However, these were overshadowed by the discovery of a deadly poison: *kalkuta.*

In the context of competing ethnonationalisms in contemporary South Asia, each side to its own is the *deva* (the person who is right) and the other is *asura* (the person who is wrong), though they may not explicitly employ these terms. The dialectically different nation-building efforts of today's *devas* and *asuras* may create a lot that is good, yet, when these efforts become antithetical, a modern version of the *kalkuta* poison is produced: the violence of insurgent terrorism met by state terror (of war and counterinsurgency). This is true not only in the South Asian context, but other global contexts as well. In *The Terrorist,* we can see that Malli and her wounded comrade have absorbed their share of a symptomatic poison, but can they save the world? Of course not. The cyanide pill that one of them will swallow is a tragic-grotesque; the explosive the other will agree to bind to her body is the horrific-absurd. Collision between this highly motivated memory narrative with shots of daily events expresses a motivational conflict in Malli, the energies of which are in part subterranean. As opposed to the hard light used in the memory sequence, the daily event sequences are in soft light. Sivan uses fast rhythmic shifts from the blue to the brown and fleshy tones and back. The shifts of focus from danger and safety, resolve and hesitation, muscle tension and relaxation, bring forth an almost yogic, zen quality to the cinematic synchronization of Malli's inner and outer realities. Through visual shape shifting of this kind, the viewer's psychological attitude toward the story is redirected.

Clearly, when someone makes a film about a suicide bomber, he or she is not trying to persuade a viewer who thinks terrorists are "rats and roaches" and should be eliminated in the same way (Rivers, 1986, p. 31). At the other end of the spectrum are viewers who expect a film about a bomber to do the opposite, to make her or him sympathetic, as is the case with the Algerian women in *Battle of Algiers.* In *The Terrorist,* the search and shoot operation discussed above, in the context of which Malli meets her lover, shows that counterinsurgency operations do engage in elimination processes. However, the filmmaker does not condemn; nor does he condone. He distracts the viewer's attention by engaging it elsewhere. Not only that, he individualizes the soldiers as much as he individualizes the rebels. The first soldier that Malli kills is shown at a moment of vulnerability, his face covered in blood (just like Malli's lover's), a tremor in his voice. When Malli and Surya cross a checkpoint, we see a dead soldier being covered up in white cloth, with big blots of blood seeping through. Malli can see all this through the corner of her eye, as she carries a bundle of wood over her head. In the same shot we see another soldier, both of whose legs have been shattered in a blast.

The informant of the opening scene, likewise, is individualized. He is very young, like many of the insurgents, and he looks terrified when the soldiers capture Malli's friend. Again, an out-of-focus shot is used to distance the beating followed by a closer view, where the focus is on his physical struggle to swallow the pill. When the soldiers come to get Surya, an out-of-focus shot is used to frame their approach through a cluster of trees. The reaction shot of Malli watching their approach makes the out-of-focus movement diegetic. Surya's posture is still, like a portrait. He is lost in thought, watching Malli depart. His back faces the death march of uniforms and his brutal end can only be inferred from an extended reaction shot of Malli's face. In the earlier scene, when Malli was shown leaving her station to march to the lair of the escaped soldier, the motion of her body gliding through the landscape was out of focus in the same way. Her female friend called out to stop her and watched the receding form. An ethically symmetrical distribution of bodies-in-motion *mise-en-scene* depicts the "us" and the "them" of this conflict in equal, not relative terms. The parity effect does not neutralize ethical concern, it underscores a need for proportionate evaluation and an individualized focus on human agents as human.

This particular aspect of *The Terrorist* brings to mind a point that Howard Zinn has made recently. Drawing attention to the very effective, timely, and healing humanization of victims of the Trade Center bombing shown in *New York Times'* "Portraits of Grief" section, Zinn goes on to point out that this should be done when any tragedy occurs and no tragedy should be summed up as a statistic. Zinn asks why the victims of the bombings in Afghanistan are not similarly humanized. The reasons for an absence of attention to victims of the bombing are obvious to everyone. However, once a statement like this is made, one begins to envision a world in which such humanizing could happen as a matter of routine (Zinn, 2002, p. 33). Perhaps a proportionate attention to human suffering as human suffering occurs more often in art than in life. From Greek drama to modern and postmodern literature (as well as film), in other forms of literature from other antiquities of the world to the present, writers have dealt with cultural anxieties, fears, threats, and questions of conscience. Santosh Sivan's *The Terrorist* is a world classic of this type. Its focus on human faces—of soldiers, traitors, suicide bombers, farmers from fishing hamlets—individualizes and humanizes from a perspective of reasoned compassion. The filmmaker avoids a vicarious, voyeuristic engagement in violence that is a common feature of mainstream cinema and media today.

THE WORLD AS FAMILY

Malli's four days of rehearsals and waiting for the day of the assassination, ironically, synchronize with the unraveling of a safely anchored familial world ready to take her in. Through images of lush jungles filled with landmines, we had seen earth, water, and vegetation as if they bore witness to human events: horrific and sacrificial. In contrast, Vasu's farmhouse depicts a network of normal human relations, anchored in indigenous tradition. Vasu tells Malli that an orphan is not a person who has lost her parents, but one who has them but refuses to reach out to them. The Vedic affirmation of the *vasudhaiva kutumbham* principle (the earth [universe] is my family), informs Vasu's world view and conduct. This is an *other-directed* ethical attitude that goes against the *self-interested* rhetoric of ethnonationalistic concepts that establish cultural and national hegemonies, as well as global imperialist practices that do the same. Gopal and Vasu draw upon the *vasudhaiva kutumbham* ethos in a very functional, viable manner to establish an easy relation with Malli. They represent a value system and a living tradition in relation to which the "symptomatic meaning" of this section of the film can be formulated.

Vasudha in Sanskrit means "the earth," or "the universe." *Kutumbam* means family, in the sense of a group of people whose survival is co-dependent. The suffix, *aiva*, added to *vasudha*, implies, "it alone is." Moreover, this particular word used for earth characterizes "earth as that which gives" (*dha*). Through a saying like this, the Vedic imperative demands of us, as human beings, that we regard all people and all nations of the worlds as our family. If put into practice in today's world, what it would mean is that every country's national interest is important, but that importance can never, under any circumstances, be an absolute thing. It is necessarily conditioned. For survival, all nations and people are tied to each other by principles of co-dependence. If all life is sacred, then it follows that these ties are sacred. More importantly, the co-dependency oriented *vasudhaiva kutumbam* ethos would dictate that conflict resolution in a global setting has to emerge from everyone's sense that the other, no matter how weak and how poor, or how rich and how powerful, is also a part of this world family. And, the good resides in recognition of the interdependent nature of it all. *Vasudhaiva kutumbam* is a practical idea, not an idealistic philosophy. Members of a family have a common stake in certain ventures, just as nations have. Global peace could, if articulated in these commonsense terms, within frameworks of an extended world-family ethos, become a guiding principle for threat reduction in today's uncertain world. As a substitute for bullying, swaggering, hate mongering, accusing, blaming, and thus, instilling fear in each other, nations and ethnic groups could, as they sometimes do, try to understand each other's fears.

In *The Terrorist,* Vasu's farmhouse—its inner and outer spaces—exudes an aura of fear dispelling trust, safety, and peace. It is simple, unglamorous, not rich, and it stands for peace, not war. The safe house that was used for the 1991 assassination of Rajiv Gandhi had been acquired by means of coercion and blackmail. The inmates of the house became accomplices. As opposed to the rural quality of Malli's safe house location, the actual suicide bomber crew inhabited urban areas. There were many more people involved and they plotted for nearly a month. Dhanu, the suicide bomber, was accompanied by another girl, Shuba, and their escort, Shivarasan. Sivan reduced the number of people involved to three. Malli is alone most of the time and does not stir outside of Vasu's home. Far from being accomplices, the inmates of the house are protected from the knowledge of her violent mission. The reasons given for Malli's brief stay with them are so clearly lies that their suspicion takes a more predictable direction. They think she must be pregnant and Perumal must be the father. The two, they think, are plotting an abortion as a way out of this situation.

Only Vasu's comatose wife, Padmavathy, watches the rehearsals with unseeing eyes. Only she knows, if she knows anything, what is going on. A window in the wall connects her room with Malli's. The uncanny aspect of Padmavathy's reclining figure in the other room, Malli's fear of it at first, her growing interest, and finally her emotional connection to this half-dead mother, as well as many other aspects of *mise-en-scene* logic foreshadow non-accomplishment of the suicide mission. The absent mother is made present. The family's functionality, its viability, supercedes the expediencies of history and ideology. It is clear that the viewer is not encouraged to think of Vasu in terms of the "garrulous old man" stereotype, which is introduced when Perumal briefs Malli on the arrangements for her stay. He says people call him "mad Vasu." Again, the internal rhetorical framing is reinforced when Malli reports to Perumal that the old man has been asking questions. Vasu had surprised her in the middle of the night under the pretext of catching a thief, and said to her, "I know what you are trying to do." Perumal expresses annoyance with this "interfering old man." Thyagu promptly asks: "Should we get rid of him?" Clearly, Vasu, who offers trust and safety to others, has no awareness of the danger they pose to him. The filmmaker has deftly moved his suicide bomber into a relation of co-dependence with this familial world that offers her what she most needs. Ironically, it is this world to which the larger implications of her mission pose a threat.

The film frame where Malli confronts Vasu about his stated suspicion (and implicit accusation), once again, brings in aspects of nature to endow them with an awareness. Vasu and Gopal are digging in the backyard. As she approaches, Vasu walks toward her, light becomes brighter around him, darker where she is standing. In a standing posture that is a cross between stylization and individualization, Vasu resorts to an extended agricultural analogy to tell her what she may suspect, but does not know for sure. He says the earth is a mother like a woman is. To be pregnant is to be like the earth, to nurture the seed and bring forth the fruit (of the womb). For this, he says, a man becomes a father and woman becomes a mother. He draws attention to her vomiting the other day and other signs. In this scene, the filmmaker inserts a story element that interferes with the viewer's anticipation of a bomb blast ending; it engages him or her in another problem. From the perspective of progressive modernity, with emphasis on reproductive rights, Vasu's opposition to Malli's supposed "plans" may come across to some as very conservative. From an indigenous point of view, however, Vasu represents an orthodox liberalism. He opposes an oppressive, self-righteous, parochial morality that prohibits premarital sex and out of wedlock conception. In this context, his ideology is a progressive ideology.

Moreover, the new life in this case is hardly an unwanted life. The last fragment of Malli's embedded memory is projected when she is taking a shower. This is the third day of her stay at Vasu's house. A harsh rhythmic shift from memory schema to the action of her taking a shower cuts from the monochromatic color design to flesh colors followed by Malli's return to the site of trauma, where the embedded romantic tragedy nears its end. She can almost see it, staring in front with an expression of terror and horror, seeing nothing of what is around her: the gentle spray of a natural shower in a shady place. This shot is followed by the next in which one large, round tear forms itself as if after a long time, after a fierce struggle to block it. It is like a dewdrop on a water lily. In the course of the film, the viewers have seen Malli's face covered in beads of sweat, rain, and shower sprays. The redemptive teardrop is different from all these; it exonerates her from an old vow: "We shall shed our blood, not our tears." Subsequent frames show Malli crouched on the ground—much like Antigone of Thebes who defies an uncle-king's decree to bury her traitor brother—trying to cover in fresh red earth the mangled, disgraced body.

Subsequently, she makes a confession to Vasu. At a time when they are both are in Padmavathy's room, Malli says, "He is dead." "Who," asks Vasu. "The child's father." Again, the configuration of a family—father, mother, daughter, a dead father, an unborn child—is suggested here. In a matter-of-fact way, Vasu says he will "shoulder the responsibility," supplementing with "commitment" an earlier gesture of "care" when he had gone to the temple to pray as a grandfather does for a daughter and her baby. A kinship-forming motif was first introduced by Surya who had said: "Malli, I like you. You are my sister." Gopal reinforces it further when he stops by Malli's window, hesitantly at first, wipes off the glass so as to see her clearly and says: "I heard you will be a mother," and then, with a stylized hand gesture, he says: "My blessing." Malli's own induction into Vasu's family is marked by her growing sense of absences that denote presence. For example, Padmavathy's absence is suggested by the banana leaf placed for her at mealtimes. Likewise, Malli lives and sleeps in Vasu's son's room, not knowing the son is dead and the room is a shrine to his memory. This room is, at the same time, a photo archive where a history of oppression (of her people) can be witnessed. On the last day, when he serves her food, Vasu tells Malli his son died seven years ago and in shock his wife became the way she is now.

Notwithstanding the representational unrealism of Padmavathy's prolonged life, her reclining figure in the next room makes sense in connection with Malli's problem. In metaphorical terms, Malli is herself a living corpse, a death machine, whose image links up with young suicide bombers anywhere in the world. Padmavathy's condition externalizes what is internal to Malli, and by extension, what might be internal to any suicide bomber: a comatose life logic. In the context of public life in Sri Lanka and India, as well as any other nation-state, the semi-dead mother-woman is a paradoxical figure. Named after the goddess who brings good fortune, she represents a life-force that is in abeyance and yet exerts an influence on everything. When Malli is about to depart for the assassination site and comes in to say a final good bye, in an uncanny gesture Padmavathy grabs hold of Malli's hand, trying to restrain her.

The iconography of assassination of a male politician by a female suicide bomber is in itself an uncanny rite, resonant with the contradictions and tensions of geopolitical life. Its culture specific aspect in *The Terrorist* is the flowery format that is similar to an Indian wedding ceremony where the bride places a garland on the neck of the groom. The conventions of ceremonial welcome (of an election candidate) simulates this ritual. In the case of an assassination, such as the one that killed Rajiv Gandhi, a sacrificial rite brought together the assassin and the head of the state. In Sivan's film, the daily drill of this death rite progresses to the point where Malli chooses *not to do it*. She does not push the button; the explosive, covered in plastic, tied to her waist does not detonate because the world that such a detonation would, symbolically, threaten has been brought into the life and mind of the suicide bomber. If, as Ashis Nandy has said, "every political assassination is 'a joint communiqué' between the state and the assassin, then, Sivan's suicide bomber chooses not to play this role any more" (Nandy, 1980, p. 70).

The counter role of motherhood is not for her a regressive alternative; it is a refuge, a rebirth. The cinematic subject, Malli, separates herself from the state; she finds her anchor in the family. As we have seen, it is not the conventional bourgeois family, but a truly extended family: the *vasudhaiva kutumbam*. Rose petals of the welcome celebration fall into her cupped hand that looks much like the hand of the drowning man whom she had rescued, the father of her child. The two cuts to black screen that are inserted between the moment of doubt and the moment of faith suggest temporal extension. The real time it takes Malli to *not do it* is much longer than the time required *to do it* (in a real-life situation). The nondiegetic sound of a fisherman's song brings to mind the river scene, with hills in the distance, the mesmerizing soft blue that marks her in white, as she is sits at the edge of a rowboat. The visible frame in its closeup format is similar to Ramu's funeral. Yet, it is not the same. The noise of loud announcements, the patriotic band, contrast with the sacrificial serenity of Malli's brother's funeral. Rituals of death, of life, of sacrifice, celebration of electoral victories, campaign rallies resemble one another in this nation of many nations that, in terms of this film, can rise from death, resurrect itself.

DISCUSSION QUESTIONS

1. Do you see any similarities between the frustrations of the Tamil rebels and other terrorist groups?
2. Review the role of culture in this essay and discuss the interplay between culture and nationalism.
3. Explain why Malli did not carry out the planned terrorist attack. In this context, what factors could have prevented the September 11 terrorists from going forward with their plans?

REFERENCES

ALI, T. (2002). *The clash of fundamentalisms: Crusades, jihad and modernity*. New York: Verso.

AVTAR, R. *The theory of Indian ragas*. (n.d.). New Delhi: Pankaj Publications.

BORDWELL, D., & THOMPSON, K. (2001). *Film art: An introduction*. New York: McGraw-Hill.

BRAUDY, L., & COHEN, M. (Eds.). (1999). *Film theory and criticism: Introductory readings*. New York: Oxford University Press.

EBERT, R. (2000). The terrorist. *http://www.suntimes. com/ebert_reviews/2000/O3/0331*.

HOBERMAN, J. (2002). Times of tumult. http://www/villagevoice .com/issues/2002/hoberman.php.

HOWE, D. A captivating "Terrorist." (2000). *http://www.washingtonpost.com/wp-srv/entertainment/movie*.

IYPE, G., & NADAR, G. A. (2002). *India Today*, April 19, 2002.

JOHNSON, A. G. (2000). Despite an interesting look, "Terrorist" fails to hit the mark. *http://www.sfgate.com/cgi-bin/article.cgi?f=/e/a/2000/o3*.

LEDEOUX, J. (2002). *Synaptic self: How our brains become who we are*. New York: Viking.

NANDY, A. (1980). *At the edge of psychology: Essays in politics and culture*. Delhi: Oxford University Press.

O'BALLANCE, E. (1989). *The cyanide war: Tamil insurrection in Sri Lanka 1973–88*. London: Brassey's.

RIVERS, G. (1986). *The war against the terrorists: How to win it*. New York: Stein and Day.

ROTBERG, R. I. (1999). *Creating peace in Sri Lanka: Civil war and reconciliation*. Washington, DC: Brookings Institution Press.

SIVAN, S. (1998). *The terrorist*. Phaedra Cinema.

TAMBIAH, S. J. (1986). *Sri Lanka: Ethnic fratricide and the dismantling of democracy*. Chicago: University of Chicago Press.

WALSH, D. (1998). An interview with director, Santosh Sivan, and leading actress, Ayesha Dharkar, of The Terrorist. *http://www.org/arts/1998/int-.09.shtml*

WILSON, J. A. (2000). *Sri Lankan Tamil nationalism: Its origins and development in the nineteenth and twentieth centuries*. Vancouver: UBC Press.

ZINN, H. (2002). *Terrorism and war*. New York: Seven Stories Press.

7

A Philosopher Looks at Terrorism: Evil, Religion, and World Ethics

Eric Kraemer

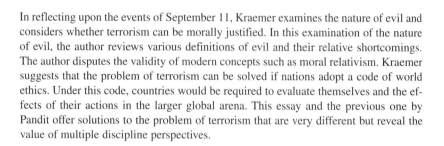

In reflecting upon the events of September 11, Kraemer examines the nature of evil and considers whether terrorism can be morally justified. In this examination of the nature of evil, the author reviews various definitions of evil and their relative shortcomings. The author disputes the validity of modern concepts such as moral relativism. Kraemer suggests that the problem of terrorism can be solved if nations adopt a code of world ethics. Under this code, countries would be required to evaluate themselves and the effects of their actions in the larger global arena. This essay and the previous one by Pandit offer solutions to the problem of terrorism that are very different but reveal the value of multiple discipline perspectives.

The four coordinated plane hijackings and subsequent horrifying attacks on the World Trade Center and the Pentagon of September 11, 2001 raise disturbing questions. They force U.S. citizens and their supporters to look carefully at a set of important philosophical issues. Americans regard these events as acts of unmitigated evil, yet they are also painfully aware that some groups in other countries greeted the very same actions with cheers and celebration. Initially, it might have been possible to dismiss these events as the unfortunate result of peculiar behaviors by clinically abnormal individuals. The available evidence, however, of the planning, determination, courage, and religious devotion of those who engaged in the plane hijackings makes it ill-advised to interpret the four plane hijackings and subsequent crashes as the acts of cowards, unbalanced loners, irreligious people, or individuals out for personal gain. If the actions cannot be so dismissed, how are they to be explained? How is one to make sense of actions that U.S. citizens and their allies regard as horribly evil but that the hijackers and their supporters considered as instances of remarkable moral heroism by fighters for a just cause? What justification could possibly have been sufficient to convince the hijackers that their actions were worth the terrible cost in human life and suffering, both to themselves and their families as well as to others and their families? Was the reasoning of those who carried out these attacks flawed or were there just irreconcilable differences of moral opinion between the perpetrators and their victims?

These questions suggest several basic questions that need to be considered:

1. What is the nature of evil and why is terrorism such a strong example of it?
2. Can terrorism be morally justified and does religion play a special role in this?
3. Is there a reasonable moral solution to the problem of terrorism?

This chapter will discuss these three questions and provide answers that explain certain aspects of the events of September 11. The structure of the chapter is as follows. First the nature of evil is examined and attempts are made to analyze the disturbing evil features of terrorist actions. Second, serious efforts to justify some evils as necessary are presented, and several general reasons to justify acts of terrorism are explored. Applying these insights to the attacks of September 11, the discussion moves to consider what sort of claims would be required to provide sufficient justification for them. It is suggested that certain religious claims might be sufficient to justify these attacks but that these claims do face serious objections. Discussion then turns to a more general concern, namely the worry about the potential for conflict between one's religious obligations and one's moral duties. Tackling the thorny question of determining the appropriate procedure for deciding what to do in cases of conflict between religion and moral duty, an argument is presented that the September 11 attacks are to be faulted for failing to use such a procedure. The conclusion develops a suggestion as to what might be done philosophically to help prevent further terrorist attacks.

THE NATURE OF EVIL

In this chapter, terrorism is defined as *the systematic use of terror as a means of coercion.* Given this definition, the events of September 11 were clearly acts of terrorism. They involved the systematic use of terror. Their apparent intention was to intimidate and coerce the United States. Still, those who organized and undertook these actions regarded them as good things to have done. This presents a confusing situation, as the September 11 attacks have also been widely regarded as a remarkable instance of great evil. How could things that are considered to be so evil also be considered good? Before attempting to answer this disturbing question one should first consider a more basic preliminary question, namely, What is evil?

A common approach is to urge that, while evil cannot be defined, one can still provide a long list of items that everyone would agree count as instances of evil. A serious problem for the list approach account of evil is that it leaves unanswered the deeper question of why certain items make it onto the list and why others do not. To help find a more satisfactory account of evil, it is useful consider four common but flawed conceptions of evil, namely the simple "badness" theory, the wickedness theory, the rule-breaking theory, and the bad-consequences theory. Examination of these faulty approaches will help define the parameters for a more adequate account of evil.

The "badness" theory of evil is an obvious starting point. According to this view, "evil" is just another term for "bad." To attribute evil to some item is just to think of it as a bad thing. The main advantage of the view is that one does find the concept of evil being applied to lots of bad things. A serious problem the view faces, however, is that many bad things are not plausibly construed as evil. Examples include unforeseen accidents and genetic diseases. These unfortunate items, though bad, just do not seem to count as instances of evil. Something crucial is lacking. (The reader is encouraged to speculate just what might be missing.)

The wickedness theory, as articulated by Midgley (1992), flows from a traditional religious context, in which evil is seen as being contrary to the will of God. The view finds supporters among those who point to horrible things that have been done in disobedience to God. Still, the theory is inadequate. It is of no help if one wishes to use the concept of evil but is uncertain about the existence of God. It also blocks attempts by serious religious critics (e.g., Spong, 2001) to classify some acts traditionally ascribed to God as evil. Further, those who claim that God approved of the September 11 attacks would be able to deny that the attacks were evil. Most critically, the wickedness theory makes investigating the nature of evil incomprehensible, as God could have commanded any action. If one agrees with Plato's classic (1961) critique in his dialogue, *The Euthyphro,* that God must have a good reason for commanding some things and not others, one must reject the wickedness theory.

Some take the rigid following of rules to be the essence of morality and the breaking of rules to be the essence of evil. Moral developmental theorists claim that human beings naturally go through a period of identifying evil with the breaking of rules. In favor of this account of evil, we should admit that many rule-breakers and rule-breakings are surely evil. On the rule-breaking account of evil, however, it is impossible to ask what rules one should follow. Moreover, some claim to be able to find moral rules that the perpetrators of the September 11 attacks followed in carrying them out. This view also makes it impossible to explain why rule-following can sometimes be evil. (One remembers the famous refrain from many who participated in the Nazi Holocaust, "I was just following orders!") Further, significant rule-breaking (such as civil disobedience against unjust laws during the civil rights movement of the 1960s) can sometimes not be evil, but morally praiseworthy.

The most plausible of the initial accounts of evil is the consequences theory, the view that actions that bring about bad consequences are evil. Support for this view is evident in commonly cited examples of evil, genocide, slavery, torture, and so on. But, this simple view cannot explain why the same consequences can sometimes be part of an evil action and sometimes part of a non-evil action. While appeal to consequences is part of the correct approach to evil, it is inadequate as a complete account. To demonstrate this claim, imagine two horrible events, the September 11 attacks and a terrible hurricane, say hurricane Andrew. Suppose both involved the same amount of death and destruction. While it is natural to call the first event evil, it does not seem appropriate to regard the second event as evil. Why not? The answer is that the existence of evil requires an agent's intending to cause harm or suffering. The hurricane is not evil, because neither it nor the damage it created was caused by anyone's intention. The hurricane is considered to be an event that just happened. The September 11 attacks, on the other hand, did not just happen. They were intentionally carried out for the express purpose of causing harm and suffering. That is why they are commonly regarded as evil. Were it to be discovered that the hurricane had been caused by human action as part of a deliberate plot to control weather patterns and extort money, it, too, would be considered evil.

Although the above four attempts to characterize evil are either inadequate or face serious objection, they do point in the direction of a more adequate theory of evil. The theory of evil proposed in this chapter is the following:

> An agent is evil just in case the agent intentionally causes suffering and harm to others.
> An action is evil just in case an evil agent causes it.

This theory of evil has important advantages over those proposed above. It captures the importance of intention in evil, it clearly demarcates evil things within the larger category of bad things, it explains why the breaking of some rules counts as evil and the breaking of other rules does not, it recognizes the importance of consequences, and it does not restrict evil only to contexts involving God, so that those who are not believers may also make meaningful use of the concept. This account of evil, like those already mentioned, must be scrutinized further to see if it can withstand critical inspection. One challenge is to see if one can think of any clear-cut cases of evil that would not count as evil under this definition. Another challenge is to see if one can think of cases of the intentional infliction of harm and suffering on others that do not count as cases of evil. If persuasive examples of either sort can be produced, the proposed theory of evil would need to be modified. These important challenges are left as exercises for the reader. With a tentative theory of evil in hand, the discussion now turns to consider why terrorist actions, such as the September 11 attacks, are such remarkable examples of evil.

THE EVIL OF TERRORISM

It is a truism that acts of terrorism are designed to induce terror in those who experience them. It is the experiencing of terror that helps give a terrorist action its especially profound sense of evil. But what does this deep sense of evil really involve? Is it really correct to hold that terrorist actions are more evil than nonterrorist actions? It would be a mistake to claim that terrorist actions are intrinsically more evil that other evil actions. A terrorist action and a nonterrorist action might both involve an intention to harm as well as the same number of victims and the same amount of harm and suffering. In such a case it would seem purely arbitrary to claim that one action had to be significantly more evil than the other. Consider, for example, the famous Nazi-led genocide of the Holocaust. Those who carried out the Holocaust took steps to limit the terror its victims experienced so as to make the operation more efficient. The Holocaust, nonetheless, was certainly as morally heinous as most any human endeavor could be.

What does seem correct is that a terrorist action involving directly harming, say, ten people would, in fact, be more evil than a nonterrorist action that directly harmed the same ten individuals. The reason is that a terrorist action not only aims at direct harm but it also aims at producing indirect harm as well in the form of the induction of prolonged fear (terror) in many others. So, a terrorist action that directly harms ten will indirectly (and to a lesser extent) harm many more than ten. It is the additional terror that makes a terrorist bombing, for example, worse than a nonterrorist killing.

The intention of creating terror is often as much aimed at the bystanders, observers, and fellow group members of the victims of the action as aimed at its victims. Moreover, acts of terror are typically not aimed at specific victims, the way that most evil actions are. Most people who commit evil actions aim to deprive specific people of some specific thing. Evil actions targeting specific individuals are easier for us to comprehend than those that are aimed at destroying just anyone who happens to be in a particular place. It is easier to understand an intention to steal from someone, or even to kill a specific person, than to commit random actions of death and destruction. Individual base motives of wanting something that someone else has (greed) or wanting to get rid of a rival (competition) or to hurt a specific person who has harmed one (revenge) are all emotions experienced early in development, and against which one is typically taught to strive. Acts of terrorism, on the other hand, when not motivated by greed or by obvious competition or a clear line of revenge, are harder to understand. The motives involved must include an abstract ideological component, one with which the observers of the event have little sympathy or awareness. This lack of understanding is an important element behind what makes terrorist acts such as the September 11 hijackings seem so profoundly evil. An evil action that one does not grasp, that follows no patterns of behavior with which one is familiar, will strike one as purely gratuitous.

A second important element that makes terrorist actions such as the September 11 attacks seem so deeply evil comes from a consideration of the victims of terrorism. As the victims of terrorist actions are not specifically chosen individuals, those who identify with the victims, either in terms of ethnicity, religion, nationality, or social class, naturally come to feel that they, too, might have been victims of that particular terrorist attack, that the terrorists were aiming just as much at them as at the actual victims. A person naturally feels that had he or she been at the right place at the right time, he or she would also have been targeted. It is this sense of a terrorist action's aiming at an abstract group, not at specific individuals, that makes the evil, for being impersonal, seem even more inhumane, as the action is interpreted as a potential attack against oneself as well as an actual attack its actual victims.

A third important factor concerns the perception of the randomness of the choice of victim of most acts of terrorism. Most acts of terrorism these days are not aimed at specific people for what they have done but rather at members of a particular group who happen to be in a particular place at a particular time. Terrorist activity increases the randomness of an environment. One can no longer plan on going to a particular place, using a particular method of transportation, shopping, eating, drinking, or being entertained in normal way, without the increased possibility of serious problems for the traveler or consumer. The greater the amount of perceived randomness in one's environment, the less predictable the immediate future is, the more disturbing one's life will be. A sense of order and pattern is required for the making of life plans. The insertion of unpredictable, random evils into one's environment calls into question the reasonableness of any plans one might have made about the future. It puts all of one's immediate life plans on hold.

These three factors help the reader better understand why so many feel so deeply about the September 11 attacks. The discussion now set its sights on to the task of trying to understand why they happened. This is not an easy matter. It is not plausible to construe the attacks as acts of mass hysteria, the result of food poisoning or some other natural, non-human cause. It also seems clear that these events did not just happen but were deliberately brought about by careful planning and training. Given that the actions were deliberate, it is important to try to ask the important question, Why? Why did they happen? This question is ambiguous between asking, What caused the actions? and What reasons motivated the actions? Speculation as to what factors caused the nineteen hijackers to act as they did is better left to forensic psychologists. To ask, however, for persuasive reasons that might have made the September 11 attacks seem reasonable to their perpetrators, and then to examine whether those reasons really were good reasons, is to request philosophical help.

THE JUSTIFICATION OF TERRORISM

What sort of justification might plausibly be given for the September 11 attacks? It is widely accepted that actions such as the September 11 hijackings were evil. Even those who supported the crashes have claimed that similar actions against members of their own culture were evil. Still, it does not follow from the simple fact that a set of actions produces evil that these actions should not be carried out. It is always possible for someone to defend an evil action as a good thing to do. How might such a defense proceed? One can defend an evil action as a good thing to do by claiming that there was a very good reason for doing the action. Producing such a reason and demonstrating that the reason was in fact a good reason is what is involved in giving an explicit justification for doing a particular evil.

One attempt to justify the September 11 attacks involves an appeal to differences in cultural practices. Some may point out that terrorist practices are customary in some cultures but not in others. Those who embrace *moral relativism,* the view that morality consists of following the customs of one's own culture, will suggest that terrorism is justified for members of cultures that advocate it. If the perpetrators of the September 11 attacks come from such cultures, then, according to the moral relativist, their actions were morally justified. But as critics (e.g., Moody-Adams, 1997) have noted, moral relativism is not a satisfactory theory. Why should slavery, female genital mutilation, and killing of twins upon birth, which are still practiced in different cultures, be respected? Why should terrorism being acceptable in some cultures make it morally permissible to inflict terror on cultures that reject terrorism? In addition, moral relativists confront the related difficulty that they cannot explain what should happen when different cultures with different customs come into conflict over those customs. Moral relativists have no resources within their view for resolving such conflicts.

Defenders of moral relativism typically defend their view by appealing to (1) the importance of tolerating differences and by claiming that (2) the great diversity of cultural practices makes it impossible to find any nonarbitrary distinction between good practices and bad practices. Both arguments merit further scrutiny. First, the argument from tolerance is powerful for Americans because U.S. culture officially values tolerance. Tolerance, however, is not highly regarded in all cultures. In fact, anyone who engages in terrorism is clearly guilty of not respecting tolerance. So, it is ridiculous to appeal to tolerance to justify terrorism. Second, to defeat the claim that there are no nonarbitrary ways of determining what is good or bad, one only needs to mention some powerful nonarbitrary ways of distinguishing good practices from bad practices. Two of the most common examples are (1) the appeal to fairness, and (2) the appeal to consequences—promoting good consequences and minimizing bad ones. These are both widely regarded as important features of nonrelative, objective morality. So, attempts to defend common attempts to defend moral relativism seem to fail. Since the view also faces serious objections, if an evil is to be justified, some other approach is required. It may help to look at some clear cases of justified evil.

There are many ordinary examples of doing evil that are typically taken to be justified. One obvious example involves the harm inflicted on an assailant to protect oneself or others from harm. A person is typically taken to be justified in harming someone if this harm is necessary to for self-defense to protect other innocent people. (Only the amount of harm necessary for protection is allowed, however.) Another example concerns the infliction of short-term harm and suffering on someone for the purpose of bringing about some greater good for that person. Thus, children receive painful inoculations against dreadful diseases even though the measures used involve the infliction of some suffering. There are many medical procedures in which a short-term infliction of pain and suffering is justified in the name of increased health for which the suffering is necessary. A third example has to do with the punishment of individuals who have broken legitimate rules and have hurt others. The punishment of children by their parents is typically justified by parents claiming that it is in the long-term interest of the children to be punished so as to improve their behavior in the future, which in turn will bring about a more productive and thus happier future for the children. The punishment of criminals is justified by the state with claims that it is important to have a means of deterring further crime, of preventing further crime by the same individual, and of attempting to rehabilitate the criminal by improving how the criminal will behave in society. A fourth example involves the extreme case of sacrificing a part in order to save a larger whole. Thus, commanders in time of war will often knowingly sacrifice one unit for the sake of saving the rest of an army. Many of the most heroic individuals involved in the aftermath of the September 11 attacks included those who sacrificed themselves for the sake of saving others. All of these different instances involve an evil, a case of intentionally caused harm and suffering. But, in each case the harm and suffering are given a specific reason, typically in terms of fairness or good consequences, which serve to justify the action.

An important historical example of justifying state-sponsored terrorism relates to the destruction of Hiroshima and Nagasaki with nuclear weapons by U.S. bombers at the end of World War II. Defenders of these actions, which caused the deaths of over 250,000 civilians, argued that the terror caused by the nuclear bombings would induce the Japanese government to surrender. A Japanese surrender, it was argued, would in turn save the lives of at least a million people. The greater good of the surrender was used to justify the evil of the huge number of horrible deaths caused by the bombings. Whether this justification of the bombings is really compelling continues to be a matter of heated controversy to this day.

An interesting religious example that appears to fit the definition of terrorism is the story from the Book of Exodus of God's inflicting ten plagues on Egypt in order to cause the Pharaoh of Egypt to allow the Israelites to return to their homeland. The express purpose of the plagues, including locusts, cattle sickness, and death to first-born males, was to create sufficient terror to coerce the ruler of Egypt to change his mind about allowing the Israelites to leave Egypt. The justification given for inflicting plagues on the Egyptians was the greater good of freeing the Israelites from bondage. What is significant about this example is that it appears to be an act of divine terrorism, terrorism directly performed by God. For religious believers who contemplate performing acts of terrorism, knowing of powerful examples of God's performing similar actions provides strong support. It is again worth noting that some religious authors (e.g., Spong, 2001) do not agree with the adequacy of the proposed justification of the plagues inflicted upon Egypt.

Any attempt to justify a specific evil is part of an important perennial philosophical worry that has bothered humans at least since the discovery of monotheism. Monotheism is the view that there is one God. Monotheists (hereafter, theists) include Jews, Christians, and Muslims. Their three religions, Judaism, Christianity, and Islam, account for about half of the world's population. Theists typically endow their deity, God, with very impressive attributes including the features of being all-good, all-powerful, and all-knowing. What is traditionally called the Problem of Evil for theists is the difficulty of making sense out of why God, a being who is supposed to be all-good, all-powerful, and all-knowing, would allow evil to exist in the world. Since an all-good being would not want evil to exist, and an all-powerful being would be able to prevent evil and an all-knowing being would know what evil to prevent, any being that had all three features should be able to create a world without evil. Yet, there is evil in the world. Why does God allow it? This, as classically presented by Hume (1998), is the Problem of Evil.

The existence of evil is not a problem for the atheist. If there is no God, only humans could cause or prevent evil, and it is well known how limited humans are in their abilities to prevent suffering to others. In fact, the atheist typically takes the problem of evil to support the claim that there is no God. If there is no God, it is even more difficult to find any good reason that might justify the September 11 attacks. If the atheist cannot appeal to God to justify the attacks, some other element needs to be found to constitute some greater good item that the attacks would produce, such as, perhaps, self-protection from the United States or perhaps an end to oppression against certain cultures by the United States. But, it is hard to see how the September 11 attacks were connected to either a legitimate right to self-defense or to a reasonable effort to end oppression. The victims of the attacks were not directly engaged in attacking other cultures, not does the link between the attacks and ending oppression seem at all clear, let alone defensible. For the typical atheist the horrific events of September 11 could and should have been avoided. The perpetrators of the tragedy, however, were not atheists, but were devout theists. Therefore, for them there must have been reasons to justify their actions that would be consistent with their theism. So, the rest of this section will pursue the perspective of the theist who is serious about trying to explain why evil in general exists.

Some have attempted to avoid the Problem of Evil by asserting that evil is an illusion or by claiming that God is either not all-powerful or not all-knowing or not all-good. These strategies are not convincing. The traditional theist does not wish to weaken God for fear of being left with a being not worthy of worship. The claim that evil does not exist is hard to take seriously, especially when one considers events such as the September 11 attacks. Why did God allow these events to take place? God surely knew about them, knew them to be evil, and could easily have prevented them (by making the perpetrators fall asleep on their airplanes after takeoff and have them wake up upon arrival). If human beings can easily imagine a safe and painless way to interfere to prevent the September 11 tragedies, God could have done as well. So why did they happen? This is a specific version of the Problem of Evil. The traditional religious believer would like to discover a convincing reason for God to allow evil, including the events of September 11. The question then to be faced is whether defenders of the September 11 attacks can also use a similar justification, or whether some other reason might be found.

Among the more common reasons to justify God's allowing the existence of evil in the world are the following:

1. Evil is necessary for moral knowledge; without evil one would not know the difference between right and wrong.
2. Evil is part of a test by God to determine whether one merits a good or bad after-life.
3. Evil is the result of human free will, and it is better that humans act freely and cause evil than not cause evil but be deprived of free will.
4. Evil is a part of God's plan according to which everything works out for the best; human beings are too limited to understand God's plan.

It is easy to see why (1) is inadequate. It is implausible to suppose that the September 11 plane crashes were necessary for anyone to get adequate moral knowledge of the difference between right and wrong. Thousands of lives did not have to be sacrificed to make the point. The witnessing of relatively few deaths would have made the matter clear to anyone capable of having moral knowledge.

With a bit more effort one can also see that (2) is not satisfactory. The basic problem here has to do with the unfairness of the test given to those who suffered directly as a result of September 11 plane crashes compared to the relatively easy test given to many others. To claim that everyone suffers equally in this world seems to ignore the obvious fact that many have much better lives than others. Were this not so, no one would ever envy anyone else.

One of the most common attempts to explain away evil involves (3), the appeal to the value of human free will. The basic problem with this strategy for dealing with evil is that while free will is widely regarded as valuable, it is not the only thing of value. Often one is willing to sacrifice some freedom for the sake of other values. For example, in the United States children are required to attend school for their own good until the age of 16. They are not permitted to choose whether they wish to attend school. While one may value one's own freedom very highly, it is clear that most do not also highly value the freedom of criminals and convicted felons. Otherwise they would not be imprisoned. And, as Kraemer and Jones (1986) argue, it is worth questioning whether the freedom of the nineteen hijackers to cause the September 11 attacks was really worth thousands of innocent lives.

These complaints should make it clear why attempts to demonstrate clearly why God allows evil in the world encounters three standard problems: (1) There is too much evil to be explained away, (2) God could achieve good results without evil, and (3) The alleged good proposed to justify evil is not worth the evil it requires. With these three objections lying in wait for any direct attempt to explain away the evil one finds in the world—including acts of terrorism—the theist will often opt for another, indirect strategy. The appeal to God's plan and human ignorance of it is the answer to which traditional theists are typically forced when trying to defend against the Problem of Evil. According to this strategy, God does have a plan according to which everything works out for the best. Human beings, however, are ignorant of what God's plan is. Moreover, according to the standard version of the strategy, humans are just not able to comprehend the enormous complexity of the divine plan. While not wholly satisfactory, it turns out to be harder to demonstrate as conclusively as in the previous three cases that the appeal to God's plan cannot be a serious answer. After all, human beings are limited in what they know and can understand. And, certainly, God must be much more knowledgeable than any human. It is not surprising that many find it comforting to think that there must be some reason beyond human comprehension that justifies the September 11 attacks. The appeal to God's plan, nevertheless, does not provide one with understanding as to why a particular tragedy strikes. This strategy does not clearly explain, for example, why the September 11 plane crashes occurred. One cannot satisfactorily explicate why it should not have been better for the four flights in question all to arrive safely at their destinations. This strategy does make clear, however, why one cannot get rid of one's ignorance about the existence of evil. That is what gives the strategy wide appeal. It appeases the human quest for knowledge with the proposed remedy that many (e.g., Plantinga, 2000) have suggested, human beings must be humble because some knowledge lies beyond them.

To be sure, there are objections to this strategy. Some may urge that if humans are smart enough to build space stations and go to the moon then they are smart enough to understand why there has to be as much evil as there is in the world. Others may argue that this strategy sounds like a conspiracy to hide the truth about evil from humans. Still others may wonder whether an all-powerful, all-knowing, and all-good being would be unable to teach human beings well enough to understand why evil exists. While these complaints may make some theists (e.g., Kelly, 2002) uncomfortable, most will probably continue to hold their ground and reassert with confidence their ignorance of God's plan.

There is, however, a further consideration that many should find disturbing. The defenders of the September 11 attacks may also insist, in spite of the incredulity of millions, that the plane crashes really were not only justified as part of God's plan, but, further, that they really were good actions to have carried out because of some hidden feature that most human beings, especially those who do not follow the correct religious faith, are too limited to comprehend. That is, if the traditional theist can use the appeal to God's plan as a strategy for explaining why evil in general occurs, including the September 11 hijackings, then the Taliban defender of the goodness of the attacks would be justified in using the same strategy to defend the basic goodness of actions that Americans, because of their ignorance of God's plan, mistakenly take to be a horrible tragedy. This result should be quite disturbing for theists who wish both to defend God and to condemn the September 11 attacks. Although many might claim that there is an important difference between their own use of the strategy and a Taliban supporter's use of the same strategy, until a clear, non-question-begging difference is presented there is no good reason either to accept or reject the strategy.

An additional attempt to justify the September 11 plane crashes has been proposed. Some religious fundamentalists argue that one is justified in using any manner of evil against an infidel (someone who does not adhere to the correct religious faith) when doing so is necessary to promote a holy cause. So, if the application of terrorism will serve to further God's purposes and no other means will work as well or better, terrorism is justified. For some, this seems the appropriate moral justification to give for the September 11 attacks. Such an argument is not limited to some followers of Islam. The same reasoning is powerfully present in the Old Testament as a justification for the removal of the Canaanites in favor of the Israelites in the Promised Land. Since Jews and Christians accept the Old Testament, it would be inconsistent for them to deny the use of this principle to others. It should be remembered that this principle has played an important historical role in Christianity, as the Crusades, Inquisition, Wars of Religion, and the continuing conflict in Northern Ireland demonstrate. The principle that it is right to use evil against infidels to further holy purposes has also played a major role in Jewish history, and some in Israel today insist on making it part of current state policy.

Theists who accept the principle that it is right to use evil against infidels to further holy purposes but also take the September 11 attacks to be an unnecessary evil must also reject the claim that the September 11 attacks were legitimate applications of this principle. A daunting difficulty these theists face is that of showing that the September 11 attacks were, in fact, contrary to God's plan and that there was no holy cause to be furthered by carrying them out. If these theists also admit that God's plan is hidden, it then turns out to be enormously difficult to demonstrate on religious grounds alone that the September 11 attacks were an unnecessary evil and served no holy cause. If God's plan is really hidden, then, for all anyone can say, any action, even an act of terrorism on the scale of the September 11 hijackings, may, for all humans can determine, have been sanctioned by God.

In this section two explicitly religious reasons have been proposed to justify the September 11 tragedy that do not face obvious decisive refutation from theists. Further, theists have typically used these reasons. Thus, it would be disturbingly inconsistent for theists to claim that there are no powerful reasons to justify the September 11 plane crashes if the reasons that are being offered are the very sorts of reasons they appeal to in other contexts. Controversy certainly remains as to whether the two principles, "God's hidden plan explains evil," and "Evil may be inflicted on infidels for holy purposes," have been correctly applied to the September 11 attacks. But, no purely religious procedure has yet been discerned that would help all theists decide the controversy.

There is a further point worth considering. Suppose the nineteen perpetrators of the September 11 attacks held what many take to be incorrect beliefs, namely the belief that God has commanded the destruction of the World Trade Center and the Pentagon and the belief that destroying these buildings will bring about a valuable spiritual renewal of Islamic tradition. Is it is really appropriate to blame individuals who happened to hold these two religious beliefs and act on them? It might be appropriate if all human beings had significant control over which beliefs—including religious beliefs—they hold. But, this is controversial. For many it seems largely a matter of luck, based primarily on culture, family upbringing, or chance experience with other faiths, that a given religious system will exert the greatest influence. This realization should make it much harder to continue to condemn personally those who thought they were being devout while engaging in evil actions. Instead, it seems, one should criticize the religious system that influenced their evil behavior. But, how are religious systems to be criticized? What kinds of criticisms are fair from those who also hold strong religious views? How can one attack the religiously influenced views of someone else without also opening oneself up to the same sorts of criticisms that one is giving of others? These are difficult problems. The discussion now moves to consider the difficult question of terrorism and religious differences.

RELIGION AND TERROR

The connection between terror and some religions should not be surprising. Many important world religions serve as a potential source of inspiration for terror, hence, for some, of terrorism as well. These would seem to include religions that emphasize the details that will follow in an "afterlife," especially religions that detail horrible punishments (Hell) that non-believers and religious transgressors will receive for not behaving as required by religious teaching as well as those which specify wonderful rewards (Heaven) for those who "smite the infidel." It should be expected that some religious practitioners would identify with the religious force that metes out horrible punishments to nonbelievers, viewing efforts to copy these behaviors as religiously sanctioned. A study of history also reveals the disturbing tendency of many to employ terror to coerce those who do not behave as prescribed by a particular religion as a means to providing their victims with a better afterlife, as well as providing perpetrators of acts of terror with a better afterlife than they might otherwise receive.

When contemplating an alleged religiously justified act of terrorism one needs to step back and ask some hard questions. For simplicity, consider only those who claim to have been authorized by their own God to commit a terrorist action, X. The questions then to ask are the following. (1) How strong is the evidence that God has commanded X or X would meet God's approval? (2) Is the evidence of God's support for X something that is widely shared or is it limited? (3) Are there strong nonreligious reasons not to commit X even if X meets God's approval? And, finally, (4) should one commit X if there are both strong nonreligious reasons not to do so as well as a religious reason for doing so? Each of these questions merits further examination.

One perennial problem for those who claim that they have been asked by God to engage in a special mission of terror is the difficulty of convincing others of the request. What is taken to be religious evidence occurs in a variety of ways. In addition to reliance on special religious texts, there are those who claim to have had special dreams, seen visions, experienced deep mystical states, or had special religious perceptions. For each of these ways of getting evidence, the skeptic will issue hard challenges. Is the religious text really clear in commanding X or are there other, equally plausible interpretations? Similarly, are the dreams, visions, mystical states, and religious perceptions all equally unambiguous? Are the texts and various experiences all trustworthy and completely unambiguous, or is there good reason to doubt their authenticity or interpretation? There are several reasons why these questions are indeed serious. First, human beings are fallible; they make mistakes of interpretation. Second, having evidence is required for knowledge—it is obvious that merely wanting some claim to be true is not a sufficient reason for thinking that in fact it is true. Third, a quick study of history reveals evidence of past hoaxes and fraud regarding claims to special evidence. Thus, with respect to any person's claim to have been commanded by God to do X, it is always possible to ask whether the evidence is sufficient, whether there might have been a mistake in interpreting the evidence, or whether there might be some fraud involved.

This then leads to the second concern, whether there is shared evidence. One crucial way to check one's claims to have knowledge is to see what support one can find from others. If several people all claim to have acquired strong evidence to do X, this tends to make the claim more reasonable to accept. Because there are well-documented cases of mass hysteria, however, one cannot assume a group asserting a claim makes it necessarily correct. Still, if there are several independent supporters of a given thesis, this does strengthen the proposal by making it less likely that misinterpretation was involved in the claim. A further feature by which to judge the claim of a group in favor of a particular thesis is the relative heterogeneity or homogeneity of the group. The claim of a group that consists only of members with very similar backgrounds is much weaker that a similar claim from a group with very different members.

A third consideration to be addressed by those contemplating doing terrorist action X is whether there are other reasons that might be adduced against doing it. What reasons might these be? First, one should ask whether there are also general religious reasons against doing X. Most religions have general prohibitions against killing and inflicting harm against others and against endangering the religious community. A second kind of reason to consider is what ethical reasons might be given against doing X. If the contemplated action is evil, if it involves inflicting great harm and suffering on others, this counts strongly against doing it. A third kind of reason is prudential. Is X contrary to its perpetrator's self-interest? Is X likely to provoke reprisals that will harm the perpetrator's community? Positive answers to any of these queries are important countervailing forces against religious reasons to do X.

The fourth and most difficult question now commands attention. Most acts of terrorism having religious reasons in their favor will also have ethical and prudential reasons *against* committing them. This presents a conflict between different kinds of reasons. When there is such a conflict, which side, the religious or nonreligious, should prevail? Many, perhaps including the perpetrators of the September 11 attacks, would assert that, in cases of conflict between religion and ethics, religion should always prevail. Those who follow the primacy of religion approach (e.g., Quinn, 1995) will argue that religious loyalty transcends all other commitments, as one's religion is the most important force in anyone's life. The difficulty for terrorists who embrace this approach is that they have no means of arguing coherently against those who wish to perform, based on alternative religious reasons, the same action against the terrorists' own community. The primacy of religion approach in a religiously diverse world condemns the world to perpetual violence.

Others, though, will assert that in cases of conflict ethics should prevail over religion. A typical argument for this view is that one should reject any religious claim that conflicts with an ethical claim as being suspect, since ethics is primary, and since religion is only acceptable if it supports ethics. This approach, while attractive and avoiding the problem faced above, is probably too idealistic to hope for its widespread acceptance. Most human beings identify themselves as being members of a specific faith community. And, the political and economic forces of religion, as Barber (1995) observes, are very strong; frequently, religion is tied to group identity. Criticism of a religion for being unethical is often interpreted, usually incorrectly, as a criticism of the members of the religious group.

A third alternative would be to insist, following important work by Audi (2000), that any action one contemplates doing must have the agreement both of one's strongest religious reasons as well as one's most persuasive ethical reasons. In cases in which there is no agreement, the individual should refrain from acting. This approach seems like a more realistic candidate for widespread acceptance. First, it does not pose a direct rejection of religious reasons, only a tempering of religion with ethics, while allowing religion its due role. Further, in a world in which the importance of human interdependence is widely recognized, it accords to others the same ethical status one would want to have accorded by others to oneself. Thus, there is an element of fairness that can be used to justify the policy. Also, if one realizes that one cannot survive well unless others in other groups do too, this recognition may help temper ill treatment of others. So, this policy also has the advantage of prudence to recommend it. The policy also affords an additional measure of fairness by requiring a common ethical standard for all.

With so much support, it seems reasonable to propose a procedure that one who accepts this third approach should follow in considering whether to perform a particular terrorist action. Whenever anyone is considering performing any evil action such as an act of terrorism, one needs first to ask what possible justification could be given to demonstrate that the action was, overall, good, that is, either required or praiseworthy instead of being overall bad, that is, defective or worthy of criticism. If no reasons can be found, either religious or ethical, then the action should not be performed, since by hypothesis it is evil. Suppose, however, that both religious and ethical reasons can be found. One then collects the various reasons that can be offered, both the reasons that the planned action is good and that the reasons that the planned action is bad. After examining the reasons, one needs to decide which reasons are religious and which are ethical. One then needs to determine whether the policy recommended by one's strongest religious reasons match up with the policy recommended by one's strongest ethical reasons. If there is no such agreement, one should not proceed with the planned terrorist action.

One criticism that can be brought against the perpetrators of the September 11 attacks and their supporters is that they failed to follow such a procedure. Had they done so, the absence of agreement between their religious and nonreligious reasons would have prevented the attacks from taking place.

This section ends with a plea to those who are considering the use of terror, including Americans and their allies, as well as their enemies. The plea is that any would-be terrorist seriously ponders in every case whether there might be alternative methods that would better achieve the terrorist's goals. Some of the most impressive changes in the past century were accomplished not by means of terror, but by its opposite. (Here one thinks of the powerful examples of the work of Gandhi and Martin Luther King, Jr.) On the other hand, it is hard to think of many situations in which the use of terror produced a lasting and peaceful improvement. The problem with terror is that it tends to produce retaliation in kind among the survivors. Once retaliation commences, as Northern Ireland, Israel, and the West Bank demonstrate, it become very difficult to stop.

TERRORISM AND WORLD ETHICS

The tragic events of September 11 raise a final important concern with which to end this exercise in applied moral philosophy. This is the concern of how large groups of peoples, nations, religious groups, ethnic groups, and so on should interact with each other.

While it has already been argued that the attacks of September 11 are not morally justifiable, that the arguments that attempt to justify the attacks are seriously flawed, and that those who support these attacks are guilty of either a remarkable ignorance, considerable moral self-deception or blatant hypocrisy, it does not follow that there is nothing more to be said about the matter. For one thing, it has been suggested that the same criticism of supporters of the September 11 hijackings also apply to many who would urge certain retaliatory actions against other groups of people and that the same bad arguments are being made to rationalize these unjustifiable actions.

There is still the nagging question of why so much hatred of the United States has been created, whether there are factors that those in the United States should be ashamed of, factors that would have played a role in creating individuals able to do what the perpetrators of the September 11 attacks did. Simple-minded explanations that have been bandied about (the hijackers were jealous, they did not have the correct religion, they were raised in a different way, they value human life differently, etc.) are not sufficient. So it is important to keep asking about this incident, as one should continue inquiring about other, seemingly inexplicable horrors such as the Holocaust and the institution of slavery, for deeper, more satisfying explanations, ones that will really fit all the pieces of these puzzles together. As an essay in philosophy, however, this discussion will not attempt to offer such an explanation. From reading some of the other essays in this volume, from reading additional literature that is suggested, from keeping current on additional information that is discovered, it seems likely that the reader will become better informed in the future as to why these horrible actions occurred. But, one also needs to admit that one may not be happy with the explanations that are put forward. Some of them may turn out to contain elements that will make Americans uncomfortable.

Suppose the United States had been a totally insignificant country with very little wealth or power. Or, suppose the United States had been a country with no history of ever interfering in the internal affairs of other countries, with no record of defending U.S. business interests abroad using tactics that are not domestically acceptable, with no record of U.S. citizens attempting to export their religion, customs, franchises, and so on elsewhere to compete with local cultures. Or, suppose the United States to be a country with a record of doing what ever good it could in any way it could no matter what the expense, with a commitment to using a really significant portion of its gross national product to combat disease, poverty, and malnutrition outside its boarders, then the events of September 11 would have been harder to comprehend. While it is true that the United States does do and has done much good, it is not these good things that cause others to attack. The question "Why did September 11 happen?" is a nagging one that refuses to be silenced with easy answers. For now it is important to consider developing a new mindset with which better to appraise additional information, a new perspective with which to try to evaluate both terrorism and attempts to respond to it.

Much of traditional ethics concerns individual relations. Political philosophy is mainly devoted to discussion of relations between individuals and the state. But, what about relations between states, relations involving the whole world? It seems that traditional philosophy has not had much interest in this topic. Yet, this may be the most important ethical concern that all human beings will face in the twenty-first century. Call the concern "World Ethics." What should be the perspective on ethics that would emerge from the viewpoint of the whole world? Suppose one were to try seriously to take every person, every group, every significant ethical stakeholder into account when we ask about moral-ity. Suppose one were to try to include not just oneself, one's family, friends, co-religionists, region, or country, in one's moral deliberation, but were to try instead to encompass the whole of the world. This, as Rachels (1992) urges, should also include nonhumans. This perspective, though daunting in its scope, is clearly in agreement with the teachings of most of the world's great religious and moral traditions. It is not, however, the standard ap-proach that is advocated in international affairs.

If one follows a common view in political theorizing, an approach clearly articulated early in Plato's classic, *The Republic,* justice is not a matter of acting fairly but just "the advantage of the stronger" (Plato, 1961). While Plato rejects this view as applied to an in-dividual state, it has been a dominant outlook in international relations, and it continues to cause problems. What the view entails is that when it comes to disputes one can only look to force to resolve them. The stronger party will win out over those who are weaker. This approach to international or interregional relations abandons all hope of trying to ask who should be doing what for whom. It gives up on the attempt to figure out what is a fair dis-tribution based on a decent basic minimum set of consequences for all. It says that while a group may have a standard of right conduct for its own culture, it will not be concerned to apply the same standard to those who are outside of one's own group. Instead, the only concern will be either to dominate other groups or at least avoid being dominated by them. Such an approach will perpetuate the tendency to commit acts of terrorism which is al-ready much too prevalent.

There is, perhaps, a lesson to be learned from the official "War on Terrorism" that the U.S. government quickly declared in the aftermath of September 11. One way of try-ing to understand this phrase is to see it as merely organizing acts of aggression against all those who aggress against others by committing terrorist actions. This perspective is not consistent with a world ethics perspective, for it pits one group, the victims of terrorism, against another group, the perpetrators of terrorist acts, valuing only the first group. If this is all that the official "War on Terrorism" comes to, then it is probably doomed to failure. The reason is that it employs the wrong model for the cause of terrorism. It assumes an analogy with the germ theory of disease, according to which there are special "bad" agents, germs that cause diseases and need to be eradicated to bring about a cure. Terrorists, however, are not special "bad" agents, such that getting rid of all currently ex-isting terrorists will mean the end of terrorism. Most terrorism, as Merlou-Ponty (2000) noted, is caused by oppressive political and social contexts. So, if the "War on Terrorism" aims not against individuals but instead attacks the social and political conditions that cause terrorism to appear, such a war seems to have a much better chance of success. This approach, however, uses a different model, namely a health model, according to which everyone, if exposed to the right conditions, can be helped to experience health. This ap-proach to terrorism, like the "War on Poverty" from the 1960s, aims at social and political change as the key. Such an approach is consistent with a world ethics perspective, as it does not create separate categories of individuals with different moral standards to apply to each.

The world ethics perspective is one that seeks to avoid the selfishness typical of in-dividual nations or groups (which mirrors the selfishness typical of certain individuals). It also attempts to avoid only being wholly altruistic, in the sense of always putting others above oneself (as is characteristic of some, noble self-sacrificing individuals), but includes a proper inclusion of one's own group in moral calculations. Nagel (1991) has complained that such an approach is not possible, since it is not possible to consider everyone in any moral calculation nor is it possible to satisfy every group's stated interests. These are important criticisms, but they may suggest that the doing of world ethics requires devising new approaches for dealing with groups or using factors not traditionally considered in typical concerns about matters of individual ethics. And, it does seem possible for people to communicate across cultures, to become familiar with and appreciate different cultures, to understand what fairness means in different cultures, and to figure out the long-range consequences of many actions for all concerned. If all of these things are possible, world ethics, though difficult, should still be possible. As a further point, if a world ethics perspective is not possible, attempts to resolve conflicts between cultures will then retreat back to the advantage-of-the-stronger conception of justice that Plato deplored.

Some will object that there is nothing new about taking a world ethics standpoint, that anyone who worries about fairness for all or the good and bad consequences of actions for all concerned already does take such a perspective. To some degree such a critic is correct. Still, although there is much lip service paid to considering the concerns of "all" in proper moral accounting, too often in practical application, however, one's actual moral calculations seem mysteriously to stop at one's own societal boundaries. In a sense, world ethics is not really new—rather, it is something that should have been emphasized in practice all along. There is certainly much more to be said about how to develop an adequate approach to applying considerations of fairness and concern to promote good, not bad consequences to the whole world. Many thorny problems remain, such as how to balance interests of different groups and how to respect cultural differences without interfering with basic rights. Still, the promise of the world ethics approach is strong enough to motivate further effort towards its development.

Consider, in particular, the concerns in this chapter with religion, social justice, and terrorism. Taking a world ethics perspective on religion would mitigates against any religious group attempting to supplant all other religious groups and in favor of maintaining religious diversity. Giving charity only to members of one's religious group would also be frowned on from a world ethics perspective. Social justice, although traditionally defined, as Miller (1999) points out, in terms of fair distribution within a single society, would on a world ethics perspective be transformed into a cross-societal notion, such that minimal but meaningful world standards for distribution would need to be adopted. Terrorism would be generally regarded as morally inappropriate from a world ethics perspective. The sole exceptions might be those in which a strong case could be made that no alternative procedure would work to provide basic self-defense and that terrorism would in fact work to remedy the problem, not make things worse. Adopting a world ethics perspective should also help alleviate situations that are currently considered to be the causes of terrorism. If terrorism is interpreted as a sign that the world system is not working for certain segments, and not as a sign that dangerous cancerous individuals have been produced who must be controlled, then attempts to improve the system should have greater, long-term effects for reducing terrorism.

This chapter concludes with three final reasons for taking a world ethics perspective seriously. First, embracing such a perspective does force one to compare one's own position and one's society's position with the positions of other people in other societies in the rest of the world. Singer (1972) has forcefully argued that such a comparison should be morally disturbing for most Americans. It will most likely reveal important ways in which the moral obligations of U.S society should change with respect to the rest of the world, in spite of the excellent opinion many Americans may have of their past track record. Second, trying on the world ethics perspective should make one more sympathetic to a number of individuals one has previously categorized as being hopelessly immoral by making one aware of disturbing similarities with them one may find to one's own rationalizations and behavior. And, third, putting a world ethics perspective into practice as best one can is probably the only real hope one has in a diverse world of demonstrating to those who contemplate or feel driven to acts of terrorism that there is a better alternative. May *all* human beings have the moral courage to embrace it![1]

DISCUSSION QUESTIONS

1. Why do the September 11 attacks seem more evil than other violent acts, e.g., wartime bombing of civilian targets?
2. The author discusses moral relativism, a contemporary philosophical framework guiding interactions with other cultures. Do you agree with this approach, or would you argue that certain actions are universally considered "good" or "evil"?
3. Outline the main elements of the world ethics perspective developed in the chapter. What would be the advantages from universal adoption of such a perspective? What problems do you anticipate in implementation of this perspective?

REFERENCES

AUDI, R. (2000). *Religious commitment and secular reason.* London: Cambridge University Press.

BARBER, B. (1995). *Jihad vs. McWorld.* New York: Random House.

HUME, D. (1998). *Dialogues concerning natural religion.* Indianapolis, IN: Hackett Publishing Co.

KELLY, J. (2002). *The problem of evil in the western tradition.* Collegeville, MN: The Liturgical Press.

KRAEMER, E., & JONES, H. (1986). Freedom and the problems of evil. *Philosophical Topics, 13,* 33–49.

MERLEAU-PONTY, M. (2000). *Humanism and terror.* Trans. John O'Neill. New Brunswick: Transaction Publishers.

MIDGLEY, M. (1992). *Wickedness.* London: Routledge.

MILLER, D. (1999). *Principles of social justice.* Cambridge, MA: Harvard University Press.

MOODY-ADAMS, M. (1997). *Fieldwork in familiar places: Morality, culture and philosophy.* Cambridge, MA: Harvard University Press.

NAGEL, T. (1991). *Equality and partiality.* New York: Oxford University Press.

PLANTINGA, A. (2000). *Warrant and Christian belief.* New York: Oxford University Press.

---

[1] I am very grateful for discussion on these topics many years ago with my late colleague, Hardy Jones.

PLATO. (1961). *The collected dialogues of Plato.* (E. Hamilton and H. Cairns, Eds.). Princeton, NJ: Princeton University Press.

QUINN, P. (1995). Political liberalisms and their exclusions of the religious. *Proceedings and Addresses of the American Philosophical Association, 69,* 35–56.

RACHAELS, J. (1990). *Created from animals.* New York: Oxford University Press.

SINGER, P. (1972). Famine, affluence, and morality. *Philosophy and Public Affairs, 1,* 229–43.

SPONG, J.S. (2001). *A new Christianity for a new world.* New York: Harper Collins.

PART III

INSTITUTIONAL
AND BEHAVIORAL RESPONSES
TO TERRORIST ATTACKS

8

Media Portrayals of September 11, 2001 and Beyond

Mary M. Step and Ronda L. Knox

❖

As the magnitude of events of September 11, 2001 became known, the media assumed a new prominence in the following days and weeks. Step and Knox explain that through radio, television, and over the Internet, the media played an important role not only in the dissemination of information, but also in shaping perceptions and perspectives about the events of that day. Subsequent attitudes and positions held by many about the relationship between the United States and the rest of the world have come to be patterned by images and interpretations presented by the media. Certain images, such as the American flag being raised among the rubble of the World Trade Center or the recurring picture of the United Airline jet slamming into the north tower, remain embedded in most Americans' remembrances of that day. But the media offered more than visual summaries, as highly charged rhetoric such as the "Attack on America" and "America Fights Back" was communicated to U.S. households. The images and commentaries contributed to the sense of a nation under siege and, as the authors point out, may have tempered any dissenting views about the events. In the conclusion, the authors caution the reader to be aware of the role of the media and urge a more sophisticated analysis of the information received from the media during periods of crisis.

The images were terrifying to watch, yet the coverage was strangely reassuring simply because it existed with such immediacy, even when detailed information was scarce. Imagine how much worse the nightmare would have been if broadcasting had been destroyed. On the day of death, television was a lifeline to what was happening.

—Caryn James, The New York Times

As many people made their way to work or school on September 11, 2001, others wound up their morning television routine with the seemingly benign, breaking news that an airplane had hit a tower at the World Trade Center in New York City. Many assumed that a small craft might have lost its way, resulting in a localized accident. Few could imagine the ferocity and scale of the events that were just beginning to unfold.

September 11 was the ultimate media human-interest story. On September 11, 2001, millions of people across the United States and around the world watched in real time as the World Trade Center was attacked and fell, the Pentagon was partially destroyed, and Flight 93 crashed in Pennsylvania. Many more listened to radios and surfed the Internet in disbelief, seeking information, and attempting to understand how it could happen. The overwhelming nature of this disaster caused television and radio stations across America to preempt all regularly scheduled programming as they attempted to make their audience aware of what was happening. Over 60 million people tuned into the four broadcast networks and another 15 million chose cable news sources (Consoli, 2001). Although they did not turn on a television for the Vietnam War, the Challenger explosion, or the Oklahoma City bombings, even cloistered monks watched television on September 11 (Rimer, 2001).

From the beginning of broadcasting, a variety of crisis events have stunned audiences. The destruction of the Hindenburg at Lakehurst, New Jersey; the assassination of President John F. Kennedy; and the Challenger explosion stand out as devastating, unexpected events that burst into most people's consciousness via the broadcast medium. On September 11, when the United States experienced four airline crashes within 90 minutes, the feeling was much the same as those previous national tragedies—a crisis of such magnitude as to preempt commercial broadcasting and grip viewers and listeners around the world. Analysis of the media perspective is important for several reasons. First, we learn a great deal about how one of the major institutions in society functions during a crisis. After all, the media play a crucial role in shaping public perceptions of the magnitude and significance of potential threats. Second, we learn how the media use specialized conventions and practices to present reality in millions of households, miles away from the actual event. Third, we can understand more deeply how media organizations were impacted by this unprecedented event. These media organizations control much of what we know about all aspects of the event. This has resulted in great debates about censorship, free speech, and even entertainment choices. Finally, we learn about media audiences. Mediated disasters often become frozen memories for listeners and viewers because of their shocking and emotionally driven content. What kind of impact can heavy viewing of this content have on audiences?

Media involvement can include both cognitive and emotional participation with media content. Involvement with media is a common process and even desirable from the perspective of media producers. However, in the case of disaster coverage, emotional involvement may be a much more encompassing event, coloring our thoughts, attitudes, and actions for an indeterminate time. Although researchers have studied various media processes immediately following a disaster or crisis, few have focused on audience responses to mediated versions of the event. For most people, television and radio are the primary sources used to understand events outside the local community. As real as these events can seem, they are still perceived through mediated channels. This fact, however, does not make response to them any less real. Viewers experienced deep emotional responses to the mediated events associated with the attacks on September 11. Therefore, it is important that audience members understand the dynamics and limitations of the coverage.

Communication involves sharing information, attitudes, and experiences. In face-to-face communication a sender and receiver interact with one another. Mass communication is much more one-sided. Audience members have little control over the content of the message and limited ability to give feedback to the senders of the message—in this case, the media. The media make command decisions about form and content about messages and select what experiences the audience should be allowed to share. Most people have come to expect entertainment, but in general, the perception seems to be that the primary function of the media is to convey information. This is evident in the heavy reliance by the public at large on round-the-clock news products and the amount of resources devoted by media organizations to the provision of ubiquitous coverage of events. Routine information like weather and sports may be easy to report. On the other hand, traumatic and emotional events create challenges for the media organizations as well as audiences. The events of September 11 raised the stakes for what the media were expected to do.

DISASTERS AS MEDIA EVENTS

Disasters have been defined as "overwhelming events and circumstances that test the response of community or individuals beyond their capability, and lead, at least temporarily, to massive disruption of function for community or individual" (Raphael, 1986, p. 5). Disasters can be man-made such as chemical spills or natural occurrences; however, both types are threatening and demand a return to stability. Disasters not only disrupt a community, but also tend to bring people together. Researchers have found an increased willingness among respondents to become involved with others following an unanticipated news event (Kubey & Peluso, 1990). Following the Challenger disaster, those who experienced stronger emotional reactions to the news were more likely to inform others, talk in order to feel better, and spend more time discussing the event (Riffe & Stovall, 1989).

Disasters and unexpected crisis events are major news stories that captivate audiences. These stories break media routines, are high in uncertainty, and are rooted, at least at the onset, in eyewitness versus official facts (Fensch, 1990). During a disaster, media outlets rely on the "command-post" orientation. This reflects a heavy reliance on experts like the police or agencies such as the FAA and FEMA to provide credible information. On September 11 there was a departure from this practice. Instead, journalists relied on a steady parade of eyewitnesses fleeing Ground Zero for a story that was eventually to span the globe. Another concept associated with media coverage of disaster stories is the idea of "open gatekeeping." This concept refers to opening the gates of information flow to any source with information about the disaster. This routine is a departure from the typical command-post perspective. Interestingly, some research showed officials as less credible sources to citizens faced with disasters. On September 11, not only did reporters use the general public as experts, but also major networks brought in amateur videotapes of the disaster.

In a normal situation, there is more news available than can be used, placing reporters and news processors in the role of determining which stories should be presented to the public. At a time of crises this balance is reversed. The need for information is greater than the availability of information. In this case, all of the available news is used by the media, and the majority of the news originated from the public affected by the crisis. Not only did average citizens supply news about the disaster but they continued to play feedback roles when situations changed or were reported inaccurately. The process described above is in direct opposition to what media personnel prefer at times of disaster. The media's preference is a command-post perspective. However, the command-post and open gatekeeping perspectives may exist simultaneously. In a content analysis of television network news stories, there was equivalent use of victim and nonvictim sources in coverage of Hurricane Hugo and the Loma Prieta earthquake. This finding supports the coexistence of command-post and open gatekeeping perspectives. The general public is more likely to be relied upon as a source at the onset of a disaster when the event is at its most ambiguous. Victims of a disaster may be portrayed and perceived as more credible sources of information in the initial aftermath of a disaster.

The credibility of an information source has been shown to affect perceptions and behaviors associated with a disaster event. When faced with hurricane warnings, only 3.5 percent of Galveston Island residents said that official sources influenced their decision to evacuate. Forty-three percent reported being unconvinced that the storm would actually affect them until one day before the event. The factor that accounted for the most variance in evacuation decision making was personal experience. Personal experience with a natural disaster can be considered influential in determining response to an impending natural disaster. Disaster coverage is also event-oriented and characterized by uncertainty. Initially, those in the media tend to focus on the impact of a disaster, such as stories about injuries or fires and disregard the larger context of the event (Wilkens & Patterson, 1987). Disasters also strain the resources of media organizations and force them to change newsgathering routines. Fensch (1990) documented the change in routine experienced by wire-service staff during the crash of Delta flight 1141 in August 1988. The uncertain situation forced reporters to follow hunches and be creative in tracking down information about the event.

Similarly, the attacks on September 11 affected the media and how reporters were able to do their jobs. The majority of New York City's television stations had their antennas on top of the World Trade Center. Only two of New York's stations were able to stay on the air because they had backup antennas on top of the Empire State Building. Critical radio, cellular, and microwave links were also housed at the World Trade Center. Reporters could not use their cell phones to send in updates so they typed text messages on pagers that anchors would read on the air (*Broadcasting & Cable,* 2001).

Yet, uncertainty is typical in emergent disaster situations. High stress and rapid change alter the balance of information needs and available information, forcing media to rely on the public, rather than officials, for facts about the event. For audiences, high levels of informational uncertainty are accompanied by dramatic sound or video footage. This results in an emotionally involved audience motivated to find the most current facts in a rapidly changing situation. As you might expect, people made distinct choices about the media they used during and after the attacks on September 11.

MEDIA OPTIONS

Differences existed in coverage of the attacks and how information was sought on the Internet, in print, radio, and television. With newspapers, the headlines set the agenda of what people were to believe. Photographs that were used brought out a sense of realism.

The front pages such as the one on the *New York Post* on September 12, 2001 of the three firemen raising the American flag in the rubble were very dramatic and will have a lasting legacy. Graphic images such as these trigger what are referred to as flashbulb memories (Conway, 1995). Flashbulb memories are vivid recalls of stressful, emotional, and often historic events. These clear memories serve as psychological reference points and help organize memory. Although not always accurate, people hold firm to their version of reality surrounding a flashbulb event. People may index their recollections as occurring before or after September 11. The amount of television watched per day during the disaster will most likely affect the accuracy of flashbulb memories. Flashbulb memories may also tie specific emotions to specific images. For example, for many, the image of the crumbling towers will be forever connected to the most intense emotion they had that day (Step et al., in press).

Radio coverage was also important because some listeners heard the initial reports live. The attacks began at a time when some people were still driving to work. As reported by Lebo and Wolpert (2002), approximately 16 percent of Americans learned about the attacks from the radio. On September 11 almost all of the radio stations in the United States were providing news coverage of the terrorists attacks. Stations were commercial free for at least three days. When commercials returned on air, most stations sorted through those that seemed "too upbeat or had jingles" (Romano, 2001, p. 24). Radio listeners supplied their own mental images based on what was heard. Television, however, made those images more real.

"The vast majority of Americans found out about the attacks on television and that is where they stayed" (Lebo & Wolpert, 2002, p. 2). Lebo and Wolpert (2002) found over 56 percent of Americans first learned about the attacks by watching television, while less than 1 percent learned of the news over the Internet. Nielsen Media Research reported that 79.5 million viewers watched television news between 8 P.M. and 11 P.M. on September 11 (*Broadcasting & Cable,* 2001). An online poll was conducted with 621 subjects between 1 P.M. and 5 P.M. on September 11 with 91 percent reporting television as their number one source of information. In the same study, 61 percent of the respondents said they also went online for news information (Multichannel News, 2001).

Although Americans preferred television as their primary news source, the Internet was employed for social support. More than 100 million Americans sent or received email messages of concern or emotional support (Lebo & Wolpert, 2002). In addition, people around the world used email and the Internet to give their sympathy and contact U.S. friends and colleagues. Email was used to bring people together in the crisis. In addition to news, rumors were also circulated over the Internet. Some of the stories that email users may have encountered after the attacks include: 1) versions of a Nostradamus prophecy allegedly anticipating the attacks, 2) pictures of the burning buildings interpreted to reveal the face of Satan, and 3) a coded message predicting the attacks using the Microsoft "Wingdings" font. O'Leary (2001) argued that people spread these rumors over the Internet because they were trying to make sense of the world around them. Such rumors reflect attempts to deal with the uncertainty and helplessness that followed the attacks. Many people watched the events unfold in real time, mediated by whatever channel they chose to bring them news or rumors. On September 11 the media needed to be able to react quickly and offer a context for the footage that audiences around the world were watching.

TELEVISION CONVENTIONS

Television conventions include format, image, and recurrent patterns in the form and content of the visual and verbal communication. The term *visual literacy* generally refers to the interpretation of the formal structure of television and carries with it the notion that the interpreter has knowledge of the use of camera angles, lighting, edits, and so forth. However, audience members may interpret many television conventions with no previous experience in examining media conventions. For example, when seeing a character filmed from a low camera angle, even naive viewers can understand that the character is meant to appear powerful because viewers are accustomed to looking up to powerful people. Television conventions resulting from September 11 included the screen crawl, recycled tape sequences, and other production choices. The image of the jet hitting the south tower was in heavy rotation, and it was repeated up to 30 times-per-hour (Uricchio, 2001). Major networks used similar visual imagery. Anchors were on screen and then would voice-over live video footage that was gathered throughout the day. Eventually, reporters were also used to give vivid descriptions of Ground Zero.

The media seemed to have little difficulty in conveying the tragedy and sense of loss from the September 11 attacks. The issue in newsrooms was how much horror should be aired. CNN and *The New York Times* as well as other newspapers chose to run victims leaping from the World Trade Center. CNN's head of newsgathering rationalized showing the footage by stating, "We don't want to shield people from the horrific reality. If you show only the smallest snippet in the body of a story about the horror, that's more appropriate than showing one person going to the ground" (Trigoboff & McClellan, 2001, p. 5). Other stations chose not show the footage. Instead, ABC showed two women on the ground screaming as their eyes followed the decent of a person jumping. An ABC spokesperson said the network thought that was a better way to show the horror of the situation without being gruesome.

Media outlets were quick to label their coverage in thematic ways. Examples of titles that flashed across television screens included: "Attack on America" and "America Fights Back." By September 15th, the new theme was "America at War." Theme music was also included later in the week, but was deliberately missing the first two or three days of coverage (Uricchio, 2001). The framing of the events were predominantly domestic—as far as the U.S. media was concerned, this was an American story. In the process, the reference to "world" in the World Trade Center, may have been diminished somehow. When projections of the missing started to come in, over 1000 nonnationals could not be accounted for. Another global issue that received attention was the businesses that were housed in the World Trade Center.

Still another recurring theme reflected the simple struggle between good and evil, exemplified in coverage speculating terrorist responsibility for the attack. Osama bin Laden quickly became the face and name of evil. Television conventions allow the media to turn uncertain emotional events, like September 11, into predictable recycled taped sequences. Visual imagery such as an American flag graphic and production choices like live shots of Ground Zero are examples of television conventions used that day. The examination of media conventions is important because journalistic choices frame how we perceive reality and have great influence over our interpretation of events. The media also influenced our emotional involvement.

EMOTIONAL INVOLVEMENT

Media sources have been regarded as crucial in determining audience response in that it is the source that defines reality. It is this reality that subsequently influences the public's attitudes and beliefs about the event. Raphael (1986) reviewed several types of response by victims of a disaster. These include excitement, shock, helplessness, abandonment, and even release of tension. One may infer that those of us who watched the events surrounding September 11 also experience some of these emotional responses.

Emotional involvement is the degree to which a media user is emotionally engaged with a media experience, content, or characters (Perse, 1990). This engagement is constituted by experiencing any of a number of distinct positive or negative emotions in response to media stimuli. Importantly, these emotional responses can vary in intensity and duration.

Emotions are responses to our environmental assessments. The unprecedented event of September 11 was a unique opportunity for audiences to have intense emotional involvement with media on a large scale. On an individual level, emotion intensity is determined by media use. The initial reaction of most was surprise followed by sadness, fear, interest, and anger. As the events of September 11 unfolded, the feeling of surprise was replaced by interest in the events and sadness (Step, Finucane, & Horvath, in press).

On an interpersonal level, co-viewing also provided an opportunity for testing emotions during the attacks. Co-viewing is simply watching television with others. Whereas the media provided information and a link to the events as they transpired, many people also turned to others who were viewing with them. Television viewing, once thought to be a passive activity, is more often a social activity. Viewers co-construct a shared reality through their common experience. Media use as a shared experience, rather than an individual one, shifts the focus from mass communication to interpersonal communication. Traditionally, co-viewing has been thought to offer viewers an opportunity to open a conversation, demonstrate competence, provide a context for talk, or bring people together in a common activity (Finucane & Horvath, 2000). Co-viewers may have facilitated or inhibited their responses to the emotionally charged event witnessed by hundreds of millions of television viewers.

Live coverage, like that on September 11, is more likely to emphasize emotional responses of victims. Viewers of September 11 coverage were deeply affected by the emotional intensity of the reports, leading to a greater desire to co-view and share their own thoughts and feelings. Although previous research has identified multiple functions for co-viewing within close relationships, the September 11 coverage presented a unique viewing situation. Specifically, mediated disasters are emotionally involving and motivate interpersonal discussion.

When disaster occurs, many people turn to the media for information. As stated earlier, almost 80 million people in the United States watched coverage of the September 11 attacks (*Broadcasting & Cable,* 2001). When that information became overwhelming emotionally, viewers turned to others for support, reassurance, and sharing (Finucane, Horvath, & Step, 2002). Although a medium of choice (radio or television) offers an explanation of the event/crisis, it is a one-sided mediated interaction. People turn to other people to process the explanations, to share fears and concerns, to assuage fears of being alone at a time of disaster or crisis, and to help comfort others.

In the days following the attacks on the World Trade Centers and the Pentagon, the focus seemed to shift from facts to sentiment. There were vigils held around the world for the victims and their families, tribute concerts were put on to raise money, and personal stories were featured on many news and talk shows. After the shock and disbelief wore off, reality set in and we were exposed to constant reminders of that day. In addition to the media's influence on us, the media and entertainment industries were also affected by the attacks.

NEWS AND ENTERTAINMENT PERSPECTIVES

As regular programming resumed after the attacks, the impact of commercial-free programming was reported. Over $300 million in advertising sales were estimated to have disappeared in the first week (Higgins & Romano, 2001). Major networks lost between $35 and $55 million. Not only were networks losing money in advertising, but they were also spending unexpectedly to cover the attacks. The cost of covering the event was enormous, and the networks were not bringing in any money. Investors also sold their media shares. When the stock market opened Monday after the attacks, politicians and television personalities were asking investors to show financial patriotism by not selling their shares or even buying stocks. By the closing bell, the market experienced its largest point drop (not percentage) ever (Higgins & Romano, 2001).

Along with the modifications that were made to the Emmy Awards, several other programs made changes to their shows that involved references to the World Trade Center or New York. Before episodes of "The Real World: New York," MTV had a statement about how the episodes are going to be aired unaltered as a "testament to this great city" (Tilton, 2001, p. 2). There were also discussions about the possibility of altering opening shots of the popular sitcom "Friends" because of pictures of the towers in the credits. In addition to preempting programs on their own, the networks had to fill gaps over the weekend after the disaster because of postponed sporting events. With no sporting events to show on Thursday night after the attacks, Fox Sports Net ran a still shot of an American flag with a streamer announcing postponement of NFL and MLB games. Regularly scheduled movies were also changed. Fox originally was going to run *Independence Day* (the White House is blown up in the film), but replaced it with the family movie *Mrs. Doubtfire*. A "Seinfeld" episode in which George's fiancée dies from licking envelopes was also deemed too risky and was withheld from rotation in syndication. Simple adjustments like these were discussed throughout the industry because the media recognized the need for serious reflection on the events happening around the world.

Following the attacks, the media responded the only way that they knew how. The content aired was based on the idea of public opinion—people pay attention to issues that have a direct effect on their own safety. This event threatened all Americans and the way that the media responded to it proved just that.

The adjustments that were made to the entertainment industry also proved that money was not the only issue, but rather how we are looked at and how we respond to certain events. The media gave the public what they wanted and during all of this chaos came a certain simplicity in that we did not have to look very far to find out the facts and then respond in the ways that we did.

The changes made in Hollywood in response to the attacks prompted many to wonder about the sincerity of these efforts. There is some concern that "today's media-saturated Americans will settle down into viewing the disaster as just another prime time special" (Overstreet, 2001, p. 2). This may indeed be the case. CBS aired a two-hour documentary in March 2002 with never-before-seen footage. Although there were concerns from victims' families, the network chose to show footage inside the towers as rescuers arrived.

Similar to the surge in patriotism during World War II, Hollywood quickly offered heroic and inspirational films including *Black Hawk Down*, *We Were Soldiers,* and *Windtalkers*. Hollywood was not the only industry affected by the events of September 11. The music industry was impacted "with songs being pulled from airplay for questionable content, and the artists themselves making last minute changes to their work" (Smith, 2001, p. 1). Examples like these weighed heavily on the issue of censorship. Since the attacks, what people said and did became a major issue because the threat of further attacks still remained.

CENSORSHIP

Many media outlets self-censored because of requests from the administration. "Government censorship of information at any time, whether direct or indirect, violates the concept of freedom of speech that is highly valued in the United States and central to a functioning democracy" (Media Alliance, 2001, p. 1). People understood, for obvious reasons, music, movies, and events that were altered, postponed, or cancelled altogether. However, censorship was also an issue with newsworthy events, including civilian casualties caused by U.S. bombings, peace protests, and communications from Osama bin Laden. Even the White House was accused of violating the spirit of the First Amendment.

Bill Maher, the host of "Politically Incorrect," made a comment on the show soon after the attacks, "We have been the cowards, lobbing cruise missiles from 2000 miles away. That's cowardly." Maher added, "Staying in the airplane when it hits the building, say what you want about it, it's not cowardly" (Reeves, 2001). On September 26, 2001, Ari Fleischer, the President's press secretary, attacked the comedian and talk show host with the comments "Americans need to watch what they say, watch what they do, and . . . this is not a time for remarks like that; there never is." Although Maher's remarks were offensive to some, Fleischer's statement set off warning bells to many members of the public and press (Reeves, 2001). The episode signaled to the press to renew their "watchdog" function of the government.

Others argued that the watchdog role was nonexistent. There were causes for concern of the media's coverage. For example, the government tried to control news content by arresting photographers near Ground Zero and trying to keep messages from Osama bin Laden off the air. In addition, the media coverage sounded like statements of U.S. government policy rather than objective information about the events following September 11. In addition there was little photographic coverage of the war in Afghanistan even after months of U.S. bombings.

The World War II model of journalistic reporting was collaborative with the government. In the Vietnam War, journalists were more skeptical. During the Gulf War, the media, again, was pro-government. Because of the pro-government reporting, public opinion was in favor of the Gulf War. Based on the patriotic approach of the media in reporting events surrounding September 11, public opinion was in favor of retaliating against the terrorists.

Another side of agenda-setting is the potential influence on terrorism. There is no doubt terrorism is capturing headlines and gaining priority in the media's agenda. Weinmann (1987) argued that terrorists may actually stage events that will attract the media and raise the visibility of the issue the terrorists are representing. Another example of agenda-setting is that the media tend to ignore terrorists activities that are initiated by U.S. agencies. The media are blamed for publicizing terrorists' messages and not reporting certain types of terrorism (Weinmann, 1987).

CONCLUDING REMARKS

In summary, the media played a central role in the dissemination of information on September 11, 2001. Further, media outlets continue to construct and influence the post-September 11 reality around the world. For most people, understanding of this tragic event is provided through the lens of the favorite or most accessible media outlet. For this reason, it is important to remain aware of media conventions, industry competition, and the tendency of audiences to become emotionally involved with coverage. In many instances, media outlets provide the only look at important and complex events taking place in distant locations. As more is known about information is constructed and presented, especially in crisis situations, the more informed audiences will be in the their roles as citizens.

DISCUSSION QUESTIONS

1. To what extent did the media set the agenda on September 11, 2001? How were the most important stories selected? What was very clear at the end of the day? What was not clear at all at the end of the day?
2. What images of September 11 do you remember most vividly? How important are those images in shaping your perceptions of what happened that day, what the causes were, and what should be done about the attacks?
3. Does the entertainment industry have special responsibility in a time of crisis? Under what circumstances should economic concerns override social responsibility in deciding the content of media coverage?

REFERENCES

Broadcasting & Cable. (2001, September 17). Black Tuesday: Made for TV. pp. 3–8.
CONSOLI, J. (2001, September 17). Advertising takes a back seat in wake of terror attacks. *Adweek, 42,* 4–5.
CONWAY, M. A. (1995). *Flashbulb memories*. Hove, UK: Erlbaum.

FENSCH, T. (1990). *Associated Press coverage of a major disaster: The crash of Delta flight 1141*. Hillsdale, NJ: Lawrence Erlbaum.

FINUCANE, M. O., & HORVATH, C. W. (2000). Lazy leisure: A qualitative investigation of the relational uses of television in marriage. *Communication Quarterly, 48*, 312–321.

FINUCANE, M. O., HORVATH, C. W., & STEP, M. M. (2002, April). *Sharing and support: The functions of coviewing on September 11, 2001*. Paper presented at the annual meeting of the Broadcast Education Association, Las Vegas, NV.

HIGGINS, J. M., & ROMANO, A. (2001, September 24). The new economics of terror. *Broadcasting & Cable*, 4–5.

KUBEY, R. W., & PELUSO, T. (1990). Emotional response as a cause of interpersonal news diffusion: The case of the space shuttle tragedy. *Journal of Broadcasting & Electronic Media, 34*, 69–76.

LEBO, H., & WOLPERT, S. (2002). *Study by UCLA Internet project shows e-mail transformed personal communication after Sept. 11 attacks*. Retrieved July 8, 2002, from UCLA, Office of Media Relations Web site *http://www.ccp.ucla.edu/pdf/ucla-Internet-report-2002.pdf*

Media Alliance. (2001). Action alert: Call on TV networks to resist U.S. government pressure to censor coverage. Retrieved February 14, 2002, from *http://www.media-alliance.org/action/*

Multichannel News. (2001). *Myers polls news viewers during tragedy*. Retrieved October 17, 2001, from *http://www.tvinsite.com/multichan*

O'LEARY, S. D. (2001, October 5). Rumors of grace and terror. *Online Journalism Review*. Retrieved October 9, 2001, from *http://ojr.usc.edu/content/print.cfm?print=648*

OVERSTREET, J. (2001). *Shock waves tear through a shock-value industry: How can we think of movies in the wake of the September 11 terrorist attacks?* Retrieved February 7, 2002, from http://promontoryartists.org/lookingcloser/shockwaves.htm

PERSE, E. M. (1990). Involvement with local television news: Cognitive and emotional dimensions. *Human Communication Research, 16*, 556–581.

RAPHAEL, B. (1986). *When disaster strikes*. New York: Basic Books.

REEVES, R. (2001, October 1). Patriotism calls out the censor. *The New York Times*, p. A23.

RIFFE, D., & STOVALL, J. G. (1989). Diffusion of news of shuttle disaster: What role for emotional response? *Journalism Quarterly, 66*, 551–556.

RIMER, S. (2001, October 21). On Sept. 11, even monks watched television. *The New York Times*, p. A16.

ROMANO, A. (2001, September 17). Radio news: E pluribus unum. *Broadcasting & Cable*, 24.

SMITH, J. W. (2001, October 1). *Rippling sounds: The entertainment industry reacts*. ArtsEditor. Retrieved February 7, 2002, from *http://artseditor.com/html/october01/oct01_music.shtml*

STEP, M. M., FINUCANE, M. O., & HORVATH, C. W. (in press). Emotional involvement in the attacks. In B. S. Greenberg (Ed.), *Communication and terrorism: Public and media responses to 9/11*. Cresskill, NJ: Hampton Press.

TILTON, A. V. (2001, October 7). The show didn't go on: 11th hour cancellation of Emmy Awards. About.com. Retrieved February 7, 2002, from *http://celebritynews.about.com/library/weekly/aa100701a.htm?terms=%22the+show+didn%27t+go+on%22*

TRIGOBOFF, D., & MCCLELLAN, S. (2001, September 17). How much is too much? Victims leaping from flames tests news judgement. *Broadcasting & Cable*, 5.

URICCHIO, W. (2001, September 16). Television conventions. *Television Archive.* Retrieved July 11, 2002, from *http://tvnews3.televisionarchive.org/tvarchive/html/article_wu1.html*

WEINMANN, G. (1987). Conceptualizing the effects of mass-mediated terrorism. *Political Communication and Persuasion, 4,* 213–216.

WILKENS, L., & PATTERSON, P. (1987). Risk analysis and the construction of news. *Journal of Communication, 37*(3), 80–92.

9

Psychological Responses to the Terrorist Attacks

Carmen R. Wilson Van Voorhis

To large sections of the population, media coverage of September 11 served to provide much-needed information about the events of that day. On the other hand, the images and associated commentaries continue to shape the collective perception of the terrorist threat and, in the process, may have contributed to the increased incidence of stress-related disorders and symptoms. Drawing on two recent traumatic events—the Oklahoma City bombing of 1995 and the September 11 attacks—Van Vorrhis examines the effects of various factors in determining vulnerability to stress. Under sociocultural factors, the author examines the effects of proximity, severity, and duration of trauma on vulnerability. Psychological factors examined include previous distress, coping styles, and thoughts about the traumatic events and exposure to trauma. Finally, the author looks at coping strategies and ways to help others suffering from trauma-induced stress.

Even as I sit in my office in La Crosse, Wisconsin, listening to a National Public Radio program about the new Office of Homeland Security, there is an air of insecurity. Colleagues and students have a new vocabulary, one that includes "terrorists" and "America" all in one sentence. While much of the early intense anxiety and tension of our nation has dissipated, some effects are permanent. Consider the cases of the following two individuals.[1]

Twenty-four-year-old Naomi lives in Minneapolis. She has shared an apartment with two other women since they all graduated from college two years ago. Naomi graduated with

---

[1]While the case of "Naomi" is hypothetical, the details have been compiled from the real stories of many individuals. "Ben" (not his real name) is a real person. I have made no changes to his story. I would like to thank him for sharing this information.

147

a bachelor's degree in finance, but continues to work in retail sales as she finds the business world to be too stressful. All her life, people have described Naomi as "high strung" and a "worrier." Since September 11, however, Naomi's anxiety has become much worse. Even though the attacks were several months ago, Naomi continues to have nightmares about anthrax and airplane disasters. Fireworks were included as part of a recent neighborhood celebration. Unaware of the festivities, Naomi thought the explosions were bombs, and she began to scream and cry. Her roommates spent the next several hours comforting Naomi until she was able to go to sleep. Naomi used to enjoy traveling, and she especially liked to fly. Since the attacks, however, she is terrified of airplanes and of flying. Every time she sees or hears a plane, her heart beats rapidly, her breathing becomes shallow, and she begins to feel nauseous. Her boyfriend lives several states away, and they have not been able to see each other as frequently as in the past because Naomi refuses to fly. Additionally, they often argue about his intentions to fly to see her. Finally, Naomi has become obsessed with watching the news. While she used to prefer science fiction and fantasy programming, she now watches news stations exclusively. She falls asleep with the news and turns it on as soon as she wakes. Her roommates have long since grown weary of her constant conversations about the attacks and possible future attacks. They avoid her at home and no longer invite her to social events as others regularly fail to enjoy themselves in her company.

Ben is 32 and lives in New York. He moved there from the Midwest about one year before the September 11 terrorist attacks. During the attack on the World Trade Center, Ben was working at the Statue of Liberty. At first, he just heard the World Trade Center was on fire. As he watched the first tower burning, he noticed a plane flying in at an odd angle. At that point, he realized the plane was going to crash into the second tower, and terrorism was to blame. He immediately became enraged, cursing the air. Everywhere around him, people began to scream and cry. As Ben was in a supervisory role at the park, he "stepped out of the moment." He took control, and as quickly and calmly as possible, closed the park and safely escorted all visitors out of the park. He and his colleagues remained at the Statue of Liberty for over two days. Thousands of ambulances and volunteers assembled at the park due to its easy access to the World Trade Center. For the first time in years, Ben started smoking again. Over the next six months, Ben coped, in part, by turning to his "vices." He continued to smoke and gained about twenty pounds. Early on, Ben had trouble when he saw planes coming in to land at the airport. The landing planes fly in at the same angle as the plane that struck the second tower, and Ben could not help but see the crash over again in his mind. That has since gone away. Mostly, Ben's life has returned to normal. In fact, sometimes Ben is afraid that things returned to normal too much and too quickly. He continues to worry when large crowds come to the park for special celebrations, like the Fourth of July. Mostly, though, at this point, Ben is saddened and angered by the thought that the safety he and many others previously took for granted collapsed with the towers.

Consider the responses of Naomi and Ben. Are they "normal"? What is the "normal" response? (*Is* there a "normal" response?) What leads to the differences in Naomi's and Ben's reactions? Think about the cases of Naomi and Ben throughout this chapter as I discuss *clinical* (i.e., diagnosable) and *subclinical* (i.e., not diagnosable) stress-related disorders and symptoms, differences in individuals' vulnerability, and, finally, coping mechanisms and treatment options.

PSYCHOLOGICAL CONSEQUENCES OF STRESS

Stress-Related Clinical Disorders

Most people have heard of **PostTraumatic Stress Disorder** or **PTSD.** The critical feature of PTSD includes (1) experiencing or witnessing an event involving actual or threatened death or serious injury or (2) learning about the unexpected death or serious injury of a family member or friend. After the traumatic event, the individual responds with fear, helplessness, or horror. Additional symptoms are grouped in three categories. The first category consists of *reexperiencing the event* in one or more ways. The event may be reexperienced in the form of distressing dreams or nightmares, intrusive thoughts or images, or flashbacks or hallucinations of the event. Individuals also might experience severe psychological distress or physical discomfort in response to either memories or external cues, such as news broadcasts, of the event. *Avoidance of cues* associated with the traumatic event and a *numbing of general responsiveness* comprise the second category of symptoms. Avoidance symptoms include attempts to avoid thinking or talking about the event, efforts to avoid people or places associated with the event, or an inability to remember aspects of the trauma. Numbing symptoms include a reduced interest in activities that previously were enjoyed, a sense of not being connected to other people, restricted emotional responses, and a sense of a foreshortened future. Individuals must experience three or more avoidance or numbing symptoms to meet criteria for diagnosis. The final category consists of symptoms of *increased arousal*. Increased arousal is indicated by sleep difficulties, irritability, and concentration problems. Some individuals are startled easily or have a need to constantly be highly aware of what is going on around them. Individuals must experience two or more increased arousal symptoms to be diagnosed with PTSD. Finally, individuals must experience these symptoms for more than one month (American Psychiatric Association, 2000).

Clearly, PTSD is serious and can be a debilitating disorder; fortunately, in the general population PTSD typically is rare. Undeniably, Naomi is experiencing significant psychological difficulties, yet she does not (from the information given) meet the criteria for PTSD. In any given year, about 3.6 percent of United States adults will experience PTSD (Department of Health and Human Services, 1999); about 8 percent of adults will experience PTSD at some point in their lives (American Psychiatric Association, 2000). Phone interviews with Manhattan residents one to two months after September 11 revealed that 7.5 percent could be diagnosed with PTSD (Galea et al., 2002). These rates are similar to those found in a study of Oklahoma City residents after the bombing of the Alfred P. Murrah Federal Building in 1995. Six months after the bombing, 254 randomly selected Oklahoma City residents were surveyed about their reactions to the bombing. About 8 percent of the sample qualified for a diagnosis of PTSD (Sprang, 1999).

Interestingly, while the rate of PTSD among the Manhattan residents post–September 11 is about twice that expected if there had been no terrorist attacks, it is still much lower than PTSD rates among terrorist attack victims in other parts of the world. Gidron (2002) reviewed six studies investigating PTSD prevalence rates among terrorist attack victims in France, Northern Ireland, and Israel. Rates ranged from a low of 5 percent among Northern Ireland police officers involved in terrorist attacks between 1993 to 1994 to 50 percent among 26 survivors of the 1987 Enniskillen bombing in Northern

Ireland. Gidron suggests that the mean prevalence rate of PTSD in response to terrorist attacks worldwide is about 28 percent, clearly much higher than the rates after the September 11 terrorist attacks.

PTSD is not, however, the only stress-related psychological disorder. A second disorder, **Acute Stress Disorder,** is similar to PTSD in that it is the result of a similar type of traumatic event to which the individual responded with fear, helplessness, or horror. Additionally, the type of symptoms are similar to those of PTSD, including general numbing of responsiveness, an inability to remember parts of the trauma, reexperiencing the trauma, avoiding cues of the trauma, and increased arousal. Acute Stress Disorder differs from PTSD in duration; Acute Stress Disorder lasts from two days to four weeks. Individuals who experience symptoms longer than four weeks are diagnosed with PTSD (American Psychiatric Association, 2000).

Unfortunately, Acute Stress Disorder has not been studied as thoroughly as PTSD. The prevalence rates in the general population are unknown. A few studies of individuals exposed to severe trauma suggest between 14 and 33 percent experience Acute Stress Disorder (American Psychiatric Association, 2000). A group of Brown University researchers surveyed psychiatric patients and general medical patients two to three weeks after the terrorist attacks in September. Thirty-three percent of psychiatric patients and 13 percent of general medical patients reported enough symptoms to be diagnosed with PTSD (Franklin, Young, & Zimmerman, 2002). By meeting the diagnostic criteria for PTSD with a duration of less than one month, these patients would qualify for a diagnosis of Acute Stress Disorder.

Subclinical Reactions to Stress

Most people did not develop a clinical stress disorder in response to the terrorist attacks of September 11. Almost everyone, however, experienced at least some level of psychological turmoil. The psychiatric and medical patients in the study mentioned above were asked about their emotions on the day of the attacks. Ninety-three percent of all patients reported being upset, 86 percent were shaken, 87 percent were depressed or saddened, 71 percent were angry, and 69 percent were anxious. These reactions remained unchanged on the day after the attacks (Franklin et al., 2002). Schuster and colleagues (2001) surveyed a random sample of 560 adults living in the United States between three and five days after the attacks. Fully 90 percent of individuals reported experiencing one of five stress symptoms at least "a little bit." The symptoms included feeling very upset, disturbing memories, difficulty concentrating, difficulty sleeping, and feeling irritable. Clearly, virtually all of us were upset in the days immediately after the terrorist attacks, yet for most of us, those intense emotions dissipated relatively quickly over the weeks following the attacks. So, were we *really* impacted by the attacks? Did we *really* experience any significant stress reactions? What other types of reactions are stress related? I would argue that, in fact, most people did experience some enduring stress reactions that they failed to attribute to the stress our nation was undergoing.

Most importantly, no reaction is *wrong,* and the number of individuals in the United States likely represents the number of different types of reactions that occurred. Certainly, however, typical patterns of reactions exist. First, we experience both physical and psychological reactions to stress. Second, these reactions are inextricably intertwined.

In the 1950s, Canadian scientist Hans Selye discovered a pattern of reactions to stressors that he termed the **general adaptation syndrome (GAS)** (Selye, 1956). The GAS consists of three phases. Phase 1 is the *alarm reaction.* The alarm reaction phase consists of immediate reactions to the stressor. Physically, the body shifts into its "fight-or-flight" reaction. In part due to an increase in adrenalin, our heart rate accelerates, our blood pressure increases, our digestion slows, and blood flows to our large muscle groups. Additionally, the burst of adrenalin leaves us emotionally keyed up and on edge. The anxiety and anger experienced by the psychiatric and medical patients in the first couple of days after the attacks would fit in this stage. This level of physical and emotional tension, however, cannot persist. Skipping phase 2 for the moment, phase 3 is *exhaustion.* Eventually, if a stressor is severe enough and continues long enough, the body's physical and emotional defense mechanisms collapse and individuals become susceptible to physical and emotional illness and possibly even death. For a variety of reasons, some individuals are more susceptible to exhaustion than others, and therefore reach exhaustion sooner. Individuals who developed PTSD in response to the terrorist attacks might have experienced the beginning stages of the exhaustion phase.

Phase 2 of the GAS is *resistance.* Given that the stressor continues (for example, continued threats of anthrax exposure), our stress reaction continues. During the resistance stage we cope, both physically and emotionally, with the stressor. Individuals use a variety of mechanisms to resist stress. These mechanisms are varied in effectiveness and include, for example, how we think about the event, how we express our emotions, if we exercise, if we use substances, and much more. This phase includes the subclinical reactions to the terrorist attacks that most of us experienced to some degree. In general, the reactions during the resistance stage can be divided into five categories: emotional, physical, behavioral/motivational, cognitive, and social.

Emotional reactions include our feelings about the stressor. Obviously, a primary emotion includes fear and anxiety. For example, individuals might fear future attacks, the effects of anthrax, or the threat of war. Sixty-one percent of students surveyed one to two days after September 11 reported they were "moderately" or "very much" scared because "we might go to war" (Murphy, Wismar, & Freeman, in press). Quite commonly, individuals feel anxious about being in situations that are similar to the traumatic event. For example, some individuals may become fearful about being in places with large crowds of people, large buildings, or airplanes. Again, among students surveyed one to two days after the attacks, 56 percent were at least "moderately" more afraid of flying than they were before the attacks (Murphy et al., in press). Emotional reactions, however, are quite varied and not at all limited to fear and anxiety. In addition to fear, many individuals might feel furious, horrified, shocked, sad, helpless, hopeless, guilty, empty, alone, confused, frustrated, and/or something else. Anger is especially common. In the days after the attacks, 24 percent of general medical patients and 47 percent of psychiatric patients reported difficulty with anger outbursts or irritability (Franklin et al., 2002). After the bombing of the Alfred P. Murrah Federal Building in Oklahoma City, residents reported a wide assortment of feelings. Individuals felt shocked and unsafe. Some individuals felt guilty that they asked for help when others were affected more severely. Yet other individuals felt embarrassed that they failed to feel lucky that they were not affected severely. Finally, many experienced feelings of disbelief that an attack of such magnitude could happen in the United States (Sprang, 1999). At least in terms of injuries and deaths, the attacks of September 11 were of far greater magnitude than the Oklahoma City bombing.

Physical reactions include any physiological changes in response to the stressful event. Physical reactions can include headaches, stomachaches or other gastrointestinal distress, or backaches. Some individuals might feel fatigued, like they have no energy. They might find themselves sleeping more than usual. Alternatively, other individuals might feel restless and have trouble sleeping. About 45 percent of psychiatric and general medical patients reported sleep difficulties in the days after the attacks (Franklin et al., 2002). Finally, research clearly supports a relationship between stress and immune system functioning. Even minor stressors impair the body's immune system to some degree. For example, the ability of students' bodies to heal wounds is significantly slower during exams than during summer vacations (Kiecolt-Glaser et al., 2002). If taking exams can affect the immune system, certainly, the stress of the terrorist attacks has the potential to leave us susceptible to colds, flus, and other illnesses.

Behavioral/motivation reactions include any things we do, or do not do, in response to the stressor. The list of stress-related behaviors in which people engage likely is endless. Yet again, some behaviors are more common than others, and some are healthier than others. For example, some individuals exercise when they feel stressed, while others may increase their substance use. In a survey of victims of the Oklahoma City bombing who used alcohol, 40 percent reported their alcohol use increased after the bombing (Pfefferbaum & Doughty, 2001). Other individuals may find themselves eating more than usual or having trouble eating at all. Some people might find themselves impulsively engaging in activities they might otherwise avoid, such as excessive shopping, gambling, or risky sexual encounters. Alternatively, some may find it difficult to do much of anything. For these people, everything seems like a chore; even previously enjoyed activities are avoided. They have trouble beginning and completing activities and are less efficient in their daily tasks. Going to work or school or studying can become quite difficult.

Cognitive reactions include how we think, not just *what* we think about, but also our *ability* to think and concentrate. Some of the cognitive reactions may be directly related to the traumatic event. For example, some people may forget aspects of the trauma or stressful event. Others may find they cannot stop thinking about the trauma and experience intrusive images or memories of the event. Other cognitive reactions may be more general. When individuals are stressed, they often have trouble focusing and concentrating. For example, in one study, researchers surveyed students one to two days after September 11. Fifty-eight percent reported some academic problem, with 26 percent reporting difficulty concentrating (Murphy et al., in press). Concentration problems were also reported by 37 percent of general medical patients and 56 percent of psychiatric patients in the days following the attacks (Franklin et al., 2002). Additionally, people may become forgetful about daily activities. For example, after the September 11 attacks, I heard many students and colleagues report they had forgotten meetings, misplaced papers, computer disks, car keys, and so on. Finally, some people have trouble making decisions.

Social reactions involve our relationships with other people. Like all of the other categories of reactions, social reactions are varied. Some individuals have trouble making and maintaining their social contacts. They withdraw from friends and family members. Conversely, others have trouble being alone and find themselves needing contact with friends and family members more frequently than they needed before the stressful event. In a survey of college students one to two days after September 11, 36 percent had given at least some consideration to going home (Murphy et al., in press). Overall, different individuals will exhibit completely different profiles of symptoms during the resistance phase. For example, one person might experience primarily emotional symptoms, while another experiences both physical and cognitive symptoms and few emotional ones. A final individual might be affected in all areas. If a severe stressor continues, however, eventually individuals will no longer be able to resist the stressor and will move into the exhaustion phase where they will be susceptible to both physical and mental illness.

Mass Sociogenic Illness

All of the above stress reactions, clinical and subclinical, can occur to any stressor or traumatic event. Some traumatic events might have only one victim—for example, a sexual assault; others, like the terrorist attacks, affect the entire nation. Events that affect entire cultures and nations lead to a unique, group-level psychological consequence. That consequence is **mass sociogenic illness,** in which large numbers of people share the same delusions (thoughts that are not true) and hallucinations (sights, sounds, smells that are not real). Mass sociogenic illness was first reported in Europe during the Middle Ages. One form was called *tarantism.* Believing they had been bitten by the tarantula, people affected by tarantism would suddenly start to jump around, dance, go into convulsions, and tear off their clothes (Comer, 2001).

The incidence of mass sociogenic illness increases during times when a culture is under stress. During the Middle Ages, the plague was the culprit; today, it is the threat of terrorist attacks. Just as the threat is more modern, so is the mass reaction. People no longer jump and dance naked in the streets (at least not as a mass reaction to stress), but since September 11, several incidents of mass reactions have been reported. In one incident in a Washington State middle school, paint fumes instigated a bioterrorism scare. One teacher and sixteen students went to the hospital. Another example occurred in a Maryland subway station. A man sprayed an unknown substance from a bottle into the air; thirty-five people experienced sudden headache, sore throat, and nausea. The substance was later determined to be window cleaner (Wessely, Hyams, & Bartholomew, 2001).

Of all the psychological reactions I have discussed, none are more "right" than others. Some are more severe than others, some are more debilitating, but none are "wrong." What leads to the variations in types and severities of reactions? What makes some individuals more vulnerable than others to severe symptoms? Again, the different individual reactions are the result of multiple individual and social factors. Much of what we know about individual responses to terrorist attacks is the result of research regarding the bombing of the Alfred P. Murrah Federal Building in Oklahoma City in April 1995.

EXPLANATIONS ABOUT INDIVIDUAL DIFFERENCES IN VULNERABILITY

Sociocultural Factors

Proximity, Severity, and Duration of Trauma.   While many people who were not in Washington, DC, New York, or Pennsylvania experienced severe reactions in response to the terrorist attacks, *proximity,* or being close to the attacks, increases the risk of symptoms. Schuster and colleagues (2001) conducted a phone survey of a random sample of adults living in the United States three to five days after September 11; more people living closer to the attacks experienced severe stress reactions than those living in other parts of the country. Sixty-six percent of people living within 100 miles of the World Trade Center experienced substantial stress in response to the attacks, compared to 48 percent living between 101 to 1000 miles away, and 36 percent living more than 1001 miles away. This is consistent with research of other traumatic events. Sprang (1999) compared post-bombing reactions of Oklahoma City residents to those of Kentucky residents, who lived about 800 miles away. She found that six months after the bombing, about 8 percent of Oklahoma City residents could be diagnosed with PTSD as compared to 1 percent of Kentucky residents.

The *severity* of a trauma can be measured in numerous ways. First is the severity of the event itself. Rubonis and Bickman (1991) found that the death rate of a traumatic event is related to the severity of individuals' reactions. Those events with higher death rates lead to more severe reactions, in part because more individuals are exposed to the threat of death. Also, however, stress reactions are more severe because they are complicated by the grieving process of those who lost friends and/or family members. The terrorist attacks took exponentially more lives than have been lost in any other acts of terror committed on U.S. soil. Previous to September 11, the most deaths from any terrorist attack were 168 in the bombing of the Alfred P. Murrah Federal Building in Oklahoma City in 1995. Including all those on the airplanes, in the Pentagon, and in the World Trade Center, about 3000 people were killed by the terrorist attacks on September 11.

Severity also can refer to the severity for the individual. Individuals who are personally affected by a traumatic event through personal injury, knowing someone who was injured or killed, or loss of personal resources typically are at increased risk for stress-related disorders and symptoms. For example, in a sample of Oklahoma City residents, being personally injured during the bombing was strongly related to the severity of PTSD symptoms. In other words, the more severely a person was injured, the more severe their symptoms (Tucker et al., 2000). Similarly, Oklahoma City residents who reported hearing, seeing, or feeling the explosion experienced more distress than did those Oklahoma City residents who did not hear, see, or feel the blast (Sprang, 1999). Sixth-grade youth who personally knew someone killed or injured by the bombing experienced more PTSD symptoms and had more trouble functioning than those youth who did not know someone killed or injured (Pfefferbaum et al., 2000). Finally, again among victims of the Oklahoma City bombing, losing both material resources (e.g., car, furniture) and experiential resources (e.g., time for sleep, daily routine) was related to higher levels of distress both two months and one year after the bombing (Benight et al., 2000).

Duration simply refers to how long the traumatic event lasts. In general, longer traumatic events lead to more severe symptoms. The initial airplane attacks were over relatively quickly. The duration of the terrorist attacks, however, did not end at that point. The cleanup stage continued for many months. The anthrax threat was immediate for several weeks. Depending on place of employment and residence, some individuals are constantly reminded of the threat of future attacks through increased security measures that have an impact on their daily lives.

We also know, however, that as the traumatic event moves further into our past, we experience fewer symptoms. One group of 44 Oklahoma City residents who reported clinical or subclinical PTSD symptoms were surveyed at six, nine, twelve, fifteen, eighteen, and twenty-four months after the bombing. Both clinical and subclincal levels of PTSD symptoms decreased over time, with most symptoms subsiding by twelve months (Sprang, 2001). Similarly, PTSD symptoms among 27 bombing victims decreased significantly between surveys conducted at two months and twelve months after the event (Benight et al., 2000). Most people will experience less distress related to the September 11 terrorist attacks as time passes. Moving beyond the first year anniversary of any traumatic event often is a notable turning point in the healing process. Not only is the trauma that much further in the past, but also a year-of-firsts is over. As of September 11, 2002 we will have made it through the first New Years celebration, the first Super Bowl, the first 4th of July, the first anniversary of the attacks. In general, "seconds" do not generate emotions as intense as "firsts."

Social Support.   The support we receive from friends and family members is a crucial component of our mental health. After a traumatic event, individuals who have others to talk with, to listen to, to support and be supported by tend to recover more quickly. Research has consistently found that immune system functioning is significantly less impaired among individuals experiencing stress if they also have solid social support (Kiecolt-Glaser et al., 2002). Victims of the Oklahoma City bombing who felt their work environment was supportive had fewer distress symptoms than those whose work environments were not supportive. Also, victims who sought therapy to deal with their reactions to the bombing reported that the therapy helped (Tucker et al., 2000).

Social support can vary dependent upon the type of trauma. For example, friends and family members tend to withdraw their support of a victim of repeated domestic violence (Epperson et al., 1992). Domestic violence is an "individual" trauma. The victim is generally one individual, or possibly a few if children are involved. The terrorist attacks, however, victimized thousands of people. When large numbers of people are victimized by the same trauma, people are more supportive. In general, people of our nation (and many other countries) were extremely supportive of victims and their loved ones. We saw the support through monetary donations, blood donations, the flying of the American flag, candlelight vigils, prayer services, and more. Anecdotally, I heard many conversations about the terrorist attacks that focused on a desire for the United States to retaliate. Some students and friends, however, expressed concern over the potential reactions of the United States. They were not sure that the best way was to "make someone pay." These individuals also often reported they felt alone and unsupported in this position, and they usually were hesitant to express it. In some ways, this dilemma parallels that of the protesters of the Vietnam and Gulf wars. Can people protest a war while still supporting the soldiers? Can people protest against a "war" on terrorism while continuing to support the victims of the attacks?

Psychological Factors

Previous Distress.   Individuals who have some emotional or mental health problem previous to a traumatic event are more likely to experience stress-related symptoms than those without prior emotional or mental health problems. In a national survey conducted three to five days after September 11, 56 percent of those with prior emotional or mental health problems experienced a substantial stress reaction compared to 42 percent without prior problems (Schuster et al., 2001). In a more extensive study, Franklin and colleagues (in press) compared the reactions of psychiatric patients to general medical patients. Primary diagnoses of the psychiatric patients included depression, anxiety, and impulse control disorders (e.g., gambling addiction, alcoholism). The psychiatric patients experienced more PTSD symptoms than the general medical patients. Specifically, the psychiatric patients were more likely to avoid people, places, and activities that reminded them of the attacks; to feel distant and cutoff from others; to experience a dulling of their emotions; to be hopeless about their future; to experience anger outbursts; and to have concentration problems (Franklin et al., in press). Clearly, a wide variety of previous emotional difficulties increases an individual's vulnerability to stress-related symptoms after a traumatic event.

Coping Styles.   Both coping styles and confidence in coping abilities are related to symptoms experienced after a trauma. In general, thinking about the traumatic event some of the time seems preferable to trying to avoid all thoughts of the event or thinking about the event constantly. Much research has found that individuals who use an *avoidant coping* style experience more symptoms in response to stress. Avoidant coping mechanisms include substance use, excessive sleep, escapism, and so on. Among a group of self-identified alcohol users who lived in Oklahoma City at the time of the bombing, increased alcohol use after the bombing was associated with more PTSD-related symptoms (Pfefferbaum & Doughty, 2001). So, using alcohol to forget and escape the trauma failed to alleviate symptoms; in effect, just the opposite occurred. Those individuals who drank more had more symptoms.

Alternatively, thinking about the trauma too much can be harmful as well. Coincidentally, some researchers were investigating the coping mechanisms and emotional well-being among a group of students just before the 1989 San Francisco earthquake. The researchers were able to return to the school and survey the students again just ten days and seven weeks after the earthquake. Children who reported a *ruminative coping* style showed more PTSD and depression symptoms both at ten days and seven weeks after the earthquake than children who used other forms of coping (Nolen-Hoeksema & Morrow, 1991). A ruminative coping style involves chronically focusing on and thinking about the event and any related symptoms while not actively doing anything to alleviate the symptoms.

The other aspect of coping that relates to symptom expression is *coping self-efficacy,* or individuals' confidence that they have the ability to cope with a traumatic event. Coping self-efficacy includes beliefs about the ability to carry out daily tasks and to manage thoughts, images, and feelings related to the event. Both at two months and at one year after the Oklahoma City bombing individuals who had high coping self-efficacy also reported less distress (Benight et al., 2000). This certainly makes sense. Individuals who feel confident in their abilities to handle the stress typically experience fewer stress-related symptoms than those who perceive the stress as overwhelming.

Thoughts about the Trauma.   A major component of coping is thinking or *cognition.* Cognitive components of coping include our ability to manage intrusive images or alter distressing thoughts. Most of us likely have had the image of the planes crashing into the towers and people jumping from the burning buildings take over our thoughts without warning. Some people may find themselves entrenched in the image, unable to shake it.

Others find a way to leave the image behind, at least temporarily. Individuals who tend to perceive themselves as victims in some way generally experience higher levels of distress than those who do not see themselves as victims. Perceptions of victimization can be quite varied. For some, their perceptions of victimization center on the grief of losing a loved one. For others, it is the sense that the situation is out of their control. Yet others may be concerned about their future safety. In two studies of Oklahoma City residents after the bombing, Sprang (1999, 2001) found that those who considered themselves personally victimized in some way experienced more PTSD symptoms than other people. Additionally, Murphy and Calleagues (in press) found that students who knew someone who lived near the three attack sites experienced more academic difficulties than other students.

Alternatively, if individuals can find some meaning in a traumatic event, make the event make some sense, or focus on some positive outcome, they typically experience fewer stress-related symptoms. For many, this process involves searching for comfort in religion or spirituality. In the days immediately following the September 11 attacks, 75 percent of people reported turning to prayer, religion, or spiritual feelings at least a little bit (Schuster et al., 2001). Others may seek counseling services. Therapy often involves working to think differently about an event. Therapists frequently try to help clients feel in control and less victimized. Among people who were directly victimized by the Oklahoma City bombing, individuals who were in therapy were much less likely to view themselves as victims than people who were not in therapy (Sprang, 2001). The challenge, of course, is finding some positive outcome or meaning in the terrorist attacks. As difficult as the task seems, preliminary results of an ongoing study found than many people reported feeling closer to family members and a greater appreciation of our country's freedoms (Dittmann, 2002). In short, people who can learn a lesson from the trauma tend to experience fewer stress-related symptoms.

Exposure. Especially now, when we have access to a wider variety of media outlets than ever before, people have the ability see and hear information about a traumatic event literally 24 hours a day. Fifty-eight percent of adults watched *thirteen or more hours* of television about the terrorist attacks on September 11 (Schuster et al., 2001). While information can help people cope—for example, through correcting misinformation from rumors—too much exposure can be harmful. Pfefferbaum and colleagues (2000, 2001) surveyed middle-school-aged children both in and about 100 miles away from Oklahoma City after the bombing. In both groups, television exposure was related to PTSD symptoms. Specifically, the more bomb-related programming the children watched, the more stress-related symptoms they experienced. While most but not all of the children living in Oklahoma City felt or heard the bombing and knew someone killed or injured, none of the children in the distant city were related to anyone killed or injured. Therefore, negative effects of high levels of media exposure are not just a risk factor for those personally affected or living near the trauma site.

Actually visiting the site also is a form of exposure. Those individuals who more frequently visited the remains of the Alfred P. Murrah Federal Building in Oklahoma City after the bombing experienced more PTSD symptoms than others (Tucker et al., 2000). One possible explanation is that those people who feel the need to visit more frequently are doing so in order to master feelings of distress related to the bombing. Another possibility is that the people who visited more frequently did so in their jobs as rescue workers or volunteers. The volunteers, in particular, may not have received adequate training to help them cope with the grotesque scene of the bombing. The site of the World Trade Center has become somewhat of a tourist site, with many people making vigils from across the United States to pay their respects. While a single visit is not likely to increase stress symptoms, on the contrary, a single visit might be just the closure some people need, multiple visits might in fact be harmful. Certainly individuals who live near or work at or near the attack sites or who just visit frequently are likely at risk for more severe stress symptoms.

Clearly, many of the psychological factors may interact with one another. Individuals with some previous history of emotional difficulties likely have difficulty coping in general. Their struggles with coping may be, in part, contributing to their mental health struggles. Additionally, anxiety, in particular, has been related to an inability to effectively disengage from information about the trauma. Interestingly, this difficulty is true even for people with subclinical levels of anxiety (Fox et al., 2001). Therefore, people struggling with anxiety might have an especially difficult time turning off the news about the attacks or staying away from the attack sites. In the end, not only do these individuals struggle with coping, which leads to higher anxiety, but they also overexpose themselves to information that then exacerbates their original anxiety. And so a vicious circle begins. The question becomes, what can be done? How can we help ourselves and others avoid experiencing serious consequences from an event as traumatic as the terrorist attacks of September 11, 2001.

HOW TO BE HELPFUL

Professional Services

Without a doubt, anyone suffering from Acute Stress Disorder, PTSD, or clinical levels of anxiety, depression, or any other disorder should seek professional therapy. Many others, however, also would benefit from professional therapy. Unfortunately, people frequently do not seek the services of a therapist because they are embarrassed of their reactions or think their problems are not "serious enough." Among Oklahoma City residents who qualified for a diagnosis of PTSD, only 25 percent had sought and received mental health services after the bombing (Sprang, 1999). In general, therapy for PTSD and related symptoms does appear to be helpful. In one study of individuals who developed PTSD in response to a car bombing in Northern Ireland, 97 percent of treated clients improved at least a little bit. Additionally, the improvement was relatively quick. Clients for whom PTSD was the only diagnosis attained this improvement in an average of only five sessions (Gillespie et al., 2002).

A typical form of treatment after a traumatic event that affects large numbers of individuals is *Critical Incident Stress Debriefing (CISD)*. CISD is a multiphase process typically conducted within several days of the traumatic event with groups of people exposed to the event. The first phase is the introduction phase, during which the process and the guidelines are described to the participants. The second phase consists of encouraging participants to recount the facts, as they perceived them, of the event. The third phase involves participants' explanations of their most prominent thoughts and emotions regarding the event. Next, facilitators teach participants about typical symptoms and that the symptoms are normal reactions to an abnormal event. Additionally, some basic coping mechanisms, such as deep relaxation training, are explained. Finally, individual therapy might be recommended to participants who appear to be experiencing more severe reactions (Jordan, 2002).

While CISD is the current practice of choice in disasters such as the terrorist attacks, some recent research suggests CISD might not be helpful to all individuals. Indeed, one study found that CISD had no effect in preventing future PTSD symptoms among a group of trauma survivors (Gidron, 2002). Coping self-efficacy theory suggests, in fact, that CISD could actually be further traumatizing to some people. CISD may be particularly risky for those with low coping self-efficacy. For individuals who feel ineffective in managing thoughts, memories, or images of the traumatic event, CISD may exacerbate their distress as they are asked to discuss those things in detail (Benight et al., 2000). Clearly, more research is needed to investigate CISD.

Nonprofessional Helping Techniques

Most people have not required professional counseling services to help them deal with the tragedy of the terrorist attacks. Even so, many people have had to find ways to cope and deal with the events. In general, in the days after the attacks, most people were engaging in relatively healthy coping techniques. Eight-seven percent of people talked about the attacks with others at least "a medium amount," 75 percent turned to religion or spirituality, and 34 percent attended a public event in recognition of the event (Schuster et al., 2001). Just as the stress symptoms are expressed emotionally, physically, behaviorally, cognitively, and socially, our coping mechanisms also should include all of those areas.

While this chapter and text focus on terrorism, these guidelines can be useful in the event of any trauma, another terrorist attack, the death of a loved one, an assault, or anything else a person finds traumatizing. First, people need to remember that all reactions are *normal reactions to an abnormal event*. After traumatic events, it is helpful to contact friends and loved ones. Find someone who is helpful with whom you can discussion the event. Give yourself and others permission to talk about the trauma, but do not force the issue. Talking about other things is fine too. Recognize your feelings and the feelings of the person with whom you are talking. Remember, and remind others, that all feelings are legitimate and okay. If someone has trouble expressing his or her feelings, share yours with them. Sometimes people can cue each other. Most importantly, *listen* to each other. Avoid giving advice and trying to make the event seem less traumatic than it is.

Take care of your physical health. Remember that stress impairs our immune systems, leaving us vulnerable to minor illnesses. Eat regular, well-balanced meals. Get plenty of rest—maybe even take a nap! Avoid excessive substance use and get some exercise. Exercise releases the physical tension in our muscles, leaving us feeling more relaxed. Take care of your mental health. The above listed physical activities often help us feel less psychologically distressed. In addition, however, it is important to avoid adding more stress to our lives. After a traumatic event, give yourself permission to do less. Avoid taking on extra tasks; do not begin new major projects. Be informed, but not overinformed. Notice your anxiety level as you read about, watch, and listen to information about the trauma. If you find yourself becoming overanxious, take a break. Actively replace unpleasant images, thoughts, and memories with more pleasant ones. Think of a time you had fun, maybe before the trauma. Of course, repressing all memories all the time is not helpful either, but it is healthy to pace yourself.

Finally, find some fun activities in which to temporarily escape. Eat a special dinner with friends or family, watch a movie, read a book, take a drive, ride a bike, play a game, watch silly television, listen to music, smile, give or receive a massage, try deep breathing or deep relaxation techniques, sing, dance, go to church or synagogue or temple, play with a pet, the possibilities are endless; most importantly, give yourself a break!

Unfortunately, we will never be able to go back to the security we felt before September 11, 2001. The threat of future terrorism on American soil will persist and, at some point, likely occur again. Knowing all the information available about psychological consequences of the trauma, risk factors that increase an individual's vulnerability to the trauma and possible treatment or helping techniques will not prevent people from experiencing distress in response to the trauma. By definition, traumatic events are distressing. The key is to do everything we can, to the best of our ability, to reduce individuals' distress as much as possible.

DISCUSSION QUESTIONS

1. Reread the cases of Naomi and Ben. What sorts of symptoms did they experience? What are some possible reasons Naomi is experiencing more psychological difficulties than Ben? If Naomi and Ben were your friends, what suggestions would you give them?
2. Think back to the days immediately after September 11, what stress-related symptoms did you see in the people around you? In what types of activities were people engaging to cope with the event?
3. Listen to one of the following National Public Radio pieces and identify any stress-related symptoms, factors that might influence individual vulnerability, and any coping mechanisms. All can be accessed online at *http://www.npr.org/archives*
   a. Recovering from 9-11 (*Weekend Edition*, Sunday, November 24, 2001)
   b. 9-11 Psychological Aftermath (*All Things Considered*, Wednesday, November 27, 2001)
   c. 9-11 Stress (*Morning Edition*, Wednesday, January 23, 2002)

REFERENCES

AMERICAN PSYCHIATRIC ASSOCIATION. (2000). *Diagnostic and statistical manual of mental disorders DSM-IV-TR (Text Revision)*. Washington, DC: Author.

BENIGHT, C. C., FREYALDENHOVEN, R. W., HUGHES, J., RUIZ, J. M., ZOSCHKE, T. A., & LOVALLO, W. R. (2000). Coping self-efficacy and psychological distress following the Oklahoma City bombing. *Journal of Applied Social Psychology, 30,* 1331–1344.

COMER, R. J. (2001). *Fundamentals of abnormal psychology* (3rd ed.). New York: Worth Publishers.

DEPARTMENT OF HEALTH AND HUMAN SERVICES. (1999). Mental health: A report of the Surgeon General [Online]. Available: *http://www.surgeongeneral.gov/Library/MentalHealth*.

DITTMANN, M. (2002, July/August). Research on 9-11: Study finds that tragedy continues to have psychological impact. *APA Monitor,* p. 20.

EPPERSON, D. E., WILSON, C. R., ESTES, K., & LOVELL, R. (1992, May). *Third-party responses to relationship violence: Impact of respondent gender, victim-perpetrator relationship, and the severity and frequency of abuse.* Paper presented at the annual meeting of the Midwestern Psychological Association, Chicago, IL.

FOX, E., RUSSO, R., BOWLES, R., & DUTTON, K. (2001). Do threatening stimuli draw or hold visual attention in subclinical anxiety? *Journal of Experimental Psychology, 130,* 681–700.

FRANKLIN, L., YOUNG, D., & ZIMMERMAN, M. (2002). Psychiatric patients' vulnerability in the wake of the September 11 terrorist attacks. *The Journal of Nervous & Mental Disease, 9,* 833–838.

GALEA, S., AHERN, J., RESNICK, H., KILPATRIC, D., BUCUVALAS, M., GOLD, J., & VLAHOV, D. (2002). Psychological sequelae of the September 11 terrorist attacks in New York City. *The New England Journal of Medicine, 346,* 982–987.

GIDRON, Y. (2002). Posttraumatic stress disorder after terrorist attacks: A review. *Journal of Nervous & Mental Disease, 190,* 118–121.

GILLESPIE, K., DUFFY, M., HACKMANN, A., & CLARK, D. M. (2002). Community based cognitive therapy in the treatment of posttraumatic stress disorder following the Omagh bomb. *Behavior Research and Therapy, 40,* 345–357.

JORDAN, K. (2002). Providing crisis counseling to New Yorkers after the terrorist attack on the World Trade Center. *The Family Journal: Counseling and Therapy for Couples and Families, 10,* 139–144.

KIECOLT-GLASER, J. K., MCGUIRE, L., ROBLES, T. F., & GLASER, R. (2002). Psychoneuroimmunology: Psychological influences on immune function and health. *Journal of Consulting and Clinical Psychology, 70,* 537–547.

MURPHY, R. T., WISMAR, K., & FREEMAN, K. (in press). Stress symptoms among African American college students following the September 11, 2001 terrorist attacks. *The Journal of Nervous & Mental Disease.*

NOLEN-HOEKSEMA, S., & MORROW, J. (1991). A prospective study of depression and distress following a natural disaster: The 1989 Loma Prieta earthquake. *Journal of Personality and Social Psychology, 67,* 92–104.

PFEFFERBAUM, B., & DOUGHTY, D. E. (2001). Increased alcohol use in a treatment sample of Oklahoma City bombing victims. *Psychiatry, 64,* 296–303.

PFEFFERBAUM, B., NIXON, S. J., TIVIS, R. D., DOUGHTY, D. E., PYNOOS, R. S., GURWITCH, R. H., & FOY, D. W. (2001). Television exposure in children after a terrorist incident. *Psychiatry, 64,* 202–211.

PFEFFERBAUM, B., SEALE, T. W., MCDONALD, N. B., BRANDT, E. N., RAINWATER, S. M., MAYNARD, B. T., MEIERHOEFER, B., & MILLER, P. D. (2000). Posttraumatic stress two years after the Oklahoma City bombing in youths geographically distant from the explosion. *Psychiatry, 63,* 358–370.

RUBONIS, A., & BICKMAN, L. (1991). Psychological impairment in the wake of disaster: The disaster-psychopathology relationship. *Psychological Bulletin, 109,* 384–399.

SCHUSTER, M. A., STEIN, B. D., JAYCOX, L. H., COLLINS, R. L., MARSHALL, G. N., ELLIOTT, M. N., ZHOU, A. J., KANOUSE, D. E., MORRISON, J. L., & BERRY, S. H. (2001). A national survey of stress reactions after the September 11, 2001, terrorist attacks. *New England Journal of Medicine, 345,* 1507–1512.

SELYE, H. (1956). *The stress of life.* New York: McGraw-Hill Book Company.

SPRANG, G. (1999). Post-disaster stress following the Oklahoma City bombing: An examination of three community groups. *Journal of Interpersonal Violence, 14,* 169–183.

————. Vicarious stress: Patterns of disturbance and use of mental health services by those indirectly affected by the Oklahoma City bombing. *Psychological Reports, 89,* 331–338.

TUCKER, P., PFEFFERBAUM, B., NIXON, S. J., & DICKSON, W. (2000). Predictors of post-traumatic stress symptoms in Oklahoma City: Exposure, social support, peri-traumatic responses. *The Journal of Behavioral Health Services & Research, 27,* 406–416.

WESSELY, S., HYAMS, K. C., & BARTHOLOMEW, R. (2001). Psychological implications of chemical and biological weapons. *British Medical Journal, 10,* 878–880.

10

Hate Crime as a Reaction to the Terrorist Attacks of September 11, 2001

Kimberly A. Vogt

❖

Various segments of the population react differently to traumatic events. The last chapter explored responses related to internalization of the effects of the traumatic events. This chapter examines a form of external expression—the increase in the incidence of hate crimes against targeted groups in the aftermath of September 11. Vogt provides a sociological explanation of why hate crimes occur. Using the McDevitt, Levin, and Bennett (2002) framework, Vogt discusses recent attacks against Muslims and members of Middle Eastern communities as retaliatory hate crimes. The perpetrators of these crimes attack innocent members of certain groups out of a sense of powerlessness against the true offenders. In this respect, the author suggests that perpetrators of hate crimes and terrorists are similar because both groups are engaged in violence against innocent civilians and use the notion of collective liability to justify their actions.

The terrorist attacks of September 11, 2001, at the World Trade Center in New York, the Pentagon, and United Airlines flight 93 in Somerset County, Pennsylvania, brought the realities of the consequences of terrorism into the homes of Americans like no other incident in recent history. We reacted to the horror of the unfolding events with feelings of fear, incredulity, anger, helplessness, and for some, hate. One response to the terrorist attacks was an increase in hate crimes against people of Muslim or Middle Eastern descent in the United States. The hate crimes occurred in big cities, small cities, and towns across the nation. Why would some Americans respond to the terrorist attacks by harming members of their own community or neighborhood? Why do people commit hate crimes?

This article provides a sociological framework for understanding why hate crimes are often committed in response to threats or attacks by people whom we see as "different." Using McDevitt, Levin, and Bennett's (2002) typology of hate crime as a tool for understanding hate crime perpetrators' motives, incidents of anti-Muslim and anti–Middle Eastern hatred are examined.

DEFINING HATE CRIMES

Defining exactly what we mean by the term *hate crime,* like all socially constructed concepts, has involved both social and political debate. The debate centers on disagreement over the creation of laws that specifically identify hate or bias motivated acts as offenses that are separate and distinct from the underlying offense—for example, a robbery or homicide. States that have enacted hate crime legislation have laws that allow for enhanced penalties if a crime such as assault is motivated by hate or bias rather than treating hate crime as a separate criminal offense. The majority of states today have some form of hate crime law that allows offenders who commit criminal acts because of bias or hatred to be held accountable for their actions (Partners Against Hate, n.d.). States that have enacted hate crime laws differ from one another with regard to the inclusion or exclusion of protected groups, most notably gender, disability, sexual orientation, and gender identity (Boeckmann & Turpin-Petrosino, 2002).

Criminologists broadly define a hate crime as an offense that is directed against a member of a specific group, solely because of membership in that group (Levin & McDevitt, 1993; Perry, 2001). Historically, stigmatized groups such as racial and ethnic minorities, Jews, gay men, and lesbians are common targets of hate crime. Although a broad definition of hate crime is useful from a sociological perspective, legalistic definitions such as the definition used by the Federal Bureau of Investigation (F.B.I.), must be more specific so they can be utilized during legal proceedings.

The F.B.I. defines hate or bias crime as ". . . offenses motivated in part or singularly by personal prejudice against others because of a diversity—race, sexual orientation, religion, ethnicity/national origin, or disability" (F.B.I., 2001). For the purposes of this article, the F.B.I. definition is used. Hate crime, as defined by the F.B.I., includes all types of traditional criminal acts such as murder, assault, rape, robbery, arson, intimidation, and vandalism. What makes them distinct is their *motivation* based on hatred or bias.

Sociological Factors Related to Hate Crime

Hate crimes have long been used by members of dominant social groups to assert their power over weaker social groups. Hate crimes are used to maintain the current balance of power by reinforcing social boundaries that prevent oppressed groups from gaining social status or power. Hate crime is used not only to keep the individual victims "in their place," but also to send a message intimidating the minority group as a whole. Hate crimes create widespread fear and vulnerability among the victim's social group. The fear that results from hate crime stems from the fact that victims are chosen for characteristics over which they have little or no control, such as race, ethnicity, religion, gender, sexual orientation, or national origin. These characteristics are components of what sociologists have termed *social location.* An individual's social location is based on the power (or lack of power) that you possess based on your position(s) in the social structure.

People, who are members of historically dominant social groups such as males, European Americans, and young- to middle-aged adults, all enjoy social rights and privileges (power) solely because of their membership in that particular group. When we, as an individual or a group, have power and social status, we try to keep it. When we feel that we are losing social status or power, we fight to retain it. One way to retain power is to oppress others. By keeping someone else in a less powerful position, an individual can maintain—or feel as though he or she is maintaining—a position of power or control.

Hate crimes are tools used by individuals and organized hate groups in attempts to maintain a position of superiority or power over another social group. The violence, property destruction, and generalized fear that hate crime creates can be an effective empowerment tool for those who feel threatened and powerless. Americans have historically used crimes of violence based on bigotry and bias to oppress others. It is only recently that we have identified these acts as hate crimes.

Hate crime occurs because an individual feels that his or her position in the social structure, or his or her access to scarce resources, is being threatened (Levin & McDevitt, 1993; Perry, 2001). The loss of a high-paying manufacturing job, the perception that social status has been eroding for people like myself, or perceived competition from newcomers in my community are all examples of the types of social change that are viewed has threatening to the typical hate crime offender. Hate crime offenders, frustrated because of their loss of status (whether perceived or real), look to blame others for their diminished social position and engage in a form of self-help (violence or intimidation as a way of solving a problem)—hate crime (Black, 1983). People who differ from the offender by race, ethnicity, gender, sexual orientation, religion, or nationality are considered outsiders who threaten to take the place of the offender on the social structural ladder of success. As hostility fostered by bias toward a social group grows, hate crime becomes a way to regain status or to punish "outsiders" for their difference (Perry, 2001). Unlike other forms of crime, the individual who becomes a victim of a hate crime is selected solely because he or she is a member of the hated group. The lack of specificity when selecting a victim during a hate crime is best explained using the concept of collective liability.

COLLECTIVE LIABILITY

Hate crime is unique when compared to nonhate crime (e.g., a typical robbery) because the victims are selected for very different reasons. The victim of a typical robbery is selected because he or she appears to the offender to be vulnerable or to have a resource, such as cash, that the offender desires. Victims of hate crime, however, are chosen *solely because they are members, or are perceived to be members,* of a hated group. The offender relies on negative stereotypes of the characteristics and behavior of the members of the despised group to help reduce empathy toward the victim, making it easier to commit the crime. The offender may be so biased against the targeted group that the victim is not even seen as a legitimate member of society but as an object that does not even merit recognition as a human being (Levin & McDevitt, 1993, p. 22).

The actions and attitudes of individuals within the hated group are mixed together in the offender's mind so that individual actions are deemed irrelevant. To the offender, all members of the hated group are held *collectively liable* for the behavior of *all other* group members (Black, 1983; Scully & Marolla, 1985). For example, if the offender is biased against Muslims, individual conduct makes no difference. A Muslim shopkeeper's actions have no effect on whether he or she becomes the victim of a hate attack. *As a Muslim,* he or she is held accountable for the actions of *all* Muslims, and therefore is perceived to be a valid hate crime target in the eyes of the offender.

Collective liability is also important in our understanding of the hateful and violent reactions on the part of some Americans to the terrorist attacks of September 11, 2001. How many hate crimes were committed in response to the September 11 attacks? How many hate crimes occur in any given year in the United States? Who are the most frequent victims of hate crime? In order to better understand the acts of hate crime that were committed in response to the terrorist attacks of September 11, 2001, we need to become familiar with the general etiology of hate crime.

CHARACTERISTICS OF HATE CRIME IN THE UNITED STATES

The most comprehensive data on hate crime in the United States comes from the Federal Bureau of Investigation's annual report, *Hate Crime Statistics*. The F.B.I. has been responsible for collecting data on hate crimes since congress passed the Hate Crimes Statistics Act in 1990 (F.B.I., 2001). Before passage of the Hate Crime Statistics Act, no single or consistent source of data was collected or reported on a broad range of hate crimes covering the United States as a whole. Data was gathered by advocacy and civil rights groups such as the Jewish Anti-Defamation League, the National Gay and Lesbian Task Force, and the Southern Poverty Law Center, or by individual researchers. The data from these organizations often have a narrow focus and rely on media reports as a source of data on hate incidents. The data often only cover a single region or city such as New York and only gather information on a particular category of hate crime. Data might be available for hate crimes against gay men and lesbians, for example, but nonexistent for other groups (e.g., hate crimes against Asians, Native Americans, or Muslims).

With the inception of the 1990 Hate Crimes Statistics Act, the United States began collection of hate crime data on a national level using a consistent set of hate crime categories. The F.B.I., in conjunction with its Uniform Crime Reporting (UCR) program, solicits information on hate crime from law enforcement agencies throughout the nation. State and local law enforcement agencies submit data on crimes that have been reported to the police and are identified by law enforcement officers as hate or bias incidents. Participation in the UCR and hate crime data collection programs is voluntary, and not all law enforcement agencies participate. Therefore, hate crime data reported by the F.B.I. is an underestimate of hate crime in the United States. In the year 2000, 11,690 law enforcement agencies, covering a population of 236,929,512 people, filed reports on hate crime activity in their jurisdictions (F.B.I., 2001, pp. 1–2).

According to the F.B.I., there were 9,430 incidents of hate crime with 9,924 victims in the year 2000 (F.B.I., 2001). Almost two-thirds of reported hate crime incidents were person-to-person crimes (65.0%), while 34.4 percent were crimes against property. Intimidation (34.9%) was the most frequent type of hate crime reported to the police, followed by destruction or vandalism (29.3%). Simple assault (17.1%), aggravated assault (12.6%), and other crimes (6.1%) made up the balance of reported hate crime (F.B.I., 2001, p. 5).

As can be seen in Table 10.1, the majority of hate crime incidents are crimes of racial bias. The second and third most prevalent forms of hate crime are religious bias and sexual orientation bias, followed by ethnic/nationality bias and disability bias. In recent years, hate crimes against Asian Americans, gay men, and lesbians have been increasing.

Table 10.1   Hate Crime Single-Bias Incident Characteristics, by Bias, United States, 2000

Offense Type	Incidents (%)	Victims (%)	Known Offenders (%)
Race	53.8	54.5	59.2
Religion	18.3	17.2	7.7
Sexual Orientation	16.1	15.7	19.2
Ethnicity/National Origin	11.3	12.3	13.5
Disability	0.4	0.4	0.5

(Source: F.B.I., 2001, p. 7.)

The hate crimes of interest for the purposes of this chapter—hate crimes against people who are or are perceived to be Middle Eastern or Muslim—have historically made up a small percentage of reported hate crime. Because of the reporting categories used by the F.B.I., hate crimes against separate ethnic groups, with the exception of Hispanics, are not presented in the annual report. The F.B.I., does, however, separately report anti-Islamic hate crime, making this the only category where a significant proportion of hate crimes related to negative reactions to the terrorist attacks of September 11 can be identified. For the years 1995 through 2000, the F.B.I. reported 165 anti-Islamic hate crimes, averaging 28 per year *(http://www.fbi.gov/ucr/ucr.htm)*. The events of September 11, 2001 triggered a surge in anti-Middle Eastern and anti-Islamic hate crime. Hate crime statistics for the years 2001 and 2002 should report significant increases in two categories: anti-Islamic religious bias and anti-other ethnicity/national bias.

Hate crimes, in comparison to other types of crime, are more damaging to property and more brutal in the level of physical harm caused to the victims (Levin & McDevitt, 1993, p. 11). In addition to being more costly and damaging, hate crimes are also more likely to be committed by strangers than are other types of interpersonal violence, which most often occur between people who are acquainted with one another. Hate crimes are also unique because they are more likely to be committed by a group of offenders when compared to similar crimes without bias motivation (Levin & McDevitt, 1993, pp. 13–19).

Offender Characteristics

The typical offender in a hate crime is a European American, young adult, or adolescent male, from a working-class background, who commits his crime with a small group of peers. In 2000, the F.B.I. reported that of offenders, who were known or identifiable through victim reports, 64.4 percent were white, 18.7 percent were black, and 7.2 percent were of another race (F.B.I., 2001, p. 16). Although hate crime offenders can come from any social class or racial or ethnic background, members of society who are disenfranchised or are experiencing eroding social status are at the greatest risk of offending.

Two pervasive features of U.S. culture can help us to understand the cultural influences behind the motivations of hate crime offenders: ethnocentrism and a culture or subculture of violence. Like all other members of our society, perpetrators of hate crime are influenced by U.S. cultural beliefs and practices. Ethnocentrism is the belief that one's culture is superior to other cultures. Ethnocentrism is problematic when one person uses the values and practices of his or her culture to judge the values and practices of another culture. Ethnocentric beliefs are the foundation for prejudice, discrimination, and oppression. The historical domination and power of the United States has fostered ethnocentric beliefs regarding the superiority of U.S. cultural values. Cultures that differ significantly from U.S. culture are devalued. For example, Americans highly value individualism. Cultures that value the collective good over individual freedom are often viewed as inferior. In its extreme form, ethnocentrism can turn to hate. Hate crime offenders espousing views of racial or religious superiority, for example, rely on their ethnocentric worldview to justify their harmful actions. In addition to ethnocentrism, the U.S. cultural norms that support the use of violence as a means to solve problems and disputes contributes to the high rate of hate crime in the United States.

Many hate crimes are crimes of violence. Using violence as a means to solve individual problems has a long history in the United States and is deeply engrained in the U.S. social fabric. The culture of violence in the United States reinforces and passes on the values, attitudes, and beliefs that promote violence as an appropriate, and sometimes necessary, response to perceived or real threats to a person's character, actions, or beliefs (Wolfgang & Ferracuti, 1967). Violence in many forms, including hate crimes, was and is widely socially sanctioned. Historically, for example, "taking the law into your own hands" through vigilante actions such as lynching is a form of hate crime that was fostered by the U.S. culture of violence. Even today, many people continue to support the actions of hate crime offenders, either implicitly or explicitly (Levin, 2002). Hate crime offenders, particularly members of organized hate groups, can increase their social standing in the group by engaging in acts of violence. For many hate crime offenders, violence is culturally normative, and responding to feelings of frustration, anger or embarrassment with nonviolent means is rarely an option. Awareness of the relationship between social forces such as the culture of violence and hate crime offending provides a basis for understanding these crimes.

In recent years, to better understand hate crime, social scientists have studied hate crime offenders and their motives. McDevitt, Levin, and Bennett (2002), using the earlier work of Levin and McDevitt (1993), present a typology of hate crime that is very useful in understanding the motivations of hate crime offenders. Using their typology, we can gain a greater understanding of the hate crimes triggered by the September 11, 2001 terrorist attacks.

MCDEVITT, LEVIN, AND BENNETT'S TOPOLOGY OF HATE CRIME

The hate crime typology developed by Levin and McDevitt (1993), and expanded by McDevitt, Levin, and Bennett (2002), was created for use by both social scientists and criminal justice agencies to assist in better understanding the motivations of hate crime offenders. The authors created the typology (see Table 10.2) based on analysis of hate crime offenses and offenders in Boston, Massachusetts. The typology consists of four ideal types that describe the motivations used by offenders: (1) thrill-seeking hate crime, (2) defensive hate crime, (3) retaliatory hate crime, and (4) mission hate crime.

Table 10.2   McDevitt, Levin, and Bennett's Typology of Hate Crime

Hate Crime Type	Characteristics
Thrill-Seeking Hate Crime	Perpetrator is looking to have some fun, inflict pain, or get a sadistic thrill.
Defensive Hate Crime	Perpetrator takes a defensive stand against a perceived threat from an "outsider."
Retaliatory Hate Crime	Perpetrator believes that his/her group has been dishonored and seeks to punish the offending group.
Mission Hate Crime	Perpetrator believes that it is his/her mission to eliminate "evil."

(Source: McDevitt, Levin, & Bennett, 2002.)

Thrill-Seeking Hate Crimes

Thrill-seeking hate crimes were the most prevalent type of hate crime in the Boston study (Levin & McDevitt, 1993). The offenders in this type of hate crime often act in a group and rarely make plans ahead of time. Their crimes are spur of the moment activities—going out and hurting something or someone whom the offender sees as inferior and socially unworthy. Thrill-seekers are often young people who are trying to impress members of their peer group or neighborhood with their actions. They feel socially rewarded—from their friends or those in their community—for engaging in acts of hatred. Thrill-seeking hate crime offenders engage in indiscriminant hatred. Oftentimes, they do not have a deep-seated hatred of any particular group. The offender is more likely to be biased *in general* toward many groups such as gay men, African Americans, and Jews. Because of the offender's lack of specialization in their biases, any hated group is a valid target.

Defensive Hate Crimes

Defensive hate crimes are emotionally charged acts that express the offender's fear, anger, and hatred at a threatening group (McDevitt, Levin, & Bennett, 2002). Oftentimes, the offender perceives of him- or herself as a defender of a territory—neighborhood, workplace, or community. The hate crime is an attempt to frighten away members of the threatening group and return things to "the way they were." The majority of defensive hate crimes are racially biased hate crimes (Levin & McDevitt, 1993, p. 75). Vandalizing the home of an African American family that has moved into a predominantly European American neighborhood is an example of a defensive hate crime.

Retaliatory Hate Crimes

Retaliatory hate crimes accounted for approximately 8 percent of all hate crimes in the Boston study (McDevitt et al., 2002, p. 309). Retaliatory hate crimes are defined as hate crimes that are committed in response to a perceived affront or attack (McDevitt et al., 2002). An example of a retaliatory hate crime is the assault of a European American youth by an African American youth, in response to an earlier hate crime incident, where the victim was an African American. Retaliatory hate crimes are a form of revenge used by members of the victimized group to avenge the affront. The majority of the hate crimes that were committed in response to the September 11, 2001 terrorist attacks were retaliatory hate crimes.

Mission Hate Crimes

Mission hate crimes are crimes that are committed by an offender who sees it as his or her goal in life to eliminate a particular group of people. Individuals who commit mission hate crime are more likely to be members of an organized hate group, or to be mentally ill, than are offenders of other types of hate crime (Levin & McDevitt, 1993, p. 89). Mission hate crime is extremely rare and made up less than 1 percent of the hate crimes in the Boston study. As will be presented shortly, terrorism is an example of an extreme form of mission hate crime.

McDevitt, Levin, and Bennett's typology, particularly the categories of retaliatory hate crime and mission hate crime, are useful in understanding the response of some Americans to the September 11 attacks and the actions of the terrorists.

HATE CRIME AS A REACTION TO THE TERRORIST ATTACKS OF SEPTEMBER 11, 2001

In the weeks and months following the terrorist attacks of September 11, a significant increase in the number of hate crimes against people of Arab descent or Muslim/Islamic faith occurred in the United States (Southern Poverty Law Center [SPLC], 2002). In the eight months following the attacks, September 12, 2001 to May 31, 2002, over 250 hate-related incidents that appeared to be triggered by the terrorist attacks were reported in the media (SPLC, 2002). The incidents vary in severity; from Muslim parents keeping their children home from school because of threats to arson and even murder (SPLC, 2002). For the first time for many Americans, on September 11, 2001, the United States experienced a large scale, multiple-site terrorist attack. The terrorist attacks created fear, anger, and uncertainty. As information regarding the individuals who were allegedly responsible for the attacks was reported by the media, the face of terror took on a specific image: that of an adult male of the Muslim faith from the Middle East. Despite pleas from government leaders, including President Bush, a barrage of hate incidents against those perceived to be Middle Eastern or Muslim swept through the United States (Serrano, 2001).

The majority of the hate crimes that occurred in the wake of the terrorist attacks of September 11, 2001, were retaliatory hate crimes. Offenders relied on stereotyped images of the terrorists, drawn from very little factual knowledge, and responded to the attacks by victimizing people who were Middle Eastern or Muslim and vandalizing homes, businesses, and places of worship. For example, on September 30, 2001, an Arab American convenience store owner in East Reedley, California, who had received earlier death threats, was murdered in his store. Witnesses identified the perpetrators as a car full of teenagers (Nieves, 2001).

Non-Muslim and non-Middle Eastern individuals were also victimized by hate crimes triggered by the September 11 terrorist attacks. Many reported hate incidents indicated that the offenders perceived the victims to be Islamic or Middle Eastern, when in fact they were not. For example, an Indian American man in New York State was attacked and his business set on fire, while the assailants yelled "Go back to Afghanistan!" (SPLC, 2002).

Many victims of retaliatory hate crime were of Asian or Indian descent or the Sikh religion. Several examples are illustrative of the ignorance among hate crime offenders regarding Middle Eastern, Asian Pacific, and Islamic cultures and the subsequent victimization that those who resembled the terrorists suffered. In Colorado, on September 13, 2001, a Sikh American family's car and driveway were vandalized with the word "terrorist" and the phrase "terrorist on board" (SPLC, 2002). Because males of the Sikh religion often have long beards and wear turbans, they were frequently mistaken for Muslims and attacked. In Arizona, a Sikh American gas station owner was shot to death while at work. The offender, on a killing spree, also attempted to murder a Lebanese man at another gas station and fired shots at the home of an Afghan family (SPLC, 2002).

Examples such as these illustrate how collective liability puts people at risk of hate crime victimization. The victims were chosen because they resembled the people identified as responsible for the terrorist attacks. It made no difference whether they were U.S. citizens or that they had not harmed anyone. Offenders see all Middle Easterners and Muslims as threatening and therefore as valid targets for attack. Perpetrators of retaliatory hate crime feel superior to those in the hated group and feel entitled to seek retribution.

Retaliatory hate crimes, like those in the wake of September 11, resemble what Levin (2002) describes as protest by proxy. When people cannot seek revenge against those whom they see as truly responsible for offending against them, they aim their aggression at someone else. In order to gain a sense of superiority over those whom they find threatening and to provide justification for their actions, these offenders create an image of an enemy (e.g., evildoers) who deserves punishment (Levin, 2002). Americans who engaged in retaliatory hate crimes as a response to the terrorist attacks of September 11 were seeking revenge against members of al-Qaeda but were powerless to aggress against them. Frustrated, all people who appeared to be Middle Eastern or Muslim, including members of the offender's own community, were now seen as dangerous and evil.

Several incidents serve as examples of retaliatory hate crime in response to the terrorist attacks:

- In Seattle, Washington, on September 13, 2001, a man was charged in the attack of a mosque and its worshipers. The man pointed a gun at worshipers and poured gasoline on cars in the parking lot. While fleeing the scene, he fired a handgun at worshipers. The accused offender admitted that he was angry over the events of September 11 (Serrano, 2001).
- A Sikh man who owned a gas station was shot to death. His alleged perpetrator is reported to have said: "I stand for America all the way!" (Serrano, 2001).
- In Washington State, "A bomb was detonated outside the home of a family of Middle Eastern descent." (SPLC, 2002).
- In Meadville, Pennsylvania, ". . . a man attacked a female high school student of Middle Eastern descent with a knife, yelling, "You're not an American! You don't belong here!" (SPLC, 2002).

- In Illinois, a taxi cab driver was assaulted after being chased by several offenders on motorcycles. During the assault they yelled, "This is what you get, you mass murderer!" (SPLC, 2002).

In the previous examples, the core components of a retaliatory hate crime are evident: The crime is a punishment for an earlier event that caused dishonor, and the victims are held collectively liable for actions over which they had no control. The victim can be any man with a turban, any person with olive-colored skin, or any member of a mosque.

THE RELATIONSHIP BETWEEN HATE CRIME AND TERRORISM

The terrorist attacks and the retaliatory hate crimes that occurred in response to them, share similarities regarding the goals of the offenders. Levin and McDevitt suggest that, "In their intended effect, [hate crimes] are very much like acts of terrorism, meant to send a signal by means of fear and horror" (p. 77). Both the hate crime offenders who engaged in retaliation and the September 11 terrorists used violence to provoke reactions of fear and insecurity in a collective group of people. Retaliatory hate crime offenders and terrorists both rely on collective liability to rationalize the validity of their actions. Retaliatory hate crime offenders felt justified in striking out against innocent Muslim and Middle Eastern Americans. That justification was fueled by feelings of helplessness. The September 11 terrorists chose to victimize people in the World Trade Center, the Pentagon, and on U.S. airlines simply because they were American. The terrorists held all Americans collectively liable for the actions of the Americans that they viewed as harmful to their way of life. Hate crime is related to terrorism in that the emotions of frustration, anger, and hatred fuel the perpetrators of both types of crime. Both hate crime offenders and terrorists feel powerless to change what they see as wrong or unjust in their world through legitimate avenues. They seek to right wrongs, or bring about "justice" through illegitimate or extralegal means (Gibbs, 1989; Levin & McDevitt, 1993).

According to Black (1983), terrorism is a means of self-help. Self-help is ". . . the expression of a grievance by unilateral aggression" (Black, 1983, p. 34). Both terrorists and reactive hate crime perpetrators hold grievances against the targets of their aggression. By definition, terrorism is ". . . violence employed for sub-revolutionary purposes of intimidation, vengeance, or punishment" (Hamm, 1994, p. 105). Terrorism can be categorized as an extreme form of mission hate crime. Like terrorists, people who engage in mission hate crime are often associated with an organized group whose members share their values and goals. Terrorist groups such as al-Qaeda can be described as a form of organized hate group that engages in mission hate crime. The al-Qaeda terrorists share some characteristics with other types of organized hate groups. The leadership and core members adhere strongly to the values and beliefs of the group. Hatred and violence is a career, not a recreational activity (Levin & McDevitt, 1993). The members are willing to engage in violent, destructive, or threatening acts in support of the group's cause. Like other mission hate crime offenders, the September 11 terrorists believed that it was their "mission" to eliminate an evil that they saw as threatening to their belief system. In this case, the evil was the United States—Americans, whose Western values and practices were destroying the Islamic way of life.

There are some differences between other mission hate groups and terrorist groups. Terrorists often target large political or governmental entities, whereas most mission hate crime offenders, target categories of people such as Jews or African Americans. In addition, it appears that many al-Qaeda terrorists, unlike more typical mission hate crime offenders, are willing to die for their cause. Both terrorism and hate crime are violent acts that instill fear and distrust. The victims of the terrorist attack of September 11, 2001 and the victims of retaliatory hate crime are all victims of hate and prejudice. Hate crime statistics from the years 2001 and 2002 will unfortunately provide a permanent record of the increased levels of hatred and discrimination experienced by people in the United States of Middle Eastern descent and Muslim faith. The anger and frustration that many Americans felt after the terrorist attacks of September 11, 2001 are comprehensible; the acts of hatred in reaction to the terrorist attacks by some, are not.

DISCUSSION QUESTIONS

1. In the wake of September 11, 2001 did you witness or hear about any acts of prejudice or hatred in response to the terrorist attacks? In one or two paragraphs, describe what event or events you observed or heard about. Describe your response to this incident/incidents. Do you think your response would have been different if the acts you observed or heard about had not been related to September 11? Why or why not?
2. Go to the Southern Poverty Law Center's Web site *http://www.tolerance.org*. Go to one of the activities listed under *Do Something* or *Dig Deeper.* In one or two pages, describe (a) the activity/exercise you explored and (b) what you learned through the exercise that is related the topic of hate crime. Be prepared to discuss your completed assignment in class.
3. List five to ten core or dominant social-cultural values of U.S. society (e.g., individualism, democracy). What core/dominant U.S. values can help us understand or explain the surge in retaliatory hate crimes in the months following September 11, 2001? How do those values assist in explaining or understanding the increase in retaliatory hate crime?

REFERENCES

BLACK, D. (1983). Crime as social control. *American Sociological Review, 14,* 34–45.

BOECKMANN, R.J., & TURPIN-PETROSINO, C. (2002). Understanding the harm of hate crime. *Journal of Social Issues, 58,* 207–225.

FEDERAL BUREAU OF INVESTIGATION (F.B.I.). (2001). *Hate crime statistics, 2000.* Retrieved January 17, 2002, from *http://www.fbi.gov/ucr/cius_00/hate00.pdf*

GIBBS, J. P. (1989). Conceptualization of terrorism. *American Sociological Review, 54,* 329–340.

HAMM, M.S. (1994). A modified social control theory of terrorism: An empirical and ethnographic assessment of the American Neo-Nazi Skinheads. In M.S. Hamm (Ed.),

Hate crime: International perspectives on causes and control (pp. 105–149). Cincinnati, OH: Anderson.

LEVIN, J. (2002). *The violence of hate: Confronting racism, anti-Semitism, and other forms of bigotry.* Boston: Allyn and Bacon.

LEVIN, J., & MCDEVITT, J. (1993). *Hate crimes: The rising tide of bigotry and bloodshed.* New York: Plenum.

MCDEVITT, J., LEVIN, J., & BENNETT, S. (2002). Hate crime offenders: An expanded typology. *Journal of Social Issues, 58,* 303–317.

NIEVES, E. (2001, October 3). California death is called a hate crime. *The New York Times,* p. A18. Retrieved April 24, 2002, from LEXIS-NEXIS Academic Universe *http://web.lexis-nexis.com/universe/*

PARTNERS AGAINST HATE. (n.d.). *State and local responses to hate crimes.* Retrieved August 24, 2002, from *http://www.partnersagainsthate.org/reference_center/database/*

PERRY, B. (2001). *In the name of hate: Understanding hate crimes.* New York: Routledge.

SCULLY, D., & MAROLLA, J. (1985). "Riding the bull at Gilley's": Convicted rapists describe the rewards of rape. *Social Problems, 32,* 251–263.

SERRANO, R. (2001, September 28). Response to terror. *Los Angeles Times,* p. A19. Retrieved April 24, 2002 from LEXIS-NEXIS Academic Universe *http://web.lexis-nexis.com/universe/*

SOUTHERN POVERTY LAW CENTER (SPLC). (2002). *Violence against Arab and Muslim Americans.* Retrieved June 18, 2002 from *http://www.tolerance.org/news/article_tol.jsp?id=280*

WOLFGANG, M., & FERRACUTI, F. (1967). *Subculture of violence.* London: Tavistock Press.

11

The Impact of the September 11, 2001 Terrorist Attacks on Civil Liberties

Patricia Brady

Different in tone from the other chapters, this article was written by a legal practitioner. Brady offers an overview of the "sources" of civil liberties and continues with a discussion of the threat to many civil liberties in the aftermath of September 11. In readable prose, she reviews the USA PATRIOT Act and its implications for members of the university community. She also discusses the potential loss of civil liberties by stifling public debate. Brady offers excellent examples of how those who dissented from the popular view regarding the causes of September 11 were met with public outrage. Further, many individuals believed to be Muslim were subjected to verbal and, at times, physical abuse. She concludes that in spite of the threat of terrorism, the university community must persevere in its mission to understand the events that surround us even if that means challenging the consensus.

The horror of the September 11, 2001 terrorist attacks on the World Trade Center and the Pentagon prompted an immediate and virtually unanimous reaction among the U.S. public that the United States should take whatever steps necessary to strike back at the terrorists and to prevent recurrences of such events. Since September 11, we have prosecuted a war on the supporters of terrorism and have adopted a number of legislative and governmental responses directed to improving our national security and preventing future terrorist attacks.

As these measures have been implemented, however, it has become apparent that the urgent effort to combat terrorism may require U.S. citizens to accept limits on certain freedoms that, in this very free and open society, have generally been taken for granted. Some of these restrictions—notably those associated with heightened security in airports and other places of public accommodation—may be no more than minor social inconveniences, readily accepted for the sake of improved public safety. Other responses to terrorism, though, create more significant intrusions, implicating the freedoms of speech and religion, privacy interests, protections for criminal defendants, and immigration practices.

To what degree should Americans be willing to accept limits on civil liberties in the name of achieving victory over terrorism? To accept any and all limits presents the painful irony that a war being waged in the name of democracy and civilization will erode those core values that are central to democracy and civilization. On the other hand, to accept no limits may undermine the effort to defeat terrorism and to impair the national security.

In this troubling environment, it is crucial to understand the nature and sources of civil liberties; to be aware of which of those liberties may be affected by our current responses to terrorism; and to consider how to resolve inherent tensions between preserving liberty and effectively prosecuting the war against terrorism. Likewise critical is the ability of the academic community to provide information and foster debate about these questions, since open discussion on these matters offers, in the end, the surest means of securing our democratic freedoms.

SOURCES OF "CIVIL LIBERTIES"

The events of September 11 generated enormous pressure to expand the powers of law enforcement authorities and the military to respond to the crisis and to improve national security. At the same time, public outrage over the attacks combined with a newly aroused patriotism to create an atmosphere hostile to reasoned discussion and debate about the underlying issues. In this kind of environment, the rights of individuals are particularly vulnerable to being sacrificed to greater community needs. Our own national history is replete with examples of wartime actions inimical to civil liberties, from the suppression of German language teaching in World War I to the internment of Japanese citizens during World War II. As such actions demonstrate, in times of grave national crisis, there is a heightened need for concern about the preservation of civil liberties.

What do we mean, though, when we refer to *civil liberties?* What does the term encompass, and what are the sources of these freedoms? In its most general sense, "civil liberties" may be said to include the entire range of civic freedoms afforded by a free society, from those individual rights secured by the United States Constitution and parallel provisions in state constitutions, to legislatively created protections embodied in statutes and rules, to ordinary social freedoms that reflect our national culture and customs.

There is, of course, a hierarchy of importance in this range of liberties and a parallel hierarchy of concern accompanying threats to their exercise. Those rights accorded constitutional protection—reflecting, as they do, the core values of our society—are of paramount importance; consequently, those responses to terrorism that impinge on constitutional rights are of greatest concern. Limitations on legislatively established protections and the curtailment of various social activities are of correspondingly less importance, despite the fact that they, too, may result in the diminution of personal freedoms.

As the principal source of civil liberties, the Constitution affords protection for a number of individual freedoms, most importantly those enumerated in the Bill of Rights (the first ten Amendments). Under the First Amendment, the Constitution guarantees the rights of religious freedom, free speech and association, and freedom of the press. The right to be free of unreasonable, warrantless searches and seizures is established by the Fourth Amendment. The rights to due process of law and to be safe from double jeopardy and self-incrimination are afforded by the Fifth Amendment. Various additional rights of criminal defendants, including the right to a speedy and public trial, are provided under the Sixth Amendment.

In addition to these explicitly described rights, the courts have interpreted the Constitution to afford protection for additional rights not named, but considered to be within the *penumbra* of constitutional provisions. Academic freedom—the idea that universities, their faculty, and students have the freedom to seek truth freely and without interference—is in this category. In the "loyalty-oath cases" arising during the Cold War era, the United States Supreme Court recognized the importance of academic freedom in a democratic society and identified academic freedom as a special concern of the First Amendment. Justice Frankfurter's concurring opinion in *Sweezy* v. *New Hampshire,* 354 U.S. 234 (1957) emphasized the "dependence of a free society on free universities," and discussed the freedoms of a university to determine who may teach, what may be taught, how it shall be taught, and who may be admitted to study. Subsequently, in *Keyishian* v. *Board of Regents of the State of New York,* 385 U.S. 589 (1967), the Supreme Court stated that academic freedom is "a special concern of the First Amendment, which does not tolerate laws that cast a pall of orthodoxy over the classroom."

Other individual rights are afforded by statutes and regulations. This category of legislatively based protections includes the expectations of privacy established under statutes such as the Family Educational Rights and Privacy Act ("FERPA").[1] FERPA's basic provisions protect student records from being disclosed without their consent, while assuring that students themselves have the ability to inspect the contents of their records. Also of importance are the rights provided by the statutory scheme governing immigration to the United States and the treatment of aliens entering the country either as guests or as applicants for permanent residency. Additionally, in this category are statutory protections such as those found in Titles VI and VII of the Civil Rights Act of 1964, prohibiting discrimination on various bases, including race and national origin.

Finally, at the most general level, there are the liberties that we enjoy and expect as a natural part of life in a free society. Among the most common of these are our freedom of access to places of public accommodation: airports and other transportation hubs, government buildings, streets, and places of business.

As quickly became apparent after September 11, the effort to defeat terrorism has potential consequences for this entire range of civil freedoms. In assessing the impact, however, it is also necessary to consider the relative importance of the rights that are affected, and the sources of limitations.

LIBERTIES AFFECTED BY OUR RESPONSES
TO THE TERRORIST ATTACKS

Following September 11, perhaps the most dramatic new limitations on freedom were those affecting air transportation. Changes in airport security that were implemented just after the attacks have now permanently altered the way we travel. Similar security measures

---

[1]Privacy has itself been held to be among the "penumbral" rights protected by the Constitution, see *Griswold* v. *Connecticut,* 381 U.S. 479 (1965).

adopted to manage entry into public buildings, from government offices and museums to heavily trafficked private facilities, followed shortly on the heels of the airport measures and have also remained in place. Yet such changes were, and continue to be, at the margin in terms of seriously impinging on individual rights. The inconveniences associated with heightened security measures—while clearly affecting the *ease* of travel and access to various facilities—did not significantly inhibit the *ability* to travel or gain access to places, and public acceptance was rapid. Because these enhanced security measures generally affect only social convenience, their impact on civil liberties has been negligible.[2]

Two other kinds of responses to the events of September 11, however, present more substantial threats to civil liberties having greater importance in the hierarchy of core rights. The first of these is Congress' comprehensive legislation aimed directly at discovering and eliminating terrorist activity, the USA PATRIOT Act ("the Act").[3] The other is the more insidious, indirect threat posed by public intolerance of free inquiry, debate, and discussion about the issues raised by or related to the attacks. Both of these kinds of reactions have constitutional implications and also jeopardize long-established legislatively granted rights.

The USA Patriot Act

The Act raises a number of troubling questions about the deprivation of civil rights. In the Act, Congress expands governmental activity in a number of areas, with the stated purpose of deterring and punishing terrorist acts in the United States and around the world, and enhancing law enforcement investigative tools. On matters of particular concern to the academic community, the Act includes provisions that affect privacy and student rights provided under FERPA, immigration, surveillance of electronic communications and tracking of computer usage, detention of certain individuals, and research activities.

A brief summary of key provisions of the Act demonstrates the potential difficulties. With regard to student privacy and FERPA, the Act permits an Assistant United States Attorney General or higher-level official to obtain a court order requiring the production of student education records relevant to a terrorism investigation, by certifying "specific and articulable facts" in support of the application. Educational institutions do not violate FERPA by complying with such orders, are not liable for good faith disclosures of information under these provisions, and need not make records of such disclosures.

The Act further steps up the monitoring of foreign students. It calls upon the government to implement fully existing laws that allow it to collect from colleges and universities information about foreign students, except for those holding immigrant visas, including their names and addresses, visa status, enrollment status, and any disciplinary actions taken against them resulting from criminal convictions. These laws have not previously been enforced, but compliance is now expected, and colleges and universities will be charged with maintaining and being able to produce the necessary data. Still other pro-

[2]This is not to say, though, that heightened security activities might not lead to violations of other kinds of rights, as where individuals are selected for additional screening processes based on race or ethnicity. In such instances, though, the individual rights implicated are those related to freedom from illegal discrimination, rather than freedom of access to public places.

[3]The Act is officially titled "Uniting and Strengthening America by Providing Appropriate Tools Required to Intercept and Obstruct Terrorism Act."

visions of the Act expand the government's ability to detain aliens, and—importantly—to deport them for certain associations with organizations designated as "terrorist groups."

Surveillance of electronic communications and computer activities by law enforcement authorities is made easier under the Act. Providers of communications services—which may include universities—are *allowed* to disclose information to law enforcement authorities if they believe there is an immediate danger of death or serious injury based on either the content of an electronic communication or information about a particular user. Providers *must disclose* information about voice-mail and user records in response to a warrant, subpoena, or similar court order. The Act also authorizes the use of certain technological devices designed to track Internet use by individuals.

Research activity is affected, as well, by the Act. The knowing possession of a biological agent, toxin, or delivery system of a type not "reasonably justified" by research is made punishable by fine and/or imprisonment up to ten years. Further, the Act makes it a crime for nationals of countries that support terrorism and certain others to possess defined "select agents" such as anthrax.

The broad expansion of government authority and activity under this statutory scheme has obvious constitutional implications. Increased information-gathering powers raise concerns about individual privacy and the right to be free of unreasonable searches and seizures. The provisions regarding detention and monitoring of aliens raise similar questions, as well as issues related to the adequacy of the process afforded to the detainees. Restrictions on associations with terrorist groups have implications for the right of free association guaranteed under the First Amendment.

Moreover, many of these provisions have direct consequences for institutions of higher education. Institutions have added obligations to ensure that their data collection practices as to foreign students are adequate and in full compliance with immigration requirements. Students are particularly vulnerable to having personal educational information revealed, as a result of the relaxation of FERPA protections and the expansion of electronic surveillance capabilities. The electronic tracking devices and surveillance activities, however, also more generally threaten all university employees, who may be subject to monitoring and whose Internet usage can be tracked. Even library patrons may be subject to these kinds of intrusions, altering previous understandings about the confidentiality of library use records.

Issues related to the First Amendment and academic freedom arise in connection with the law's regulation of "select agents." The government's ability to determine what quantities and types of toxic substances are "reasonably justified" as being kept for research purposes impinges on academic freedom in research.

These kinds of constraints go beyond the minor inconveniences to personal freedom resulting from heightened security measures. Both in terms of the extent of government intrusiveness and the importance of the civil rights implicated, the Act causes concern and raises questions about whether its limitations on freedom are necessary or justified by the war effort, or can be legally supported under the Constitution.

"Chilling Effects" on Expression and Debate

The provisions of the USA PATRIOT Act raise, in a direct manner, constitutional problems with the government's response to terrorism. Less direct—but also significant—are the societal effects of popular reaction to the September 11 attacks. Of special concern are the consequences of an overzealous patriotism that leads to intolerance of different viewpoints, peoples, and religions while chilling First Amendment and related freedoms of religion, expression, debate, and inquiry. Although here the evidence is of an anecdotal nature, the impacts on civil liberties are nonetheless real.

Public outrage at the September 11 attacks immediately precipitated acts of religious intolerance. Individuals perceived to be Muslims were subjected to verbal and sometimes physical assaults and other forms of overt discrimination. Islam, as a religion, was vehemently criticized as encouraging or justifying the attacks.[4]

At the same time, strong public sentiment favoring patriotic displays such as the recitation of the Pledge of Allegiance and the singing of patriotic anthems created pressure on individuals to express religious and other views that might not have been their own. In Madison, Wisconsin, a controversy developed over the manner in which the local school district should comply with a legislative requirement that students recite the Pledge of Allegiance each day. Despite well-established constitutional limitations[5] on prayer in public schools and related concerns about compelled expression, the school board's efforts to accommodate students not wishing to participate were ridiculed and attacked as unpatriotic. The strength of public reaction effectively overwhelmed legitimate concerns about forcing students to participate in an objectionable expressive activity.

Other expressions of disagreement with government policies responding to the September 11 attacks were greeted with similar anger. When several faculty members at the University of Wisconsin-Madison suggested, in a local newspaper forum, that the United States and its foreign policy bore some responsibility for the attacks, a guest editorialist opined:

> Those professors, . . . have lost all common sense. . . . We've all had to listen to teachers, professors and the American Civil Liberties Union tell us what is right for this country for years. Now those people are starting to learn where the real majority in this country stands. We don't stand on top of the flag; we stand under it—united. Professors, go to Afghanistan and make your speeches. . . . (*Wisconsin State Journal,* October 28, 2001.)

Of course, the writer's last sentence does make the point: In Afghanistan, such an exchange of views would not be possible. The difficulty is that the writer also suggests that we should not permit it to occur here, either.

It is but a short step from this sort of reaction to more direct threats against unpopular speakers. For example, in the aftermath of September 11, the University of South Florida initiated proceedings to terminate a tenured professor, Sami Al-Arian, for pro-Islamist/anti-Israel statements made in 1988. Although the First Amendment does not afford an absolute guarantee that any and all speech by faculty members is protected (laws governing defamation of character, pornography, commercial speech, and public broadcasting all place limits on free speech), it *does* require that government demonstrate a compelling reason for limiting speech on matters of public concern. Absent such a compelling

---

[4]The recent controversy over the University of North Carolina's requirement that first-year students read a book about the Qur`àn reflects the ongoing nature of this problem.
[5]*Engel* v. *Vitale,* 370 U.S. 421 (1962).

interest, speech on issues of public interest cannot be grounds for adverse employment action against faculty members.

As these and similar incidents demonstrate, rights of free speech and religion are jeopardized not only by direct governmental action, but by the power of popular sentiment to chill their exercise. In this environment, there is a real danger that free and open debate about matters of the gravest public importance will be stifled. What is lost is not only the individual freedom to speak on matters of public importance, but the critically important need for public debate about the underlying issues.

ROLE OF THE ACADEMIC COMMUNITY IN PROTECTING CIVIL LIBERTIES

What is the appropriate response to such governmental and societal threats to our most important civil liberties? Again, there is a range of likely reactions. At the most basic level, there will be litigation about individual deprivations of rights, and courts will be called upon to decide, in cases affecting individuals, whether the Constitution permits specific governmental actions. More broadly, the media and individual speakers can continue to present to the public a variety of views on issues related to the September 11 attacks.

Colleges and universities, too, can play a pivotal role in protecting civil liberties and fostering debate, and that role is especially important given the many direct effects of September 11 on the academic community. As Justice Frankfurter emphasized in *Sweezy, supra,* our democracy depends upon free universities: "To impose any straight jacket [sic] upon the intellectual leaders in our colleges and universities would imperil the future of our Nation." It is, therefore, critically important that universities continue freely to pursue knowledge and truth in relation to the causes of terrorism, and to encourage the expression of diverse views about the terrorist attacks and related political issues.

In the end, it is through the expansion of information and the vigorous exchange of ideas that civil liberties will be preserved and terrorism defeated. Another anecdote illustrates the point. My daughter is a college student in New York City and was there on the day of the attacks. One of her courses for the semester was about Islamic civilization. When classes resumed after September 11, the professor challenged the students to consider whether U.S. foreign policy had contributed to the causes of the attacks. The immediate reaction of the students was anger and derision, but over the course of the ensuing weeks, a reasoned discourse emerged, informed by greater knowledge of Islamic culture and history, as well as more careful consideration of U.S. policies. By stimulating the students to deeper thought about the attacks, the professor successfully led them to a better understanding of a complex and frightening situation.

As our nation continues to struggle with the impact of the terrorist attacks on civil liberties, the need for knowledge, debate, and discourse about the underlying issues has never been greater. The academic community's role in answering this need is central. When Richard Ely, a University of Wisconsin professor, was threatened with dismissal for his support of labor activities, the Board of Regents declared: "Whatever may be the limitations which trammel inquiry elsewhere, we believe that the great state university of Wisconsin should ever encourage that continual and fearless sifting and winnowing by which alone the truth can be found." It is this sifting and winnowing process that offers the hope that civil liberties can be preserved, even as we fight terrorism.

DISCUSSION QUESTIONS

1. To what extent do U.S. liberties offer protection for the activities of terrorist and extremist groups?
2. In the protection of civil liberties, what role does the author see for universities?
3. In your opinion, what rights are Americans willing to give up to prevent future terrorist attacks?

PART IV

EMERGING TRENDS IN INTERNATIONAL TERRORISM

12

Technology and the Transformation of Terrorism

Jess Hollenback

This chapter examines how technology can be used to transform small, maliciously inclined groups of nonstate players into major terrorist threats. Hollenback surveys the history of biological warfare and notes that, in general, biological weapons had only marginal military significance until recent technological advances in weaponization of pathogens and genetic engineering of harmful microbes. The author makes the point that emerging technologies have been used not only to increase offensive capabilities, but also to make it easier for potential terrorists to avoid detection, block out potential infiltrators, and elude capture. In this regard, the challenge of fighting terrorism in the twenty-first century lies not only in the development of technologies to counter the terrorist threat, but also in the establishment of safeguards to prevent new technologies from getting into the wrong hands.

The tragic events of September 11, 2001 mark a deeply unsettling watershed in our nation's history and are pregnant with very disturbing possibilities for the future. The immediate impacts that this terrorist "Pearl Harbor" have had upon our nation's collective psyche, sense of security, and economy are obvious and horrifying enough. This nation's soil was unexpectedly and most brutally violated by stealthy foreign enemies with a loss of life as large as that sustained by this country as a result of the Japanese attack on Pearl Harbor. The sheer savagery and hatred made manifest in these attacks and the fervent exuberance that the murderous actions of the terrorists ignited in much of the Islamic world made it clear to everyone that this country is passionately hated in much of the Muslim world. These things were a tremendous shock to the American public. The dreadful events of September 11 were clear proof that something was terribly wrong with both our foreign policy in the Middle East and with our relationship to the wider Muslim world.

However, there was something even more troubling about these events—it quickly became clear that the vicious acts of terrorists were no longer a mere nuisance, a small-scale violent background noise that powerful nation-states simply had to put up with as the cost of doing business in the world. Instead, terrorism was now revealed as major menace to civilization and humankind. As one scholar of terrorism noted, "Yesterday's nuisance has become one of the gravest dangers facing mankind" (Laqueur, 1999, p. 4). The September 11 terrorists who shocked the world with their ghastly demonstration of the deadly power of fully fueled passenger airplanes and the anonymous bioterrorist(s) who sent the anthrax spores through the mails showed that modern technologies are developing in ways that make all of us increasingly vulnerable to both catastrophic losses of life as well as catastrophic infrastructural and economic damages. These can be perpetrated not just by enemy nation-states and their terrorist proxies but also by small, independent, secretive, privately financed, and well-organized groups of criminals, terrorists, and even aberrant individuals (e.g., Timothy McVeigh or the Unabomber). These losses of life and massive damages to both the economy and the nation's infrastructure inflicted by small cells of terrorists have the potential to be just as devastating in magnitude as the losses that would be expected in a major war with a technologically proficient enemy nation-state. Equally unsettling, our vaunted geographical isolation offers us little protection against such malicious nonstate actors. In short, September 11 revealed that modern technologies spawned by the information sciences, molecular biology, chemistry, and atomic physics have greatly expanded both the reach and lethal power of terrorists by giving them greatly enhanced access to weapons of mass destruction.

OBJECTIVES OF THIS STUDY

This chapter focuses on the links between technology and the growing menace that terrorism poses to civilization and humankind. This study sets about this task with three principal objectives:

1. It will highlight the specific ways that recent advances in technology are carrying the grave risk that weapons of mass destruction will no longer be the monopoly of nation-states but will increasingly also be in the hands of small extremist groups, criminal organizations, and possibly, even aberrant individuals. As a result, these technologies are transforming small, maliciously inclined groups of nonstate actors into major threats to civilization.

2. This analysis will also draw attention to the fact that new technologies have not only shrunken the size of lethal adversaries but they have also made it easier for them to avoid detection, to avoid infiltration by the targeted nation's spies or informers, and to elude punishment. Furthermore, the smaller size of these terrorist and criminal groups carries another danger—precisely because of their very small size, these groups are much more likely to be committed to extremist political agendas than nation-state actors who have to appeal to much larger political constituencies.

3. This chapter will conclude by drawing the reader's attention to the ways that advances in both biotechnology and the embryonic science of nanotechnology have the potential to enormously amplify the destructive power of terrorists.

THE DANGEROUS IMPACTS OF BENIGN
TECHNOLOGIES: A BRIEF HISTORICAL OVERVIEW

There is certainly nothing unusual in history about the fact that seemingly harmless new technologies often have unexpected, and even lethal, consequences. For example, when the Neolithic peoples of the ancient Near East first domesticated cattle and oxen around 6000 B.C., no one imagined that these valuable labor-saving creatures and sources of milk, meat, and leather would ultimately be responsible for the near annihilation of New World peoples and civilizations after the Spaniards made contact with the Native Americans in the sixteenth century. It was through the domestication of cattle that two diseases, smallpox (Diamond, 1997, p. 207) and measles (Diamond, 1992, pp. 70–71), appear to have jumped from cattle to human hosts and became established as crowd diseases endemic to many peoples and cultures of the Old World. When these two long-established crowd diseases of the Old World originating from cattle first infected the dense populations of Native American peoples in Mexico and South America, the medical consequences of this microbial contact were catastrophic. Jared Diamond cites an example from 1837 where a steamboat coming up the Missouri River to a Mandan Indian village of 2,000 people happened to be carrying a passenger who was sick with smallpox. This sick passenger infected the Indians of that village with the result that within a few weeks only 40 Indians were left alive, a fatality rate of 98 percent (Diamond, 1992, p. 71). In a similar vein, no one would have ever imagined that Thomas Midgley's invention in 1928 of a more efficient and chemically inert refrigerant called freon to replace the dangerously reactive, poisonous, and even explosive gases that had been used in early refrigerators would be anything but an unalloyed blessing. Nevertheless, fifty years later scientists discovered—almost by accident—that this seemingly innocuous and benign refrigerant gas was a grave menace to the ozone layer that shields all land-based animal and plant life from lethal ultraviolet radiation (Molina & Rowland, 1974). Even the quest for medicines can sometimes have unexpectedly lethal consequences. Thus the search of Chinese alchemists for an elixir of immortality that combined sulfur (a common remedy for a variety of skin diseases), saltpeter (helpful for lowering fevers), and charcoal did appear to have some beneficial effect in treating ringworm and a variety of other skin problems (Shaffer, 1997, p. 850). However, the medicinal qualities of this drug were quickly eclipsed by something else that these early Chinese pharmacists and alchemists had also noted about it—it was both explosive and a fire hazard. This medicine that the Chinese called "firedrug" is today better known as gunpowder. It is hard to imagine any invention that has killed more people or had a more revolutionary impact on the character of warfare and the fate of nations than this drug that originated as a remedy for skin diseases.

As one would expect, the explosive acceleration of scientific discoveries and technological innovations in the twentieth century have led to a correspondingly explosive increase in the number of inventions with unexpectedly dangerous or undesirable side effects. Recent inventions and discoveries in the information sciences and molecular biology have been particularly relevant in generating dangerous side effects that have the potential to greatly amplify the destructive power of both individual terrorists and small terrorist groups.

TERRORISM AND THE INFORMATION SCIENCES

Scholars who study present-day terrorism have often drawn attention to the manifold ways that recent advances in computer technology and software design could benefit individual terrorists, criminal organizations, and small extremist groups and give them the potential to wreak great havoc upon the vital infrastructures and services of a nation-state (Arquilla & Ronfeldt, 2001; Cordesman & Cordesman, 2002). What makes cyberterrorism so potentially threatening is that many of our nation's most critical infrastructures—such as electrical power grids, nuclear power plants, air traffic control systems, missile defense, banks, and stock exchanges—depend upon networked systems of computers and, as a result, are vulnerable to penetration by the viruses, worms, and other forms of disabling programs that hackers and terrorists could introduce into those networks. In his testimony before Congress in 1999, George Tenet, the Director of Central Intelligence, told the Senators that any enemy that succeeds in seriously disrupting our networked informational systems and infrastructures "will have the potential to weaken us dramatically or even render us helpless" (quoted in Cordesman & Cordesman, 2002, p. 24).

Moreover, cyberattacks designed to destabilize, cripple, or permanently damage these vital infrastructures by corrupting the software that permits them to function smoothly could be launched from anywhere by lone, anonymous individuals who have the advantage of surprise, who can reconnoiter their targets from a remote location with little risk of detection, who can, after a successful attack, cover their tracks and escape detection and punishment. No massive investment of a nation's resources is required to launch a successful attack. Indeed, as one scholar has observed, "Tomorrow's terrorist may be able to do more with a keyboard than with a bomb" (Denning, 2001, p. 282). All that is required is a computer hooked up to the Internet. Furthermore, unlike explosives or chemical and biological weapons, cyberweapons do not require the terrorist to expose himself or herself to physical risk or the danger of being arrested with the incriminating materials.

There can be no question that cyberterror poses a very real threat to this nation's security. For instance, in the year 1999 the Department of Defense detected over 22,000 attempts to penetrate its computer networks with the intent to probe their contents, to disable them, or to infect them with viruses or worms. Approximately 600 of those attempts caused temporary shutdowns or other forms of damage (Cordesman & Cordesman, 2002, pp. 114–115). It is clear that computer networks vital to our national defense, power grids, and economic system are locked in a constant evolutionary struggle against continually evolving cyberpathogens. If our vital infrastructures are to avoid succumbing to crippling virus infections or other forms of disabling cyberattacks in the future, the computer networks that sustain them must ensure that their electronic immune systems always stay one jump ahead of the swarms of rapidly evolving viruses and worms that hackers and would-be cyberterrorists are inventing every day.

Despite the constant hostile probings and virus infections that the nation's vital computer networks receive from hackers and cyberterrorists, scholars who have studied cyberwarfare emphasize that, *at present,* the danger of an "electronic Pearl Harbor" is just a theoretical possibility (Cordesman & Cordesman, 2002, pp. 2–3). Thus, Cordesman notes that "Those directly involved in cyber-offense . . . generally seem to feel that carrying out a successful major cyber-attack is far more difficult than those outside the national security arena recognize" (Cordesman & Cordesman, 2002, p. 3). Moreover, up to the present time (2001), ". . . there have been few, if any, computer network attacks that meet the criteria for cyberterrorism" (Denning, 2001, p. 281). Nevertheless, there is no reason for complacency. For one thing, official audits of government computer security networks by the General Accounting Office (GAO) in 1999 showed very serious security lapses. These led one official charged with providing the results of these audits to the Senate to conclude that the federal government "is not adequately protecting critical federal operations and assets from computer-based attacks" (quoted in Cordesman & Cordesman, 2002, p. 133). Another GAO auditor wrote that "'our audits have repeatedly identified serious deficiencies in the most basic controls over access to federal systems'" (quoted in Cordesman & Cordesman, 2002, p. 77).

The most persistent security lapses that these auditors and inspectors found involved inadequate protection of passwords and overly broad access privileges. For example, passwords were often posted in plain view of others or shared with other people. In many departments investigated, authorization to access vital information or information systems was often given far too broadly. Far more users than necessary had access to information systems for the purposes of browsing or scanning what was in them. What was even more worrisome, the auditors recorded instances where people without an essential right to know had access to important systems that entitled them not only to browse the contents of that system but also to modify or delete even sensitive or critical information within it (Cordesman & Cordesman, 2002).

Another serious security problem that the GAO auditors found in the Department of Defense computer systems was that most of the hackers had gotten access to their networks by vulnerabilities in the software that the Department of Defense purchased from various private companies. There are millions of lines of code that have to be tested, and it is a daunting, if not almost impossible, task to be sure that this code does not have weaknesses that could be exploited by hackers and cyberterrorists (Cordesman & Cordesman, 2002, p. 115). While most of these weaknesses appeared to have been unintentional defects in the software, the auditors and inspectors did note a few instances of what appear to have been intentionally designed "'trapdoors' deliberately left by the authors of the software to allow intrusions" (p. 115). Compounding this problem is the fact that much of the computer code for this commercially acquired software is written abroad in places like India, Israel, or Ireland. One security lapse by the FAA serves as a glaring example of the government's carelessness in allowing potentially hostile foreigners to gain intimate access to critical infrastructures. In this particular instance, "the FAA subcontracted critical air control systems to a firm staffed largely by Chinese nationals" (Cordesman & Cordesman, 2002, p. 150). This lapse was especially worrisome not only because the subcontracted systems were critical to the operational integrity of the nation's air traffic control systems but also because it is well known in intelligence circles that mainland China has "made cyber warfare a critical part of their military doctrine" (Cordesman & Cordesman, 2002, p. 12).

Recent advances in computer technology and information processing have certainly amplified the potential power of malicious individuals and small terrorist groups to wreak havoc on our nation's critical infrastructures by making the functional integrity of those essential infrastructures dependent on computer networks that are vulnerable to corruption from hackers, computer viruses, and worms, and other forms of rogue software that alter or delete critical data. It will certainly be a Herculean task to be both continually on the alert for the newly minted viruses and worms that hackers and terrorists will constantly attempt to introduce into these vital networks and to enforce throughout those vast networks the rigorous electronic security measures that are necessary to protect those systems from cyberattack. Scanning the enormous mass of computer code that could hide electronic "trapdoors" for the cyberterrorists and protecting the software from being outsourced to potentially hostile foreign or domestic programmers is an additional daunting challenge that our nation's computer security experts must somehow overcome.

The computer revolution has also made us more vulnerable to malicious individuals and small terrorist groups by enhancing both the security and the scope of their communications. With regard to the first item, commercially available encryption programs are now being produced that are virtually unbreakable (Zanini & Edwards, 2001, p. 37). This has enabled terrorist cells to communicate more securely with each other over the Internet. Even the most sophisticated national intelligence agencies are finding modern encryption devices extremely difficult to decipher. For example, Israeli counterterrorist agents admit that they cannot easily trace or decode the contents of messages between Hamas operatives (Zanini & Edwards, 2001). Terrorists and criminal organizations can also communicate over the Internet using a cryptographic tool called "steganography," where secret data or messages can be hidden by embedding them in a picture file (Zanini & Edwards, 2001, p. 38). In addition to providing terrorists with these cryptographic enhancements to their communications, the Internet also gives them immediate access to a global audience for the twin purposes of easier recruitment and propaganda. It also makes it easier for such groups and individuals to locate and disseminate information that enables them to construct not just bombs and other conventional explosive devices but even weapons of mass destruction. As Jessica Stern has noted in her study of contemporary terrorism, "how-to manuals on producing chemical and biological agents are advertised in paramilitary journals sold in magazine shops all over the United States, as well as on the Internet" (Stern, 1999, pp. 50–51). Stern found that one publishing house was perfectly willing to sell her a book on how to poison people and even asked her if she would also like to purchase books on how to construct bombs and silencers as well (Stern, 1999, p. 51 n.8)!

The Internet and the recent advances in computer technology and encryption that have developed in tandem with it have spawned new modes of warfare, namely, (1) cyberwarfare (already described above) where the goal is the destruction of a computer-regulated infrastructures by means of corrupting the software in those computers and (2) netwar, a new mode of conflict where the enemy protagonists that a nation's military and police forces must fight are not just the traditional nation-state actors and their proxies but are, instead, more likely to be rather diffuse groups of decentralized networked individuals or privately financed terrorist or criminal groups "who communicate, coordinate, and conduct their campaigns in an internetted manner without a precise central command" (Zanini & Edwards, 2001, p. 30).

The crucial feature of netwar is that the protagonists have a much more flexible and decentralized command structure than the militaries of their nation-state adversaries. Though each local cell may receive strategic guidance from the core leadership of the terrorist group, each cell still preserves a high degree of tactical independence (Zanini & Edwards, 2001, p. 32). As we are presently finding out, terrorist and criminal organizations such Osama bin Laden's al-Qaeda network are not easily destroyed by the superior military force that a technologically advanced nation-state is able to bring against it. The surprising and disturbing resilience of these groups employing netwar tactics stems, in part, from their decentralized command structure. If the main core of leadership is destroyed, the leftover cells can easily and securely communicate with each other through encrypted emails, faxes, steganography, and cell phone conversations, regroup, and if necessary, re-create a new nucleus of leaders. Two other factors powerfully enhance the resilience of such groups: their financial independence from nation-state sponsors and the sophisticated means of commercially available encryption that assure them secure lines of communication as well as command and control.

The almost unbreakable encryption programs that protect their communications across the network not only assure that they have secure lines of communication between the various subgroups in the organization, but they also preserve anonymity and deniability, making it extremely difficult to determine which particular group originated a terrorist act in the absence of anyone claiming responsibility. One of the other potentially dangerous consequences that this encryption-assisted anonymity poses to its victims is that the terrorists can arrange the details of an attack to make it seem as though the assault came from a foreign government rather than from the actual perpetrators (Denning, 2001, p. 276). In a similar fashion, a terrorist attack from an U.S. right-wing extremist group can be configured in such a way as to make it appear that it originated from a Muslim extremist group and vice versa.

Both cyberwar and netwar pose serious and difficult challenges to the military forces, the police, and intelligence agencies of nation-states. First of all, nations must now fight widely dispersed enemies who attack with both cyberweapons and chemical and biological weapons that bear no return address (Stern, 1999, p. 77). In many cases, it will be difficult to establish who actually carried out an attack, and it will be easy for the netwar enemy to make it seem as though another group was the perpetrator. Second, these non-state actors now have the advantage of possessing communications that can be protected with almost unbreakable encryption software (Zanini & Edwards, 2001, pp. 37–38). These facts will put a premium on gaining reliable intelligence about the activities and plans of these groups, a task that will be made more onerous than ever before due to the sophisticated encryption of their communications, the small size of these groups, and the consequent difficulties that their small size will pose to intelligence operatives who attempt to infiltrate their ranks.

BIOTECHNOLOGY, BIOLOGICAL WARFARE, AND TERRORISM

One of the most unsettling aftershocks associated with the September 11 tragedy was the series of lethal bioterrorist attacks using tiny amounts of anthrax spores that killed a number of people in Florida, Washington, DC, and several other areas along the eastern seaboard. These attacks were exceptionally frightening for the following reasons: (1) They showed that the United States was incredibly vulnerable to serious disruption from even a very small-scale bioterrorist attack. There was almost nothing the U.S. government or Post Office could do in the short term to protect the mail, postal workers, or postal recipients from lethally contaminated letters or packages that might either contain such anthrax spores or have made accidental contact with other items of mail that contained them. (2) The attacks revealed an alarming lack of preparedness on the part of the U.S. government for biological warfare.

The U.S. government was simply unable to offer its citizens any significant degree of protection from the menace of biological terrorism. If this anthrax attack had involved pounds of fully aerosolized anthrax spores instead of a mere gram or two, there would not have been enough anthrax vaccine or antibiotic on hand to have protected the exposed populace. For instance, Osterholm and Schwartz have pointed out that in 1999 the city of Baltimore had 69,000 capsules of the anthrax antibiotic ciprofloxacin in stock in all the metropolitan hospitals and pharmacies. That was only enough medicine to complete the treatment regimen for 575 infected patients (Osterholm & Schwartz, 2000, pp. 128–129). (3) The attack also showed the extraordinary difficulty of locating and punishing the perpetrator(s) of a biological attack. Even after eight months of intensive effort, the F.B.I. and police forces are still unable to discover who did it. It is impossible to use the threat of overwhelming mass destruction as a deterrent against an enemy that one cannot even identify. As a consequence, there is an escalating risk that one's enemies will be tempted to use such untraceable but extremely disruptive biological weapons of mass destruction. (4) Apart from the extraordinary human costs, the anthrax attacks also showed how economically disruptive bioterrorism could be. It was a Herculean and very expensive task to decontaminate the Capitol and the affected postal facilities from the minute amounts of anthrax spores that were involved. The economic costs of decontamination—and the lengthy disruption of commercial activites—that would be necessary were a much larger-scale release of anthrax spores to take place would be mind-boggling.

Biological warfare is nothing new in history. As early as two thousand years ago, Scythian archers dipped their arrows into manure or rotting corpses in order to make sure that the wounds made with these weapons would become lethally infected (Miller, Engelberg, & Broad, 2001, p. 37). During the North American French and Indian War, Jeffrey Amherst, the British commander of Fort Pitt, was involved in a scheme to exterminate the Indians of western Pennsylvania by giving them smallpox-infected blankets (Ewald, 2000, pp. 178–179). Both in World War I and World War II, biological weapons were used from time to time, although they played only a very marginal role in the conflict. For example, the Germans in World War I deliberately spread the equine disease glanders among the horses of the Allied troops in order to weaken their cavalries (Miller et al., 2000, p. 38), and there is also good reason to believe that the Soviet Union released tularemia microbes on the German armies as they approached Stalingrad in the late summer of 1942. Evidence indicates that, at first, only the Nazi troops got sick with the disease but that very shortly afterwards, the disease also spread to Russian soldiers and civilians in the area. In this case, biological warfare backfired on its perpetrators (Alibek, 1999, pp. 29–31). It was the Japanese who developed biological warfare tactics and experimentation more fully than any of the other belligerents of World War II. The Japanese army's infamous Unit 731 conducted fiendish medical experiments on Chinese and American prisoners and dropped anthrax, plague-infected fleas, and typhoid on Manchurian towns and cities (Miller et al., 2001, p. 40). As hideous and systematic as their biological warfare researches were, the results did not appreciably affect the outcome of the Chinese campaign.

In short, despite the long history of their use in warfare, biological weapons had only marginal military significance prior to the end of World War II, and their dreadful potential as terrorist weapons of truly catastrophic destructive power was still undeveloped. However, after 1945 two technological advances began to transform biological weapons into increasingly menacing agents of mass destruction and terror: (1) advances in the weaponization of pathogens and (2) advances in the genetic engineering of harmful microbes.

The first postwar advances that greatly amplified the lethal power and potential of biological warfare agents were those related to the weaponization of microbes. Even during World War II, techniques of biological warfare were still very crude. For example, the Soviets' methods of disseminating tularemia against the Nazi invaders on the outskirts of Stalingrad ended up backfiring since they not only infected Nazis but also their own troops and civilians (Alibek, 1999, p. 30). As already noted, the Japanese Army's Unit 731, despite its lengthy, systematic, and gruesome studies of how to enhance the lethality of its germ agents, still ended up employing very primitive methods of spreading them, such as dropping porcelain canisters of plague-infected fleas onto the Chinese. Although wartime China was devoid of any significant public health infrastructure and would therefore seem to have been exceptionally vulnerable to catastrophic infection from the plague, the crude techniques of dissemination that the Japanese used appear to have inflicted "only" thousands of casualties rather than the millions of victims that the Japanese military had hoped for (Alibek, 1999, pp. 36–37). What was missing in the biological weaponry of World War II was knowledge about how to stabilize the microbial pathogens so that they would remain viable in the presence of dry air and ultraviolet light from the sun and also knowledge about how to disperse them in aerosols so that they could travel long distances without losing their lethal potency. As one scholar of biological warfare has observed, growing germs in large quantities is usually not very difficult. The hard part of designing effective bioweapons lies in "the subtleties of biological engineering—drying germs, encapsulating them in special coatings, making them hardy and stable enough for wide dissemination by aerosol sprayers, [and] learning how to extend their shelf life" (Miller et al., 2001, p. 35).

These "subtleties" of bioengineering pathogens were, unfortunately, successfully mastered by both the Americans and the Soviets in the decades immediately after World War II as they both engaged in massive research efforts to develop more sophisticated and effective weapons of biological warfare. For example, both superpowers learned how to weaponize anthrax bacteria—that is to say, they learned how to dry anthrax bacteria into a powder of bacterial spores (in much the same way that the baking industry has learned to powder dry yeast for breadmaking). Then they learned how to coat these tiny spores so that they would not clump together. This difficult task of learning how to make the spores avoid clumping ensures that the lethal spores are light enough to float long distances through the air and that they are tiny enough to lodge deeply into the lungs of their intended victim, triggering the extremely deadly respiratory form of anthrax. If the spores stick together, they might not float to their intended destination or, once there, they might be picked up by the cilia in the nose and not make it to their intended target. Furthermore, if spores clump together, they will not be easy to spray from a crop duster.

There is presently considerable debate about whether small groups of terrorists currently have the ability to weaponize and aerosolize pathogens in the manner described above. William Patrick, the man most responsible for developing the U.S. biological warfare arsenal in the 1950s and 1960s, contends that terrorists do not yet have that ability to dry, mill, and fully aerosolize bioweapons. "I know how to make a weapon . . . Ken Alibek [the expatriate Russian scientist who was instrumental in the Soviet Union's massive bioweapons program during the 1970s and 1980s] knows how to make a weapon. I don't think our domestic terrorists have the capability to make a weapon yet . . . it takes some doing, it really does" (quoted in Miller et al., 2001, p. 102). On the other hand, D. A. Henderson, the man who led the final successful effort to eradicate smallpox and head of the Johns Hopkins University Center for Civilian Biodefense Studies, contends that "Even groups with modest finances and basic training in biology and engineering could develop . . . an effective weapon at little cost" (quoted in Miller et al., 2001, p. 105). Those who would argue that present-day terrorists *do* have the requisite technology to weaponize pathogens point to the fact that sophisticated technology for aerosolizing pathogens is easily available on the Internet and that many commercial technologies such as crop dusters, photocopying machines, and medical inhalant sprayers and nebulizers use devices that can deliver tiny particles of any desired size. They claim that converting these sprayers, inhalants, and nebulizers into effective delivery systems for liquid or powdered bioweapons would be very easy to do (Miller et al., 2001, pp. 113–115). In any case, even if one agrees with William Patrick that terrorist groups *currently* cannot produce the most highly milled and refined types of anthrax spores, there is still the grave risk that they could get the most deadly forms of weaponized anthrax from sympathizers with access to the Russians' massive germ warfare arsenal or from sympathizers or fifth columnists who have access to the biowarfare arsenals of countries like Iraq, North Korea, or Iran. Terrorists might even be able to steal such weapons. For instance, when Dr. Peter Jahrling, an internationally famous expert on infectious diseases, visited the former Soviet Union's Vector plant in 1998 where one of the world's only sites of stored smallpox virus resides, he was appalled at the flimsy security arrangements there. He said, "There is no doubt in my mind that the smallpox sample is not secure. I saw the site. The only apparent security was one pimply-faced kid who looked about fourteen with a Kalashnikov rifle" (Miller et al., 2001, p. 109).

There is also the grave risk that wealthy terrorist groups like Osama bin Laden's al-Qaeda or Aum Shinrikyo could purchase the weaponizing expertise of unemployed germ warfare experts from the former Soviet Union. Thousands of them are currently out of work, and it is well known that the Iranians have been actively attempting to recruit them to jumpstart their own biological warfare program. These Iranian recruiters were interested not only in biological weapons that could be employed against human beings, but they were also interested in bioweapons that could be useful against food crops and livestock (Miller et al., 2001, p. 206). If the Iranians and Iraqis are actively seeking the expertise of these former Soviet germ warfare experts who know how to maximize the deadliness of the pathogens and the systems that disseminate them, it is almost certain that terrorist groups are doing so as well.

While the advances in the technology of weaponizing microbes just described radically transformed biological agents from being weapons of only marginal military utility into cheap and extremely lethal weapons of warfare and mass destruction, there has been a second technological innovation that shows ominous promise of further amplifying the already staggering killing power of microbial weapons, namely, genetic engineering. Although splicing the genes of pathogenic microbes to enhance their killing power is only in its infancy, this technology is almost certain, in the long run, to render us even more vulnerable than we are now to catastrophic attacks from small terrorist groups and lone biological Unabombers. Individuals or groups who possessed expertise about how to alter the genetic material of microbes in order to create entirely novel pathogens or more lethal forms of familiar ones would be an *extremely* dangerous threat not only to the country or countries that they targeted but to all of civilization. Similarly, individuals or groups who genetically altered microbes to resist antibiotics, to resist vaccines, or to cripple the host's immune system would be equally menacing. Indeed, such attempts to genetically engineer ever more virulent forms of pathogenic microbes might very well be the greatest potential threat to the survival of the human race that we have ever faced—eclipsing even nuclear weapons in their potential to inflict lasting harm to our species.

There are many ways that genetically altered "designer" pathogens could inflict massive casualties. First of all, if a genetically altered pathogen differed sufficiently from any presently existing microorganisms, no one in the targeted population would have any naturally existing immunity to it. Such a novel microbe would find itself infecting an epidemiologically virgin population of hosts. It is well known that new infectious agents unleashed into a virgin host population can sometimes rage with exceptional virulence. For example, Native Americans had never been exposed to smallpox before the voyages of Columbus. Smallpox was a terrible enough killer even among those Old World cultures whose populations were forced to endure repeated epidemics of it, but among the epidemiologically virgin peoples of the Americas it was far more lethal. One will recall Jared Diamond's example of the Mandan Indian village that encountered smallpox in 1837 and within several weeks suffered a staggering mortality rate of 98 percent (Diamond, 1992, pp. 72–73). In a similar vein, when Brazilian myxomatosis was first introduced to the rabbits of Australia who had never been exposed to this virus, the initial outbreak killed 99.8 percent of the Australian rabbits that were infected (Diamond, 1997, p. 209). Even among plants, the introduction of novel microbial pathogens into virgin populations can inflict horrific casualties. This was what happened when the fungus that carries European chestnut blight came over to the United States and almost completely wiped out the native American chestnut tree. From these examples it should be evident that the human race would be extremely vulnerable to any terrorist group or individual that could manufacture or otherwise acquire sufficiently novel "designer" pathogens.

A second way that genetically altered designer pathogens could inflict enormous casualties is by crippling the effectiveness of antibiotics. Soviet technicians were already apparently *successful* in their attempts to create antibiotic-resistant strains of deadly bacteria. Two highly placed Russian scientists who had worked in the former Soviet Union's biological weapons program, Ken Alibek (Alibek, 1999, pp. 160, 167) and Gennady Lepyoshkin (Miller et al., 2001, p. 175), have independently told Western investigators that the Soviet Union had genetically engineered antibiotic strains of anthrax. Lepyoshkin told U.S. scientists that the most virulent of these genetically altered anthrax strains was "three times as lethal in both dry and liquid form" as the anthrax produced in massive quantities at other Soviet biological warfare laboratories. It also needed fewer spores to cause infection (Miller et al., 2001). Alibek reported that one team of scientists in the Soviet Union had produced "a genetically altered strain of anthrax resistant to five antibiotics" (Alibek, 1999, p. 167). Vladimir Pasechnik, another top Soviet biologist scientist who had worked at a high level in that nation's massive biological warfare program and later defected to Great Britain, told his interrogators that the Soviet scientists had taken plasmids, small snippets of bacterial DNA, and created a genetically altered form of superplague that was resistant to both existing antibiotics and vaccines. He went on to say that this superplague "was no mere laboratory curiosity. The Soviets had packed a dry, powdered form of the germ into bombs, rocket warheads, and artillery shells. . ." (quoted in Miller et al., 2001, p. 95). Alibek seems to confirm Pasechnik's claim that the Soviets did indeed develop antibiotic-resistant strains of plague bacillus (Alibek, 1999, pp. 160, 281). Fortunately, not all attempts to create antibiotic-resistant strains of microbial pathogens succeed. Alibek reports that one Soviet scientist was indeed able to alter the genome of the tularemia microbe to make it resistant to three of the antibiotics that have traditionally been used to treat it. However, in doing so, it lost much of its infectiousness (Alibek, 1999, pp. 160–161). Indeed, for many years after the technology for recombining DNA was first discovered, most attempts to hybridize pathogens in the laboratory resulted in variants of the microorganism that were weaker in virulence than their counterparts in nature (Miller et al., 2001, p. 84). Nevertheless, there is no reason for complacency because, as the Soviet scientists have shown, pathogens that have been genetically altered in the laboratory sometimes do possess enhanced virulence and other dangerous features such as antibiotic resistance or vaccine resistance.

A third and most alarming way that genetically engineered designer pathogens might inflict massive numbers of casualties is by crippling or otherwise damaging our immune systems. There is now very good evidence that it is indeed possible to alter microbes genetically so that they cripple the host organism's immune system. In February 2001 the scientific community was shocked when a group of Australian scientists published a paper in the *Journal of Virology* (Jackson & Ramshaw, 2001, pp. 1205–1210) that showed that during the course of genetically altering mousepox viruses to sterilize mice as a rodent control mechanism, they had accidentally stumbled upon a unsettling side effect: The genetically engineered mousepox virus not only sterilized the infected mice, but it also killed them AND destroyed their immune systems. Even those mice that had been previously vaccinated against mousepox and, for that reason, would normally have been expected to resist infection by mousepox, died just like the unvaccinated mice (Miller et al., 2001, pp. 310–311). In short, this new form of mousepox virus was vaccine-resistant. This meant that vaccination was useless against it. The scientists immediately recognized that this same mechanism for crippling the immune systems of mice might also be applied to the genome of a very similar cousin of the mousepox virus, the human smallpox virus, and create a genetically altered form of human smallpox that would likewise be resistant to vaccination. There was a concern that, were terrorists to get a hold of a sample of smallpox virus and alter that virus by inserting a gene for the expression of interleukin-4 in the same way that the Australian scientists had increased the virulence of the mousepox virus, they might be able to obliterate what is currently our only effective check on smallpox (Cohen, 2002, pp. 114–115).

Whereas the Australian scientists' alterations of the mousepox virus killed the host organism by *crippling* its immune system's ability to make effective antibodies to that virus, Soviet scientists have discovered ways to alter microbial DNA so as to *hyperactivate* the host's immune system instead of crippling it. The results are the same—the death of the host organism from the genetically altered microorganism. Sergei Popov, a Russian scientist who was involved at the highest levels in the former Soviet Union's biological weapons program, defected to Great Britain in 1992 and subsequently told Western scientists about the nature of his genetic engineering research when he was still working for the Soviet Union. In one experiment he discovered a way to transform the *Legionella* bacterium that causes mild symptoms of pneumonia in guinea pigs into a lethal killer that produces a form of multiple sclerosis in the infected animals. He found that if he inserted a gene for the production of the brain and nerve protein myelin into the *Legionella* bacterium's genome, the genetically altered organism triggered an autoimmune response to myelin in the infected guinea pigs. In other words, the infected animals' immune systems turned on themselves and they became allergic to the myelin that surrounds their brain and nervous tissue. This infection-induced allergic reaction caused their nerves to lose their myelin, and, as they did so, the infected animals suffered a progressive brain degeneration and paralysis that killed almost 100 percent of the infected guinea pigs (Miller et al., 2001, p. 302). What was even more unsettling, this genetically altered killer bacterium was also extremely infectious. "With normal *Legionella,* many thousands of bacteria are required to sicken lab animals. But the recombinant *Legionella* was active with only a few cells" (Miller et al., 2001).

At present scientists have only created genetically altered microbes that cripple or hyperactivate the immune systems of laboratory animals. So far as we know, they have not yet done this with microbes that afflict humans. Nevertheless, the experiments of both Popov with *Legionella* and the Austalian scientists' experiments with genetically altered mousepox are a clear warning that we may be standing at the threshhold of a new and even more dangerous era of biological terrorism. Their experiments have demonstrated beyond any doubt that so-called "designer" pathogens are now a laboratory reality rather than just the product of science fiction writers' imaginations. It is almost certainly just a matter of time before some scientist, technician, or terrorist uses gene-splicing techniques to create novel antibiotic-resistant or vaccine-resistant designer pathogens that are intended to kill or maim humans rather than laboratory animals.

The increasing automation of the gene-splicing process and the rapidly increasing speed with which these complicated operations can now be performed certainly has ramifications for our vulnerability to bioterrorism. In a short "News Scan" article in the January 2002 issue of *Scientific American,* W. Wayt Gibbs observed that recent advances in biotechnology are "quickly speeding up, shrinking down, and automating the work of genetically engineering microorganisms. 'You can now finish before lunch projects that used to consume a Ph.D. thesis'" (Gibbs, 2002, p. 14), noted one scientist who works for the Johns Hopkins University Center for Civilian Biodefense Studies. DNA sequencers and DNA synthesizers are the automated machines that have made much of this process so much easier for scientists and laboratory technicians. Using these sophisticated and automated tools, Gibb points out that "dozens of geneticists are working to create stealthy viruses that can deliver artificially engineered payloads into cells without detection by the immune system" (Gibbs, 2002, p. 14). Other scientists have discovered that infectious influenza viruses "can be assembled from just eight short loops of DNA, easily synthesized by a machine" (Gibbs, 2002, p. 14). These scientists referred to in the above quotes are not evil scientists bent on creating vaccine-resistant bioweapons, though it might sound like it. They are instead trying to discover ways of helping the victims of genetically transmitted diseases. Nevertheless, it ought to be evident that the very same technologies that show so much promise for treating intractable genetic diseases like Huntington's chorea or cystic fibrosis can very easily be perverted so as to accelerate the process of manufacturing antibiotic-resistant or vaccine-resistant designer pathogens. This is one of the poignant ironies of the recent biotechnology revolution. The same technologies that are necessary to more effectively combat disease, to make human insulin from bacteria, and to enhance the yields of food crops are the very same technologies that bioterrorists can use to enhance the lethality and infectiousness of their weapons of mass destruction. As a result, some scientists are now becoming concerned about the currently easy access to these automated DNA sequencing and synthesizing machines, and they are proposing that the government regulate their export to minimize the risk of them falling into the hands of terrorists (Gibbs, 2002).

The growing speed and automation of the process for genetically engineering microbes is not the only thing that might make it a lot easier for terrorists to create "designer" pathogens. Much of the necessary information is in the public domain for the terrorists' easy perusal. Ken Alibek pointed out in his testimony to Congress in 2000 that, for the cost of hiring a translator, a bioterrorist could browse the scientific literature published in Russia over the last few years and learn the techniques to "genetically engineer vaccinia virus and then transfer the results to smallpox; to create antibiotic-resistant strains of anthrax, plague, and glanders; and to mass-produce the Marburg and Machupo viruses" (Drexler, 2002, p. 256). The "methods" sections of such journal articles delineate how and where the authors purchased their materials and how they performed their techniques of gene manipulation in the laboratory. For these reasons, many experts in bioterrorism contend that it is no longer a question of *whether* a massive terrorist attack with biological weapons will take place but, instead, a question of where or when they will strike (Osterholm & Schwartz, 2000, pp. xvii–xviii).

Prior to the revolutionary developments in genetically engineering microbes that have developed over the last thirty years or so, a prudent defender had the advantage in biological warfare provided that that nation prepared itself by stockpiling antibiotics and vaccines that were antidotal to the weaponizable human pathogens that they had reason to believe their enemies might use against them in war. The possible biological agents that had to defend against were in nature. However, with the advent of genetically engineered microbes designed to resist antibiotics, resist vaccines, or otherwise harm our immune system's ability to mount an effective resistance to these pathogens, even the most technologically advanced nations might suddenly find out that their most elaborate efforts at stockpiling antibiotics and vaccines are useless, a kind of present-day "medical Maginot Line" (Miller et al., 2001, p. 268). Now the advantage in biological warfare may reside with the attacker, since defenders will find it much more difficult, if not impossible, to anticipate which particular biological agent will be employed against them.

Another concern about genetically engineering designer microbes for use in terrorism or biological warfare is that while a terrorist or nation-state enemy might very well be able to fashion antibiotic-resistant or vaccine-resistant microbes in a matter of just a few weeks or months, the search for safe antidotes or vaccines to counter that new pathogen is a far more time-consuming and tedious process that could take many years, assuming that it can be done at all. As the long and presently unsuccessful search for a vaccine and cure for the AIDS virus shows, when a new pathogen emerges, whether it originates naturally or in a laboratory, even bringing the full panoply of economic and scientific resources to bear on the problem of eradicating or neutralizing it does not necessarily guarantee success.

CONCLUDING REMARKS

The foregoing analysis should make it clear that the tragic events of September 11, 2001 and the anthrax attacks that followed it are symptoms of a radical and ominous transformation of terrorism that will profoundly and forever change the way we live. These attacks—together with the Japanese nerve gas attack carried out by terrorists from the Aum Shinrikyo cult—proved that even the militarily strongest and most technologically advanced nations can suffer catastrophic casualties from the violent actions of small, stealthy, decentralized, privately financed terrorist groups and possibly, in the case of the anthrax attacks, from solitary terrorists acting on their own. We have entered a new age of warfare known as netwar where the enemy is not a nation-state but rather the lone individual bearing a violent grudge, or a small, independent, decentralized, privately financed group of nonstate actors functioning as a terrorist group, or such terrorist groups acting as the proxies of a rogue nation-state. Massive military strength in the form of anti-missile shields, drone weapons, ballistic missiles, and huge, well-equipped armies, navies, and air forces may offer excellent protection against aggressive nation-states. However, they offer surprisingly little protection against this new form of warfare and this new breed of non-state enemy. It is clear that in the wake of these particular terrorist attacks the nature of warfare and military strategy must undergo a major and lasting metamorphosis.

We have shown that two technologies played crucial roles in enabling this new form of warfare and this new breed of terrorist. These enabling technologies were computer networks together with the sophisticated encryption programs that keep communications on those networks secure and recent developments in biotechnology, especially those related to genetic engineering. We saw that computer networks enabled terrorism and netwar in a variety of ways. First of all, they are susceptible to serious disruption by such electronic pathogens as computer worms and viruses. Devastating attacks that might even shut down the entire Internet or a nation's crucial infrastructures could be launched by solitary hackers or small groups of them working as part of a terrorist group. In this sense, computer networks have greatly increased our vulnerability to terrorist attack. Second, these same computer networks and the secure encryption programs that are now commercially available enable terrorists to recruit new members much more easily from a global audience, access the latest scientific knowledge and technology that might be necessary to perfect their weapons of mass destruction, and communicate with each other and plan and coordinate their attacks with a high degree of security. This makes tracking these groups very difficult; it also enables them to operate with a very decentralized command structure.

Developments in biotechnology have enormously enhanced our vulnerability to both solitary terrorists and small terrorist groups because the technologies needed to produce both fully weaponized "natural" pathogens and novel genetically engineered "designer" pathogens are becoming much more accessible. Furthermore, genetically engineering microorganisms is also becoming increasingly easy, automated, and quicker. As more and more scientists and technicians learn how to genetically engineer microbes, the chances increase that someone will use this knowledge to design bioweapons that resist antibiotics or cripple a victim's immune system. And finally, since this bioengineering technology has so many legitimate and beneficial applications, its use is bound to become more widespread. As this technology proliferates, it will become increasingly difficult for watchdog agencies to separate the scientist who may be requesting this equipment for terrorist purposes from the scientist who has a legitimate reason for its use.

The twenty-first century looks like it will be a century that will be dominated by three technologies: computer and information processing technology, biotechnology (especially genetic engineering), and nanotechnology, the manipulation of matter by tiny, microscopic machines that, when this currently embryonic technology finally matures, will ideally become both programmable and self-replicating. All three of these technologies share a common characteristic that should give all of us cause for concern—each of them can be perverted by a malicious human operator into churning out rapidly proliferating self-replicating pathogens that have the potential to cause mass destruction of either infrastructures, people, or the environment. Computer networks are susceptible to humanly created self-replicating cyberpathogens like computer viruses and worms, genetic engineering can be perversely used to create self-replicating "designer" microbes, and nanotechnology—should it develop into a viable technology—will carry the risk that some individual either accidentally or with malicious intent could create programmable, self-replicating microscopic machines or nanopathogens that could run amok like cancer cells and smother the planet with copies of themselves. This latter possibility is the so-called "grey-goo problem" that nanotech visionaries have warned us about (Drexler, 1986, pp. 171–190). To a very significant extent, the security and survival of civilization in the twenty-first century will depend upon how well human beings learn to control the self-replicating entities spawned by these technologies. Technological visionaries like K. Eric Drexler (1986.), Ray Kurzweil (Kurzweil, 1999, pp. 140–142), and Bill Joy (Joy, 2000, pp. 236–262) have repeatedly warned us of the grave dangers that self-replicating entities pose to the well-being of both our species and this planet. For instance, K. Eric Drexler has noted that

> [r]eplicators can be more potent than nuclear weapons: to devastate Earth with bombs would require masses of exotic hardware and rare isotopes, but to destroy all life with replicators would require only a single speck made of ordinary elements. Replicators give nuclear war some company as a potential cause of extinction, giving a broader context to extinction as a moral concern. (1986, p. 174)

Technologies that can spawn self-replicating entities are dangerous not only because self-replication enormous amplifies their destructive potential but also because this potential destructive power is knowledge-enabled rather than being activated or enabled by the combination of extremely rare and difficult-to-manufacture isotopes as nuclear weapons are (Joy, 2000, p. 242). These technological visionaries have also emphasized that these technologies that generate self-replicating entities are very dangerous for a third reason: They threaten to put us at the mercy of extreme individuals and small terrorist groups. As Bill Joy put it in his recent prescient and controversial article on future trends in technology, "I think it is no exaggeration to say that we are on the cusp of the further perfection of extreme evil . . . on to a surprising and terrible empowerment of extreme individuals" (Joy, 2000, p. 242). These disturbing reflections led him to make the controversial suggestion that the potential risks of these replicant-producing technologies might far outweigh their admittedly great benefits and that, as a result, it might be a good idea if societies refused to develop these technologies and suppressed access to the kinds of scientific information that would permit someone to develop them (Joy, 2000, p. 254). How one would enforce or verify that such a relinquishment of technology had indeed taken place is another matter!

From these reflections, it is clear that fate of humankind in this century and in subsequent centuries may very well rest upon our ability to fashion effective institutional "immune systems" that prevent self-replicating entities from running amok. Seen from the perspective of evolutionary biology, terrorist groups and aberrant individuals who spawn and then unleash malignant self-replicating entities, whether they be designer viruses or nanopathogens, are part of an old evolutionary struggle between predator and prey, parasite and host, that has been going on since the dawn of life itself. This struggle will never end as long as life persists on this planet. However, this age-old evolutionary struggle has accelerated by many orders of magnitude as human beings have begun, through genetic engineering, to tamper with the chemical and biological mechanisms that are behind the evolutionary process itself. Our struggle with the "new" terrorism will accelerate this evolutionary struggle to a fever pitch as sometimes suicidal but technologically sophisticated terrorists hurl increasingly stealthy and increasingly lethal challenges to the survival of nations, species (through agricultural terrorism, for example), and even the human race itself. Will the institutional "immune systems" of nations and civilizations be able to keep ahead of these technologically sophisticated predators and pathogens, these new terrorists in our midst?

From this very broad evolutionary perspective, it is clear that the terrorist tragedies of the fall of 2001 were far more than just than the calamitous results of a failed relationship between the West and the Arab Muslim world. At a deeper level, these terrorist actions and the deeply felt dread they invoked were harbingers of a new and unsettling form of warfare, of a transformed, deeply ambivalent relationship to computer technology and self-replicating systems, and of a growing vulnerability of peoples, nations, and even animal and plant species to the vicious and catastrophic acts of aberrant individuals and small groups of terrorists. It is no exaggeration to say that this "new" breed of technologically enabled terrorist is one of the gravest threats that civilization has ever faced. We have entered the grim new age that one writer has called the age of "catastrophic terrorism" (Osterholm, 2000, p. xix) where the human race must live from now on under the threatening shadow of yet one more potential cause of our species' extinction.

DISCUSSION QUESTIONS

1. The author explains how technology can be used to transform small groups into formidable terrorist threats. Are the arguments made in support of this claim convincing? Why is this a major concern in the war against terrorism?
2. What do you learn from this article about how terrorists can use technology to avoid detection? What policies would you suggest to keep emerging technologies away from terrorists and other malicious groups?
3. What are some of the potential difficulties with the use of information technology and biological weapons to conduct acts of terrorism? Do you agree with the assessment by some experts that a cyber or biological attack is imminent?

REFERENCES

ALIBEK, K. (1999). *Biohazard.* New York: Delta Books.

ARQUILLA, J., & RONFELDT, D. (2001). *Networks and netwars: The future of terror, crime, and militancy.* Santa Monica: RAND.

COHEN, J. (2002, July-August). Designer bugs. *The Atlantic Monthly, 290,* 113–124.

CORDESMAN, A., & CORDESMAN, J. (2002). *Cyber-threats, information warfare, and critical infrastructure protection: Defending the homeland.* Westport, CT: Praeger.

DENNING, D. (2001). Activism, hacktivism, and cyberterrorism: The Internet as a tool for influencing foreign policy. In J. Arquilla & D. Ronfeldt (Eds.), *Networks and netwars: The future of terror, crime, and militancy* (pp. 238–288). Santa Monica: RAND.

DIAMOND, J. (1992, October). The arrow of disease. *Discover, 13,* 64–73.

DIAMOND, J. (1997). *Guns, germs, and steel: The fates of human societies.* New York & London: W.W. Norton & Company.

DREXLER, K. E. (1986). *Engines of creation: The coming era of nanotechnology.* New York: Doubleday.

DREXLER, M. (2002). *Secret agents: The menace of emerging infections.* Washington, DC: Joseph Henry Press.

EWALD, P. (2000). *Plague time: The new germ theory of disease.* New York: Anchor Books.

GIBBS, W. (2002, January). Innocence lost: Is enough being done to keep biotechnology out of the wrong hands? *Scientific American, 286,* 14–15.

JACKSON, R., & RAMSHAW, I. (2001, February). Expression of mouse interleukin-4 by a recombinant ectromilia virus suppresses cytolytic lymphocyte responses and overcomes genetic resistance to mousepox. *Journal of Virology,* 1205–1210.

JOY, B. (2000, April). Why the future doesn't need us. *Wired, 8,* 238–262.

KURZWEIL, R. (1999).*The age of spiritual machines: When computers exceed human intelligence.* New York: Penguin.

LAQUEUR, W. (1999). *The new terrorism: Fanaticism and the arms of mass destruction.* Oxford, UK: Oxford University Press.

MILLER, J., ENGELBERG, S., & BROAD, W. (2001). *Germs: Biological weapons and America's secret war.* New York: Simon & Schuster.

MOLINA, M., & ROWLAND, F. (1974, June 28). Stratospheric sink for chlorofluoromethanes: Chlorine atom-catalyzed destruction of ozone. *Nature, 249,* 810–812.

OSTERHOLM, M., & JOHN SCHWARTZ, J. (2000). *Living terrors: What America needs to know to survive the coming bioterrorist catastrophe.* New York: Delta Books.

SHAFFER, L. (1997). A concrete panoply of intercultural exchange: Asia in world history. In A. Embree & C. Gluck (Eds.), *Asia in western and world history* (pp. 810–866). Armonk, NY: M.E. Sharpe.

STERN, J. (1999). *The ultimate terrorists.* Cambridge, MA; London: Harvard University Press.

ZANINI, M., & EDWARDS, S. (2001). The networking of terror in the information age. In J. Arquilla & D. Ronfeldt (Eds.), *Networks and netwars: The future of terror, crime, and militancy* (pp. 29–60). Santa Monica: RAND.

13

Cyberterrorism: A New Reality in the Information Age

Karin A. Bast and Kuang-Wei Wen

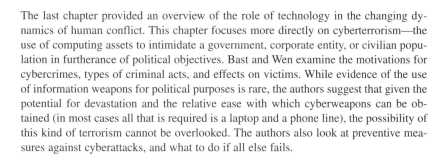

The last chapter provided an overview of the role of technology in the changing dynamics of human conflict. This chapter focuses more directly on cyberterrorism—the use of computing assets to intimidate a government, corporate entity, or civilian population in furtherance of political objectives. Bast and Wen examine the motivations for cybercrimes, types of criminal acts, and effects on victims. While evidence of the use of information weapons for political purposes is rare, the authors suggest that given the potential for devastation and the relative ease with which cyberweapons can be obtained (in most cases all that is required is a laptop and a phone line), the possibility of this kind of terrorism cannot be overlooked. The authors also look at preventive measures against cyberattacks, and what to do if all else fails.

It takes tremendous effort and determination for a suicide bomber to sneak into a target locale to detonate explosives. However, while many innocent victims could be murdered in such an act of physical terrorism, the supply of fearless martyrs would also dwindle as the crime is repeated. Now consider the twenty-first century scenario: five feet of water roaring through the city of Phoenix from all the floodgates on the Roosevelt Dam remotely opened by a 12-year-old preteen who was hired by a terrorist group via the Internet. A more catastrophic consequence is created in this latter case, but no known terrorist has been killed, harmed, or even identified—thanks to the power of information technology and the convenience of the Internet. What we are describing here is a form of cyberterrorism, among many others, that uses cyberspace as the means to carry out physical attacks.

Al-Qaeda members reportedly used encrypted email to communicate; steganography to hide encoded messages in Web images (including pornography), Kinko's and public library computers to send messages, underground banking networks called "*hawala*" to transfer untraceable funds, and a host of other information technologies like rented cell phones, online travel agencies, and flight simulators (Der Derian, 2002). The loss of communications infrastructure caused by the terrorist bombings of the World Trade Center "threatened the country's economic stability" according to Breton Greene, deputy manager at the National Communications System. This organization is responsible for the telecommunications networks that have national security significance (Verton, 2002d).

As recently as early 2001, most scholars and technology experts would have said that the potential for cyberterrorism existed but that it hadn't been used by individuals or groups for political, ideological, or theological reasons. However, shortly after the September 11 terrorist attack against the United States, "hacktivists" (hackers with activist intentions) took to the Internet to voice their rage with attacks supporting both sides of the ideological spectrum. For example, websites representing both sides were defaced, Arabic banks with suspected ties to Osama bin Laden were hacked, and denial of service (DoS) attacks against sites such as the Iranian Ministry of Interior, the Presidential Palace of Afghanistan and Palestinian ISPs were reported. "The cyberattacks arising from the events of September 11 reflect a growing use of the Internet as a digital battleground" (Denning, 2001).

This increased use of and dependence on technology to conduct business and wage war means that understanding how technology can be used for terrorist purposes is increasingly important for all citizens. The more we rely on computers, telecommunications, and the Internet, the more vulnerable and valuable they are to attack. The collective term for these attacks is *cyberterrorism*—the convergence of terrorism and cyberspace. It is generally understood to mean unlawful attacks and threats of attack against computers, networks, and the information stored therein when done to intimidate or coerce a government or its people in furtherance of political or social objectives (Denning, 2000).

Officials of the U.S. government are aware of the potential threat. "Our enemies will use our technology against us, just as the hijackers used our planes," said White House cybersecurity chief Richard Clarke in a February speech (National Security, 2002). The Internet is also vulnerable to physical attack at major connection points for telecommunications such as bridges or tunnels or beside isolated rail lines.

These threats may sound like science fiction and were considered unlikely at best just a few months before the September 11 attacks. We now realize that the use of technology for terrorism is all too real and citizens of this new century must have proper knowledge about cyberterrorism in their survival kit. Having been motivated by this new reality, the current chapter is intended to provide a multifaceted understanding of cyberterrorism, discuss available defense measures against it, explore the role of information technology in the evolutionary cyberwar, and suggest proper actions for the day after, should all defense options fail.

THE MANY FACES OF CYBERTERRORISM

Motivations and Their Seriousness

Why would someone want to purposely inflict harm to cyberspace or the physical world via cyberspace? The answer contains at least six distinguishable motivations, though a combination of several of them could also propel cyberterrorism: curiosity, excitement/publicity, monetary/personal gains, revenge/hatred, activism/patriotism, and religious causes. Depending on the underlying motives and the technical sophistication of the means, the seriousness of an attack varies widely. While teens vandalizing their school's website might not create much harm to society, the same teens could also cause havoc if they were to reverse all the A and F scores in the school's academic database. If the terrorists were actually motivated by a combination of patriotism and religious causes, the only limit on the catastrophe of their attacks is their imagination.

Early computer enthusiasts were called "hackers" because their curiosity led them to investigate as the Internet grew. In most cases of early hacking, no malicious damage was done. In many cases, no one even knew they had been inside the computer's defenses. A number of hackers enjoy the challenge and have made it their mission to test computer security flaws at companies like Microsoft, The New York Times, WorldCom, and Yahoo. One, Adrian Lamo, has a moral justification for his actions—alerting companies to flaws in their security. He claims to break into company networks using "only an old Toshiba notebook that's missing seven keys, a Web Browser, and rented network connections at Internet cafes or copy shops" (Hulme, 2002).

Benign hacking for the purpose of personal satisfaction rarely goes beyond creating a sense of insecurity and anxiety on the part of the victims. But cybercrimes for monetary or personal gains could cause financial and other hardships to a large segment of our society. This is especially true when extortion or blackmail is involved. However, if the motivation for the crimes is the perpetrators' own self-interest, deterrence measures should be effective in discouraging them.

If terrorism is propelled by hatred or revenge, irrational or illogical criminal acts might occur. Sabotaging an ex-employer's computing facility as a revenge for being laid off is a typical example. But as the motivation progresses to activism and patriotism, two new dangerous dimensions are added to cyberterrorism: collectivity and conviction. Making a loud political statement in cyberspace requires support from comrades, and waging war against a foe that is a nation-state or a strong group of adversaries entails long-term commitment and perseverance. With peer support and strong personal conviction to the causes, the seriousness of cyberterrorism could increase exponentially.

Religious conviction has been responsible for countless human conflicts and mass destructions in history. When conquering or eliminating heresies becomes a religious motivation *Jihad*-justified cyberterror attacks could be as bloody as any battle in the Crusade.

Types of Criminal Acts

Using the infrastructure of the Internet to commit crimes is sometimes called *cybercrime*. Some of the possible ways the Internet may be used to commit crimes include computer hacking or breaking into systems without authorization with the intent of causing harm or stealing information. In some cases the information on websites is defaced as a way to protest or to cause disruption. Identity theft is a way to obtain information about an individual for use in impersonating that individual with banks, credit card companies, or other businesses. Thousands of viruses are created by individuals to disrupt activity, including some that are very destructive not only to individual files but to the computers that host websites on the Internet. A new method of causing disruption is called a *denial of service (DoS) attack*. A computer or group of computers sends multiple requests for information to a server. If enough requests occur, it may cause the recipient machine to halt from the overload. Popular Internet sites such as Yahoo, eBay, and Amazon.com were attacked in February 2000. They were required to shut down operations until they developed a method of stopping the attack at a cost of $1.2 billion in lost revenue (Security incident planning, 2002). Another method of attacking computer systems is to cause a buffer overflow that exploits a known vulnerability in the computer's operating system to cause a system crash.

Those committing cyberterrorist acts have a significant advantage over terrorists operating in the physical world. They do not need to be physically close to the target of terrorism and may be halfway around the world from their target. All they need is a laptop and a phone line to commit cyberterrorist acts. They have devised ways to make their identity unknown by using anonymizers or systems that mask their Internet addresses so they are not in any physical danger from proximity or threat of exposure.

Hackers may even be politically neutral and available for hire to anyone for any purpose anywhere in the world, whether for criminal or cyberterrorist intent. Terrorists involved in the World Trade Center attack on September 11, 2001 demonstrated their willingness to spend long periods of time in the United States training for that attack. It is also plausible that some students in computer-related fields in the United States and other countries are involved in obtaining training for future cyberattacks either by attending universities and colleges in person or taking online courses using the Internet rather than the classroom. Cyberterror Virtual University with all its classes offered online in cyberspace is technologically possible and may already be a reality.

Some individuals and organizations are attempting to use the Internet to commit acts of terrorism not just within cyberspace but in the physical infrastructure connected to cyberspace by computers such as energy grids, telecommunications and emergency response systems, dams, water and sewage systems, rail, and air traffic control systems. Many critical systems have Web-based connections for supervisory control and data acquisition (SCADA). These segments of our critical infrastructure are vulnerable to disruptions and attacks in cyberspace (Verton, 2002e). According to a 2002 survey by Riptech Inc., a provider of security monitoring services, the highest percentages of total attacks were experienced by power and energy, financial services, and high tech firms, in that order. Among the 400 companies surveyed, the average company experienced 32 attacks per company per week. One in three attacks was targeted at a specific company with the remainder involving finding and exploiting vulnerabilities of organizations over the Internet (Smith, 2002).

VICTIMS AND THEIR VULNERABILITY

Information Infrastructure

"The USA PATRIOT Act defines critical infrastructure as those systems and assets, whether physical or virtual, so vital to the United States that the incapacity or destruction of such systems and assets would have a debilitating impact on security, national economic security, national public health or safety or any combination of those matters" (National Strategy for Homeland Security, 2002). One of these critical infrastructures is the information and telecommunications network that includes the Internet.

The Internet had its origins in the 1960s as a way to tie sophisticated supercomputers located at sites across the United States together. In the early 1990s the Internet was opened to commercial traffic for the first time. Today the Internet is comprised of millions of host computers in more than 250 countries, and the number is growing rapidly each year.

This new infrastructure called cyberspace is the result of connecting the various research institutions, businesses, and military installations together. This infrastructure is comprised of a *backbone* or a set of communication links that use high capacity telephone lines, including fiber optic cable, satellites, and microwaves to connect computers at various sites all over the world. The Internet is often defined as a network of networks where each individual network is under the control and administration of separate individuals, educational institutions, or organizations. Management of cyberspace is by a group of volunteer board members through an organization called ICANN that acts as a governing body for the Internet. Many companies, called Internet Service Providers (ISPs), provide the connections necessary to enable the communications from an individual computer to the Internet.

Because of the distributed nature of the Internet, it is difficult to imagine being able to disrupt it in any major way. However, there are 13 top-level access points called root servers that point to the .com, .biz, .org, and .net addresses that route or send packets of information on their way. These are vulnerable since they are so few and also so integral to the operation of the Internet addressing system. Any major disruption of the telecommunications infrastructure of our telephone system would also make Internet connections impossible.

Many companies today are setting up virtual private networks (VPNs) to allow use of the Internet for information flow but with protection including an encryption system for e-mail and documents. Many telecommuters working from their homes or cars use VPNs to secure information.

End Systems

Not only the utilities and information and telecommunications infrastructure are vulnerable to attack through the Internet. Many corporations have elaborate websites and information systems designed for internal, customer, and business partner use. Much of this information is also a gold mine to cyberterrorists. Critical industries might find themselves targets and have inadvertently provided information to make those attacks easier. Not only can a cyberterrorist use the Internet to perpetrate an attack through a DoS attack, a virus, or hacking, but considerable information is available online to facilitate that attack.

Corporate systems are designed to take advantage of the Internet's flexibility and ease of use. Companies may have widely dispersed branches around the world and employees who are only "present" virtually—using the Internet to connect to corporate data and communications. Assuring that these employees connecting are really who they purport to be and authorized to have access to information requires sophisticated procedures many companies have not yet realized are important. Note that the wireless systems becoming very popular for employees on the go have almost no security and can be monitored by someone with unsophisticated equipment simply by being in the physical location using a simple monitoring device.

Physical Infrastructure

The U.S. energy infrastructure is highly reliant on technology and makes an easy target for a well-placed attack, according to the Union of Concerned Scientist (U.S. energy supplies, 2002):

> A disruption at a key power plant, refinery, transmission hub, or pipeline can break the flow of power or fuel to millions of customers and create costly energy price spikes. A major accident at a nuclear power plan could kill tens of thousands and contaminate an area the size of Pennsylvania.

Telecommunications infrastructure is also vulnerable to attack and information about the infrastructure is readily available online. A survey by Computerworld of eight national and local telecommunications service providers in 2002 showed that there was enough information available to produce fairly accurate detail about the backbones serving businesses:

> In addition to network maps, the survey found detailed information on the locations of current and planned Internet data centers, router locations, major nodes of metropolitan-area networks. Virtual tours of data centers, maps depicting East Coast termination points of all long-haul undersea communications cables and street-level maps of fiber-optic networks are also available (Verton, 2002b).

Department of Energy (DOE) websites also revealed the approximate locations for nuclear waste storage facilities, reactors, and surplus plutonium storage sites, according to Verton. Most of the information was required by regulatory bodies and for business promotion according to Ed Badolato, president of Washington-based Contingency Management Services Inc. and the former Deputy Assistant Secretary for Energy Emergencies at the DOE (Verton, 2002a). "Many websites constitute a gold mine for potential attackers . . . ," according to Eric Friedberg, managing director at the New York-based firm Stroz Associates and a former crime coordinator at the U.S. Department of Justice, and "audits have found descriptions of physical locations of backup facilities, the number of people working at specific facilities, detailed information about wired and wireless networks. . . . Other sites give graphical representations of floor plans, cabling connections, and ventilation ductwork" (Verton, 2002c).

Not only are our energy, water, and telecommunications infrastructure easy targets, but so also are our emergency systems like 911 that depend on telecommunications to work. A number of individuals have predicted that an attack on a U.S. icon in the future like the World Trade Center attack on September 11, 2001 might also include a disruption of the emergency response infrastructure so those in need of fire and ambulance assistance will not be able to reach help. The World Trade Center buildings collapse destroyed a number of high-speed switches and circuits located in the basement of the building, according to Mark Marchand, a spokesman for Verison Inc. of New York. Worldcom and Spring Corp. also lost switches and circuits in the basement of the buildings (Brewin, 2001). Cell and wired voice communications were overloaded by the emergency prompting discussion about separate channels for emergency calls with priority in the future.

A new infrastructure carrying Internet traffic is the cable system. Unfortunately, cable is not regulated in the same way as the telephone system, so there are more possibilities for abuse and infiltration with cable than there are with the use of the telephone system.

What do these various infrastructures have in common that make them vulnerable? First, they are often distributed over large geographic locations, so monitoring and any kind of physical protection is difficult. For example, power lines may have remote monitoring equipment that is polled or called on a regular basis.

COUNTERMEASURES AND THEIR EFFECTIVENESS

In traditional information systems criminology, the standard approach to effectively fighting crime has been the simultaneous deployment of two measures: prevention and deterrence (Straub, 1990). The objective of deterrence measures is to create a cost or psychological hurdle to discourage criminal motives in the first place. If deterrence does not work, a defensive shield is needed to prevent attack. This general approach shall apply well in the war against cyberterrorism.

Preventive Measures

Awareness, introspective information, and system security are the three key ingredients for effective preventive measures. Although system security has been the main focus of discussion on preventing cyberterrorism, the other two ingredients are prerequisites for any successful system defense. An organization must be aware of the existence and potential threat of cyberterrorism to have any incentives for acquiring and deploying system defenses. As of today, many stakeholders and employees of companies still have not sensed the importance of the issue. There are still others who believe they are invincible to any cyberattack. Regardless of its source, the low level of awareness is a clear and present danger to current cyberdefense because it could lead to underuse of preventive measures. Even if the motivation for self-defense exists, the lack of introspective information could hinder the establishment of system security. An individual owning and operating a home computer connected to the Internet might have little difficulty knowing where the critical security points are. But this would not be the case when a large corporation running national or international business with tens or even hundreds of units or sites linked by the Internet is in question. The diverse nature of the technology platform across all units and the complex internal telecommunications networks tend to hamper the firm's ability to understand its own security weaknesses. Since we know we must defend the Internet itself and the critical infrastructure connected to it in a cyberattack, details of these crucial elements of the national economy must be collected, compiled, maintained, and kept up-to-date. Unfortunately, convincing industry to share proprietary internal information with the government has been a daunting task, given the private sector's longstanding of distrust of the government. However, some significant effort for this task has been spearheaded by the federal government recently and impressive progress made.

Assuming both the motivation for defense and the introspective information are present, we will still need to take a comprehensive approach to addressing system security.

A computer-based and networked system always consists of hardware, software, data, telecommunications linkages, people, and policies and procedures. All these components can be breached during a cyberattack. Protecting software and hardware alone does not suffice to ensure system security. For example, a disgruntled employee can leak access codes to a rival firm or terrorist group. To achieve a high level of security, the integrity of the nonmachine components of a system must also be guaranteed.

Traditionally, security has been an afterthought rather than part of planning in many organizations' information systems. The open flow of information, formerly segregated in small, local area networks, but now available to employees, business partners, and alliance members worldwide through the Internet has been the paramount goal. Often, some kind of intrusion or attack has been required to awaken organizations to the dangers to their data and the privacy of the information they disseminate. Many organizations have a militaristic approach to security that has been prevalent for many years: protect the perimeter, only let known and authorized personnel have access, and install programs like antivirus software that are able to detect known "enemies." While one can carry the analogy too far, it is useful to understand how organizations have approached security.

A common first line of defense is a firewall. Firewalls are software or the combination of software and hardware used to determine which messages are allowed through from the Internet or from a remote user calling in. A simple firewall might just screen incoming traffic to assure that the message is from a known machine provided by the company. In some cases, incoming calls are not allowed but a call-back system records the request for connection and uses an internally stored phone number to call the requester back. Packet-shaping software can be installed inside a firewall to block or allow certain kinds of Internet messages and information. Messages from certain addresses might be categorically refused. Most organizations and individuals now have access to antivirus software to protect from inadvertent downloads of viruses. This is still a perimeter defense.

Authentication systems can be added to the firewall by requiring that all computers attempting to connect must identify themselves using one of a variety of methods. The simplest is a username and password. More sophisticated methods, such as a smart card, require that the user carry a battery-operated card about the size of a credit card with a number generating program. Every 60 seconds the number required to connect may change. A computer at the receiving end has the same software and compares the two numbers. In combination with a login and password, smart cards are a very common way to authenticate users. Technology is now allowing the use of *biometrics* for authentication. Biometric systems scan certain unique parts of the human anatomy: iris of the eye, handprint, thumbprint, voice, face or a combination. This scan is then checked against a baseline scan to determine if this is an authorized person.

Many organizations resort to a demilitarized zone or an area outside the firewall as a place to store information they are willing to make available to the public. Email needs to be outside the firewall, as do most websites that are accessible to the public. Since the computer is outside the perimeter, security doesn't need to be as strict.

Cryptography or encryption is also a way to protect valuable data. Messages are first passed through some kind of encryption program to convert them into secret code. A similar process in reverse converts the message back into readable text at the receiving end. VPNs are used as a means of protecting data using encryption and extra protection before sending messages over the Internet.

While many organizations are using a militaristic approach to security, many hackers and cyberterrorists have adopted a more biological or internal approach. The goal is to pass through the perimeter defenses and operate from within the organization. The most obvious is a virus, a program that is used to cause damage to another computer. Viruses are often carried through email or an Internet download and thus can penetrate the perimeter. They usually try to use your computer to replicate and spread themselves to new hosts by infecting other programs on your computer inside the firewall. Some destroy the program they infect by overwriting some of the original code, in other cases, the virus carries a worm or additional program. The worm tries to spread copies of itself to other computer systems through email contact lists or other Internet connections. The worm may stay dormant until something triggers its activity. Some viruses are actually hidden in another software program. These are called Trojan Horse viruses. The program performs an unexpected or unauthorized and often malicious action, such as erasing files, formatting the hard drive, or displaying messages. A new method of breaking through the perimeter is the use of *steganography,* a method of incorporating encoded messages in Web images such as photographs and the popular .GIF graphic images.

Another popular way to cause damage from inside the perimeter is to leave a backdoor into the computer after infection from a virus that can later be exploited. In most cases detection is impossible since it is not part of the perimeter defense system and the intruder has a valid password. Using a system log cleaner, an intruder can erase all evidence of activity that would normally be recorded in log files before leaving the system.

Defending against cyberterrorists who have penetrated the perimeter will require new ways of thinking about security. Thinking of these problems as similar to autoimmune attacks where the organism attacks itself from within will require focusing on how to modify and make more flexible the immune system so it can react to new invaders it has not seen before. The strategy may require distributing defenses to all important parts of the organism rather than just concentrating on the perimeter and using monitoring of what is normal and expected as a way of deciding locally when some suspicious activities are found.

To gain a broad understanding of the prevalence of security breaches, the "Computer Crime and Security Survey" is conducted annually by the Computer Security Institute (CSI) with participation by the San Francisco Federal Bureau of Investigation's (F.B.I.) Computer Intrusion Squad. Patrice Rapalus, CSI Director, said that "There is much more illegal and unauthorized activity going on in cyberspace than corporations admit to their clients, stockholders, and business partners or report to law enforcement. Incidents are widespread, costly, and commonplace" (Power, 2002). "Probably every machine on the Internet is touched multiple times a day by one type of a scan or another, according to Jeff Carpenter, a manager with the Computer Emergency Response Team. . . ." (Cyberspace Invaders, 2002). Bruce J. Gephardt, the FBI's Executive Assistant Director, commented that:

> The United States' increasing dependency on information technology to manage and operate our nation's critical infrastructures provides a prime target to would-be cyber-terrorists. Now, more than ever, government and [the] private sector need to work together to share information and be more cognitive of information security so that our nation's critical infrastructures are protected from cyber-terrorists. (Power, 2002)

Ninety percent of respondents detected computer security breaches within the last year, according to the 2002 survey, but only about a third reported the intrusion to law enforcement. Eighty percent acknowledged financial losses due to computer breaches (Power, 2002).

An organization needs to commit itself to information security according to Power (2002). The information security team should report to the CIO or higher, and the author recommends one information security professional for every thousand users. Of course, training and budget dollars are important, too.

Deterrence Measures

The best deterrent to any crime is the existence of a perfect, impenetrable defense shield. However, such ideal protection cannot possibly exist in the evolutionary cyberwar, and the involvement of humans in the security system further complicates the picture. Since terrorists already know that all systems are vulnerable, the only way we can effectively deter them from engaging in cyberattack at will is to establish credible threats of punishment. Even if the terrorist has no fear of any harsh reprisal, the class of hackers-for-hire would be scared away, thereby effectively decoupling technology from terrorism. After all, very few terrorists are master hackers who can on their own penetrate a carefully constructed security system.

How can credible threats of punishment be established? The answer lies in three important steps: timely detection, successful conviction, and enforceable punishment. Given the volatile nature of electronic data communications, it should be clear that we must be able to instantly detect the occurrence of a cyberattack in order to initiate the follow-up investigation. To result in successful conviction, forensic evidence must be collected and undeniably linked to the terrorist. And finally, enforceable criminal laws must exist to impose harsh punishment on the convicted perpetrators.

Currently, the detection of cyberterrorism relies heavily on timely reporting by the private sector, since the government does not control the Internet and cannot tap into computer systems of companies. However, many companies and organizations have been reluctant to report cyberattacks. Publicizing their vulnerability may leave them open to further attack. The CIO Cyberthreat Response and Reporting Project is a collaboration among industry professionals, law enforcement, and *CIO Magazine* to develop guidelines for reporting computer security incidents to law enforcement that was created in October 2001 to make incident response coordinated especially for attacks on information systems or data. Things to report, as recommended by the project, include the primary systems involved, information about the attack itself, how the company mitigated or remedied the attack, any idea about who the suspect might be including whether it is a current or former employee, and any evidence that might help in any investigation (CIO cyberthreat, 2001).

Organizations to contact in case of cyberattack include the F.B.I. field office electronic crimes investigator, National Infrastructure Protection Center (NIPC), Electronic Crimes Branch of the U.S. Secret Service Headquarters, State Attorney General office, InfraGard, Electronic Crimes Task Force, Information Sharing & Analysis Centers (industry specific information sharing for critical infrastructure sectors), and the Forum of Incident Response and Security Teams for the private sector.

Even in the seemingly borderless and lawless cyberspace, it may be possible to trace the perpetrators if law enforcement is notified immediately. In this regard, the NIPC has published the following advice to help individuals and companies report any cyber-attack:

- Do not stop systems or tamper with files if you suspect an intruder.
- Use a wired telephone line to report any intruders since email may be monitored.
- Copy damaged or altered files and keep backups in a secure location.
- Be conscious of the need to establish chain-of-evidence custody of evidence so it may be used for prosecution; evidence loses its value if it is not properly controlled.

Once an attack is detected, forensic or identification capability will be the most crucial factor dictating the success of prosecution. But at this stage of the cyberwar, our ability to accurately identify and locate cyberterrorists and provide admissible evidence to the court is still very limited. How to develop irrefutable proof of the source of the attack remains as a challenge for current and future research. Recently, the RAND Corporation (a top policy think-tank) has recommended to the Defense Advanced Research Project Agency (DARPA) some approaches to solving the identification problem in cyberspace. The first is to develop a "cyberspace hot pursuit" capability to help back-track incidents and locate perpetrators. Appropriate laws authorizing such pursuit and cooperative agreements with foreign governments were identified as the necessary conditions for this suggestion. The second approach proposed the development of a "tamperproof black box" recording device to preserve the trails of criminal acts that would allow for later investigation (Tirenen, 2002).

When it comes to legal protection in cyberspace, slow but steady progress has been made in this country. So far there exist three federal statues that prohibit computer hacking and other unauthorized uses of computers and computerized information: the Computer Fraud and Abuse Act (CFAA) of 1984, the Electronic Communications Privacy Act (ECPA) of 1986, and the Economic Espionage Act (EEA) of 1996 (Fein & Heaphy, 2001). The focus of the CFAA is on the protection of computers and computer networks. Data are covered only in the form of digital records stored in computer systems. But the ECPA was a specific law protecting personal and proprietary data; it was an extension of the 1968 Wiretap Statute to the digital media and data communication channels. Both criminal charges and civil actions could apply to the perpetrators under the ECPA. The last statute, the EEA, criminalizes the theft of trade secrets and other proprietary information. The definition of "trade secrets" under the EEA is so broad that virtually all aspects of a company's information system are protected. Along with the passage of the EEA was the National Information Infrastructure Protection Act (NIIPA), an important amendment to the CFAA to provide extensive coverage for computer intrusion affecting interstate commerce. "Thanks to enactment of the NIIPA, the federal criminal code now penalizes not only the release of worms and viruses into computer networks systems, but also a broad range of hacking, hijacking, and generally disruptive and destructive breaches of e-commerce and other business networks. . . . they will face up to 20 years in prison and [fines] up to $250,000," said Mark Rush and Lucas Pagila, lawyers of Kirkpatrick & Lockhart LLP (Rush & Pagila, 2001).

While the above statues have established the legal ground for severely penalizing cy-bercriminals, vigilant protection of information systems still is the precondition for prose-cution. For example, the EEA requires that the company take "reasonable measures" to preserve the integrity and secrecy of its systems to ensure coverage. In other words, com-panies that are ignorant of safeguarding their own systems cannot ask for legal protection against cyberterrorism. As the cyberwar evolves in the future, it is certain that more tech-nology-specific cyberlaws will be enacted in the United States. Yet, on the other hand, we must also hold back our optimism at the same time for the development of any kind of use-ful international cyberlaw. Different nation-states have distinctive justice systems to pro-tect their own peoples (for example, see Evers, 2002), and many are not concerned with cyberterrorism the same way we are. How to pursue a terrorist abroad where extradition treaties do not exist, or even the evidentiary requirements for conviction are different, will be a very difficult issue needing feasible resolutions.

THE PIVOTAL ROLE OF IT IN THE FUTURE

IT as a Crime Weapon

"In reality, the Web sites and Web applications are probed continuously and hacked with frightening ease," according to Eric Hemmendinger of the Aberdeen Group, a market analysis firm specializing in helping information technology vendors. "The issue is not whether—but when—the enterprise will receive the unwanted attentions of a crafty hacker" (Hemmendinger, 2002). In fact, the attention of cyberterrorists has been evolving in a more subtle and deliberated way over time. Initially, destroying many valuable com-puter systems or networks using malicious programs like viruses or worms was the inten-tion. Then, a new objective of disabling online services by means of mass disruption (e.g., the DoS attack) was created. While the IT industry has been striving to develop cures for these serious problems, the nasty commercial application of spyware programs is now pos-ing a threat in our war against terrorism.

A user might, for instance, download a game to play. Meanwhile, as the user is play-ing the game, ads appear and the spyware goes about the process of investigating the player's computer system and reporting back what it finds. If the user were accessing Web pages in an intranet or password-protected site that stored user information on the local machine, the user could pass this information in unencrypted form over the Internet with-out realizing it through the spyware. If the spyware were controlled by a terrorist who seeks to gain access to computer systems that manage our critical infrastructure such as the hospital's emergency dispatch system or the air traffic control system, we would lose our ability to respond to a brutal attack on the physical world.

The rapid proliferation of cyberweapons has taken a toll on our ability to defend all critical computer systems and infrastructure. One well-known testimony to this claim was the Nimda attack in 2001, during which 2.2 million systems were infected within 24 hours of the virus's release. Because the perpetrator embodied the virus with a mixture of four known cyberweapons, most servers failed to stop the infection using traditional anti-virus techniques (Response strategies, 2002). The use of this new kind of hybrid cyberweapon capable of carrying out multivector attacks has opened up a new possibility in cyberwarfare: automated offense supported by artificial intelligence.

Unlike using humans to stalk the target and initiate deadly attack at a certain time in physical terrorism, cyberterrorism can be carried out without any set timetable, since software-based terrorists can stay dormant indefinitely. Why do terrorists choose cyberspace over other means of attack? There are a number of reasons. One of the obvious ones is that the individual or individuals involved can remain anonymous by using an intermediary service. This is called an *anonymizer.* Their email or computer hardware identification can be masked by any of a number of Internet sites so it's impossible to trace the actual perpetrator. Secondly, the terrorists may be anywhere in the world other than the actual site targeted for the terrorist act. The personal safety of the terrorists is not jeopardized, so no plans for a get-away or threats of giving away the plan by nervous or other inappropriate behavior are necessary. The third reason is that the very nature of the Internet makes small- or large-scale attack possible. Just the unlimited threat of attacking major businesses or key physical infrastructures through such an untraceable means makes this fit nicely with terrorist objectives. The fourth reason is that much of the infrastructure in the United States is vulnerable through this means because of poor security through the Internet. There may be fences and other physical barriers to the actual site but very poor security through computer systems, making this means of attack the easiest.

If these malicious programs were made intelligent enough to optimize their own decisions of target selection, self-reproduction, attack methods and timing, and even self-destruction for eliminating evidence, we would be put in the worst possible position to defend our systems. Today's information technology already has the capability to produce software robots (called *bots*) that can act as agents to perform many network and Web functions. These autonomous programs are valuable aids to us in dealing with the scale and complexity of the Internet; they also could help companies handle large volume of e-business activities online. However, the same technology could also produce disguised agents that have a normal virtual appearance but have a deadly terrorist's intention. And once released to the Internet, they will carry out their missions in the best way they see fit, thereby leaving no specific attack patterns for detection. Should this technology fall into the hands of terrorists, the cyberspace Armageddon would not be too far away.

IT as a Defense Shield

Firewalls and antivirus software are two obvious defenses that any organization or individual can deploy to help defend its systems against attack. Intruder detection systems watch for unauthorized activity on computer systems and respond to unusual or suspicious activity by analyzing packets of information passing through the network or by monitoring log files and data on individual computers. Companies providing operating systems like Windows XP® may release security updates regularly to fix known software security problems. Key employees can subscribe to email notification of patches to fix known problems and alerts about newly discovered vulnerabilities. Companies can use VPNs and encryption as well as sophisticated authentication systems. Cyberinsurance companies can conduct audits of a company's security measures to assess whether system administrators are able to detect and deflect various forms of cyberattack.

Scalet and Berinato (2002) recommended these best practices: identifying your company's most critical information assets so you can spend your time and energy protecting what's most important, making sure the top levels of management value security, give someone responsibility for coordinating security, develop and implement a security policy and make sure employees are educated about it, conduct a security audit, make sure computers and other equipment are physically secure, be vigilant for internal threats and threats from former employees who may be disgruntled, subscribe to warning alerts, and have a business continuity plan.

Companies should also implement caller ID on remote access telephone lines and consider installation of keystroke monitoring software. In addition, self-assessment of vulnerability is also important. SPI Dynamics program WebInspect® is an automated Web application vulnerability testing program that examines Web content from the perspective of the hacker. It examines all vulnerabilities to show how a hacker could breach the defenses. Programs like this might help organizations become more proactive in handling security (Ware, 2001).

There are programs that could prevent unauthorized programs from communicating with the Internet. Some malicious programs will give themselves the same name as a trusted program. Two programs, PestPatrol® and LeakTest®, prevent masquerading programs and eliminate the hacker tools, spyware, and Trojans from a PC or network (Flore & Francois, 2002).

A broad strategy of President George W. Bush is to use the government's advanced technology to detect and prevent terrorism. He has created the Critical Infrastructure Protection Board and developed a National Strategy to Secure Cyberspace. A key component of this strategy is to ensure that federal agencies have compatible technologies so they can share information. The information sharing will have to include local, state, and federal levels of government as well as the private sector, which owns the majority of the nation's critical infrastructure. This may include smart borders that use IT-enabled sensors and monitoring equipment for securing shipping and biometric authentication systems for secure buildings, airports, and other infrastructure facilities.

It is necessary to have an early warning system at the national level to avert large-scale, catastrophic cyberterrorism. Conventional thoughts would base the system on a comprehensive, public-private information sharing system and a real-time reporting system. However, neither of the underlying systems seems feasible at this juncture due to severe differences in the industrial and political cultures among various sectors of U.S. society. As an alarming example, the U.S. Postal Service declined to participate in Operation TIPS, a program proposed by the Homeland Security Office to have postal workers report suspicious activities as they deliver mail (Postal Service, 2002). A change in attitude among private and public organizations or enactment of laws may be necessary to develop an effective civil watch system. In addition, artificial intelligence in a distributed fashion may help with a technology-assisted version of the watch system.

In his inspiring work, *Darwin among the Machines: The Evolution of Global Intelligence,* George Dyson (1997) portrays a world of computer systems linked by broadband communication channels. Each individual system on the network might not possess any particular intelligence, but through communication, they develop a high level of global intelligence. Based on Darwin's theory, Dyson predicted that such an intelligent network would be capable of evolving quickly and independently, and eventually outsmarting the human race. Akin to the structure of Dyson's intelligent network is our Internet, though it does not have coordinated and collective intelligence yet. But if we are willing to suppress our fear of Dyson's prediction, the Internet, or any contiguous segment of it, can be configured with distributed artificial intelligence to provide the much-needed capability of automatic attack detection. The technological potential for this cutting-edge application exists today; what we lack is firm legal basis to support overlaying a nationwide control network over the current Internet to allow uninterrupted communications among all the component devices.

Is This a Winnable War?

If you view the terrorist threats to cyberspace and, through cyberspace, to our physical infrastructure as a cyberwar, then we might ask the question: What would we need to do to win this war and would we like the results if we implement these steps? Or is winning really losing? The Internet has from its inception been loosely governed by volunteers, encouraged experimentation and innovation, and been totally uncensored. The changes that would increase security would lessen our privacy and require more regulation. We might argue that the incredible pace of technological innovation and the widespread adoption of Internet technology is in large part because of the lack of regulation. In addition, individuals are not willing to give up their privacy to facilitate national identification systems and intrusive monitoring of their actions. Much of the funding given to the private sector for the development of the Internet came from the Department of Defense. In the future the military may again need to take the lead in encouraging the development of better security by funding research. For example, use of wireless equipment such as cell phones, pagers, and wireless Internet access is commonplace even though wireless systems have very poor security. Funding to increase research on more secure wireless systems would benefit everyone.

Increased cooperation between governmental information systems at the federal, state, and local levels is long overdue in areas such as law enforcement. Gathering information about much of the critical U.S. infrastructure will require cooperation from private industry as well. Concern about keeping the information secure from competitors and preventing public disclosure due to freedom of information regulations if it is maintained by a central governmental agency has so far stifled cooperation. In the same way that national ID cards and centralized medical records cause concern because of the possibility of a security breach or misuse, giving massive amounts of data about critical infrastructure to the federal government is of great concern to industry.

Even with increased security and the aggregation of data, the likelihood of cyberattack is great. Cyberattack weapons are widely available on the Internet and the technological sophistication of the terrorists continues to increase. We see the following trends: (1) increasing sophistication of terrorism planning supported by information technologies; (2) increasing efficiency and flexibility in logistic operations of the terrorists via the Internet; (3) effective recruitment, online education, and alliance formation of the terrorist in cyberspace; (4) accelerating access to hackers-for-hire worldwide; and (5) wider recognition of the limited power of U.S. defenses under social, legal, and political restrictions. An enemy who is technically advanced, well supported by flexible, global networks, elusive in cybermaneuvers, has detailed information about all critical infrastructure of the United

States, and can control all kinds of specialty hackers to stage creative attacks both in and through the cyberspace is a formidable opponent indeed.

Can we win this war decisively? Probably not. But can we contain our enemy to minimize our casualties? Yes, definitely. As long as the nation as a whole realizes the future danger, moves swiftly to develop and implement a multifront defense strategy, and also preserves its superiority in information technology, it will be able to at least maintain a long-term equilibrium. To go beyond this equilibrium, we would need to either build a perfect terrorism prevention system at the expense of sacrificing our civil liberty or strike back with deadly countermeasures that might cause innocent collateral damages. In either event, winning is actually losing, for we have changed who we are in the end.

HOW TO LIVE IN AN IMPERFECT WORLD WHEN ALL ELSE FAILS

There is no such thing as perfect security unless you turn the computer systems off and keep them in a locked and secured location. Employees, customers, and business partners need access to data electronically, often via the Internet. Security breaches can disrupt work and cause embarrassment, but they may also cause physical or financial loss as well. What happens if all else fails and cyberterrorists succeed in breaching your security defenses and causing physical or cyberspace damage?

Every organization should have a business continuity plan, although a survey by *CIO Magazine* found that two-thirds of respondents said their company had no well-defined security plan in place. Close to one-third of the companies reported that the organization's critical information was accessible directly via the Internet. They also reported that many more employees had access to critical data than needed that access. Further, over half had no system in place to detect an infrastructure attack even within 24 hours (Ware, 2001).

A significant part of any business continuity plan should include a well-defined, companywide security policy that employees are required to review regularly. This should include an alternative physical location miles away from the main site where it is unlikely that the same disaster would strike simultaneously. The site should have the hardware and software necessary to provide continuity in case of any kind of failure, sufficient office space, and phone systems. How elaborate this alternative site needs to be depends on the critical nature of the computer support and the cost of interrupting operations. For example, the site for a bank or other financial institution may need to have computers and software running constantly with data already in place so it can take over in seconds or minutes if there is a disaster. In addition, this plan should include information about who to call, including home and cell phone numbers. Of course, copies of the plan should be widely distributed and must be kept off site as well. It is a good idea to conduct disaster drills to test the plan. Carnegie Mellon's CERT® center (*http://www.cert.org*) provides security alerts via email for attacks caused by viruses and other cyberspace software. The Carnegie Mellon Software Engineering Institute has developed a program called OCTAVE[SM] (Operationally Critical Threat, Asset, and Vulnerability Evaluation) that outlines a method for large organizations to follow to understand and evaluate their security risks. The plan has three phases: build asset-based threat profiles, identify infrastructure vulnerabilities, and develop security strategy and plans (Alberts & Dorofee, 2001).

Even simple steps like keeping backups of all original operating system software and critical data can be part of a business (or individual) continuity plan. Strict policies for changing passwords and using complex passwords requiring letters, numbers, and symbols are another simple way to safeguard data. If employees leave the organization, be sure to cancel their access. Dial-in access is more vulnerable to attack: Consider call-back systems or biometrics for authentication.

The continuity planning we have discussed would be the same whether the disaster is caused by natural causes, such as weather or earthquake, or whether the disaster originated with a cyberterrorist attack. In fact, a successful cyberattack may be indistinguishable from a natural disaster unless and until a terrorist group identifies its part in the disaster. Good planning and well-informed individuals to implement the plan are crucial in either case. People are the most important part of any information systems and care taken to hire the right people, train them, and assure their loyalty are just as important as the best plan.

As we cautioned earlier, we are fighting a war against cyberterrorism without the realistic prospect of winning. Damages and disruptions will be a part of our life as the war goes on. However, as long as we properly prepare ourselves to minimize the effects of any disaster, we can prevent the total success of any cyberattack, thereby ensuring that terrorists always fail to intimidate or coerce us for their political, social, or religious objectives.

DISCUSSION QUESTIONS

1. What are the advantages to a terrorist organization from using cyberspace to initiate an attack?
2. What fundamental rights and privileges are granted by a "free society" that might make the harboring of cyberterrorists unavoidable? What countermeasures might be required to stop the use of technology for terrorist purposes and how might that affect our freedom and privacy?
3. Given that all countries do not have the same viewpoint about freedom of speech and open access to information, what measures are available to other societies as they attempt to control access to the Internet? Are these acceptable in a free society? Are these countermeasures a violation of basic human rights, ethics, legal, or social norms in the United States?

REFERENCES

ALBERTS, C. J., & DOROFEE, A. J. (2001, December) *OCTAVE^{SM} criteria, version 2.0. Networked systems survivability program.* Retrieved July 17, 2002 from *http://www.cert.org/archive/pdf/01tr016.pdf.*

BREWIN, B. (2001, September 11) Defense dept. command and control nets unaffected by terrorist attack. *Computerworld.* Retrieved September 12, 2001 from *http://www.computerworld.com/csi/story/0,1199,NAV47_STO63712,00.html.*

CIO cyberthreat response and reporting guidelines. (2001). Retrieved July 19, 2002 from *http://64.28.79.79/research/security/.*

Cyberspace Invaders. (2002, June). *Consumer Reports,* 16.

DENNING, D. E. (2000, May 23) *Cyberterrorism.* Testimony before the Special Oversight Panel on Terrorism Committee on Armed Services, U.S. House of Representatives. Retrieved March 29, 2002 from *http://www.cs.georgetown.edu/~denning/infosec/ cyberterror.html.*

DENNING, D. E. (2001, November 1) *Is cyber terror next?* Social Science Research Council. Retrieved March 29, 2002 from *http://www.ssrc.org/sept11/essays/denning. htm.*

DER DERIAN, J. (2002, March 29) *9-11: Before, after, and in between.* Retrieved March 29, 2002 from *http://www.ssrc.org/sept11/essagys/der_derian.htm.*

DYSON, D. G. (1997). *Darwin among the machines:* The *evolution of global intelligence.* New York: Addison-Wesley.

EVERS, J. (2002, April 12) European Parliament says no to Web site blocking. *Computerworld.* Retrieved April 15, 2002 from *http://www.computerworld.com/ storyba/0,4125,NAV47_ST070115,00.html.*

FEIN, D. B., & HEAPHY, M. W. (2001, October 15). Companies Have Options When Systems Hacked. Connecticut Law Tribune, Vol 27, pg 5.

FLORE, F., & FRANCOIS, J. (2002, July 5) *Unwitting collaborators, part 3: Spyware.* InformIT. Retrieved July 10, 2002 from *http://www.informit.com/isapi/product_ id~{E03875BE-D0CA-49C8-B8E9-77FAFA32}.htm.*

HEMMENDINGER, E. (2002, July 12) Automated Web application vulnerability testing keeps Web applications from being hacked. *InSight,* Aberdeen Group. Retrieved July 19, 2002 from *http://www.aberdeen.com/ab_abstracts/2002/07/07020009.htm.*

HULME, G. V. (2002, July 8) With friends like this; Lamo takes a morally ambiguous stance on his hacking, but others don't. *InformationWeek.* Retrieved July 8, 2002 from *http:// www.informationweek.com/shared/printableArticle?doc_id=IWK20020705S0017.*

Minimizing your potential vulnerability and enhancing effective response. (2002). *National Infrastructure Protection Center.* Retrieved July 19, 2002 from *http://www. nipc.gov/incident/incident3.htm.*

National security is an IT concern. (2002, July 1). *eWeek.* Retrieved July 19, 2002 from *http://www.eweek.com/print_article/0,3668,a=28711,00.asp.*

National strategy for homeland security. (2002). *Homeland Security Department.* Retrieved July 19, 2002 from *http://www.whitehouse.gov/homeland/book/index.html.*

Postal Service delines to take part in terrorist tip program. (2002, July 18). *La Crosse Tribune,* A-3.

POWER, R. (2002, Spring) 2002 CSI/FBI computer crime and security survey. *Computer Security Issues & Trends,* 8(1). Retrieved July 1, 2002 from *http://www.gocsi.com/pdfs/ fbi/FBI2002.pdf.*

Response strategies hybrid threats: A new approach to protecting online information re- sources. (2002). Atlanta, GA: Internet Security Systems.

RUSH, M. A. & PAGLIA, L. G. (2001, August 20). Preventing, Investigating and Prosecuting Computer Attacks and E-Commerce Crimes. Delaware Corporate Litigation Reporter. Vol 15, pg 11.

SCALET, S. D., & BERINATO, S. (2002, February 20). The ABCs of security. *CIO Magazine.* Retrieved July 19, 2002 from *http://www.cio.com/security/edit/security_abc.html.*

Security incident planning: How to prepare and respond and recover executive summary. (2002). *CIO Focus.* Retrieved July 19, 2002 from *http://www.theciostore.com/guide_ product.asp?id=54.*

SMITH, T. (2002, July 11). How often hackers attack, and what they're after. *Internetweek.com.* Retrieved July 12, 2002 from *http://www.internetweek.com/shared/ printableArticle?doc_id=INW20020211S0001.*

STRAUB, D. (1990). Effective IS security: An empirical study. *Information Systems Research, 1*(3), 255–276.

TIRENEN, W. (2002, July 1). Deterrence Through Identification. Retrieved July 1, 2002 from *http://www.isi.edu/gost/cctws/tirenen.html.*

U.S. *energy supplies vulnerable: Report says exposed infrastructure, oil dependence to blame.* (2002, February 1). Union of Concerned Scientists. Retrieved July 9, 2002 from *http://www.ucsusa.org/releases/02-01-02.html.*

VERTON, D. (2002a, February 11). Energy, Nuclear Infrastructure Exposed. *Computerworld.* Retrieved July 9, 2002 from *http://www.computerworld.com/printthis/2002/0, 4814, 68183,00.html.*

VERTON, D. (2002b, February 11). Telecom infrastructure an open book. *Computerworld.* Retrieved July 9, 2002 from *http://www.computerworld.com/printthis/2002/ 0,4814,68182,00.html.*

VERTON, D. (2002c, February 11). Web sites seen as terrorist aids. *Computerworld.* Retrieved July 9, 2002 from *http://www.computerworld.com/printthis/2002/ 0,4814,68181,00.html.*

VERTON, D., (2002d, March 4). Digital destruction was worst imaginable. *Computerworld.* Retrieved April 13, 2002 from *http://www.computerworld.com/storyba/0,4125,NAV47_ STO68762,00.html.*

VERTON, D. (2002e, April 26). Movement afoot to beef up industrial cybersecurity. *Computerworld.* Retrieved April 26, 2002 from *http://www.computerworld.com/storyba/ 0,4125,NAV47_STO70587,00.html.*

WARE, L. C. (2001, August 12) *CIO security worksheet.* Retrieved July 19, 2002 from *http://www2.cio.com/research/surveyreport.cfm?id=21.*

14

Bioterrorism: Should I Be Worried?

William Schwan

Unlike cyberterrorism, the use of biological weapons by individuals with political grievances presents a more immediate threat. At the time of publication, not much is known about the individual(s) responsible for mailing of *Bacillus anthracis* spores that resulted in five deaths and several cases of exposure to anthrax. This chapter discusses the recent history of bioterrorism in the United States and provides a taxonomy of various biological agents. Several factors favor the use of biological weapons for commission of terrorist acts: The agents are inexpensive, easy to transport, hard to detect, and diseases caused may be transmitted from person to person. This means that biological weapons can be used to cause significant panic with minimal outlays. The author notes that in spite of these advantages, the widespread use of biological weapons is not imminent due to difficulties in weaponization and dissemination of the agents.

The date September 11, 2001 will forever be engrained into the minds of the American people. It was on this date that the threat of terrorism made an enormous impact and dissolved away many perceptions regarding the immunity of the United States to a coordinated terrorist attack. The collective sense of security was torn further as a result of the mailings of *Bacillus anthracis* spores, resulting in several cases of anthrax. Vulnerability to organisms that cannot be seen, felt, or tasted can engender fear in a lay population. The threat of bioterrorism is now a grim reality, but with greater knowledge there is less likelihood these fears will dominate daily life in the United States. This chapter will address the question "Bioterrorism: Should I Be Worried?" The study will define the term bioterrorism, distinguish between various agents and discuss what is being done to minimize the threat.

Mere mention of the word *bioterrorism* conjures up a great deal of apprehension in most people. The agents involved are typically microorganisms or products of microorganisms that most individuals know little about. It is important to distinguish between bioterrorism and biowarfare. By definition, *biowarfare* is the intentional use of disease-causing organisms or products of organisms to infect populations to attain a military objective, whereas bioterrorism is the intentional use of disease-causing organisms or products of organisms to infect humans, other animals, or plants in order to cause civil unrest and panic. To further expand this definition, the Federal Bureau of Investigation (F.B.I.) defines a bioterrorist agent as any microbe, virus, infectious substance, or biological product capable of causing death or disease in a human, animal, plant, or another living organism or having a deleterious effect on food, water, or the environment (Beecher, 2001). Thus, the main distinction between bioterrorism and biowarfare lies in the objective of the user.

What are some of the advantages from using biological weapons? Biologics as a potential weapon in the hands of a bioterrorist is a scary thought and not unreasonable. Some of the rationales favoring the use of biological agents as weapons include: The agents may be readily available; they are typically inexpensive (compared to a nuclear weapon for instance); they are highly transportable; they are not easily detected; they are invisible, tasteless, odorless; they will cause no damage to the infrastructure (whereas bombs will cause mass destruction that will have to be rebuilt); they can cause large-scale panic in a population; and there may be the possibility of person-to-person transmission that will bring additional morbidity and mortality after the initial attack has ended. All of these attributes make biological agents ideal weapons. So why haven't they been more widely used? One of the reasons is because many people think of using biological agents as morally repugnant or a socially unethical thing to do. More importantly, concerns about one's own safety when manufacturing and disseminating these agents arise because they are difficult to control. Once "Pandora's Box" has been opened, there is great difficulty in closing it up. Delivery of the agent is another roadblock that can and has impeded the use of biological agents as terrorist weapons.

Although the disadvantages noted above dissuade most people from becoming bioterrorists, there are individuals or groups that will persist. It takes money and resources to develop and carry out a biological attack. If the bioterrorist group or individual has developed the right agent and has overcome many of the technical obstacles along the way, how might the attack unfold? It would come as either an overt event or a covert event. This distinction is critical for how effective the response would be against the attack. In an overt event, the people perpetuating the event will announce it, people in turn will fall ill or die as a result of the exposure, microorganisms are considered unconfirmed, and any hoaxes are assumed to be real and are treated as such. Conversely, a covert event will have no prior warning. This type of attack will be manifested through patients falling ill or dying from unknown or unusual causes, combined with an unusual geographic clustering of cases from an undetermined causative agent. Examples of overt events would be the wave of anthrax hoaxes that surfaced in the late 1990s, targeting abortion clinics across the United States. Hundreds of these events occurred, precipitating responses that included the use of hazardous material or HAZMAT teams to decontaminate the facilities as well as the people exposed (Tucker, 1999). Covert attacks are more foreboding because the targeted areas are unaware that an attack has taken place due to the properties associated with biological agents (i.e., they are invisible, odorless, tasteless, etc.).

A BRIEF HISTORY OF BIOTERRORISM

There is a long history associated with biowarfare. From as far back as the Romans, biological agents have been used to achieve military objectives. Probably the most famous historical case would be during the siege of Kaffa on the Black Sea in present-day Ukraine.

A Tartar force catapaulted bodies of individuals who had died of the plague into the city. An outbreak of plague within the city took place, and some of the hired mercenaries fled to Italy. This may have precipitated the spread of the plague throughout Europe in what became known as the "The Black Death" (Block, 2001).

Although biowarfare has been practiced for hundreds of years, the history of bioterrorism is relatively short. Very few cases have surfaced, in part due to the difficulties linked with biological agents. Table 14.1 shows some of the incidents of bioterrorism that have been reported. Among the incidents noted are the Rajneeshee Cult's release of *Salmonella enterica* var. Typhimurium onto the salad bars in ten different locations in The Dalles, Oregon, in September 1984 (Torok et al., 1997). The cult, located in rural Orgeon, was trying to affect a local county election. As a result of their covert biological assault, 751 people became sick with diarrhea. What is really striking is that, at the time, the event was considered a benign foodborne illness outbreak, presumed to be the result of natural contamination. *Salmonella enterica* var. Typhimurium is relatively easy to obtain naturally, and there are fewer hazards associated with working with this agent, as will be discussed in more detail later. Until the late 1990s, there were few restrictions in place for obtaining biological agents from supply houses like the American Type Culture Collection then

Table 1.   Specific incidents of bioterrorism/biocrimes-related activities around the world

Person/Organization	*Year*	*Agent Used/Procured*	*Outcome*
Rajneeshee Cult	1984	*Salmonella enterica* ser. Typhimurium	Cult members arrested after cult collapsed
Aum Shinrikyo	1990–1995	*Bacillus anthracis* and botulinum toxin	The attacks failed because of inadequate preparation of the agents
Thomas Lavy	1993	Ricin toxin	Stopped at the Alaska-Canada border and agent confiscated
Larry Wayne Harris	1995	*Yersinia pestis*	Arrested after illegally receiving the agent
Diane Thompson	1997	*Shigella dysenteriae*	Arrested and serving prison term
Larry Wayne Harris & Joe Leavitt	1998	*Bacillus anthracis*	Arrested on suspicion of possessing agent
***Bacillus* mailings**	2001	*Bacillus anthracis*	No perpetrator found yet
Islamic militants	2003	Ricin toxin	British government arrested members

located in Rockville, Maryland. Changes were forthcoming after the arrest of Larry Wayne Harris in 1995. Harris was a trained laboratory technician from Ohio with microbiology experience who also was a fervent member of the Aryan Nation (Kaplan, 1997). He was able to obtain three vials of the bacterial species *Yersinia pestis,* which causes bubonic plague, from the ATCC. Because of this lapse in security, tighter restrictions were mandated to minimize lay people from obtaining these deadly biological agents. Three years later Larry Wayne Harris rose to notarity again when he was arrested in Las Vegas with William Joseph Leavitt, a Nevada man, on suspicion of possessing *Bacillus anthracis,* the causative agent of anthrax. It was determined that the pair were in possession of a vaccine strain of the species and their motives were to develop an effective vaccine to protect mankind (Gorman & Lichtblau, 1998). Ironically, the notarity that the Harris/Leavitt case generated may have indirectly led to the wave of anthrax hoaxes that arose throughout the United States in the subsequent months and years.

Many people have heard of the Aum Shinrikyo cult headed by Shiko Asahare as a consequence of the cult's release of sarin gas in the Tokyo subway system. What wasn't widely known was that the cult ran a biological warfare program. During a five-year time-span from 1990 through 1995, the cult carried out nine biological attacks, including several in Tokyo as well as against United States military bases (Olson, 1999). Their first attack began in April 1990 and probably represents the first biological assault by a terrorist organization. Spray trucks laden with botulinum toxin were used, but the toxin was prepared incorrectly and was rendered useless in terms of a bioterrorist agent. The group switched to *B. anthracis* following its failure with botulinum toxin, but their lack of knowledge regarding microorganisms led them to obtain a vaccine strain of the species rather than a variety that would be extremely lethal in humans. From what is known about the group, their quest to get the Ebola virus after an outbreak occurred in Africa was unsuccessful.

The biocrime instigated by Diane Thompson in 1997 was a subtler form of bioterrorism. She was a clinical lab worker from Texas who took a *Shigella dysenteriae* type 2 stock at the hospital and spread it on pastries and muffins (Kolavic et al., 1997). She announced the free food to her co-workers, who eagerly consumed these foodstuffs. Of forty-five people with exposure to the bacteria, twelve developed severe, acute diarrhea, which resulted in the hospitalization of four individuals. Eight of the patients had *S. dysenteriae* isolated from their bloody stools that matched the bacteria found in leftover muffins. Due to a quick-acting health network, Thompson was arrested and is now serving a 20-year jail sentence. From her arrest and subsequent questioning, it was uncovered that she perpetuated this incident as a result of some petty quarrel with her co-workers, so although she did not have a political agenda, nevertheless, she did use a biological agent for a covert attack on her co-workers.

CLASSIFICATION OF POTENTIAL BIOWARFARE/BIOTERRORIST AGENTS

The successful attacks by the Rajneeshee cult and Diane Thompson were accomplished with microorganisms that are less likely to cause death in humans. Biological warfare/bioterrorism agents have been categorized based on the potential risk to people in the United States and throughout the world (Centers for Disease Control, 2000a). This list was designed to assist healthcare workers and the U.S. public health system in the event one of these biological agents was released onto a population. Three categories of agents have been noted: Category A, Category B, and Category C. Those agents labeled as Category A have the highest priority in terms of posing a risk to national security, being easily disseminated or transmitted person-to-person, causing high mortality (or having major public health impact), causing public panic and social disruption, and requiring special action for public health preparedness. Some of these agents have had a significant impact on the history of the human race. The agents are noted in Table 14.2 and include the viruses responsible for smallpox and hemorrhagic fever; the bacterial agents responsible for anthrax, plague, and tularemia, as well as a toxin produced by a ubiquitous species of bacteria found routinely in soil,*Clostridium botulinum* (botulinum toxin). All told these agents have killed millions of people through the span of human history, and they remain a potential threat to human health and survival. These are the agents to which the Soviet Union and the United States devoted much time and expenditures of money for the purposes of biological warfare.

Category B agents are next in priority because they are moderately easy to disseminate, cause moderate morbidity and low mortality, and require special enhancements of diagnostic capacity and disease surveillance. The lay population is less familiar with most of these agents, which include the bacteria responsible for Q fever, brucellosis, and Rocky Mountain Spotted Fever; viruses capable of causing Rift Valley Fever or encephalitis (Table 14.2); a product that is not of microbial origin (ricin toxin from castor beans); and several other toxins of microbial origin. Most individuals are more acquainted with a subset of these agents known to contaminate food and water, including *Salmonella, Shigella,* and *Escherichia coli* O157:H7, which leads to bloody diarrhea. Until last year's attacks, these were the agents that had been successfully used in bioterrorist attacks.

Category C includes agents known as emerging pathogens about which little is known and that could be engineered for mass dissemination in the future. They are easily available, easily produced and disseminated, and could have the potential for a high number of deaths and incapacitation. Among these agents are Hantavirus and multidrug-resistant *Mycobacterium tuberculosis.*

Thus, each agent is categorized according to how much is known about it and how deadly it might be for humans. Category A agents are the hot button organisms that engender a great deal of fear and panic in a human population. Of these Category A agents, two in particular have aroused considerable interest. One is still a scourge around the world, causing death and suffering in man and other animals, whereas the other has been eradicated from the wild since 1977. These microorganisms are *Bacillus anthracis* (anthrax) and Variola major (smallpox).

THE THREAT OF ANTHRAX

Since hoofed animals roamed the Earth, *B. anthracis* has been around. The name was derived from the Greek word for coal—*anthrakis. B. anthracis* are large boxcar-shaped cells that can only be observed under a light microscope. Products that they produce include something called spores, which are resistant to harsh environments that can include boiling and even exposure to some disinfectants. Inside a mammalian body, spores

Table 2. Categorization of potential biological warfare/bioterrorism agents and their biosafety level (BSL) classification

Agent(s)	Disease	BSL
	Category A	
Bacillus anthracis	Anthrax	2/3[a,b]
Yersinia pestis	Plague	2/3
Franciscella tularensis	Tularemia	2/3
Clostridium botulinum toxin	Botulism	2/3
Variola major virus	Smallpox	4
Filoviruses (Ebola, Marburg)	Hemorrhagic fever	4
Arenaviruses (Lassa, Junin, etc.)	Hemorrhagic fever	4
	Category B	
Brucella sp.	Brucellosis	2/3
Burkholderia mallei	Glanders	3
Burkholderia pseudomallei	Melidiosis	2/3
Coxiella burnetii	Q fever	2/3
Rickettsia prowazeki	Typhus	2/3
Ricksettsia rickettsii	Rocky Mountain Spotted Fever	2/3
Rift Valley Fever virus	Rift Valley Fever	3
Alphaviruses (WEE, EEE, VEE)	Encephalitis	3
Castor beans ricin toxin	Hemorrhaging, neurological	1/2
Clostridium perfringens epsilon toxin	Diarrhea	2
Staphylococcus aureus enterotoxin B	Diarrhea, lung problems	2
Aspergillus fumigatus	Muscle ache, liver failure, bone marrow depletion	2
Red tide algae saxitoxin	Nerve damage	1/2
	Category B (Waterborne/Foodborne)	
Salmonella enterica	Salmonellosis, typhoid fever	2
Shigella	Dysentery, HUS[c]	2
Vibrio cholerae	Cholera	2
Escherichia coli O157:H7	Bloody diarrhea, HUS	2
Cryptosporidium parvum	Diarrhea	1/2
	Category C	
Hantavirus	Hemorrhagic fever	3/4
Yellow fever virus	Yellow fever	2/3
Multidrug-resistant *Mycobacterium tuberculosis*	Tuberculosis	2/3
Nipah virus	Encephalitis	2/3
Dengue fever virus	Dengue fever	2/3
Tickborne hemorrhagic fever viruses	Hemorrhagic fever	2/3
Tickborne encephalitis viruses	Encephalitis	2/3

[a]Lower biosafety level when use low number, higher level when aerosolized.
[b]BSL rating taken from the (Centers for Disease Control, 2000a).
[c]Hemolytic uremic syndrome (can lead to kidney failure).

form a capsule that will protect the bacteria from engulfment from white blood cells within that animal's body and a potent three-part toxin that leads to the complications and potentially death in the animal. The disease caused by this organism is called anthrax. During the recent biological attacks through the mail, it was a misnomer to say that anthrax was detected in several letters and postal facilities. Inanimate objects do not get anthrax. Rather, the bacteria responsible for the potentially life-threatening disease anthrax was detected. When someone is exposed to *B. anthracis,* there is the possibility of developing one of three forms of anthrax, depending upon the route of exposure to the bacteria (Inglesby et al., 1999). These three types of anthrax that can develop are *cutaneous, gastrointestinal,* and *inhalation.* Of the three types, cutaneous is the most common; this type comprised a little more than half of the cases during the 2001 attacks. One gets this form by touching or handling something contaminated with the resistant spores. Postal workers and a woman from the media got this type of anthrax by handling letters contaminated with the bacterial spores. The spores get in under the skin and change into cells that will now replicate and produce the toxin. An early symptom of this form of anthrax is a red ulceration that will blacken and swell if left untreated. A large percentage of people will heal themselves without treatment. In up to 20 percent of these untreated cases, the bacteria may enter the bloodstream. Once inside the blood vessels, a high fever and death may occur. Again, this is the most common type and was found in 50 percent of the cases during the mail assaults. If a person is treated, there are far fewer complications and only rare deaths. None of the people who developed the cutaneous anthrax during the 2001 attacks died.

Gastrointestinal anthrax is the second type and is extremely rare. In the United States, there have been few cases of gastrointestinal anthrax, although there was an outbreak a few years ago in upper northwest Minnesota linked to a family's butchering and consuming *B. anthracis*-infected livestock (Centers for Disease Control, 2000b). To get this form, one would have to ingest contaminated meat. An infection of the stomach or mouth would ensue, progressing to fever, vomiting, and abdominal pain. Entry into the bloodstream is more likely, and the chance of death would increase to 25 to 60 percent without antibiotic treatment.

It is the last form of anthrax that creates the greatest amount of fear. Inhalation anthrax occurs when one breathes in the bacterial spores. For many years, the conventional wisdom was that one needed to inhale between 8,000 and 50,000 spores with particle sizes between 1 and 5 micrometers in diameter (Inglesby et al., 1999). Based on the mail attacks with *B. anthracis* spores, the number of spores may be reduced from this estimate, although the size of the spores is critical. Particles larger than 5 micrometers may be caught in the respiratory tract and eliminated by our own body's defenses, whereas spores smaller than 1 micrometer in diameter will not stay in the lungs. After entry into the lungs, the spores are taken up by specific white blood cells in the lungs, multiply within these cells, and transit to the regional lymph nodes, where they will continue to reproduce. Early signs of this form of anthrax include fever, muscle ache, cough, and general fatigue. During this time, the disease can be mistaken for the flu or other respiratory diseases. If the disease is left unchecked and continues its destructive path, a high fever, low blood pressure, bleeding within the lungs, and nervous system failure can result. Death can occur in as little as 24 hours after entry into this terminal stage. Without antibiotic treatment, mortality is thought to be 80 to 100 percent. Even with antibiotic treatment, the numbers of deaths can be high. The fall 2001 attacks demonstrated that early intervention with antibiotics prevented a number of fatalities in the people who were exposed to the bacteria and subsequently developed inhalation anthrax. Only five of eleven patients (45%) died as a result of contracting inhalation anthrax.

Fortunately, there are several antibiotics that can limit the spread of the bacterial agent responsible for anthrax. These antibiotics include ciprofloxacin, penicillin, and doxycycline. All of them can be taken orally and they can all be easily obtained by prescription from a physician. There is a multidose vaccine that offers protection against the cutaneous form of anthrax and may offer protection against the other two forms. The Bioport Company in Michigan is presently the sole supplier of the vaccine currently used to protect our military, and there have been substantial delays since 1998 in producing more vaccine doses to meet the Food and Drug Administration regulations. The DynaPort Company has been asked to develop a better anthrax vaccine that does not need six doses to provide protection. Legislation is underway to set aside up to half of the vaccine doses for civilian use in the advent of another more widespread biological attack.

THE THREAT OF SMALLPOX

The other potentially scary bioterrorist agent is variola major that causes the disease smallpox (Henderson et al., 1999). This agent is a DNA virus with a brickshape that is related to cowpox, monkeypox, and vaccinia, which can all form skin lesions. Infection usually occurs as the result of aerosols containing the virus particles. Around 10 to 100 viruses can cause infection. The viruses will deposit on the throat surface, there will be a migration to the lymph nodes, and then multiplication of the viral population at these sites. After three to eight days, spread to other sites within the body occurs. Within seven to seventeen days, the person will develop a high fever, general fatigue, headache, and a backache. A rash then develops on the mouth, throat, face, and forearms, spreading to the trunk and legs. Within a couple of days, the rash will develop pus and a scab will form. Once the rash develops, there is a two-to three-day window where the symptoms will mimic chickenpox.

How do we distinguish between the two diseases? Smallpox lesions develop at the same pace over the entire body, whereas chickenpox develops in crops of lesions more dense over the trunk and typically found adjacent to areas already covered by the lesions. Unlike smallpox lesions, you rarely find lesions on the palms and soles of people afflicted with chickenpox. As the smallpox scab heals, pitted scars frequently emerge in the infected patients that will remain with them for the rest of their lives.

Mortality from smallpox is typically 30 percent in unvaccinated people. The variola major organism responsible for smallpox was eradicated in the wild in 1977 as the result of a successful worldwide vaccination program carried out by the World Health Organization (Check, 2001). There are only two legal depository sites for the virus: the Centers for Disease Control (CDC) in Atlanta, Georgia, and the Vektor Laboratory in the Novosibirsk region of Russia. Immunity following vaccination is supposed to persist for at least three to seven years. Since vaccination in the United States was halted in 1972, this means at least a third of the U.S. population has never been vaccinated, and those who were may not be fully protected due to waning immunity, if the agent was used today.

STEPS NECESSARY TO MOUNT A BIOTERRORIST ATTACK

To mount a biological agent with any of these agents, one must overcome several hurdles. These are broken down into four areas: obtaining the agents, growing or producing the agents, weaponizing the agents, and dispersing the agents. In the past, one could obtain cultures through the American Type Culture Collection or similar repositories for biological agents. Such federal and private facilities have in the past shipped agents like *Yersinia pestis, Salmonella enterica,* and *Bacillus anthracis* to the Rajneeshee cult, the University of Baghdad, and even Larry Wayne Harris. Additional security measures have now been installed to minimize acquisition by individuals who do not have a legitimate reason for acquiring these agents. Unfortunately, repositories outside of the United States may not have the same high degree of safeguards in place. Besides these commercial sources, some of the agents are readily obtained from nature. Livestock routinely contract anthrax and die. Rodents around the world may harbor fleas that carry *Yersinia pestis.* The foodborne Category B agents are quite ubiquitous throughout the world and are thus easily obtainable. The terrorist would not necessarily have to begin with a natural isolate. Research facilities and hospitals have some of these agents in their freezers. The former Soviet Union has several complexes where stocks of such agents are kept safe by an underpaid security force. Although the relative ease by which one could get ahold of some of these agents is a point of concern, other biological agents are harder to acquire; including the Variola virus as well as Ebola and Marburg viruses that cause hemorrhagic fever. Groups like Aum Shinrikyo and even al-Qaeda have attempted to get their hands on these agents but have failed.

Once acquisition has been successful, one must now grow and process the biological agent. For many of the Category B agents, this would require minimal scientific knowledge and not a lot of money. Our own government showed the relative ease by which this could be done in Operation Bacchus set up in the Nevada desert (Miller, 2001). It is feasible to have basement laboratories that could produce these agents in sufficient bulk to be a problem. Fortunately, some agents are harder to grow and keep viable for extended periods of time. As the Aum Shinrikyo cult found out, the right strain of *Bacillus anthracis* is needed to give rise to infection and disease in a human. Botulinum toxin can be prepared in bulk, but it must be complexed with other agents to stabilize and protect the fragile toxin. This toxin is quite readily inactivated by fluctuations in temperature and humidity. More serious concerns for the people producing these agents in bulk may include the possibility of contracting the disease associated with their particular agent, hiding the production from inspectors or other individuals, and obtaining the proper equipment and supplies to propagate the agent.

If the production has been successful, the most daunting steps now stand before those individuals inclined toward bioterrorism. Weaponizing a biological agent is no trivial matter. In part, it is dependent on what the goals are for the use of the agent. Will it be used for killing mass numbers of people or merely to create fear and panic in a population? For the latter, low tech means are available. The *B. anthracis* attacks used letters to disseminate the biological agent. Only a few letters were mailed, but the ensuing problems and fear that ensued led to the disruption of many lives within the United States. The spores found in the envelopes were determined to be milled to the proper diameter, which would require a great deal of expertise that only a handful of people possess. To widely distribute the agents, one may have to deal with powders that would clog nozzles and pumps and contend with temperature and sunlight variability that would have a dramatic impact of the viability of these agents. Also of major importance are the questions Will the agent survive an explosion? and, most importantly, Will you infect yourself? These technical obstacles in the acquisition, production, weaponization, and dispersal of biological agents have dissuaded many people from using them.

SURVEILLANCE NETWORKS AND DETECTION OF AN ATTACK

In the event of an attack, what should be done? A bioterrorist attack will most likely be covert. Several initiatives have been instituted to monitor and detect potential biological assaults. Under the Clinton Adminstration, millions of dollars were funneled into programs to bolster the health infrastructure around the United States and to stockpile needed supplies in the case of a bioterrorist attack. The pushpacks of antibiotics that have been stored at strategic locations around the United States were used during the 2001 attacks. The initial detection of such an incident will be noted by the local healthcare network of primary care physicians, local and state health agencies, and epidemiologists. Steps have been taken to prepare for biological attacks, and they are lumped into five focus areas: preparedness, detection and surveillance, diagnosis and characterization of biological agents, communication, and response (Snyder & Check, 2001).

For preparedness, heightened awareness and safety considerations have been instituted. Hospitals across the United States have formulated bioterrorism protocols to recognize potential agents, assess the biosafety of such organisms, assess the risk to laboratory personnel, maintain access to patient isolates and information, safely ship out any agents that cannot be adequately tested in the facility, provide secure clinical labs, and protect cultures or reagents from unauthorized personnel.

With these plans in place, a network of healthcare facilities have loosely linked themselves together to offer detection and surveillance capabilities for monitoring unusual infections and diseases. This network of hospitals and clinics has been formed into what is called the Laboratory Response Network (LRN). It is comprised of four levels that form a loose pyramid to track and deal with potential outbreaks around the United States (Gilchrist, 2000; Snyder & Check, 2001). Each level of this pyramid has a particular function to guard against a potential biological attack. Forming the foundation of this LRN pyramid are the Level A laboratories. Their main role is providing early detection of intentional dispersal of biological agents and investigate suspicious agents. These will include public health and hospital laboratories with low level biosafety facilities, such as Gundersen Lutheran Hospital or Franciscan Skemp Hospital in La Crosse, Wisconsin. Personnel at these places will make decisions regarding which specimens and isolates will be forwarded to higher level biocontainment facilities. As part of their current training, the staff should know proper ways to safely collect, package, and ship samples deemed to be dangerous to higher level laboratories. Most hospitals can handle what are called biosafety level 2 (BSL-2) agents and in some cases BSL-3 agents within the confines of a biosafety hood. The biosafety levels for each potential bioterrorist agent is also listed in Table 14.2.

At the next level on the LRN pyramid are the Level B laboratories. These facilities have the capacity to isolate potential bioterrorism agents and do presumptive testing of suspect specimens. They will ensure that testing is accurate, and they will perform confirmatory tests as well as determine drug susceptibility for bacterial agents. Agents beyond their capability (i.e., BSL-4 agents) will be sent to a higher level biocontainment laboratory. Examples of these places would include state or local public health laboratories, such as the State Lab of Hygiene or Marshfield Clinic in Wisconsin. These labs are typically capable of working with BSL-3 agents.

The laboratories at Level C on the LRN pyramid will have advanced capacity for rapid identification of a wide range of agents. They are able to perform advanced and specialized testing, evaluate new tests and reagents, and determine what can be transferred down to Level B labs. Biosafety level 3 agents can be tested here. These facilities will typically be state health agencies, academic research labs, or federal facilities, such as the National Animal Disease Center in Ames, Iowa.

Level D laboratories reside at the top of the LRN pyramid. They have the highest level of containment and a tremendous amount of expertise in the diagnosis of rare and dangerous biological agents. Federal laboratories at Fort Detrick, Frederick, Maryland, the National Institutes of Health, Bethesda, Maryland, and the Centers for Disease Control, Atlanta, Georgia, are the Level D laboratories in the United States. People in these facilities are capable of developing new tests and methods; maintaining a bank of the biological agents; conducting all of the tests performed in Levels A through C, as well as do confirmatory testing; and detecting genetically engineered organisms. Within these facilities, BSL-4 agents can be worked with.

What is the BSL rating and why is this important for biological agents used for bioterrorism? This safety structure was established to protect individuals who may be exposed to such agents so that they take the proper precautions (Centers for Disease Control, 1999). On the ground level are the BSL-1 agents, which are not known to consistently cause disease in humans. No primary barrier safety equipment is needed. BSL-2 agents are routinely associated with human disease. Limited access, biohazard warning signs, "sharps" precautions, and procedures to decontaminate an area are required. In addition, primary barriers will include a biosafety cabinet (hood) as well as lab coats, gloves, and face protection. All hospitals and clinics can safely handle BSL-1 and BSL-2 agents. The third level is BSL-3, usually associated with organisms that have the potential for aerosol transmission and are typically very deadly. Controlled access, decontamination of waste, physical separation from other corridors, self-closing double-door access, no recirculation of exhausted air, and a negative airflow into the laboratory are standard. Last, but certainly not least, are the BSL-4 agents, the ones that bring one's pulse up and a sweat over one's brow. These agents are very dangerous and are very life-threatening. They are easily disseminated and typically have a high death rate. Safety precautions mandated for working with these agents include a clothing change before entering the laboratory, showering on exit, all material decontaminated on exit, full-body positive pressure personnel suits, separate building or isolated zone, as well as dedicated supply and exhaust, vacuum, and decontaminated systems. Variola virus is rated as a BSL-4 agent. Specimens from a suspected smallpox outbreak would be sent on to a Level D facility for examination and confirmation.

The Laboratory Response Network is a linchpin to providing detection and surveillance capabilities to the United States. Level A laboratories are affiliated with several networks that provide surveillance for a variety of different biological agents, some of which can be used in bioterrorist attacks (Sobel, 2001). These surveillance networks are in place to help distinguish between natural outbreaks or natural foodborne contamination versus a suspected biological assault. Outbreak reporting will be picked up by observant clinicians, laboratory technicians, and local public health officials. This was the case in the *B. anthracis* attack in Florida. An astute physician made the connection between clinical signs and characteristics of the bacteria being characterized from the patient that led to a prompt detection of *B. anthracis*. Without this quick response, more people might have suffered and even died. Surveillance networks functioning in these Level A laboratories will include the Notifiable Disease System, a laboratory test-based database that is triggered when particular diagnostic tests are ordered. A fault of this system is that it is incomplete because only cases where the test is ordered will be captured. A Botulinum Surveillance System monitors every case that is suspected to be botulism. In those cases, specimens are sent to a state lab for analysis, and the CDC is immediately called to release botulinum antitoxin to that facility. If an assault were underway using botulinum toxin, this system would be the first to pick it up. Both PulseNet and FoodNet track microorganisms, generating information down to the strain level. PulseNet is invaluable because if there were an attack at different locations, molecular subtyping performed as part of this system would tell healthcare workers if it was the same microbe involved. More sophisticated types of testing, including genome sequencing, have resulted from the *B. anthracis* attacks to tell investigators exactly which strain of *B. anthracis* was used and what its lineage could have been. Coordinating this information through these networks could lead to the future apprehension of those parties involved in the bioterrorist attack.

Last, the Health Alert Network is in the formulative stage (Centers for Disease Control, 2002a). Ultimately, this will be a nationwide integrated information and communications system designed to send out health alerts, national disease surveillance based on the networks mentioned above, and electronic laboratory reporting to expedite the flow of information to those parties that need it quickly. Thus, Level A and B laboratories on the front lines during an attack will be more effectively able to deal with the health crisis following the assault. The Health Alert Network is supposed to ensure high-speed Internet connections between the CDC and local or state health laboratories. In the future, distance learning that will include information pertaining to bioterrorism will be disseminated to a vast number of facilities and the population of those communities. Information will allay many of the fears that people have regarding these biological agents.

Surveillance through these integrated networks is helpful, but it takes time for results to appear and the information to be disseminated. Quicker detection systems are being designed and tested to monitor for potential biological attacks. One of these systems is the Biological Integrated Detection System. It is designed to collect air samples and, through an immunological interaction, detect particular bioterrorist agents. Presently, the machines are designed to identify four agents and the list is expanding. Some drawbacks to this system are it is bulky, expensive, and can give too many false-positive results. Another detection system under development is the RAPID (Krane, 2001). It is rapid and portable, but it cannot continuously monitor the air. Systems being considered in the not-too-distant future may include using synthetic small detectors and genetic chips designed for each agent.

If a covert or overt attack has been detected through a surveillance network or a rapid detection system, communication will be a vital for an expeditious response. Internal communication protocols have been established to coordinate between the medical laboratory that is processing the samples, the infection control staff that must determine if the specimens can be adequately and safely examined in their facility, and the emergency room and family physicians who see the patients suffering from the agent. Within this framework, a safe environment must be provided for all those involved, patient confidentiality must be maintained, and any ethical considerations must be examined. Besides this internal communication, the institutes must contact public health facilities at the local, state, or even federal levels. Based on the assessments made, other organizations may also have to be contacted, including the CDC, F.B.I., U.S. Department of Agriculture (USDA), Department of Health and Human Services (DHHS), Department of Defense (DOD), and the Federal Emergency Management Organization (FEMA). If an investigation is warranted, the F.B.I. will take the lead in the criminal investigation, maintaining the chain of custody, analyzing evidence, and providing testimony if a case goes to trial. All other aspects of the event would be taken over by FEMA. A new Department of Homeland Security has been created by Congress for the purpose of consolidating several functions and hopefully keeping lines of communication open between the various agencies that would be involved in a biological attack.

If an attack was deemed to have occurred or there was sufficient evidence to suggest an attack may have taken place, the F.B.I. would be sent into the area to provide investigative support. Part of this operation would include bringing in a HAZMAT team with a mobile full public health lab on wheels for handling biological emergencies. This team would include a paramedic, safety officer, scientist, HAZMAT officer, and two HAZMAT technicians who would handle the samples.

WHAT WAS LEARNED FROM THE FALL 2001 ATTACKS?

Overall, the five focus areas of preparedness, detection and surveillance, diagnosis and characterization of biological agents, communication, and response all look good on paper, but what happens in a real-life scenario? We can examine the 2001 *Bacillus anthracis* attacks along the East Coast to see where we were and what more should be done.

The anthrax attacks came in two waves. The first wave began on September 18, 2001 and targeted the media. This was followed by a second wave on October 9, 2001, which was aimed at the government. Of 23 cases of anthrax, 11 were inhalation and 12 were cutaneous (Centers for Disease Control, 2002b). None of the 12 cases of cutaneous anthrax died, and only 5 of the 11 patients with the inhalation form were killed by the bacteria. Prompt antibiotic and life-support intervention saved the other 6 patients. Thirty-two thousand people were put on antibiotic prophylaxis, which prompted the release of one of the pushpacks of antibiotics. Antibiotic prophylaxis may have prevented additional cases of anthrax from arising, but more research is needed in this area. Thousands of clinical samples and hundreds of thousands of environmental samples were tested. This resulted in a tremendous strain on many public health laboratories, which were unable to accommodate the surge in specimens. Over 500 Post Offices had to be evacuated at a cost estimated at $6 billion. New molecular and immunohistological testing procedures were developed that accelerated the time it took to confirm the presence of *B. anthracis* in a sample. A need is still present to adapt these techniques to fixed tissue specimens. Lines of communication from the national to state level were good, yet dissemination down to the local level still required improvement. The CDC and lower level labs in the LRN had experts on top of things.

Lessons learned from the anthrax attacks include having the clinical laboratories knowing and carrying out the 5 Cs: competency, capacity, coordination, communication, and consultation. Several of these five areas had shortfalls, particularly the communication of useful information. The public does not want to be misled, and painting a rosy picture may not work during a crisis.

What more can and is being done? Additional doses of the anthrax vaccine are being produced, and roughly half of these doses are being earmarked for civilian use, a departure from standard practice of reserving the vaccine for the military alone. For the fiscal year 2002, a base budget of $1.4 billion with a supplemental adjustment of $3.7 billion has been appropriated. These funds are meant to enhance communication and surveillance, strengthen state and local public health facilities, allow for research and development, improve the federal response, and provide for bioterrorism preparation. Among some of the measures being proposed are quarantine processes for "attack areas" and a national vaccine strategy. The Bush Administration is moving forward with the production of 300 million doses of the smallpox vaccine that would supposedly protect every citizen in the United States. An office to oversee vaccine development may arise within the Department of Homeland Security. In Fiscal Year 2003, $5.9 billion has been set aside for bioterrorism initiatives. Local health laboratories are slated to receive approximately $1 billion. For any of these things to truly work, better coordination among agencies is paramount.

Other measures are also warranted. There is a vital need to set up contingency plans for surge labs that would contend with an onslaught of hundreds or even thousands of specimens. More scientists must get involved to increase knowledge about these dangerous microorganisms and convey this information to the masses. Increases in bioterrorism-related education, awareness, and communication are critical. New partnerships should be forged with the former Soviet Union to deal with security concerns, as well as tap their scientific expertise. A bolstering of the Biological Weapons Convention ratified by the United States in 1975 should have teeth in it rather than the unenforceable doctrine that currently exists. With these changes, we would be less concerned with potential dual-use production facilities, evolving technologies, and unstable political factors.

CONCLUDING REMARKS

The *B. anthracis* attacks, the potential for releasing Variola virus onto a virgin population, and the prospects of delivering some other Category A or B agent through a bioterrorist act may make one pause for a moment. Our fear of the unknown has the potential to paralyze us, but it should not. In the beginning of this chapter, the question "Should I Be Worried?" was raised. As educated citizens of this country, we should be concerned about the prospects of a bioterrorist attack. The likelihood that there will be another attack is relatively high. In what form and when is anyone's guess. However, it is important not to be worried to the point of helplessness. The United States has taken many steps to lessen the likelihood and the potential impacts of such events. Nevertheless, it is impossible to prevent all types of covert attacks. There will always be people who care little for human life, but if everyone remains diligent and educated about these unknown biological agents, the future may not be as bleak. If the healthcare system is bolstered and the other steps outlined above are taken, the risk from bioterrorist attacks can be significantly reduced.

DISCUSSION QUESTIONS

1. What are the advantages to a terrorist organization from using biological weapons to initiate an attack?
2. Compare the analysis in this chapter with the discussion in Chapter 12, "Technology and the Transformation of Terrorism," about the potential for a bioterrorist attack. Which discussion do you find most persuasive?
3. Do you think the U.S. health system is adequately prepared to deal with a large-scale biological attack? Why or why not? Outline three policies for improving public awareness about the threat of bioterrorism.

REFERENCES

BEECHER, D. (2001, May 21). *FBI perspective on bioterrorism.* Presentation at the American Society for Microbiology Meeting, Orlando, FL.

BLOCK, S. M. (2001). The growing threat of biological weapons. *American Scientist,* pp. *8, 28*–37. Centers for Disease Control and Prevention and National Institutes of Health. (1999).

Biosafety in microbiological and biomedical laboratories (4th ed.). Washington, DC: U. S. Department of Health and Human Services, Public Health Service.

Centers for Disease Control. (2000a). Biological and chemical terrorism: Strategic plan for preparedness and response. *Morbidity and Mortality Weekly Report,* pp. *4* (RRO4), 1–14.

Center for Disease Control. (2000b). Human ingestion of *Bacillus anthracis*-contaminated meat—Minnesota, August, 2000. *Morbidity and Mortality Weekly Report,* pp. *49,* 813.

Centers for Disease Control. (2002a, July 25). *Health alert network.* Retrieved at *http://www.phppo.cdc.gov/han/*

Centers for Disease Control. (2002b). Public health dispatch: Update: cutaneous anthrax in a laboratory worker—Texas, 2002. *Morbidity and Mortality Weekly Report,* pp. 51, 482.

CHECK, E. (2001). Need for vaccine stocks questioned. *Nature* (London), pp. *414,* 677.

GILCHRIST, M. J. R. (2000). A national laboratory network for bioterrorism: Evolution from a prototype network of laboratories performing routine surveillance. *Military Medicine, 156*(Suppl), pp. 28–34.

GORMAN, T., & LICHTBLAU, E. (1998, February 21). Anthrax case suspect has often voiced interest in germ warfare arrest. *Los Angeles Times,* p. A21.

HENDERSON, D. A., INGLESBY, T. V., BARTLETT, J. G., ASCHER, M. S., EITZEN, E., JARLING, P. B., et al. (1999). Smallpox as a biological weapon. *Journal of the American Medical Association,* pp. *281,* 2177–2137.

INGLESBY, T. V., HENDERSON, D. A., BARTLETT, J. G., ASCHER, M. S., EITZEN, E., FRIEDLANDER, A. M., et al. (1999). Anthrax as a biological weapon. *Journal of the American Medical Association,* pp. 28, 1735–1745.

KAPLAN, D. E. (1997, November 17). Terrorism's next wave: Nerve gas and germs are the new weapons of choice. *U.S. News & World Report.* pp. 26, 28, 30–31.

KOLAVIC, S. S., KIMURA, A., SIMONS, S. L., SLUTSKER, L., BARTH, S., & HOKEY, C. E. (1997). An outbreak *of Shigella dysenteriae* type 2 among laboratory workers due to intentional food contamination. *Journal of the American Medical Association,* pp. *278,* 396–398.

KRANE, J. (2001, October 20). Detecting terror: Biological weapons tough to identify. *La Crosse Tribune.* pp. E1 & E4.

MILLER, J. (2001). *Next to old Rec Hall, a "germ-making plant".* Retrieved at *http://www. nytimes.com/2001/09104/international/04BIOW.html.*

OLSON, K. B. (1999). Aum Shinrikyo: Once and future threat? *Emerging Infectious Disease,* pp. *5,* 513–516.

SNYDER, J. W., & CHECK, W. (2001). *Bioterrorism threats to our future: The role of the clinical microbiology laboratory in detection, identification, and confirmation of biological agents.* Washington, DC: American Academy of Microbiology.

SOBEL, J. (2001, May 21). *CDC's food bioterrorism response program.* Presentation at the American Society for Microbiology Meeting, Orlando, FL.

TOROK, T. J., TAUXE, R. V., WISE, R. P., LIVERGOOD, J. R., SOKOLOW, R., MAUVAIS, S., et al. (1997). A large community outbreak of Salmonellosis caused by intentional contamination of restaurant salad bars. *Journal of the American Medical Association,* pp. *278,* 389–395.

TUCKER, J. B. (1999). Historical trends related to bioterrorism: An empirical analysis. *Emerging Infectious Disease,* pp. *5,* 498–504.

PART V

CONCLUSION

15

Terorrism in the Twenty-First Century

H. Matthew Loayza

In this final chapter, historian Matt Loayza considers the future of international relations in the wake of September 11. The author reviews U.S. foreign policy in light of what has been referred to as "the first war of the twenty-first century." Loayza devotes much of his attention to what this warfare would entail. He examines the difficulty in targeting terrorist groups, as well as the type of warfare terrorists might employ against their perceived enemies. The essay is thorough in its examination of potential biological, chemical, and nuclear weapons, the likelihood of their use, and the potential destruction. But this chapter's value lies in its tribute to historical memory. The author reveals an earlier foreign policy era in which a powerful enemy was identified as a major threat to the United States and offers parallels with contemporary foreign policy. Loayza concludes with a plea that statesmen and politicians refrain from oversimplifying this challenge to world order and instead asks that foreign policy be the product of thoughtful, well-informed decision making.

In the immediate aftermath of the September 11 attacks, President George W. Bush assured the American people that his administration would marshal all of its resources—diplomatic, financial, and military—toward the goal of defeating international terrorism. The President urged Americans to shed any illusions that this task would be achieved with the relative ease of recent conflicts such as the Persian Gulf War. Rather, Americans should "not expect one battle, but a lengthy campaign, unlike any other we have ever seen" (Bush, 2001b). But what will a campaign that the President has described as the "first war of the twenty-first century" entail (Bush, 2001a)? How will it be fought, and whom will it be fought against? To answer these questions, this chapter will examine the nature of the current terrorist threat, discuss some of the tactics terrorists might use in the future, and consider how the United States might attempt to resist hostile terrorist organizations.

It is ironic that while the President urged Americans to view the terrorist attacks as the opening act in a new kind of conflict that would look remarkably different from prior conflicts, some commentators looked to a past U.S. war as a means of explaining the new predicament facing The United States. Many immediately compared the September 11 attacks to the Japanese bombing of Pearl Harbor in December 1941, since both events involved surprise attacks upon Americans that left thousands dead. Proponents of this analogy suggested that, like Pearl Harbor, the 9-11 attacks presented a clear and immediate threat to a U.S. public that had been previously indifferent to events beyond its borders. In this broader context, it was presumed that 9-11, like 12-7 before it, would unify public opinion against a common enemy.

Yet any similarities between Pearl Harbor and 9-11 are far outweighed by the significant differences in the nature of the attackers and how events unfolded subsequent to the attacks of both 1941 and 2001. In regard to the former, the United States declared war on Japan only two days after the attack on Pearl Harbor, initiating nearly four years of struggle against Japanese air, naval, and ground forces that finally ended with Japan's formal surrender to U.S. naval officers on the Battleship *Missouri* on September 2, 1945.

But whereas World War II provided Americans with clearly defined opponents and objectives, it will be much more difficult to define the basic points of reference in the war against terrorism. Although the Bush administration quickly identified al-Qaeda, the terrorist network headed by Osama bin Laden, as responsible for the attacks in New York and Washington, DC, the source of the deadly anthrax mailings that followed the 9-11 attacks remains a mystery. It seems that in the future, simply identifying the enemy will be a task in itself. Measuring tangible progress will also be difficult, as it is questionable if the U.S. military, which quickly dispatched the brutal Taliban regime that harbored bin Laden, has inflicted serious damage to al-Qaeda's ability to wage terror.

Since violent, clandestine groups such as al-Qaeda are highly secretive and elusive, "victory" will come to be defined not as the complete destruction of terrorist networks, but rather success in suppressing, harassing, and disrupting terrorist activities. It is unlikely that the anti-terror campaign will end on board a U.S. battleship with the formal surrender of an al-Qaeda delegation! In other words, upcoming counterterrorism campaigns will differ from past wars because of the major difficulties involved in identifying, locating, and retaliating against terrorist networks. Although one might argue that counterterrorism has never been easy, two recent developments have made fighting terrorism far more difficult: an increase in violence motivated by religious fervor rather than secular agendas and technological advances that allow terrorist organizations to cause far greater death and destruction than ever before.

Although terrorism is nothing new, the terrifying images of commercial airliners smashing into skyscrapers are jarring examples of a relatively recent trend—the emergence of terrorist groups motivated by religious fanaticism. As recently as the late 1970s, most terrorists had practiced violence in hopes of achieving secular, political goals. Their ideological inspiration and purposes varied, ranging from Marxist-Leninism (the Japanese Red Army and the Italian Red Brigades) to national separation or liberation (Basque ETA, Tamil Tigers of Sri Lanka, and the Irish Republican Army). However, these politically minded terrorist groups have been overshadowed during the 1990s by a rising tide of religiously sanctioned terrorism. According to one scholar, one-third of all active international terrorist groups identify religious goals as their main motivation (Wilkinson, 2001, p. 51).

Islamist fanatics such as Osama bin Laden presently dominate the media headlines and the attentions of national leaders, but it would be a mistake to assume that Islamic radicals will always occupy the center of the terrorist stage. Although the recent ascent of violent Islamist radicalism is certainly alarming, the Islamic world has no monopoly on violence inspired by faith. Aum Shinrikyo, a strange Japanese doomsday cult, unleashed the sarin nerve agent in Tokyo subways in 1995, leaving twelve people dead and thousands more injured. Prior to the sarin attack, Aum Shinrikyo had tried unsuccessfully to create a weaponized form of anthrax. Another potential danger comes from the little-known Christian Identity Movement. Its adherents, found mainly in the United States, contend that northern Europeans are the true descendants of the biblical Jews and that contemporary Jews are actually the spawn of Satan. Christian Identity doctrine maintains that all nonwhite peoples existed before the creation of Adam, the first white man. It dismisses Adam's predecessors as subhuman "mud-people" who lack souls, who might therefore be killed without incurring sin or remorse (Snow, 1999, p. 109).

Religious fanaticism and political extremism are not, of course, mutually exclusive categories. Many religious extremist groups cite political objectives as well as spiritual ones or draw considerable strength from groups that share a mutual grievance or hatred. Osama bin Laden, who has spoken of his desire to spark a radical Islamist revolution across the globe, has also cited political objectives such as expelling U.S. military forces from Saudi Arabia and ousting the Saudi royal family from power. Many disaffected Arabs and Palestinians have supported bin Laden's anti-American, anti-Israeli message, even though bin Laden has only recently emerged as a champion of the Palestinian cause (Berger & Sutphen, 2001). In like vein, several right-wing extremists and white supremacist groups within the United States are attracted to the racist theology of the Christian Identity Movement.

The emergence of religiously inspired terrorist groups is significant, since their use of violence appears to be relatively uninhibited and indiscriminate compared to that of secular terrorists, who have generally rejected mass slaughter as a tactic. Some analysts have theorized that while secular terrorists did not shy away from murdering innocent people if it suited their purposes, their ultimate goal was not to cause death, but rather to draw attention to their cause and subsequently prompt extensive changes in the political status quo. They subsequently avoided massive bloodletting because they feared that the resultant public horror and revulsion would backfire and undermine the very cause they sought to promote. On the other hand, the actions of Aum Shinrikyo and al-Qaeda suggest that religious extremists, whatever their affiliation, harbor few, if any, reservations about inflicting death on a mass scale.

Since conventional wisdom suggested until recently that terrorists would not inflict large casualties, some experts believed it unlikely that terrorists would turn to nuclear, chemical, and biological weapons of mass destruction. But the ferocity of the September 2001 attacks and past use of chemical (sarin) and biological (anthrax) weapons by terrorists illustrate the possibility that terrorists will turn to these weapons more frequently in the future. Since there are significant differences in how these armaments work and how they might be obtained, it is worth considering weapons of mass destruction separately.

Americans have lived under the shadow of nuclear annihilation ever since the Soviet Union exploded its first atomic bomb in 1949. Since Americans lived in fear of the bomb for the duration of the Cold War, it is unsurprising that people wonder if or when terrorists might "go nuclear," perhaps by smuggling a nuclear device into a major city such as New York. It would be a considerable understatement to say that such an attack would be devastating. The detonation of a relatively small 12.5-kiloton bomb (equivalent in size to the bomb dropped over Hiroshima in 1945) in New York City would immediately kill over 50,000 people. Radioactive fallout would kill up to 200,000 people and cause thousands of cases of radiation sickness in the days and weeks ahead (Helfand, Forrow, & Tiwari, 2002).

For those worried about an impending nuclear terrorist attack, the good news is that building a nuclear weapon is still very difficult. The major problem for a would-be nuclear terrorist would not be obtaining the relevant information, which is unclassified and widely available, but rather in getting hold of fissile material, the essential fuel for a nuclear weapon. Unfortunately, someone who knew absolutely nothing about nuclear fission and lacked access to weapons-grade materials could still do considerable harm with non-weapons-grade radioactive materials. Indeed, a far cheaper (and thus, more likely) alternative for a terrorist would be a radiological dispersion, or "dirty" bomb, which involves detonating radioactive materials with conventional explosives. The explosion of such a bomb would not cause a thermonuclear reaction, but it would nevertheless scatter large amounts of toxic radiation over considerable distances, causing at least 2,000 immediate and long-term deaths, as well as widespread panic and significant property damage (Helfand et al., 2002). A terrorist could also sabotage or bomb an existing nuclear facility or place highly radioactive materials in a water system in an effort to poison large numbers of people.

More attention and effort has been given to preventing the spread and use of nuclear weapons than of radiological weapons, due to the staggering destructive capacity of the former. Unfortunately, there are serious doubts about the security of the world's nuclear materials and weapons from theft or sale. Although nuclear terrorists could conceivably obtain nuclear material from any country with a nuclear program, it is the Russian nuclear program that has caused the most anxiety in this regard. The Russian government that emerged after the 1991 collapse of the Soviet Union inherited both a crumbling economy and an extensive nuclear weapons program that consumed vast financial resources. As the 1990s progressed, Moscow struggled to pay its nuclear engineers and scientists, prompting fears in the West that unpaid, disgruntled Russian scientists might sell their services to any country or group that had cash in hand.

Russia's economic woes also contributed to an alarming decline in security measures for Russian nuclear fuel storage installations. Since the aforementioned rise in unpaid and angry personnel made the possibility of insider theft more likely, the deterioration of already inadequate security measures was untimely, to say the least. It is probably unsurprising, then, that the mid-1990s witnessed isolated but confirmed instances of thefts of weapons-grade nuclear materials from Russian facilities.

Through collaborative ventures with the United States that will be discussed later, the Russians have upgraded the security of their nuclear facilities. However, these recent improvements are just that—improvements, rather than guarantees of security, and the danger that terrorists might acquire nuclear weapons or materials remains very real. Compounding the problem are the existence of several thousand U.S. and Russian tactical (battlefield) nuclear weapons that are conceivably vulnerable to theft. The task of guarding both the 1,670 U.S. tactical warheads and the estimated 3,590 to 15,000 weapons in the Russian tactical nuclear arsenal is formidable, to say the least. The doubts of Western observers that the Russians themselves have an accurate count of their tactical nuclear weapons stockpile lends credence to fears that these Soviet-era armaments are particularly vulnerable to proliferation (Stanton, 2002, p. 3). So while the obstacles involved in building or stealing nuclear bombs or materials are significant, they are by no means insurmountable. It is likely, then, that nuclear weapons are, or will soon be, within the reach of those possessing the necessary skill, determination, and financial resources.

It may be not be reassuring to point out that terrorists could reject nuclear weapons simply because other deadly weapons are both more widely available and more affordable. For example, biological weapons both rival the destructive power of nuclear weapons and are far cheaper to develop. Bioweapons might therefore be very attractive to those who wish to cause heavy casualties and public hysteria but cannot afford the option of a nuclear bomb.

Although biological warfare—the intentional spreading of disease as a weapon—has been waged sporadically for at least 2000 years, most Americans were oblivious to the threat posed by biological terrorism until a series of anthrax-laced letters appeared shortly after the initial terrorist attacks of September 2001. Yet the anthrax letters, while tragic, provided only a brief glimpse of the destructive potential of biological weapons, for anthrax is only one of several diseases that scientists have been able to harness as a weapon. Botulinum toxins, plague, Q fever, and smallpox are only a few of the more unpleasant diseases that a biological terrorist might wield in the future. A smallpox attack would be particularly devastating, perhaps resulting in as many as two billion deaths (Garrett, 2001, p. 218).

Biological weapons would not even need to target humans to cause havoc and misery. The introduction of a microbe with the ability to destroy crops or kill livestock would not only cause severe food shortages but also an increase in food prices, a drop in agricultural exports, and declining consumer confidence. The resultant shock to the financial markets would vary, depending on the severity of the attack. Since it would be impossible to place all of the herds, pastures, fields, and fishing waters within the United States under armed guard, America's agricultural resources will remain vulnerable to such an attack in the foreseeable future (Wheelis, 2000).

Population centers, unfortunately, are also quite vulnerable to biological terrorism. Anthrax is a particular cause for worry, thanks in large part to the efforts of U.S. and Soviet scientists during the Cold War. The inhalation form of the disease (anthrax can be contracted through the skin, inhaled, or ingested) became particularly important to the work of Cold War scientists, who saw the potential of using the airborne pathogen as a weapon. By the 1950s, U.S. and Soviet laboratories succeeded in drying anthrax germs and converting them into spores, a dormant state more resistant to extreme temperatures and ultraviolet radiation. Once so converted, diseases like anthrax were far better suited for use in aerosol sprayers, and thus for weapons (Miller, Engelberg, & Broad, p. 35). Until the spate of anthrax letters in 2002, which contained dried, weapons-grade anthrax, it was believed that that these techniques were beyond the capabilities of terrorist groups. Since this no longer seems to be the case, the 2002 anthrax mailings mark an unsettling watershed in the history of terrorism (Chyba, 2002, p. 127).

It is difficult to estimate how difficult it will be for terrorists to convert germs into weapons, but it will certainly be much harder than getting hold of the germs in the first place. To obtain harmful microbes, a person would simply need to pose as someone pursuing legitimate scientific research, and then approach one of the several germ banks in the country that supply a wide variety of microbes to doctors and hospitals that wish to conduct research or diagnostic tests. As an alternative, one could retrieve a germ sample from the vicinity of a natural outbreak of the disease (Chyba, 2002, p. 127).

After one obtained an original germ sample, it would be very easy to obtain the equipment needed to grow more. Pharmaceutical companies, biotechnology laboratories, and even breweries frequently use the fermentors used to produce germs (Chyba, 2002, p. 127). This raises what is known as the "dual-use" problem. Since innovations such as fermentors (not to mention countless others) can be used for both good and evil, it is nearly impossible to keep track of who owns the relevant equipment, or for what purposes they are using it. The widespread applications of dual-use technologies make it extremely difficult to monitor the proliferation of biological weapons. Whereas someone who wanted to secretly build a nuclear bomb might have to hide an entire nuclear reactor, a person who wanted to unleash anthrax on a city would only have to conceal a few pieces of lab equipment. In other words, halting or slowing the spread of biological weapons will be increasingly difficult.

One of the most frightening aspects of biological terrorism is that the improvements made in biological weapons during the 1950s pale in comparison to the breakthroughs that followed the founding of bioengineering in the early 1970s. Bioengineering, or gene splicing, involves the transplanting of genes (single strands of DNA) from one DNA strand to another. The potential health benefits of this research became evident in mid-decade, when scientists spliced the human insulin gene into bacteria and grew it, creating a renewable source of insulin (Miller et al. 2001, p. 66).

But although bioengineering will no doubt contribute many more positive innovations to medical science, the same techniques can also be used for destructive purposes. From the outset, biologists recognized that recombinant gene technology could theoretically be used to create a "superbug," that is, a microbe far more lethal and resistant to antibiotics and vaccines than the original. By the early 1990s, the revelations of Soviet defectors such as biochemist Sergei Popov confirmed that the Soviet bioweapons program had turned theory into reality. Popov revealed that the efforts of Soviet bioengineers had yielded, among other things, a "superbug" that greatly increased the potency of the plague bacteria. In a chilling prediction, the former Soviet biowarrior concluded that the use of recombinant gene technology for military purposes was still in its infancy. "I think it opens . . . more and more possibilities to create something dangerous," he warned, "to create a new kind of weapon" (Miller et al., 2001, p. 304).

Although Soviet scientists certainly mastered the ability to genetically tailor microbes into lethal weapons of mass destruction, this is most likely beyond the current capabilities of international terrorists. Even taking the "superbug" threat out of consideration, however, leaves a great deal to contend with. At present, the offensive potential of a biological assault would overpower the smaller and weaker array of treatments or vaccines available as a potential defense. Moreover, effective strategies to contain the effects of biological attacks require intricate planning, which is woefully lacking on municipal, state, and national levels.

Although chemical weapons receive less attention than either nuclear bombs or genetically enhanced diseases, they are nevertheless extremely powerful weapons. They are, like biological weapons, cheaper than nuclear arms and therefore of potential interest to terrorist groups. These weapons, which use manmade materials for lethal effect, are often discussed in the context of an *emerging* threat, such as that of the Iraqi chemical weapons program. But although it is true that Saddam Hussein has made relatively recent use of chemical weapons—first against Iranian troops and then Iraq's Kurdish minority in the 1980s—chemical weapons have a long and grisly history. One need only look back as far as World War I (1914–1918) for evidence of the deadly and horrific results of what today would be considered relatively crude chemical weapons. During the war, both sides made liberal use of lung-damaging agents such as chlorine and phosgene, as well as mustard gas, which burns and blisters skin and damages the eyes and lungs.

Although the introduction of gas masks in 1916 minimized the lethality of these attacks, the power of these early chemical weapons had already been demonstrated at Ypres, Belgium a year before. German troops opened thousands of chlorine gas canisters and, with the wind as their only delivery system, attacked French lines and managed to kill 5,000 Allied soldiers before day's end (Tucker, 1998, p. 62). By the end of the war, according to one estimate, chlorine, phosgene, and mustard gas attacks had killed up to 91,000 people (Hersh, 1968, p. 5).

Despite efforts after the war to ban the use of chemical weapons, scientific research soon introduced more complex, deadlier concoctions to the world's chemical arsenals. The work of German scientists during the 1930s resulted in the production of the first nerve agents, tabun and sarin. Nerve agents, when inhaled or absorbed by the skin, block the enzymes needed for the central nervous system to function, causing blurred vision, loss of control of bodily functions, drooling, convulsions, and very often death. By the end of the 1950s, British, U.S., and Russian scientists had made significant advances based on prior German nerve agent research. These dubious achievements resulted in the development of a new group of extremely potent nerve agents known as the "V" group, which both the United States and Soviet Union produced during the Cold War. The U.S.-produced variant VX is so poisonous that absorbing only 10 mg through the skin can case death within fifteen minutes (Federation of American Scientists, 1998, p. 2).

Aspiring chemical terrorists would find producing chemical weapons difficult, but far from impossible. The materials and expertise needed to create relatively crude World War I–era weapons such as mustard gas or phosgene are available in hundreds of countries, and the information needed to create more complex chemical substances such as sarin is also readily available. Although it would be far more difficult to obtain nerve agents such as VX and its Russian equivalent, it would be naïve to suggest that it would be impossible.

Nor would a terrorist need to resort to sophisticated military hardware to disperse harmful chemical agents. Although using rockets, bombs, or artillery shells as a delivery system would greatly increase the likelihood of inflicting mass casualties, it is worth recalling that the German attack at Ypres simply involved opening cylinders of chlorine gas downwind. Aum Shinrikyo's attacks on Tokyo subways also used a crude method of dispersal—the cultists simply punctured sarin-filled containers as they hurriedly departed the subways. The death toll would have been far higher had the cult developed a more sophisticated means of dispersing the sarin. One expert has suggested that Aum Shinrikyo's failure to produce large quantities of sarin, despite ample finances and equipment, suggests that considerable technical obstacles stand in the way of terrorists interested in using chemical weapons to inflict mass destruction (Smithson, 2002, p. 1). Nevertheless, since time, money, and the help of a sympathetic government could help overcome these hurdles, the use of chemical weapons in future terrorist attacks is a real possibility.

The prospect of nuclear, biological, or chemical terrorism is a grim one that deserves serious attention, but it should not obscure the fact that terrorist groups are presently able to inflict a great deal of death and destruction without resorting to such exotic weaponry. Indeed, a quick look at a few of the more notorious terrorist acts of recent memory confirms that clever criminals can do a great deal of harm without using sophisticated armaments. Timothy McVeigh destroyed an Oklahoma City office building and killed 168 people in April 1995 using a truck bomb. Five years later, Yemeni terrorists, using only a small boat packed with explosives, successfully disabled a U.S. guided missile destroyer, the USS Cole, killing seventeen sailors. Most recently, the 9-11 terrorists used box cutters and knives to gain control of more unorthodox weapons—passenger jets. Indeed, as has been discussed elsewhere in this volume, even the normally benign power of personal computers can be used to access and shut down essential infrastructures. So although the prospects of future attacks involving weapons of mass destruction are worthy of attention, one can expect conventional weapons to remain the mainstay of the terrorist arsenal. Bombs are not difficult to make, nor is it difficult to obtain guns in the United States.

Terrorists contemplating future strikes against the United States possess the element of surprise, a formidable arsenal, and a wide selection of targets from which to choose. These depressing facts might tempt one to conclude that the only defense against terrorist attacks is to be as far away as possible when they occur. Yet while it would be impossible to make the United States invulnerable to terrorism, there is much that can be done to contain the threat and minimize the effects of future terrorist attacks. Military strikes (both overt and covert), improved intelligence gathering, diplomatic agreements such as extradition and nonproliferation treaties, and closer attention to public diplomacy are among the many ways that the United States can respond to terrorism.

Although the United States clearly possesses the most powerful military forces on the face of the earth, military power will not alone be enough to defeat international terrorism. The U.S. armed forces have fought bravely and well in Afghanistan, but it is important to note that rather than destroying al-Qaeda's ability to wage terror once and for all, they have only destroyed al-Qaeda's ability to wage terror *from Afghanistan*. Despite the destruction of numerous enemy units and base camps, several al-Qaeda soldiers eluded their pursuers and slipped into neighboring Pakistan. These survivors have no doubt regrouped and, along with other al-Qaeda cells throughout the world, are planning future acts of terrorism.

Pointing out the inability of conventional military forces to completely root out and destroy terrorist groups is not to argue that military operations have no value in wider counter-terror campaigns. There is much to be said for harassing and disrupting terrorist organizations. Every day that al-Qaeda members spend hiding from U.S. military patrols or trying to replenish their own numbers and supplies is a day that they do not spend planning and implementing additional attacks. In addition, it is conceivable that military strikes, such as the ones in Afghanistan, could deter other nations from harboring or otherwise supporting terrorist organizations.

However, military operations against terrorist groups and their state sponsors also involve serious drawbacks that should be carefully considered before placing U.S. soldiers in the line of fire. First and foremost is the problem of "collateral damage," which in nonmilitary terms refers to the unintended deaths of innocent civilians that often result from combat. While the argument that civilian casualties are an inevitable part of modern warfare is true, it is also true that every village that is accidentally destroyed by a stray bomb and every civilian who is mistakenly shot as an enemy soldier becomes a potential public relations bonanza for the enemy. A person killed by an unfortunate error is still dead, and that person's family and friends might find the Pentagon's apologies less persuasive than the charges made by terrorists and their allies that the deaths of their loved ones were malicious, intentional, and above all else, caused by Americans. Hence, an air strike that successfully bombs one terrorist out of existence might, by inadvertently causing civilian casualties, create two more terrorists to take the place of the first one.

In addition to creating new enemies, civilian deaths could also cost the United States the support of its friends. America's allies—and even a few of its adversaries, such as Iran—responded to 9-11 with a groundswell of sympathy and support for the United States. Since any counterterrorist strategy will fail without the cooperation of other countries, the United States needs to tap this reservoir of goodwill. But, U.S. operations that kill civilians, however unintentional, will erode such support. Put simply, the United States cannot afford to be viewed by the rest of the world as a vindictive bully if it hopes to convince other nations to follow its lead in the war against terror.

Finally, before U.S. leaders use military force to eliminate governments that sponsor terrorism, they need to examine if the available alternatives are any better. U.S. officials would do well to recall the events that followed Washington, DC's selection of a fervent anticommunist named Ngo Dinh Diem to lead a new country called South Vietnam in 1954. Diem's government was corrupt and oppressive, and his opponents quickly branded him as a lackey who served his masters in Washington at the expense of the Vietnamese people. Diem turned a deaf ear toward his U.S. patrons, who repeatedly urged him to implement reforms that would make his regime more attractive to his people.

For their part, policymakers in Washington grew increasingly disgusted with Diem's penchant for accepting U.S. aid, but not U.S. advice. Washington officials, in the assumption that any change would be for the better, finally agreed to a coup in 1963 to remove Diem. Yet by 1965, shortly before the United States sent ground troops to Vietnam, the situation had actually deteriorated, with one U.S. official describing South Vietnamese politics as a "government of the week sideshow" (Olsen & Roberts, 1999, p. 121). In retrospect, it is apparent that the United States made a very poor choice of an ally back in 1954. Tragically, by the end of the Vietnam War, over 58,000 Americans had paid for this error in judgment with their lives.

The debacle in Vietnam should remind policymakers in Washington to choose their allies carefully. The United States now has a new ally in the Afghan government, Harmid Karzai—but the question remains if Karzai and his successors can provide Afghanistan with effective rule. Since Afghan warlords have traditionally resisted the authority of the central government, it would be difficult for Karzai to rule under the best of circumstances. Should Afghans fail to rally behind Karzai's government, it is conceivable that to retain power, he will have to rely more heavily on his U.S. patrons for support, resort to repressive measures, or both. Any of these developments would provide anti-American forces in the region with ample grist for their propaganda mill. It would not bode well for the future if anti-American forces could credibly label the Afghan government as corrupt and repressive, a mere lackey that catered to the whims of its masters in Washington, DC.

In addition to carrying out large, high-profile missions such as the campaign in Afghanistan, the U.S. military will also be called upon to achieve tasks with more limited objectives, such as helping friendly governments to combat terrorists. These tasks might include training, advising local police and military forces in counterterror tactics, and occasionally even participating in covert strikes against specific targets such as terrorist training camps. The public will get little, if any, chance to weigh the merits of these operations, as the military intends to keep the planning, execution, and results of its missions shrouded in secrecy (Clark, 2002, p. 250).

The success or failure of these operations may hinge upon accurate, timely intelligence gathering. Accurate intelligence is the cornerstone of any antiterrorist operation, military or otherwise. Yet in the aftermath of September 11, frightened and angry Americans wanted to know how al-Qaeda had managed to evade the considerable assets of the national intelligence community (which includes not only the Central Intelligence Agency [CIA] and Federal Bureau of Investigation [F.B.I.], but also agencies such as the Defense Intelligence Agency [DIA] and the National Security Agency [NSA]). The lack of advance warning appeared to many people as evidence of a colossal intelligence failure, prompting calls for a massive overhaul of the agencies responsible for gathering and analyzing intelligence data.

Although reforms are clearly in order, it is important to realize that no intelligence system is foolproof and that drastic reform is unlikely to transform the CIA, F.B.I., and other government institutions into all-knowing, all-seeing shields against terrorism. The most productive way to improve our intelligence gathering and analysis is not to completely remake the system, but rather to plan carefully, spend in the right areas, and improve the lines of communication between the institutions responsible for intelligence gathering and analysis.

Intelligence work falls into two categories: technical intelligence and human intelligence. Technical intelligence refers to gathering information with specialized equipment such as cameras, microphones, and satellites, while the latter refers to spies: people who infiltrate underground organizations, gain the trust of the members, and then report on their membership and activities.

Although the United States has earned high marks for its technical surveillance programs, the emergence of new technologies will make it difficult for the United States to match its past performance. Since modern criminals can communicate by cell phone and email, it is no longer possible to simply place a wiretap on a telephone and expect results. The development of technologies, such as encryption coding, promise to make it even harder to track discussions between terrorists. Since these sophisticated technologies are becoming more widely available, the intelligence agencies will require considerable funding to ensure that research and development for technical surveillance remains one step ahead of the communication technologies available to hostile organizations.

Critics of the U.S. intelligence community have charged that the strength of U.S. technical surveillance has come at the expense of human intelligence programs, and that the latter have been neglected and allowed to decay since the end of the Cold War. Although there is no doubt that human intelligence will receive more attention and more funding in the near future, money will not provide an immediate solution, as agents cannot be developed overnight. It takes considerable time to provide new recruits with an understanding of the culture, internal politics, and economic structure of the societies they are supposed to infiltrate. Even agents armed with such knowledge are unlikely to successfully infiltrate the ranks of secretive groups such as al-Qaeda (Deutch & Smith, 2002,

p. 66). In order to penetrate terrorist networks, U.S. intelligence agencies will have to recruit sources from within these organizations and turn them into informants (Campbell & Flournoy, 2001, p. 87).

Perhaps the most daunting but significant way to improve the intelligence capabilities of the United States will be to eliminate the bureaucratic walls that hinder the abilities of the intelligence and law enforcement agencies to coordinate their activities and share information in a timely and effective manner. Part of this problem is due to the sheer size of the intelligence community, which sometimes hinders the rapid sharing of information. The growth of the intelligence agencies over the years has spawned a formidable bureaucracy that has created redundant information systems and blurred lines of authority. Navigating the various directorates and divisions of the intelligence and law enforcement agencies is no easy task.

The difficulty of government agencies to coordinate their activities, assets, and information also stems from the fact that as a domestic law enforcement agency, the F.B.I. has objectives that differ significantly from that of the CIA, NSA, and DIA. Whereas the latter gathers information from overseas to discover the *future* plans of America's adversaries, the FBI collects information (at home and overseas) to prosecute *past* crimes. As a result, the agencies are often reluctant to share sources, information, and methods. The FBI fears that sharing information with other agencies could reveal its informants, thus making future prosecutions more difficult. For its part, the CIA also fears that divulging information to the F.B.I. will expose its sources and methods to public view, compromising its ongoing investigations (Deutch & Smith, 2002, p. 64).

One way to improve access to the intelligence data compiled by the U.S. intelligence community would be to modernize the database. U.S. intelligence agencies compile a comprehensive amount of raw data, but since most of it remains in paper files, the information is relatively inaccessible. The creation of an extensive, central electronic database would be an effective way to pool data and make it quickly available to those who need it most. In addition, the quality of the data could be improved by augmenting classified information with more widely available information (Campbell & Flournoy, 2001, p. 85).

Bureaucratic reorganization is an oft-discussed remedy for solving the more difficult problems of interagency rivalries and suspicions. But one expert warns that for bureaucratic reshuffling to work, those entrusted with the task of collecting intelligence must be given real authority in order to overcome bureaucratic obstacles. He observes that while the original proposals for the Office of Homeland Security provided that office with responsibility for coordinating the activities of all U.S. intelligence agencies, the 1947 National Security Act gave this same responsibility to the Director of Central Intelligence (DCI). In practice, however, the DCI wielded only limited authority over agencies such as the DIA and the NSA because those agencies fell under the auspices of the Defense Department (Betts, 2002, pp. 156–157).

The creation of the U.S. Department of Homeland Security in November 2002 was hailed as the most significant reorganization of the federal government in over fifty years. But although the new department includes a directorate charged with analyzing the data compiled by the various intelligence agencies, it remains to be seen as to whether or not the Department of Homeland Security will facilitate inter-agency coordination, or if it will merely add another layer of bureaucracy to the process. Without the power of budgetary authority over these institutions, former Assistant Secretary of Defense for International

Security Affairs Joseph Nye has argued, other government agencies will be unlikely to defer to the dictates of the new department (Nye, 2002, p. # 207).

Finally, future intelligence-gathering efforts will need to consider the issue of whether to increase surveillance within the United States. Although the U.S. people would probably be reassured to learn that the F.B.I. has significantly expanded its overseas operations over the last fifteen years, the public would likely react to any proposal to expand the F.B.I.'s domestic surveillance powers with alarm. However, since it is alleged that more extensive search and surveillance of suspects such as Zacarias Moussaoui—the infamous "twentieth hijacker" who expressed to his flight instructors an interest in flying, but not taking off or landing large jets—might have helped avert or minimize disasters such as September 11, calls for Americans to sacrifice some of their civil liberties in order to provide a greater margin of public safety will no doubt resurface time and time again (Betts, 2002, p. 153).

The likelihood of the government's seeking expanded search and surveillance powers will depend on the nature of and the frequency of future terrorist attacks. A wave of terrorist incidents, or an attack involving nuclear, biological, or chemical weapons, might quiet any significant objections to granting authorities greater leeway in investigating, searching, and apprehending suspects, whereas an extended period of terrorist inactivity would prompt calls to repeal these expanded police powers. It is also likely that U.S. citizens, who jealously guard their own constitutional rights, will tolerate increased search and surveillance powers as long as these measures are limited to noncitizens. No great outcry accompanied a 1996 counter-terrorism law that allowed the government to present *summaries,* rather than actual evidence in court, thus preserving the confidentiality of its intelligence sources and methods. This law thus eliminated the ability of resident aliens to face their accuser in court—a right guaranteed to U.S. citizens (Harmon, 2000, p. 247). In like vein, the military tribunals passed by presidential executive order in November 2001 currently apply only to non–U.S. citizens.

Therein lies the dilemma. The easing of restraints on the gathering and use of domestic intelligence and preserving may help to track and apprehend terrorists operating within the United States, but acceptance of these measures will by definition expand the powers of the state at the expense of individual rights. Furthermore, it is possible that the careless implementation or arbitrary expansion of police powers could arouse the ire of extremist right-wing groups, thereby increasing the likelihood of home-grown terrorism. So although the United States should not dismiss the importance of domestic surveillance, extreme care must be taken to strike a balance between the need for greater security and the preservation of civil liberties.

In the final analysis, the United States will not win the war on terrorism without the help and cooperation of other nations. But given that U.S. interests will not always coincide with those of other nations, and since other countries often accuse the United States of ignoring their interests, foreign support cannot be taken for granted. To enlist the support of the global community, U.S. leaders should make efforts in both multilateral and bilateral forums to reach agreements that help track, apprehend, and prosecute terrorists.

International attempts to suppress terrorism have had mixed results in the past. Multilateral efforts include the various United Nations Conventions, which have proscribed specific terrorist acts and express the international community's condemnation of terrorism. However, UN countries have had little success defining what terrorism is, let alone reaching a consensus on how to eliminate it. Since the final conventions tend to be worded in vague language and lack any real enforcement mechanisms, they usually amount to little more than statements of intent with limited practical value (Wilkinson, 2001, p. 191).

U.S. diplomats should therefore redouble their bilateral efforts, since these agreements often yield more positive and tangible results. Topics of discussion range from curbing the proliferation of weapons of mass destruction, improving ties between U.S. and foreign intelligence and law enforcement agencies, and disrupting terrorist financial networks to the swift extradition of terrorists. The potential value of bilateral agreements is illustrated by the efforts of the Russian and U.S. governments to curb the proliferation of nuclear weapons. The most significant of these measures, the Cooperative Threat Reduction (CTR), or Nunn-Lugar Program, was created in 1991 to downsize Russia's nuclear weapons stockpile and secure its nuclear weapons and materials. Through the CTR Program, the United States has helped Russia build new storage facilities for weapons grade materials, purchased Russian plutonium stocks, and helped to upgrade Russian security systems (National Intelligence Council, 2002, p. 3).

In addition to seeking specific areas of agreement with other nations that will make life more difficult for terrorist organizations, U.S. policymakers need to take steps to rehabilitate the image of the United States throughout the world. This is particularly urgent in the Middle East, where a significant proportion of the population views the United States and its policies through the eyes of Osama bin Laden and his ilk. The United States needs to do a far better job of articulating its policies to the Arab and Muslim world. More than ever before, the United States needs to make sure that it does not lose the battle for the hearts and minds of the peoples in the Middle East and elsewhere (Howard, 2002, p. 10).

Although the United States cannot restore its international reputation overnight, it should take immediate steps to counter the heretofore unchallenged voices in Arab and Muslim communities that present a hostile, distorted interpretation of U.S. actions, institutions, and values. The United States needs to regain the initiative in defining its policies to the peoples of the Middle East, rather than conceding the task to its enemies. It is possible that U.S. officials might try to inform and influence Arab and Muslim opinion by increasing the presence of state-run information programs such as the radio program Voice of America, which is currently heard by only 2 percent of the Arab population. A case can be made that investing more resources into these broadcasts will allow the United States to, in effect, raise its voice in the Middle East and elsewhere in the world (Campbell & Flournoy, 2001, p. 144).

The United States can do much better, however, than to broadcast radio shows that many foreign listeners will accurately dismiss as soft propaganda. In the long run, the United States will achieve better results by actively supporting the development of open media and democracy in the Muslim world. U.S. policymakers should instruct their diplomats to pressure Middle Eastern states to implement laws that ease restrictions on independent media. At the same time, U.S. officials can offer assistance in creating laws to regulate the print and broadcast media, as well as sponsoring training programs in journalistic standards and technical assistance. Such initiatives will not guarantee that Islamic journalists will begin to sing the praises of U.S. foreign policies, but they will help equip moderates within the Muslim world to compete with the virulent, anti-American propagandists that currently dominate the national media of many nations in the Islamic world

(Hoffman, 2002). The United States will never be able to reach out to the irreconcilable, violent elements such as bin Laden's followers, who should be brought into custody or eliminated. But the United States can and should try to reach out to the Arab world, explain its policies, and discredit terrorist groups.

Finally, the United States cannot assume that its efforts to deter, apprehend, or eliminate terrorists will put a complete end to terrorism. It is therefore essential for the United States to prepare strategies to cope with and minimize the damage caused by successful terrorist attacks. As of now, few U.S. communities have any idea as to how they might defend themselves or react to a terrorist incident (Nye, 2002, p. 203).

Defensive measures of this type would be crucial to containing a biological attack. Since biological weapons are silent and sometimes take days to take effect, an epidemic could be mistaken for a natural outbreak and quickly spread out of control. Programs that help healthcare workers identify signs of unusual diseases and improve lines of communication between healthcare workers and the appropriate authorities could be vital in identifying a biological attack in time to treat its victims and limit its spread. The creation of the Biological Preparedness and Response Program (BPRP) in 1999 introduces a framework to build an effective defense against biological warfare, but considerably more financial resources will be required to build the mechanisms for planning and implementing such a defense. So too will more funding be needed to invest in the scientific research required to develop improved antibiotics and new vaccines (Chyba, 2002, p. 131).

In the face of so many unprecedented factors and unpredictable variables, can history provide any suggestions as to what the future holds? Clearly, comparisons of September 2001 to Pearl Harbor provide at best an imprecise description of the events in question. What is needed is a broader analogy that can provide some insight as to how the United States might respond to the current threat and how its response will shape our society in the years ahead. An examination of the situation that faced the United States in early 1950, when events prompted the Truman administration to completely reassess U.S. national security policies, reveals some striking similarities to the contemporary situation. Considering how our predecessors defined and responded to what they perceived as a grave threat to national security can in turn allow us to give more informed consideration to the task confronting the United States today.

The year 1949 was not a good one for Harry S Truman. In late September, Truman learned that the Soviet Union had, far ahead of the schedule predicted by U.S. intelligence, successfully tested an atomic bomb. Only a month later, Chinese communists led by Mao Zedong toppled the nationalist government of Chiang Kai-Shek, bringing a nation of several million people into the communist bloc. Together, these two events suggested that the emerging Cold War had taken a sudden and ominous turn for the worse. In response to these unwelcome developments, President Truman ordered a thorough reevaluation of U.S. foreign policy. The National Security Council (NSC) quickly responded to Truman's directive by drafting a top secret, systematic analysis of U.S. national security policies known as NSC-68. This document branded the Soviet Union as a predatory, expansionist nation that posed a clear threat to the United States and presented four possible options for contending with the Soviet menace. The United States could: (1) continue with its current policies, (2) abandon its global interests and retreat to the western hemisphere, (3) fight a preventive war against the Soviets, or (4) militarize against Soviet expansion.

The authors of NSC-68 made a spirited argument in favor of the fourth option, militarization. Nevertheless, NSC-68 met significant opposition until North Korea, a Soviet protégée, launched a surprise invasion of anti-communist South Korea. The Korean War confirmed for most Americans that the Soviets were bent upon world domination. Debate on NSC-68 quickly ended, and the United States began to rearm.

After comparing the two time periods, a number of interesting parallels emerge. In both 1950 and 2001, the United States stood as the predominant military and economic power in the world. In both 1950 and 2001, U.S. officials identified a powerful enemy that, if unchallenged, could threaten the very existence of the United States. And in both eras, this threat did not materialize overnight. Truman was already wary of Moscow's intentions by 1950, just as U.S. officials were aware in 2001 that Osama bin Laden had orchestrated attacks on U.S. interests overseas throughout the 1990s.

Revisiting the courses of action outlined in NSC-68 reveals not only how policy perceived the Soviet Union in 1950, but also as to how the United States might respond to a very different threat in the twenty-first century. Just as the authors of NSC-68 dismissed the ability of existing policies to withstand Soviet aggression, it is evident that Americans today regard current policies as inadequate to the task of combating terrorism. Politicians, academics, and journalists alike have recently called for extensive revisions, if not a complete overhaul of military, diplomatic, and domestic security policies. It is not a question of whether existing policies will change, but rather to what degree they will change.

The authors of NSC-68 understood that since the United States had fought in World War II to ensure that the postwar world order would be one where Americans could travel, buy, and sell goods freely, retreating to the western hemisphere was not a viable option. Nor will the present administration give serious consideration to Osama bin Laden's demand that the United States withdraw from the Middle East. In 1950, a withdrawal to "Fortress America" meant renouncing U.S. economic interests and status as a superpower. Such a decision is as unthinkable now as it was in 1950.

The option of preventive war raised in NSC-68 highlights the importance of public opinion as a factor in policy making. NSC-68 ruled out waging preventive war against the Soviets on the grounds that the U.S. public would not support an attack on the Soviet Union. Although there is currently widespread support for military action against terrorist organizations and their state patrons, public support for a protracted military campaign may evaporate. Since success in the war against terrorism will require the active support of the U.S. people, national leaders will need to devote considerable time and energy not only to devising counterterrorist strategies, but also to explaining and justifying these strategies to the public.

NSC-68's appeal for drastic increases in military spending, and thus higher taxes, was initially dismissed. However, the communist assault on South Korea, which seemed to validate NSC-68's estimate of Soviet intentions, quickly silenced most critics of higher defense spending. U.S. defense spending subsequently tripled during Truman's term as president, and the defense budget continued to command a high percentage of federal dollars for the remainder of the Cold War. It is likely that 9-11 will serve, as had the Korean War, as a catalyst for increased defense spending. Our defense dollars, of course, will be spent differently than in 1950. Whereas defense budgets of the 1950s emphasized strengthening U.S. offensive nuclear capabilities, twenty-first century defense budgets will place a greater emphasis on intelligence than in the past. They will also seek to increase the ability of the military to project military power over long distances (Rumsfeld, 2002). Missile defense systems designed to protect the United States from a limited missile strike are also likely to be included in future defense budgets, despite doubts as to the viability and wisdom of deploying such a system.

One of the most important points the analogy provides is a warning against the danger of oversimplifying the threat before us. NSC-68, despite its influence, was a deeply flawed analysis, containing what one prominent historian has described as a "superficial and exaggerated" depiction of Soviet capabilities and intentions (Paterson, 1992, p. 93). Even as NSC-68 circulated through Washington in 1950, Russian experts within the State Department were saying the same thing. They urged their superiors to reject NSC-68's conclusion that Soviet leaders were intent upon spreading the Russian revolution to every corner of the world.

That these calls went ignored is highly significant. By acting on the questionable assumptions of NSC-68, U.S. leaders not only reallocated a substantial proportion of our national resources toward military spending, but also began to emphasize civil defense, loyalty programs, and the need for a public consensus that supported Cold War policies (McCormick, 1995, p. 98). The subsequent hardening of the Cold War led to a wave of anti-communist hysteria within the United States; support for a variety of unsavory, but anti-communist third-world regimes (such as Guatemala, South Vietnam, Iran, and the Philippines); a diplomatic crisis in the Caribbean in 1962 that nearly led to nuclear war; and ultimately, the disastrous war in Vietnam.

Although U.S. Cold War strategies focused upon the Soviet Union and its allies, the emergence of other international problems during the Cold War, such as the Arab-Israeli conflict, European economic integration, and third-world nationalism also absorbed the attention and energies of U.S. officials. In similar fashion, the current importance of anti-terrorism to the U.S. foreign policy agenda does not mean that officials in Washington can afford to ignore other important diplomatic matters, such as relations with China and Russia. Both of these countries have supported international efforts to suppress terrorism in the wake of September 11, and neither has offered serious objections to the military campaign in Afghanistan. Nevertheless, Beijing and Moscow are at odds with the United States on a variety of other issues, and there is no reason to believe that the war on terrorism will keep these disputes buried indefinitely. The world was a complicated and dangerous place before 9-11, and although counterterrorism will certainly become a top foreign policy priority, terrorism is still only one of several issues, concerns, and crises that will compete for the attention of U.S. policymakers.

Although it would be impossible to plot the exact course of future U.S. diplomacy, it is important to recall that while 9-11 has already been described as a turning point in U.S. history, none of the factors involved in the September 11 attacks was without precedent. Plane hijackings, terrorist bombings, and even the use of nuclear, biological, and chemical weapons all entered the historical record well before September 2001. Since attacks of such magnitude were previously unknown in the United States, it is understandable that many Americans only now grasp that their sense of invulnerability to terrorism was illusory. But although Americans may view the world far differently in light of this realization, today's world is in many respects the same world that existed before 9-11—a world of competing nation states with divergent economic, political, and strategic interests.

Given these circumstances, one should not expect future U.S. foreign policies to undergo fundamental change. As it has in the past, the United States will seek the active support of powerful nations (such as Britain, Germany, Russia, and China) for its international policies, and it will also cultivate ties with weaker nations. In the case of the latter, it is probable that efforts to forge closer relations will be dictated by expediency. For example, the U.S.-Pakistani partnership in the war against terrorism comes despite Pakistan's past friendship with the Taliban regime and despite Pakistani dictator Pervez Musharraf's disdain for democratic rule. Despite Musharraf's shortcomings, U.S. officials have concluded that Pakistan's geographic proximity to Afghanistan makes Musharraf a desirable ally in the war against terrorism (Menon, 2001, p. 102).

U.S. policymakers will encounter several hurdles in their efforts to sustain a global coalition against terrorism, and their efforts are certain to have unforeseen and unintended consequences. The United States should certainly do everything in its power to sustain the cooperation of other nations, but the efforts of U.S. policymakers to forge new partnerships and devise new strategies to fight terrorists will likely take the United States into uncharted and dangerous waters. This will be especially true in volatile regions with fragile governments, such as Central Asia. U.S. officials will need to walk a delicate tightrope in their support of unpopular regimes that have joined the campaign against terrorism, lest they further destabilize these countries and draw the United States further into the internal politics of a dangerous and unstable region.

The difficulties involved in sustaining a long-term international consensus on counterterrorism strategies mean that in all probability declarations that U.S. unilateralism ended on September 11 are premature. Although the Bush administration initially emphasized the value of an organized, multilateral campaign against international terrorism, the spirit of multilateral diplomacy was not truly tested until late 2002, when the United States initiated a campaign to isolate and disarm Iraq. The failure of U.S. officials to overcome doubts within the global community (most significantly policymakers in France and Germany) that Saddam Hussein's weapons programs and alleged ties to terrorist groups warrants military action to remove him from power has prompted skepticism on both sides of the Atlantic regarding the prospects of future multilateral cooperation. It is too soon to accurately gauge whether or not this dispute will have any far-reaching repercussions beyond the immediate issue of Iraqi disarmament. Yet given the vital importance of international collaboration in combating terrorism, not to mention an ambitious and costly project such as reconstructing a post-Saddam Iraq, it is clearly in the national interests of the United States to cultivate and sustain positive relationships with its allies across the globe.

In order to understand and respond to a crisis, it is often tempting and convenient to reduce the problem to its simplest form. However, historical precedent demonstrates that NSC-68's gross oversimplification of Soviet intentions and the threat of the Soviet Union to the United States turned out in the long run to be very costly in both human and monetary terms. To avoid making similar errors in the future, Americans need to educate themselves on the basics of the subject of terrorism. A solid grasp of the issues will not by itself make terrorism go away, but it will guard against any tendencies to exaggerate or underestimate the nature of the threat, thus helping Americans to contend with the problem in a rational and sophisticated way.

An important responsibility for prominent politicians and statesmen will be to articulate and justify its counterterror policies to the U.S. people. Since the public is more likely to support policies that it fully understands, future administrations should make a priority of educating the public about emerging threats to the United States and about what the government intends to do to thwart the plans of hostile groups. In doing so, a noted scholar of terrorism has observed, national leaders must "avoid apocalyptic language and the making of impossible promises" (Harmon, 2000, p. 236). Just as branding the Soviet Union as an "evil empire" ultimately told Americans little about how the United States might contend with its Cold War adversary, dismissing terrorists as irrational "evildoers" does not provide significant insights as to how the United States should fight these groups. Rhetoric that oversimplifies the problem or caricatures terrorist elements may inadvertently lead to an underestimation of their skills and resolve, subsequently to an underestimation of the danger they pose to society.

For their part, the U.S. people will need to get used to a world that includes terrorism and the idea that terrorism will not be defeated overnight. This does not mean that Americans should become fatalistic, only that they should be aware of the likelihood that they will be called upon to spend more of their tax dollars on intelligence, disaster planning, technological research and development, and the military. In a broader sense, the public will likely need to grow accustomed to the idea of big government. Although Americans should and will continue to debate the proper role of the government in society, they would do well to accept that the federal government has a legitimate role in that society, particularly as it pertains to defending the country against violent, clandestine organizations.

The U.S. public will also need to become and stay informed on subjects as diverse as world affairs, anthrax symptoms, and domestic intelligence policies. A better informed public will be less susceptible to the shallow and irrational arguments of political opportunists as well as irresponsible doomsday forecasts that often cause unwarranted panic and anxiety. Knowledgeable citizens will be better able and, hopefully, more willing to participate and contribute to what promises to be an ongoing, national debate on the proper courses of action in the fight against terrorism. In this way, Americans can reinvigorate a national spirit invoked long ago by John F. Kennedy, who urged Americans "to ask not what your country can do for you, but ask what you can do for your country." As they do so, Americans can take comfort in realizing that while terrorism can never be completely eradicated, the reverse is also true; terrorists can attack the United States, but never defeat it.

REFERENCES

BERGER, S. R., & SUTPHEN, M. (2001). Commandeering the Palestinian Cause: bin Laden's belated concern. In J. F. Hoge, Jr., & G. Rose (Eds.), *How did this happen? Terrorism and the new war.* New York: Public Affairs.

BETTS, R. K. (2002). Intelligence test: The limits of prevention. In J. F. Hoge, Jr. & G. Rose (Eds.), *How did this happen? Terrorism and the new war.* New York: Public Affairs.

BUSH, G. (2001a, September 13). *President pledges assistance for New York in phone call with Pataki, Giuliani.* Retrieved July 8, 2002, from *http://www.whitehouse.gov/news/releases/2001/09/20010913-4.html*

BUSH, G. (2001b, September 20). *Address to a joint session of Congress and the American people.* Retrieved July 8, 2002, from *http://www.whitehouse.gov/news/releases/2001/09/20010920-8.html*

CAMPBELL, K. M., & FLOURNOY, M. A. (2001). *To prevail: An American strategy for the campaign against terrorism.* Washington, DC: CSIS Press.

CHYBA, C. F. (2002). Toward biological security. *Foreign Affairs, 81*(3), 122–136.

CLARK, W. K. (2002). Waging the new war: What's next for the U.S. armed forces? In J.F. Hoge, Jr., & G. Rose (Eds.), *How did this happen? Terrorism and the new war.* New York: Public Affairs.

DEUTCH, J., & SMITH, J. H. (2002, January/February). Smarter intelligence. *Foreign Policy, 128,* 64–69.

Federation of American Scientists. (Updated November 8, 1998). *Special weapons primer: Chemical warfare agents.* Retrieved July 17, 2002, from *http://www.fas.org/nuke/intro/cw/agent.htm*

GARRETT, L. (2001). Countering bioterrorism: Who's in charge? In J.F. Hoge, Jr., & G. Rose (Eds.), *How did this happen? Terrorism and the new war* (pp. 217–224). New York: Public Affairs.

HARMON, C.C. (2000). *Terrorism today.* London; Portland, OR: Frank Cass.

HELFAND, I., FORROW, L., & TIWARI, J. (2002). Nuclear terrorism. [Electronic Version]. *British Medical Journal, 324 (7333),* 356–359. Retrieved July 11, 2002 from *http://bmj.com/cgi/content/full/324/7333/356*

HERSH, S.M. (1968). *Chemical and biological warfare: America's hidden arsenal.* Indianapolis, IN: Bobbs-Merrill.

HOFFMAN, D. (2002). Beyond public diplomacy. *Foreign Affairs, 81*(2), 83–95.

HOWARD, M. (2002). What's in a name? How to fight terrorism. *Foreign Affairs, 81*(1), 8–13.

McCORMICK, T. (1995). *America's half-century: United States foreign policy in the cold war and after* (2nd ed.). Baltimore: Johns Hopkins University Press.

MENON, R. (2001). The restless region: The brittle states of Central and South Asia. In J.F. Hoge, Jr., & G. Rose (Eds.), *How did this happen? Terrorism and the new war.* New York: Public Affairs.

MILLER, J., ENGELBERG, S., & BROAD, W. (2001). *Germs: Biological weapons and America's secret war.* New York: Simon & Schuster.

NYE, J. S., Jr. (2002). Government's challenge: Getting serious about terrorism. In J.F. Hoge, Jr., & G. Rose (Eds.), *How did this happen? Terrorism and the new war.* New York: Public Affairs.

OLSEN, J. S., & Roberts, R. (1999). *Where the domino fell: America and Vietnam, 1945–1995* (3rd ed.). St. James, NY: Brandywine Press.

PATERSON, T. G. (1992). *On every front: The making and unmaking of the cold war* (rev. ed.). New York: W.W. Norton.

RUMSFELD, D.H. (2002). Transforming the military. *Foreign Affairs, 81*(3), 20–32.

SMITHSON, A. (2002). *Prepared statement before the Senate Committee on Governmental Affairs. Subcommittee on International Security, Proliferation, and Federal Services.* Retrieved July 18, 2002 from *http://www.stimson.org/cbw/?SN=CB20020219314*

SNOW, R. L. (1999). *The militia threat: Terrorists among us.* New York: Plenum Trade.

STANTON, J. (2002, February). U.S. fears proliferation of "orphan" nukes. *National Defense Magazine.* Retrieved July 10, 2002 from *http://www.nci.org/02/02f/09-01.htm*

TUCKER, S. C. (1998). *The Great War: 1914–1918.* Bloomington, IN: Indiana University Press.

WHEELIS, M. (2000). Agricultural biowarfare and bioterrorism. *Edmonds Institute Occasional Paper.* Retrieved July 19, 2002 from *http://www.edmonds-institute.org/wheelis.html*

WILKINSON, P. (2001). *Terrorism versus democracy: The liberal state response.* London; Portland, OR: Frank Cass.

Index

❖